Toward Better Teaching of Home Economics

Toward Better Teaching of Home Economics

Third Edition

Henrietta Fleck
Ph.D., Sc.D. (Hon.)
Home Economics and Nutrition Department
New York University

Macmillan Publishing Co., Inc.,
New York

Collier Macmillan Publishers,
London

Macmillan Publishing Co., Inc.
866 Third Avenue, New York, New York 10022
Collier Macmillan Canada, Ltd.

Library of Congress Cataloging in Publication Data

Fleck, Henrietta Christina (date)
Toward better teaching of home economics.

Includes bibliographies and index.
1. Home economics—Study and teaching. I. Title.
TX165.F57 1980 640'.7'1 79-11222
ISBN 0-02-338240-6

Printing: 1 2 3 4 5 6 7 8 Year: 0 1 2 3 4 5 6

*To the memory of Professor Louis E. Raths,
my mentor, whose teachings are reflected
in many pages of this book.*

Preface

Most home economists do some teaching. The recipients of this teaching may be students in a classroom, employees, lay persons, audiences of mass media, or workshop, seminar, or conference participants. The necessity of being prepared for this responsibility appears obvious. This broad interpretation of teaching for the home economics profession was a major premise of the author in the revision of this text.

To fulfill the mission of the profession of improving the quality of personal and family living demands a reexamination of the educational delivery systems in home economics. Persons of all ages are clamoring for education, and home economics should be an important part of this movement. This potential for greater service is exciting.

These educational delivery systems are best planned in the light of the social changes discussed in Chapter 1. There are a number of critical areas. What can home economics contribute to the solution of environmental problems? What adjustments are necessary with population changes, such as fewer children and more older Americans? How may home economics educators help individuals and families cope with inflation, poverty, and unemployment, especially of youth? What will be the role of home economics in the new trend of parent-child education? How may the home economist assist students involved in crime; drug, child, and spouse abuse; teenage pregnancy; vandalism; and other problems? How may instruction be adapted to the many variations of family lifestyles? How will members of the profession become more aware of legislation pertinent to the profession and learn to be effective politically? What does it mean to be *professional?* What impact will these questions have on the curriculum? In this book, answers have been attempted to these and many other questions that confront the home economics educator.

Information about students has been enlarged to three chapters: teaching children, youth, and adults. Not only have age characteristics been highlighted, but there is discussion of the impact of mainstreaming, cultural pluralism, bilingual education, the interest in death and dying, moral education, the strengthening of self-concept, and the total life of the student.

Other changes in the text are new chapters on professionalism, legislation and grantmanship, and nutrition education in line with recent trends. Extensive rewriting has been done to update the information and research, to explore new theories, to describe innovative teaching strategies, and to examine the latest ideas about the teaching environment.

Appreciation is expressed to many persons who contributed to this book. Discussions with many college home economics educators, classroom teachers, home economics educators in other areas of the profession, student teachers, and college students have been most helpful. Former students shared many innovative teaching experiences. In the preparation of the manuscript, special thanks are extended to Lucy Beck, Marjorie Dunlap, Marion Herforth, and Ileen Henricksen for typing, editing, and proofreading.

A sincere hope of the author is that this text will provide suggestions for creative and inspirational teaching so that home economics education will become better and better. In this manner, the contribution of home economics is broadened and the profession and society will benefit.

H. F.

Contents

1

Home Economics in Contemporary Life

One of the first steps in the improvement of home economics instruction is the intensification of the home economist's awareness of the world in which she/he and the students, patients, clients, or customers are living. He/she must be ever alert to the rapid changes constantly taking place. More important is a knowledge about the many social phenomena that have an impact on home economics programs and their students. The world shapes home economics, and home economics contributes to the shaping of the world through its professional impact on millions of individuals and their families.

THE NATIONAL AND WORLD SETTING

The most significant realization of the contemporary era, according to Cousins,[1] is that all humanity is compressed into a single geographic area. No longer can a country focus on itself; it must share the problems of the world. These world situations are related to environment, population, economic trends, women, crime and violence, drugs, and the threat of war.

Environment

One of the shocking discoveries of the time is that the ability of this planet to sustain life is threatened. People of the world must know

[1] Norman Cousins, Editorial, *World,* Vol. 1, No. 1 (Aug. 4, 1972), pp. 1–2.

Figure 1-1 The human environment should enrich life, not impoverish it.

that existence is possible because millions and millions of factors are in precise and delicate balance. Man's intervention in this universal design has imperiled survival.

Pollution of various types is a major problem. Americans are faced annually with the disposal of millions of scrapped cars, millions of tons of waste paper, billions of discarded cans, bottles, and jars. More than a million tons of garbage pile up daily. Americans contribute over a million tons of pollutants to the air each year, over half from cars alone. More gasoline is consumed in our nation than in the rest of the entire world. The generation of electric power contributes millions of tons of air pollutants. Noise pollution doubles in volume every ten years. Billions of dollars must be spent to control pollution.

Many questions confront the people of America. What sacrifices are necessary for a clean world? What is being done about these high-priority demands? Who will pay the bills? The opinions of citizens in national polls indicate that they believe that environmental problems can be postponed. But a growing group of determined environmentalists believe that balancing our ecology is of primary importance to our survival. The problem is so large that only through the cooperative efforts of government, business, industry, and citizens can solutions be reached.

Effecting these changes in our present wasteful society will not be easy. The home economist, especially the teacher, may find this problem to be one of her/his most challenging ones—educating self, students, customers, patients, clients, and families in the community, then assuming an important role as a citizen.

In a number of communities, there is action to meet some of these problems.[2] Residents of Banitay, Florida, preserve some of their own food at a cannery sponsored by a tricounty community council. This venture saves pollution by cans in that area. At the University of Bridgeport in Connecticut, community youth take care of greenhouses that are regulated through a combination of solar and organically produced energy. Vegetables and tiny eels are grown there. Experiments for growing other fish in the greenhouse are being considered. Iron River, Michigan, has twenty-five acres of communal gardens for use in the summertime and a huge solar greenhouse for year-round use. Using windmill power, waterless toilets, and cooperatives that range from groups that share tools to fuel-buying cooperatives are a part of the plan to save energy. Growing food in the community, especially in the Middle West, means saving the energy used to transport food from California.

Home economics educators may alert students to these important social problems and consider possible solutions.

Population

Because of low fertility and mortality rates, America's population is undergoing a profound change that could alter many facets of daily living. The fertility rate of American women continues to drop.

[2] Patricia Wells, "Some Towns Are Finding Ways of Recycling Themselves," *The New York Times,* July 25, 1978, pp. B1, B16.

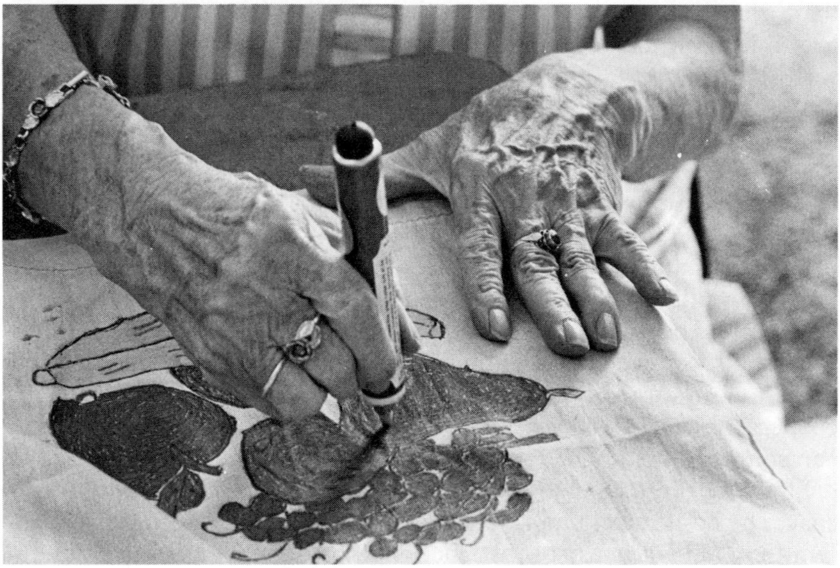

Figure 1–2 How will the increasing needs of the older population be met? (USDA Photo)

The population rise in United States is slowing and will probably stabilize by the year 2025 and reach zero population growth. Many futurists believe that a better life is in store when this stage is reached because pressures will be reduced on the environment, resources, and government services.

There will continue to be a larger proportion of elderly people: 10 per cent of our citizens are older than sixty-five, and this figure may double in the next twenty-five years. Improved medical care has resulted in a declining death rate for this age group. Care of the elderly is far more costly than care of the young, and the middle-aged citizens may bear the brunt of this responsibility. A new look at the care of the elderly is in order.

What needs of the older population must be met in light of their increasing numbers? More retirement homes and health-care facilities will be required. Many retirees are interested in continuing to make a contribution to society, so provisions may be made for part-time jobs, consultant work, and satisfying volunteer service.

The number of children under fourteen is decreasing. The result is decreasing enrollment in schools and colleges. From a productive standpoint, there will be less need for baby foods, toys, maternity wards in hospitals, and teachers. Families may become more adult-oriented than child-centered. What will these changes mean for home economics education? It may be necessary to prepare more teachers for working with the elderly than with children, for example.

The median age level in the population increases each year. In 1950, the median age was 30.2 years; in 2000, it is predicted that it will be 34.8 years; and by 2050, 37.0 years. By 2020, it is predicted that one out of every three Americans will be a taxpayer, so that the middle-aged will have the major responsibilities for society. More women are in the labor force, perhaps influenced by the rising cost of living and the women's movement. Marriage and childbearing are thus postponed. The college enrollment of women aged twenty-five to thirty-five has doubled since 1970. Older women are either returning to or entering college for various reasons, among them to prepare themselves for a job. The divorce rate is high and alarming.

Home economists are urged to acquaint themselves with current and projected data from the U.S. Census Bureau about population trends and to prepare themselves for important changes in home economics professional services.

Economic Trends

An analysis of personal and family incomes in the nation will give the home economics teacher insights into levels of living and into the possible problems encountered by consumers. This information may be received from Current Population Reports, *Consumer Income,* U.S. Department of Commerce.

A matter of concern related to income levels is the impact of poverty on children. Home economists must be concerned about the additional handicaps these children will face as youth and adults because of privations in childhood. These privations are serious not only for the individual child but also for the nation, which loses human resources.

Welfare plagues the American people. The taxpayers complain, the

Figure 1–3 Poverty is a negative factor in a child's development. (National Institute of Child Health, U.S. Department of Labor)

people who receive the aid are unhappy and bewildered, and the officials who administer the programs are distraught. The number of recipients on public assistance rolls is in the millions, and the number of food-stamp recipients is rising. Medicaid payments will soon go to an estimated 25 million persons. Many believe that finding work for welfare recipients is the answer. About 1 per cent of such recipients are able men. The largest group of working-age adults consists of about 3 million mothers, most of whom head families without men and have little or no employment potential because they have to care for small children or have mental or physical problems. For these people, welfare assistance is inevitably necessary.

Inflation haunts families. The threat of higher prices for food and other necessities is ever-present. Such influences as increased marketing costs, weather, the higher costs of imported goods, the rising costs of labor and petroleum, and the higher prices of domestically produced goods trigger inflation. There is a strong movement among all nations to find ways to beat inflation, such as reducing waste, insulating homes and other buildings, saving energy, living more simply, recycling, and countless other ways. This is an area in which home economists have expertise and may be of assistance to others.

Fetterman[3] believes that a lack of both money and the ability to manage it are among the most serious problems facing consumers. Furthermore many consumers do not know their rights under the law, nor are they familiar with the sources of information and the agencies available to them. In addition, many consumers do not read labels or use other available guidelines for making suitable decisions about purchases. The home economics teacher, along with other home economics professionals, can organize community, county, and state councils in order to reach a maximum number of people, as well as teach consumer education.

Work is an integral part of the American lifestyle. Jobs and joblessness have a strong economic impact on our society. For the poor man or woman, the chance to work is the greatest of all needs, according to Schumacher.[4]

In the ghettos of many American cities, nearly half of all minority youth between sixteen and nineteen years of age in the work force are unemployed—nearly two-and-a-half times higher than the unemployment rate of white youth.[5] Few have hope for the future and frequently turn to lawlessness and violence. In recent years, the job

[3] Elsie Fetterman, "Viewpoints: Consumerism—What Is the Issue?" *Penney's Forum* (Fall/Winter 1972), p. 9.

[4] E. F. Schumacher, *Small Is Beautiful, Economics As If People Mattered* (New York: Harper, 1973), p. 163.

[5] "To Be Young, Black and Out Of Work," *The New York Times Magazine,* Oct. 23, 1977, pp. 39–61.

Figure 1–4 A shopper seeking aid in making food buying decisions. (USDA Photo)

market for minority groups seems to have contracted. There are many reasons for this situation, such as lack of high school diplomas, licenses, and educational requirements. Other deterrents are arrest records, correctional histories, minimum wage laws that price youth out of the market, subtle discrimination, and other job barriers.

Women

The women's movement has had a significant impact not only on women but on society itself. Throughout the history of the world, there have been many events in which individuals and groups attempted to broaden the rights and privileges of women. The United Nations Charter stressed equal rights for men and women.[6] Translation into reality has been slow and uneven. Although conditions vary from nation to nation, women form the bulk of the illiterate, the poor, the undernourished, the unskilled, and the unemployed. Women have little or no say in the important decisions that affect their country, their lives, and their children.

The underutilization of approximately 50 per cent of the world's adult population led the United Nations to proclaim 1975 as International Women's Year. The objective was to define a society in which

[6] *World Plan of Action* (A Summarized Version), United Nations Decade for Women 1976–1985 (New York: United Nations, 1976).

women participate in the economic, social, and political life in a real sense. Strategies were to be planned to solve the problems that place women in an inferior position and to emphasize the participation of women in their own development. Some of the changes sought were equal opportunities in education and employment, a greater sensitivity to the needs of all women in the planning of national and international legislation, and a review of the shortcomings in present laws. The putting of more women in policy-making positions should be encouraged. The recognition of the worth of women's work, the reduction of their heavy work load, and a governmental department to oversee the integration of women at the national level were among the important recommendations. Progress in the fulfillment of these goals has been somewhat discouraging.

Crime and Violence

Among the most serious social ills are crime and violence. Although national and worldwide in scope, these ills seem to be more concentrated in cities. Cutler[7] cites the two major causes highlighted by the three national commissions that studied these problems. The first is the persistence of major social injustice, such as the inability of many citizens to hold a satisfactory stake in the life of their community or failure to heed their legitimate grievances. Second, the political framework of the criminal justice system is outmoded, rigid, and often impotent. Changes are needed. Violence must be made unrewarding, and our institutions must be able to control violence when it arises with firmness and fairness and within the law.

We are rapidly losing the right to live without fear because of crime and violence. In many communities, residents are organizing into effective lobbies for positive legislation, becoming court watchers and keeping track of sentences imposed by judges. Other projects are forming home-alert surveillance groups to "keep an eye" on each other's property and having local law enforcement agencies teach citizens how to protect their property and themselves. All of these measures and others are helpful, but the real cause of this upheaval is related to social ills, such as alienation, the impersonal urban industrial system, lack of moral idealism, drug abuse, violence on television and other media, and unemployment.

The Drug Problem

Drug abuse, which is one of the most serious problems facing families and educators, is not restricted to any segment of our society. In

[7] Lloyd N. Cutler, "Thomas Jefferson, Won't You Please Come Home?" *The Annals of the American Academy of Social and Political Science*, Vol. 396 (July 1971), pp. 25–39.

spite of the attempts by law enforcement agencies to halt it, the narcotics trade has grown into a multi-billion-dollar-a-year enterprise.

Home economics teachers can help in the prevention of drug abuse, because education is considered one of the best means of prevention. The big challenge is for the teacher to become well informed about the subject. There is considerable misinformation about drugs and their use. The National Coordinating Council on Drug Abuse and Information estimates that more than 60 per cent of the literature in circulation among schoolchildren contains at least some unsound information. Teachers are urged to evaluate all materials on this subject very carefully. Knowledge about government efforts, legal restrictions, the types of drugs being used and their possible effects (short and long term), the cost of drugs, how drugs are acquired, and the attitudes of students and the information they have are important background for the teacher. The causes of drug use should be explored. A general opinion is that addiction is a symptom of complex social forces that reflects the uncertainty and insecurity that so many young people feel. The environment in which drug users live may be a contributing factor. Exploring methods and materials for reaching students is essential. "Preaching" is of little avail. Peer-group programs in which students themselves devise ways to keep fellow students from falling prey to drug abuse have been successful. This problem is beginning to affect the pattern of all of our lives and the well-being of our youth.

Threat of War

People everywhere are concerned about the possibility of atomic and other types of war that would destroy the world and its people. Although the desire for peace is great, complex political, economic, and ideological factors have created an international setting in which small-scale confrontations in any area of the world threaten to erupt into wider hostilities. Opposition to wars as a means for settling differences has heightened, and hopefully, in time wars will be outmoded.

The United Nations has contributed in many ways to peace and to projects for improving the health and self-sufficiency of many peoples throughout the world. Many home economists have contributed to these programs, especially in the developing countries. Although the United Nations operates under great handicaps, in several countries it has restored peace when violence broke out.

Whether the people of the world can meet the test of survival in the nuclear age will depend to a great extent on their goals and values. A home economics teacher can help her/his students to be aware of the immense problems of working toward world peace and to contribute in their own ways toward its accomplishment. In education children must be prepared to support and to work for a world in which the safety of each is the safety of all.

THE FAMILY SETTING

Some family-life experts believe that two prevailing beliefs about the family should be refuted. Graubard[8] describes them as (1) the belief that the family is a weak organism, frequently under attack and unable to ward off these threats and (2) the belief that objectivity about the family is easily achieved without the influence of political or partisan outlooks. Graubard further asserts that serious inquiry into the family is of recent origin and is interdisciplinary in nature. There has been little time to implement the research that has been done. We tend to glorify the stability and order of families of the past but have little evidence that this condition existed. The family is not fragile, but as a social institution, it is often at the center of our political debates related to education, health, welfare, and other concerns. Uniformity in family life does not exist throughout nations or regions or in various classes of society. There are some commonalities, such as living together.

Family Lifestyles

Sussman[9] categorizes family types, beginning with the nuclear family, as having these possible variations: (1) nuclear family, with husband and wife and offspring living in a common household (intact) with a single career or a dual career in which the wife's or husband's career may be continuous or interrupted; (2) nuclear dyad, with only husband and wife living together, childless or with no children living at home, with single or dual career, or with wife's or husband's career continuous or interrupted; or (3) nuclear family of remarried husband or wife and offspring living in a common household, with possible career variations. Other family types are (4) the single-parent family, with the head being male or female as a result of death, abandonment, divorce, or separation and usually including small and school-aged children, with a career or living on welfare; (5) the extended family, which may be three-generational—the elderly, the parents, the children, and other relatives may live in

[8] Stephen R. Graubard, "Preface to the Issue 'The Family,'" *Daedalus,* Vol. 106, No. 2 (Spring 1977), pp. v–xiv.

[9] Marvin Sussman, "What Every School Principal Should Know About Families," "The American Family," *The Elementary School Principal,* Vol. 55, No. 5, Part I (May/June 1976), p. 32.

Figure 1–5 A migrant family has a special form of lifestyle. (U.S. Department of Labor)

one household or in close proximity, so that goods and services may be shared; and (6) single, widowed, divorced, or separated adults living alone. Experimental family styles include (1) the commune, a household of monogamous couples who live together to share resources, child care, and group activities, or (2) a household of adults and children who emphasize the one-family concept, where each adult is married to all other adults and each child has all the adults as parents.

Other alternatives in family-life systems are arrangements or relationships in which a young couple live together as a married couple but are not married and may not have plans for marriage. Sometimes these couples have children.

Within a nuclear marriage, there may be unusual arrangements. When careers are important, the husband and the wife may live a considerable distance apart for a time, depending upon their work. This has been called *long-distance marriage.* These couples may have children, and in some instances, the husband stays in the home with the children because that is where he works, while the wife is away on her job. Sometimes the mother commutes, for example, between New York and Washington, D.C. Some couples are deliberately planning not to have children or are postponing having children until the wife is well established in her career.

Quality of Family Life

The degree of satisfaction in family living is influenced by many factors. Extended dependency on parents, according to Bettelheim,[10] has resulted from the longer social and economic dependence of their children. Also affecting adults is a sharp increase in average life expectancy, which has led to the responsibility for elderly parents and has meant a longer retirement period in their own lives. Retirement may be marked by nonproductivity. Families and society have to plan to handle this situation. Although children mature in all areas of development at an earlier age than formerly, parents may continue to protect their children. This situation may evoke an open revolt of the young against their parents because of the delay in their independence. This situation can develop into a destructive phenomenon that interferes with family happiness.

The purposes of the family are changing. In the past, many believed that the principal function of the family was to provide the physical necessities, such as food, clothing, and shelter. Today's parents continue to provide these essentials, according to their ability, but some parents do not gain fulfillment from this responsibility. The purpose of the modern family, as Bettelheim discerns it, resides in less tangible achievements that are difficult to assess. These purposes include the ultimate physical, intellectual, and emotional development of each family member; the provision of every opportunity to be happy and successful; and the chance for every family member to be contented and close to all other family members. Deterrents to the accomplishment of these goals are wide variations in the interests and activities of family members and a pronounced emphasis on "a life of my own." Working parents often have limited time to spend with their children and spouse. Some families do not provide ways for children to contribute to the economic and social welfare of all, an experience that could enhance their development, their sense of self-worth, and their feeling of helping.

Some family-life professionals believe that the family is important in helping its members to identify, to clarify, and to select values that may improve their quality of life.[11] The humaneness and the psychological support that a family provides are other suggested functions of the family.

[10] Bruno Bettelheim, "The Family, Then and Now," *New York University Education Quarterly,* Vol. 8, No. 5 (Spring 1977), pp. 2–7.

[11] Betty Lane, "The Challenge of Shaping Future Families," *Journal of Home Economics,* Vol. 65, No. 2 (Feb. 1973), p. 61.

Family-Life Education

Home economics educators must be familiar with and well informed about families and their ways of living in order to develop expertise. Many professionals are concerned only with working with an individual member of a family and often fail to consider the totality of family relationships, according to Mannino.[12] Certain understandings are imperative, such as understanding variations in family lifestyles in order to identify family needs and the ways to meet them intelligently. Understanding the family's effects on and interrelationships with institutions (religious, medical, educational, work, peer-group, leisure, and the like) will enable the home economics professional to perform more effectively.

THE EDUCATIONAL SETTING

A popular pastime is to berate education. Tyler[13] offers three positive achievements of American education: (1) it is a force in maintaining a stable society in spite of strife and confusion; (2) it provides two-and-one-half times more of a chance than in other societies for youth to rise above the socioeconomic level of their parents; and (3) it provides for the education of very diverse groups of people for citizenship and productive work. The challenge for education in the present and for the future is to analyze trends, to examine the role of government and politics in education, to solve wide-ranging problems, to look outward from academia, and to concentrate on a curriculum that will meet the needs of students for lifetime learning.

Problems Facing Schools

Some of the problems listed by Goodlad and Tyler[14] are (1) reaching students who have no or little education when society demands considerable schooling (an example is an unemployed youth who is unable to secure a job because of inadequate education); (2) developing moral and ethical character during schooling; (3) helping adolescents to grow into adulthood; (4) creating greater school-community involvement; (5) reaching disadvantaged youth; (6) re-examining the meaning of equality in education; (7) analyzing the prob-

[12] Fortune V. Mannino, "An Ecological Approach to Understanding Family and Community Relationships," *Journal of Home Economics*, Vol. 66, No. 3 (March 1974), pp. 37–41.

[13] M. Frances Klein, "Tyler and Goodlad Speak on American Education: A Critique," *Educational Leadership*, Vol. 33, No. 8 (May 1976), pp. 565–570.

[14] Ibid., p. 565.

Figure 1–6 The school is only one source of education. Other sources are family, mass media, churches, youth groups, libraries, and community resources. (Bethlehem Steel)

lems related to centralization and decentralization of schools; (8) planning for a more challenging program in the final year of high school; (9) being more effective in operational procedures; (10) helping students to have greater access to, and to adjust to, a complex society; and (11) creating less segmentation and greater cohesion and interaction among all educators.

Other problems are handling violence and vandalism in schools, considering strategies for mainstreaming the special student into the classroom, and unraveling some of the serious complexities, such as recognizing and integrating the education that students are receiving outside of school from religious organizations, mass media, youth groups, families, museums, libraries, and other sources.[15]

Trends in Education

Trends that continue to gain attention in education are behavioral objectives (which are, however, contested by the humanistic educators); career and occupational education; and competency-based teacher education. There is great interest in individualized instruction, in which students may proceed according to their ability and

[15] Lawrence A. Cremin, "The Ecology of American Education," *New York University Education Quarterly,* Vol. 3, No. 3 (Spring 1972), p. 3.

inclination. Use of the community has offered another dimension to education in its enhancement of student experiences and has demonstrated a sufficiently important contribution to be continued. Financial problems have been a deterrent to educational planning and may become more serious in light of the citizen tax revolt. A strong trend toward teaching the basics is prevalent and is being encouraged by parents, the community, and others, although some objections have been raised. Accountability continues to be a major trend as it is demanded by federal, state, county, and city governments as well as school administrations.

Politics and the Role of Government in Education

For many years education was considered apolitical.[16] During the 1950s and 1960s, the federal government enlarged its role in education. Federal court decisions reflected a more aggressive posture in regard to religion in schools, racial segregation, and the rights of students and teachers. Legislation related to schools increased. Governmental commitment to education deepened with greater funding and control. Communities gained greater power over their schools.

Politics is *power* and implies control, authority, or influence.[17] In educational politics, there is a concern about how (and how much) power is exercised by government, and over whom. The growth of teacher power and union power, particularly as they relate to bargaining activities, is serious because of the element of conflict. The community, parents, taxpayers, and citizens may on occasion display a political stance.

Dahl[18] points out the need to improve skills in political analysis. All educators, including home economists, need such skills in order to function and even to survive. If educational politics involves an authoritarian allocation of resources and of power, then planned action by educators at the local to the federal levels, in professional groups, as citizens, and in other ways, is imperative. The need for political skills is equally critical. Only through being heard can greater numbers of people experience equality in education and can more families gain opportunities for self-expression and a higher standard of living.[19]

[16] Jay D. Scribner and Richard M. Engbert, "The Politics of Education: An Introduction," in *The Politics of Education,* Seventy-sixth Yearbook of the National Society for the Study of Education, Part II (Chicago: U. of Chicago, 1977), pp. 9–22.

[17] Ibid., pp. 23–27.

[18] Robert H. Dahl, *Modern Political Analysis* (Englewood Cliffs, N.J.: Prentice-Hall, 1970), p. 1.

[19] Willis D. Hawley, "If Schools Are for Learning, the Study of Politics Is Just Beginning," in *The Politics of Education,* Seventy-sixth Yearbook of the National Society for the Study of Education, Part II (Chicago: U. of Chicago, 1977), p. 334.

Curriculum Development

If constraints can be overcome, a lifelong human-needs curriculum should be created for persons of all ages, according to Shane.[20] A command of fundamental processes is necessary if one is to meet both present and future needs, such as (1) skill in human relations, group processes, and cross-cultural and multiethnic understanding; (2) neoacademic skills, such as the knowledge and use of computer language and an ability to cope with cross-disciplinary information; and (3) anticipatory skills, represented by the ability to make correlations, to act on sound data, to evaluate choices and decisions, and to understand how power functions at different levels, from the neighborhood to international capitals.

Home economics educators are challenged to determine where home economics education fits into the total pattern of education. Certainly home economics contributes to meeting the basic needs. How may we become political analysts and to what ends? How do we meet the educational needs of all ages in our field? How do the trends in our profession mesh with the trends in education? What might be next steps?

SUGGESTIONS FOR FURTHER LEARNING

1. Select a nationally known newspaper, such as *The Christian Science Monitor, The New York Times, The Baltimore Sun,* or *The St. Louis Post-Dispatch.* Read each issue of the newspaper for a week and carefully choose those news items that deal with the social problems mentioned in this chapter. Have you discovered any new viewpoints or information? What new insights have you gained? Are any of the points discussed of particular concern to the home economics teacher? Were any of your own values, beliefs, or attitudes challenged? If so, in what way? Did you discover any new social problems that were not discussed in this chapter? Have these articles stimulated you to any action? What kind?
2. Read the following references, which relate to this chapter. Find some references on your own. Become steeped in the problems of contemporary life. Select your own way of summarizing positions, issues, possible action, or whatever you believe will help you to have a global view of the situation as it affects home economic programs.

"The American Family," Parts I and II, "The Ecology of Education." *The National Elementary Principal,* **5** (May–June and July–Aug. 1976), entire issues.

Aries, Philippe, et al. "The Family." *Daedalus* (Spring 1977), entire issue.

Bernard, Jessie, et al. "Stress and the Family." *Journal of Home Economics,* **68** (Nov. 1976), 6–19.

[20] Harold G. Shane, *Curriculum Change Toward the 21st Century* (Washington, D.C.: N.E.A., 1977), p. 11.

Bettelheim, Bruno. "The Family, Now and Then." *New York University Education Quarterly,* **8** (Spring 1977), 2–7.
Bettelheim, Bruno. "Untying the Family." *The Center Magazine,* **9** (Sept.–Oct. 1976), 5–9.
Brown, Lester K., Patricia McGrath, and Bruce Stokes. *Twenty-Two Dimensions of the Population Problem.* Worldwatch Paper 5. Washington, D.C.: Worldwatch Institute, March 1976.
Bryant, Barbara Everitt. *American Women, Today and Tomorrow.* Washington, D.C.: National Commission of International Women's Year, Superintendent of Documents, March 1977.
Focus on Families, selected articles from the *Journal of Home Economics,* American Home Economics Association, Washington, D.C., 1977.
Gross, Dorothy, et al. "Improving the Quality of Family Life." *Childhood Education,* **54** (Nov.–Dec. 1977), entire issue.
Leeper, Robert R., et al. "Controversy and Education." *Educational Leadership,* **33** (Oct. 1975), 3–28.
McGrath, Patricia L. *The Unfinished Assignment: Equal Education for Women.* Worldwatch Paper 7. Washington, D.C.: Worldwatch Institute, July 1976.
McKean, Robert C., and Bob L. Taylor. "Politics and Education, New Challenges, New Problems." *Educational Leadership,* **34** (Nov. 1976), 83–112.
Ross, Heather L., and Isabel V. Sawhill. *Time of Transition, The Growth of Families Headed by Women.* Washington D.C.: The Urban Institute, 1975.
Schumacher, E. F. *Small Is Beautiful, Economics as If People Mattered.* New York: Harper, 1973.
Scribner, Jay D., et al. *The Politics of Education,* The Seventy-sixth Yearbook of the National Society for the Study of Education, Part II. Chicago: U. of Chicago, 1977.
Shane, Harold G. *Curriculum Change Toward the 21st Century.* Washington, D.C.: Curriculum Series, NEA, 1977.
"What Future for the American Family?" *Changing Times,* **30** (Dec. 1976), 7–10.
Wise, Arthur E. "The Hypernationalization of American Education." *New York University Education Quarterly,* **8** (Summer 1977), 2–6.

2

Education Through Home Economics

Home economics contributes to the education of individuals of every age. Programs dealing with personal and family development begin with prenatal care and continue throughout the life cycle. Schools, colleges, extension services, and other educational endeavors offer programs in home economics. Millions are reached through mass media, conferences, workshops, institutes, professional meetings, individual consultation, individualized instruction, adult education, and other avenues. The preparation of home economics–oriented educational materials by schools, extension services, professional magazines, professional organizations, businesses, government agencies, social welfare services, publishers, and other adds another dimension. There is considerable breadth and depth in the treatment of home economics subject matter by all of these sources and through all these avenues of communication. To serve this clientele is a challenge to home economics delivery systems.

DEFINITION AND CONCERNS

During the Fourth Lake Placid Conference, the complex nature of home economics led to a tentative definition that could be accepted today:

> Home economics in its most comprehensive sense is the study of the laws, conditions, principles, and ideals which are concerned on the one hand

with man's immediate physical environment and on the other hand with his nature as a social being, and is the study especially of the relation between the two factors.[1]

A committee of the American Home Economics Association developed a new statement (Home Economics—New Directions II) for the profession that included input from many members of the profession.[2]

Home Economics—New Directions II

Statement of Purpose

The focus of home economics is family in its various forms. Family is defined as a unit of intimate, transacting, and interdependent persons who share some values and goals, resources, responsibility for decisions, and have commitment to one another over time.

HOME ECONOMICS views the family as a major source of nurturance, protection, and renewal for the individual. As an educational force, the family significantly contributes to the qualitative development of its individual members and has the potential to prepare them for effective productivity for self and society.

From this perspective, HOME ECONOMICS works through family to effect an optimum balance between people and their environments. HOME ECONOMICS accepts the challenge of helping people to adjust to change and to shape the future.

The core of HOME ECONOMICS is the family ecosystem. It is the study of the reciprocal relations of family to its natural and man-made environments, the effect of these singly or in unison as they shape the internal functioning of families, and the interplays between the family and other social institutions and the physical environment.

New Priorities for Home Economics

These statements assume that the home economics profession recognizes the interrelationship of theory (a knowledge base for home economics) and research (scientifically structured investigations about the family ecosystem). Theory and research provide the base for application in business, education, and service programs. The implications (cost/benefits assessed in terms of people and environments) for maintaining and/or changing the family unit need to be continuously assessed in charting the future.

It is not intended that the following priorities be all-inclusive. Rather, the home economist will adapt and expand the statements to give more substantive meaning for particular situations, interests, and needs.

1. *Futuristic Thinking and Planning.* Envisions alternative designs of every-

[1] Katurah E. Baldwin, *The AHEA Saga* (Washington, D.C.: American Home Economics Association, 1949), p. 15.

[2] Gordon Blivens, Margaret Fitch, Gwendolyn Newkirk, Beatrice Paolucci, Em Riggs, Satenig St. Marie, and Gladys Vaughn, "Home Economics—New Directions II," *Journal of Home Economics*, Vol. 67, No. 3 (May 1975), pp. 20–27.

day living and critically evaluates and interprets the costs/benefits of these.

2. *Public Policy Formation.* Achieves greater input into decisions made in the public realm that impact on families.
3. *Creative Adaption to Uncertainty and Change.* Views the opportunities inherent in change and is willing to assume risks in directing change affecting families.
4. *Redistribution of Resources.* Recognizes the interdependence of resource availability and the development of human potentials, and initiates actions that lead to a more equitable resource distribution.
5. *Interrelatedness of the Professional and the Paraprofessional.* Distinguishes between the competencies of the professional and the paraprofessional and acknowledges the contribution of each to families.

The priorities are only viable when home economists critically examine the profession in relation to existing programs to ensure that they are justifiable; as changes are effected, do the existing programs require different structures and emphasis or mere additions to the present situations? The home economist must be creative and innovative in accepting the challenges that new priorities require new structures, programs, and responsibilities.

HOME ECONOMICS CONTENT

The content of home economics is a synthesis of the physical, biological, and social sciences; the arts; and the humanities as they are applied to the improvement of family living. The aspects of family living that concern home economists in general and home economics

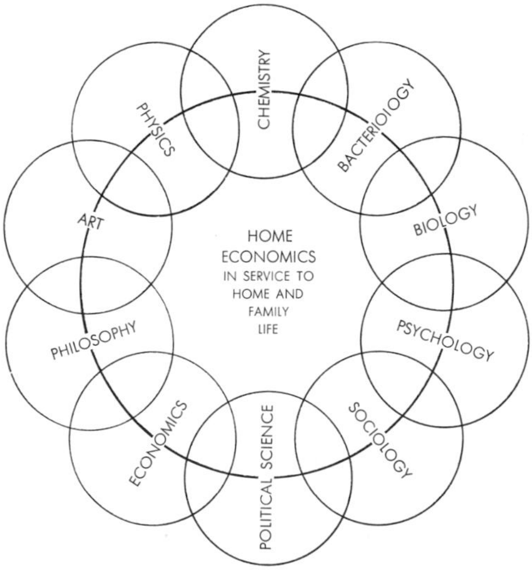

Figure 2–1 The integrating function of home economics. (Courtesy of Grace Henderson, *Development of Home Economics in United States,* College of Home Economics, Pennsylvania State University)

educators in particular include the following areas, that were developed in a series of professional workshops.[3]

The area of *human development and family* is grouped into four clusters based on a framework of major concepts and generalizations: human growth and development, families, environmental influences, and individual development. Some of the emphases are the characteristics and the orderly sequence of growth and development at different stages or ages of individuals. Studies in personal and family living may stress individual and social values, relationships, heredity, socialization, and interaction with the environment. In addition, these studies include adaptation to life situations, understanding of human sexuality and sex roles, and development of the individual in the family. Human development and family are like common threads in the subject matter of home economics and may be mentioned in the discussion of the various other areas of home economics.

Consumer education and home management have a strong interrelationship because both are related to the management of resources. Personal and family satisfactions with goods, services, and other resources may be optimized by the decisions that individuals and families make. Many factors influence the management of resources and the quality of life, such as ethnic and cultural backgrounds, lifestyles, stages in the life cycle, and basic human needs. A recognition of the concepts related to family consumption and economics is important. Knowledge about the available total resources, interdependence within the economic system, and the critical importance of consumer choices is integral to being an effective consumer and manager.

Nutrition and food management focus on the decisions related to food choices. These decisions are based on knowledge of the influence of physical activity and physiological states, the impact of culture, occupation, symbolism related to foods and nutrition, food likes and dislikes, family economic and social status, family lifestyles, and the role of the gatekeeper (the person in the family who has the most influence on the food that comes into a home and that is actually consumed). Other influences on food selection are familiarity with the nutrient density of plant, animal, and prefabricated foods; ability to distinguish among fact, fad, fallacy, and food lore; the effect of preparation, storage, sanitary measures, additives, and the service of food on the adequacy of a diet. An awareness of world hunger, of policies that might affect family nutrition, and of the management of national and world food resources is encouraged in nutrition education.

The area of *clothing, apparel, and textiles* focuses on the role of

[3] Home Economics Teacher Educators, *Competencies for Home Economics Teachers* (Ames: Iowa State U. P., 1978).

clothes in daily living. The language or meanings conveyed by clothes to the self and others, the impact of personal development, peer approval and interaction, and contribution to the quality of life are important clothing influences. The making, buying, and wearing of clothes reflect a knowledge of the application of art elements and principles and an analysis of sociological, psychological, physiological, and cultural influences. Age, occupation, health (including handicaps), lifestyle, comfort, safety, and pleasure affect the choice of clothes. Consideration of the characteristics of a specific fiber as to its durability, its range of use, its care and cost, its availability, its appropriateness for the purpose, and its assets and liabilities is basic to the selection of clothes. The selection and purchase of clothing and textiles, including those used in home furnishings, are an essential part of the study in this area. Recycling, legislation, types of markets, the impact of advertisements, and trends in clothing selection are pertinent.

Figure 2–2 Teaching an awareness of world hunger is one objective of home economics education. (United Nations)

Housing, living environments, furnishings, and home equipment include the selection, purchase, and use of any of these components with a recognition of the role of physical, psychological, economic, and sociocultural factors. Other influences are availability, design and structural form, present and future needs, awareness of the impact of attitudes, values, knowledge, skill and experience in making choices, analysis of unique needs, and the role of the family members in making decisions. Energy and ecological conservation, the role of the family in formulating and implementing public policies with regard to housing and the total environment, and a sensitivity to the impact of legislation on home environments are social concerns related to this area.

With a knowledge of the research related to each of these areas, the home economics educator can read the material available in each of them with greater discrimination and accuracy, which in turn will assure greater confidence in working with students. Further critical inquiry may be stimulated on the part of both teacher and students, and their thinking, studying, and communicating may become more rigorous in the process.

HOME ECONOMICS PROGRAMS

Home economics education can contribute significantly to the development of families and their members. The content already reviewed suggests ways in which individuals and families can acquire skills for living, such as decision making and coping with inflation and other social problems that impinge on families. Handling resources wisely, examining and clarifying values, learning to assess and establish viable goals, and wise handling of the countless other facets of everyday life can improve the quality of personal and family living. Home economics is the only profession that can offer expertise in all of these areas.

This mission of home economics is accomplished through offering education and services in a broad spectrum. This profession has something to offer for each age level and for a wide range of problems, interests, and needs. Examples of contributions of home economics are described here.

Infant-Care Centers

There are few infant-care centers in the nation, but the need for them has been demonstrated, and the number is growing. The function of these centers is to give care (often adjusted to various hours) to the infants of working women, mothers who are ill, and mothers who are unable to care for their children for other reasons. The centers work closely with parents.

Whether a mother should work while her child is still an infant may be a controversial question, but some mothers must work for economic reasons. A study on working women by the Center for Human Resources Research revealed some interesting data.[4] About 35 per cent of the white women and nearly 50 per cent of the black women who have returned to work were back on the job within five months after the birth of their child. Nearly 70 per cent of the black women were working full time shortly after the birth of their child. Of the white women 50–55 per cent returned to work full time.

Infant laboratories or centers are connected with home economics in some colleges and universities. The rationale is that young couples who have to deal with an infant child may feel quite incompetent and anxious about their abilities as parents.

Home economists may serve as administrators[5] or teachers, with nutritionists working with the pediatrician in advising on the feeding of infants. All participate in the education of parents. A teacher in an infant-care center may plan activities to stimulate learning and growth in many areas, such as seeing, feeling, hearing, and the use of the other senses. Giving a feeling of support and other infant-development tactics are important. Home economists who work in these programs have laid a strong emphasis on human development in their professional preparation.

Preschool Education

Children who are toddlers one to three years of age and those who are four to six years of age may be found in infant centers, nursery schools, part-of-a-day and all-day child-care centers, and kindergartens. Children in these programs represent all ranges of the socioeconomic spectrum. The distinction between being toilet-trained or not influences where children are placed. Children under two-and-a-half years are usually placed in infant centers. Mature two-and-a-half-year-olds and children of three to five years of age are found in nursery schools and day-care centers. Kindergarten most often begins at five years of age. Some centers are financed by government funds; some are part of a school or college or university program; and some are private and the parents must pay the full cost.

The programs consist of activities that are appropriate for each age

[4] Center for Human Resources Research, *Years for Decision*, Vol. 4 (Columbus: Ohio State University, 1978).

[5] New York University offers an interdisciplinary program (elementary education, nursing, psychology, and home economics and nutrition departments) for a master's degree in the preparation of administrators for infant- and toddler-care centers.

Figure 2–3 Preschool education contributes to child development.

level or level of maturity. Manipulative skills and other experiences are emphasized for physical growth. Social skills are strengthened through playing, sharing and learning with peers. Creativity may be stimulated through activities such as finger painting, setting up life-like situations like playing house and storekeeping, building with blocks, or storytelling.

The development of sound eating habits can be established through the serving of nutritious meals and snacks as well as through the child's being with other children who are consuming their food with relish. The teacher who can encourage children to become involved in activities that are especially stimulating is a valuable guide. The ecouragement of freedom in making choices and the availability of facilities and equipment that most homes cannot provide are other assets of these centers. Older children have activities of a more mature and complex nature to foster their development.

Some high schools operate nursery schools in which the high school students participate. The value to the high school students of this education for future parenthood and for future positions is difficult to estimate, but the students do have a chance to observe themselves realistically as they work with the children. High school boys, interestingly, tend to strengthen their masculine image. Day-care centers, with expanded services in the areas of education, health, and nutrition, will be available to millions of American children if legislation can be enacted. In addition, business and labor, community agencies, church clubs, and other charitable groups have established day-care centers. The movement is to provide care for the children of all families who desire it with cost shared according to financial ability and without cost for those who cannot afford to pay. Home economics teachers can make a special contribution as experts in child development.

Elementary Education

Home economics in organized education logically begins in the elementary grades.[6] It can be integrated into the program of any grade at the elementary level.

In some schools, home economics teachers are given released time to serve as consultants to elementary teachers. They may help to plan suitable experiences that emphasize home and family living in relation to the learning of students. For example, when a particular country is studied in social studies, questions may be raised about the way of life in that country. Some foods may be prepared, pictures of homes and clothes may be displayed, or a film about this nation that highlights family living may be shown. Other topics of interest are the use of leisure time, the games played, and the holidays celebrated. A comparison of similarities and differences in ways of life is especially valuable.

The home economics teacher may also, with the help of students, demonstrate certain nutritious foods that they can prepare at home: quick-cooked cereal, dried or fresh fruit, and dishes with milk. Cultural foods and foods not requiring cooking add a creative touch. Reading labels for nutritional information, handling an allowance, helping with home jobs, buying food, and the care and selection of clothes are other possibilities. A mobile home-economics unit, which includes cooking units, kitchen equipment, fabrics, materials for mending, detergents and other cleaning agents, and similar items, is used in some schools. It is wheeled from room to room as it is needed.

Home economics can be integrated with mathematics: measuring ingredients and studying recipes or measuring fabric for sewing projects. In literature, stories or poems may be read or told about mother's and father's work or ways to help mother and father at home. Feelings or ideas about the importance of the home can be explored through songs or artwork. In science, simple experiments can

[6] Virginia Anderson, "Home Economics and the Three R's," *Journal of Home Economics,* Vol. 65, No. 2 (Feb. 1973), pp. 15–18.

be conducted with detergents or cleansing agents to compare the ability of different brands to remove common household soils. Another experiment might demonstrate the effect of heat on protein foods. Animal experiments in nutrition may be suitable for upper grades. The possibilities are limitless.

The school cafeteria can provide many learning experiences, such as using good table manners, choosing a nutritious lunch, being a gracious host or hostess, and planning a menu. Students can be made responsible for the bulletin boards in the cafeteria, for organizing the serving and the lines for returning trays, for decorating the tables with mats and interesting centerpieces, and for actual assistance in certain tasks.

Some junior and senior high schools use the elementary grades, when they are conveniently near, as a laboratory for learning more about small children. The older students assist on the playground or in the classroom for a limited time. Observing children for certain behavior, speech patterns, eating habits, patterns of relationships, degree of maturity, and the like can be quite revealing. Sometimes pupils from the lower grades are brought to the home economics

Figure 2–4 Elementary school children making an Irish stew on St. Patrick's Day. (USDA Photo)

room, so that each student has an opportunity to work with a small child or two in a home-economics–related activity.

Middle School

One of the latest changes in the organizational structure of schools is the middle school. The middle school begins with the fifth or sixth grade and extends through the eighth grade. Within this framework there are many types of grade organization, such as 7–8, 6–7–8, and 5–6–7–8.

The major concept is to provide for the special needs of the preadolescent, particularly socially, physically, and emotionally. These students are "in-betweeners" and need to establish a consistent image of themselves, examine their values and attitudes, and determine their role in society. The middle school is an attempt to effect a gradual transition from a self-contained elementary school to a departmentalized high school.

Ideally, the middle school is student-centered, and emphasis is placed on creative exploration, self-direction, and independence. Greater flexibility in program encourages greater variability in scheduling, teaching, and group size than the junior high school permits.

The middle school presents interesting challenges to the home economics teacher. The organization permits curriculum innovations to a greater degree than does the junior high school. Both boys and girls are in home economics classes. Because students are in an important stage of growing up, the home economics curriculum should recognize the needs of these students: peer relationships, for example, are so important that some group work is essential. Some middle schools have emphasized the world of work, an area in which the home economics teacher can be especially helpful. Health is another topic that can be covered.

Every area of home economics can be profitably taught in the middle school. Examples are looking at human development within their own age range; the development of desirable food habits; assistance in family food preparation; learning clothing construction, buying, and care; decision making with regard to personal resources; buying for leisure; family relations; and social development.

Teachers in middle schools are drawn from both elementary and high schools. Elementary teachers, according to Compton,[7] are especially effective in planning and in suggesting varied activities, whereas the secondary teachers have an in-depth knowledge of the subject matter and are helpful in the development of units. Team

[7] Crystal Compton, "Getting Middle Schools Started—What We Learned," *The National Elementary Principal,* Vol. 51, No. 3 (Nov. 1971), pp. 50–54.

teaching is used frequently, and home economics teachers can be found on related-arts teaching teams or on academic teaching teams.

Junior High School

Home economics teachers reach more students at the seventh- and eighth-grade levels than at any other. Some authorities advance the belief that home economics should be exploratory in nature at this stage, but whatever the focus, the teacher must plan to meet the problems, needs, interests, and objectives of this age group.

Instruction must be planned for both boys and girls in a class. Focus should be on the area under discussion, not on sex differences. An example is hair care. Both boys and girls may wear short or long hair, so attention is given to care of various types of hair, such as curly, thin, thick, oily, and so on. Many articles of clothing have commonalities. Many boys and girls participate in the same home jobs, such as preparing meals, maintaining the home, and buying food and other household items.

Senior High School

The courses planned for students at the level of senior high school have various purposes. They may be designed for the girl or boy who marries in high school or soon after graduation, for those who wish instruction in wage earning, for boys and girls who wish to improve competencies for daily living, or for those who intend to specialize in a certain area—foods, clothing, child care, or the like. Many courses attempt to interrelate the areas that will have special meaning in the personal lives of all students as homemakers and family members. The emphasis in these courses is on preparation for marriage, family living and health, consumer education, management, and housing.

Mini or short courses or modules provide opportunities to interest high school students in home economics. Enrichment courses on Saturdays are becoming more common. Foods and clothing have been especially popular with boys, but they are also interested in other areas of home economics. In some instances, parents and children take courses together. For example, a father and son might enjoy learning about outdoor cooking, refinishing furniture, or doing crafts related to the home.

These mini courses or modules may be for boys or for boys and girls, and their length varies, but a marking period is one guide. Catchy titles may attract students. Suggestions[8] include "How to

[8] Ideas offered by the Forecast/Co-Ed Editorial Advisory Board at a meeting on May 6, 1972, in New York City.

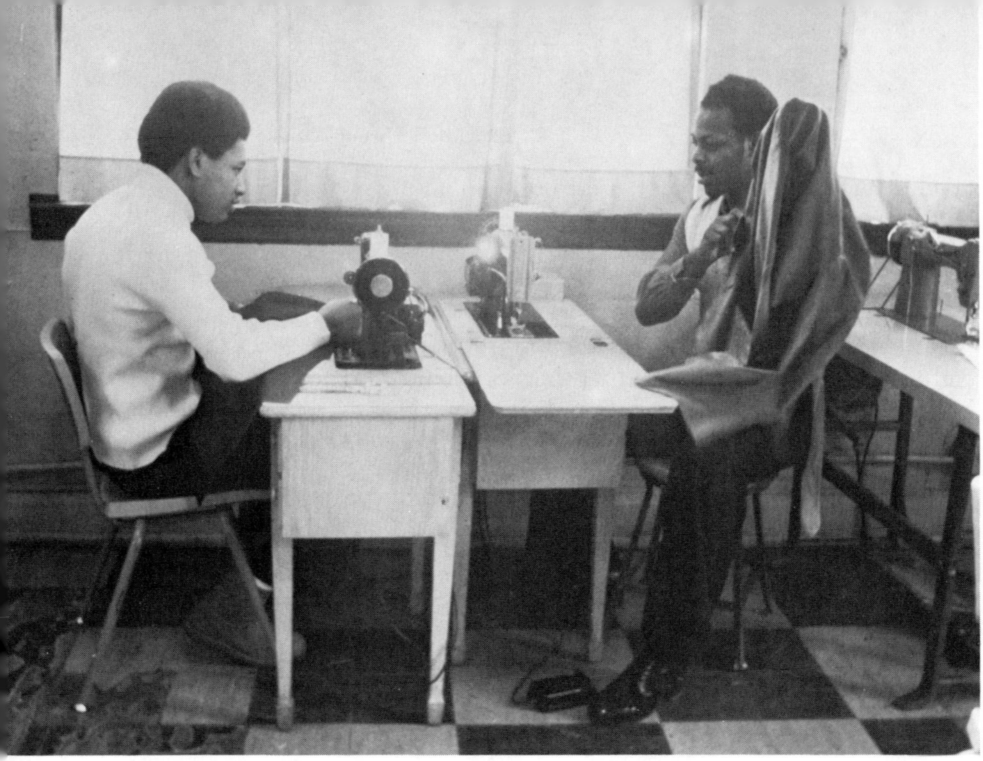

Figure 2–5 Boys enjoy making their own clothes. (Photo courtesy of Simplicity Pattern Co., Inc.)

Make and Keep Your Bread" (consumer education course); "Bachelor Survival"; "Instant Help and Where to Get It" (especially helpful for both boys and girls of disadvantaged families); and "Knitwits" (sewing boys' pants and other items using stretch fabrics).

Other suggested topics for these courses are facets of consumer education that charm the young, including the buying and care of bicycles, mopeds, and motorbikes; stereos, CB radios, and recordings; used automobiles; recreation; games to play at home; the pros and cons of health foods; quick, do-it-yourself, low-cost home furnishings; foods of other countries; and hasty meals for married students or for students who live away from home.

A course in home ecology would be exciting for students. Cooperation with the science and social studies departments is a possibility. Some topics to consider for this course might be the everyday waste that accumulates in a home and what happens to it after disposal; possibilities for recycling; the improvement of packages from a pollution viewpoint (an article, "The Packaging Problem Is a Can of Worms," by Tom Alexander in the June 1972 issue of *Fortune* may be of use here); and personal and community involvement.

A course on suggestions for making money may attract attention. Things to sell might include unusual foods (an organic or natural food dessert or a low-calorie snack); posters, such as the cover of the May 1972 issue of Future Homemakers of America's *Teen-Times;*

homemade ties; macrame wall hangings; tote bags; soap sculpture; beach needs; unusual personal services; tie-dyed articles; needlework; or collages. At the end of the course, a boutique might be set up for the sale of the items. Students may wish to set up their own little business. In the Locust Valley High School (Locust Valley, New York) students run a small bakeshop and prepare nutritious snacks for sale. Students are responsible for all the business processes, such as surveying their public, advertising their product, establishing a budget, selling tactics, and the like.[9] Establishing criteria for the marketability of products, display, packaging, and business procedures might be a part of the course. The distributive education and art staffs and students might participate.

Career and Occupational Education

The home economics curriculum may include specialized educational programs for developing attitudes and job competencies that will lead to employment. There are many variations in the development of such a program. It may be offered for students in high school who must bridge the gap between school and work. The preparation may be for positions that are home-economics related and are of the service type, such as day-care center aide, waiter or waitress, dietary aide, or upholstery assistant. Homemakers who are new to the labor market or are interested in acquiring new skills or upgrading present skills enroll in an occupational education program.

An effort is being made to serve the disadvantaged, the unemployed, and the handicapped. Other goals are to familiarize elementary and secondary school students with a broad range of occupations for which skills are required and with the requisites for careers in such occupations and to provide funds for research and experimental projects to identify new careers in mental and physical health, child care, and other fields. Funds are allocated also to prepare students for the occupation of homemaking and for the dual role of homemaker and wage earner. (See Chapter 17 for additional information.)

Future Homemakers of America and Home Economics Related Occupations

Future Homemakers of America and Home Economics Related Occupations is a national organization of home economics students in junior and senior high schools. All students who are now enrolled or who have previously taken courses in home economics are eligible to

[9] Information from Anna Marie Warren-Boulton, the teacher of the project.

join. The total membership is around 500,000 in 12,000 chapters in the United States, Puerto Rico, the Virgin Islands, and American schools overseas. Male members increased 20 per cent, to 20,000, in 1977. Three fourths of the males participate in FHA chapters and one fourth in HERO chapters.[10] The Division of Vocational and Technical Education in the Office of Education and the American Home Economics Association sponsor the organization.

Some unique features[11] of the Future Homemakers of America are

1. It operates through the framework of secondary schools at all levels.
2. It is an integral part of the home economics curriculum.
3. Affiliation is open to all public and private schools that provide home economics instruction.
4. Two types of chapters are available: FHA chapters for youth in general home economics, including family-life education, and FHA/HERO chapters for youth in classes especially designed for occupational objectives in home-economics–related occupations.
5. It provides opportunities for developing individual and group initiative in planning and carrying out activities related to the dual role of homemaker and wage earner.

Correlated classes/chapters of Future Homemakers of America provide a unique teaching tool for reaching home economics students.

Teen Times is the magazine for this organization. Article titles give an insight into the topics of concern to these groups: "Apathy"; "Child Abuse"; "Handicaps"; "Death"; "Changing Roles"; "Goal Setting"; "Teen Businesses"; "Marriage or Life Planning—Call It The Coping Kit."

Future Homemakers of America chapters concentrate on personal development by devices such as "Impact" (steps for planning); "Encounter" (examining ways to grow); "Get Out of the Boxes You Are In"; and in other ways. Involvement in community problems and improvement is demonstrated in many ways. Chapter members work with the retarded, the elderly, and delinquents and on pollution control and consumer education projects and similar activities. Many chapters work with local units of the March of Dimes, the Federation of Women's Clubs, the National Association of Retired Persons, and others in launching campaigns such as "Wanted: Better Babies." Individual members work on their own projects, such as sewing clothes

[10] Millie Riley, *Method* (Washington, D.C.: Future Homemakers of America, March 1977), p. 2.

[11] Information provided by National Headquarters, Future Homemakers of America, 2010 Massachusetts Ave., N.W., Washington, D.C. 20036.

for a child who is paralyzed from the waist down, pushing recycling, planning a pioneer meal and serving it to some elderly guests, or being responsible for creating a bulletin board on part-time jobs. Many chapters invite speakers and involved parents to rap sessions on burning topics.

Home economics teachers will wish to advise a chapter of the FHA/HERO (the largest secondary school youth organization in the nation) in order to provide opportunities for learning beyond the home economics classroom, to become better acquainted with students, and to work with youth toward improved personal, family, and community living.

Postsecondary and Two-Year Colleges

Education at the postsecondary level in home economics is in area schools, technical institutes, or two-year colleges. The following types of students may be served in occupational education:[12]

1. Youth who wish to prepare for wage earning and to complete the requirements for high school graduation.
2. High school dropouts who wish to prepare for an occupation.
3. High school graduates (youth and adults) who wish to prepare for employment.
4. Youth and adults who desire intensive occupational training to secure a job as quickly as possible.
5. Adults who need retraining for a job because their present skills are obsolete.
6. Youth and adults who have academic or socioeconomic handicaps and necessitate special training.
7. Homemakers who have never been employed and now wish to enter employment for the first time.

The two-year-college program provides several avenues for home economics. General home economics programs may provide courses in food and nutrition, child development, family and human relations, family economics and consumer education, management, housing, home furnishings, and clothing as general education and electives. Sometimes home economics supports programs in nursing, physical therapy, dental hygiene, health education, and other fields, with courses in nutrition, child development, and family relations. Special-interest or short-term programs are frequently offered to adults in the community.

[12] Pauline Garrett, et al., *Post-Secondary Education in Home Economics* (Washington, D.C.: American Vocational Association, 1967), p. 8.

Home economics prepares students in two-year colleges for gainful employment in positions such as buyer in fashion merchandise and fashion designer, food service director, day-care center assistant, home decoration assistant in department stores and specialty shops, and dietary technician. The curriculum includes courses in liberal education, specialization, supportive courses to specialization, and fieldwork, usually on-the-job experience.

Because community colleges are becoming more accessible to students, many students take the first two years of college there and then complete their degrees in a four-year college. Some students who have completed an occupational course work for a while and then enter a four-year college. Many students find positions in the areas they have studied in two-year colleges. The income helps to pay their college expenses now or later. Home economics as a profession must give thought to articulation between the two-year and the four-year college curriculums to meet the varied needs of these students.

Adult Education

Home economists employed in adult education must be proficient in both subject matter and teaching methods. All areas of home economics are represented. Sometimes full-time teachers accept this extra responsibility, and in some instances, part-time teachers are employed.

Many of the home economists in extension work with adults in various ways. The Expanded Food and Nutrition Education Program (EFNEP) utilizes paraprofessionals, called *program aides,* in a person-to-person approach to adult education.[13] The aides are selected from the low-income clientele, so that the clients will find them approachable. Although this program was designed for emphasis on foods and nutrition, in some of the projects the aides and the home economists have discovered other family problems, such as the need for family planning. According to the write-in comments of aides in a study by Brand,[14] an overwhelming 93.7 per cent of the aides found that the women and girls in the program needed information on family planning. Other kinds of assistance were also requested by clients. Extension offers many other programs. In addition to schools and extension, community agencies and industries offer an informal type of adult education through classes for employees, workshops, demonstrations, educational materials, and television, radio, and newspapers. Community agencies provide consultations for individuals, as do some home economists who free-lance.

[13] Keith Prichard and Mary R. Hall, "Attitudes of Aides and Clients," *Journal of Home Economics,* Vol. 63, No. 7 (Oct. 1971), pp. 545–548.

[14] Jean Brand, "Family Planning Information—Do Low-Income Families Need and Want It?" *Journal of Home Economics,* Vol. 64, No. 5 (May 1972), pp. 2–5.

The elderly are a segment of the population especially in need of adult education that will assist them with the many problems that confront them. Legislation has been enacted. A nutrition program has been funded. Hopefully, other programs will be funded.

Other Types of Home Economics Education

Many other professionals are home economics educators in interesting programs. A home economist in a social welfare agency may work with a single social worker or a group of workers whose case families may be having financial problems, need nutrition information, have difficulty in selecting and buying low-cost attractive clothes for family members, or need assistance in buying home furnishings or equipment. A number of home economists work in banks with individuals, couples, or entire families in financial planning and problems. Seminars, workshops, and other types of group meetings may be held for women's clubs, professional groups, or employees of companies, department stores, or other interested groups. Finance companies employ home economists for similar types of education. Pamphlets and other literature may be prepared for distribution to the public. Home economists in rehabilitation teach handicapped individuals of all ages and both sexes to become independent in their home and family living. Home economists in business, advertising, or public relations agencies, or with magazines, may prepare teaching materials, give demonstrations, talk at schools or in other institutions, participate in television or radio programs, or prepare releases for newspapers. Some companies have answering services for letters of inquiry about homemaking problems.

Home economists with utilities companies have become "energy specialists" and teach employees in their companies, groups of homemakers, other home economists, students, and others about ways to save energy. Dietitians teach hospital patients and employees about their diet. Nutritionists in health centers, clinics, and business help patients or employees with special problems in nutrition. Home economists in large department stores may plan and supervise sewing and cooking classes and demonstrations, have clothing or equipment clinics, offer nutrition counseling, or serve customers in other capacities. Pattern companies have home economists to prepare learning materials for a wide audience, from quick-and-easy sewing for beginners to tailoring or other complex processes. Pamphlets and other types of materials on sewing upholstery and making pillows, curtains, draperies, or decorative objects for the home are developed for wide distribution in stores and other outlets as well as for students in schools.

A home economist working with a soap and detergent company or for an institute of manufacturers may reach a wide audience through a newsletter or other publications about personal and home cleaning jobs. Some home economists work alone or with others as consultants. A wardrobe service specialist may help busy women in the selection, purchase, or construction of clothes. A space expert goes into offices and homes and reorganizes furniture, equipment, closets, and other living or work areas for greater efficiency and more pleasant surroundings. A money management service is another type of consultation. Many other examples can be cited of the work of home economics educators in unique programs.

Extension home economists, college faculty, and experts in institutes and councils prepare scholarly monographs, research papers, and monthly communications on recent trends in nutrition, money management, family life, and other areas of home economics. Many home economics educators are employed in government agencies, such as the Department of Agriculture, the Children's Bureau, the Food and Drug Administration, and the Office of Education to supervise and plan educational programs that have been legislated. State departments of education have nutritionists and home economists in supervisory positions to help teachers in the schools or to supervise and coordinate nutrition education programs.

Family-life educators may be located in youth service centers or may be houseparents or program directors in group or halfway houses for the physically or emotionally handicapped or for other groups needing special attention. Program directors in the Big Brother/Big Sister community-coordinated child care, Camp Fire Girls, Girl Scouts, Boy Scouts, and similar organizations may be home economists. Sometimes home economics educators are affiliated with crisis centers, help centers, schools for the deaf or blind, or mental health centers and serve as counselors or outreach workers. Senior citizen centers, YMCA, YWCA, YMHA, YWHA, Red Cross, convalescent homes, housing projects, family resort centers, and penal and/or mental institutions employ home economics educators for family-living programs.

International Home Economics

The role of the American home economist has expanded to include the improvement of home and family living in other nations through actual work abroad or through contacts with visitors, students, and home economists who come to the United States from other parts of the world. Teachers may participate through the Fulbright Teacher Exchange Program or in schools abroad for the children of American military and civilian personnel. Opportunities to work abroad are also available through international programs sponsored by churches, clubs, foundations, and the federal government, as well as through

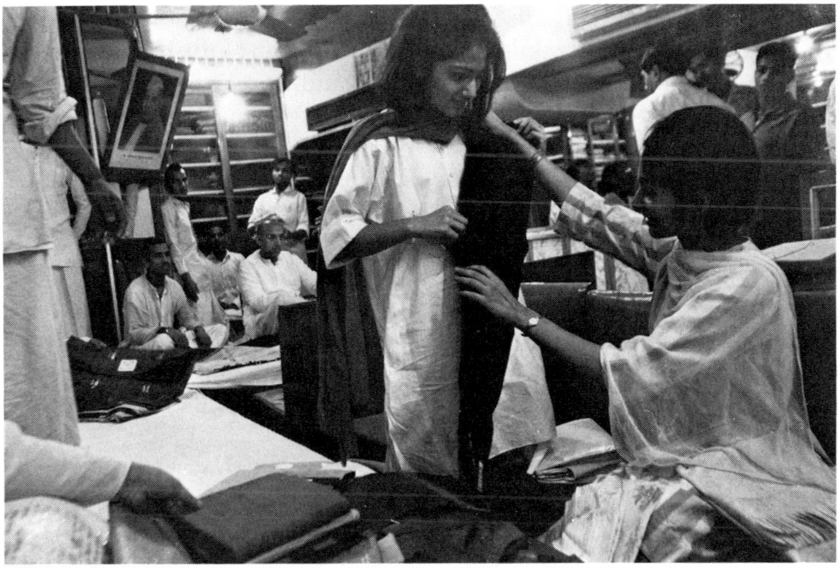

Figure 2–6 A home economics student in India selecting suitable fabric for a project.

United Nations organizations, such as the Food and Agriculture Organization; the Educational, Scientific, and Cultural Organization; and the United Nations Children's Fund. Occasionally the governments of other nations solicit the direct aid of American teachers and home economists. Teachers working abroad must show considerable ingenuity in using limited resources creatively and in planning suitable programs. The realization that programs related to economic growth and population education are more likely to succeed with the assistance of additional programs dealing with family living opens up many job opportunities in all areas of home economics.[15]

Recent legislation has important implications for international home economics. The Findley amendment to the Foreign Assistance Act of 1975[16] established education and extension programs similar to those of the American land-grant institutions for the "hungry" nations of the world. This act gives American universities an opportunity to expand present programs and to develop new ones.

The Percy amendment[17] to the Foreign Assistance Act of 1975 gives particular attention to programs, projects, and activities that tend to integrate women into the national economics of foreign countries, thus improving their status and assisting the total development ef-

[15] Cecile Hoover Edwards, "A New Look at International Service in Home Economics," *Journal of Home Economics*, Vol. 69, No. 4 (Sept. 1977), pp. 58–61.
[16] International Development and Foreign Assistance Act of 1975, Public Law 94-161, 94th Congress, H.R. 9001, Dec. 20, 1975.
[17] Ibid.

fort. This amendment calls for the help of home economists of multiple specialties, such as skills in family planning, skills in making surveys and collecting data about women and families, administrative and leadership skills, familiarity with group dynamics, and competencies in working with mass media. The women in these countries need help in vocational and career development, the formation of cooperatives, and in other areas so they may contribute to the economic development of their countries.

Many of the problems of the Third World are similar to those of poor urban families in America.[18] Some of the needs are improved housing and environmental design, nutrition, child development and day-care centers, care of the elderly, recreation, family planning, and the need for educational programs that deal with the broad spectrum of family life problems.

In addition to strong backgrounds in general home economics, plus strengths in several specializations, other skills that may be required for work abroad include fluency in languages; teaching; organization, supervision, and management; evaluation; research; doing publications; and the development of curriculum materials depending on the nature of the need.

Edwards[19] has an excellent listing of the agencies of the United States government, international agencies, and private foundations in the United States, all of which have international interests in home economics. In addition, there is an excellent table indicating the type of career, position, responsibility, and skills required for many opportunities in international service.

Great benefits would result from more direct communication and association among home economists and home economics organizations that are working on similar problems all over the world. Home economics teachers who are not members may wish to join the International Federation of Home Economics.[20] Attendance at international meetings can be a source of inspiration and challenge.

SUGGESTIONS FOR FURTHER LEARNING

1. If you were to plan a home economics program without leaning on any precedents for elementary, middle school, junior high school, and senior high school students, what innovations would you suggest?
2. In what new ways may home economics educators deliver their services? Why do you feel that these services would be important? Do any of these ways appeal to you as a career?

[18] Edwards, op. cit., p. 59.
[19] Ibid., pp. 60–61.
[20] Dues for this organization are collected by the American Home Economics Association.

3. Here are some references related to this chapter that you might enjoy reading:

   Churaman, Charlotte V. "Home Economists at Work: A Round-Up of Experiences—Family Finance Counseling." *Journal of Home Economics,* **69** (Jan. 1977), 18–21.

   Creasy, Donna Newbury. "A Husband and Wife Business." *Journal of Home Economics,* **67** (July 1975), 7–9.

   Edwards, Cecile Hoover. "A New Look at International Service in Home Economics." *Journal of Home Economics,* **69** (Sept. 1977), 58–61.

   Kunis, Beila Simon. "Family Nutritionist on the Primary Health Care Team." *Journal of Nutrition Education,* **8** (Apr.–June 1976), 77–79.

   Lind, Robert W. "Jobs for Family Life Majors." *Journal of Home Economics,* **68** (Jan. 1976), 26–28.

   Maineri, Sandra C. "How I Developed a Job Market as a Free Lance Home Economist." *Journal of Home Economics,* **68** (Sept. 1976), 51–52.

   Peck, Eileen. "Nutrition Education Specialist: Time for Action." *Journal of Nutrition Education,* **8** (Jan.–March 1976), 11–12.

   Poolton, Martha Anne. "What Does the Nutrition Education Specialist Need to Know?" *Journal of Nutrition Education,* **9** (July–Sept. 1977), 105.

   Rankine, Daryl C., and Betty Taylor. "Are Community Nutrition Programs Meeting the Needs of the Elderly?" *Journal of Home Economics,* **76** (Nov. 1975), 37–40.

   Wait, Janet Lynn. "Home Economics in Business: National Survey of Textiles and Clothing Jobs." *Journal of Home Economics,* **69** (Nov. 1977), 44–45.

4. Read the following reference about "Home Economics—New Directions II":

   Blivens, Gordon, Margaret Fitch, Gwendolyn Newkirk, Beatrice Paolucci, Em Riggs, Satenig St. Marie, and Gladys Vaughn. "Home Economics—New Directions II." *Journal of Home Economics,* **67** (May 1975), 26–27.

   What questions, if any, do you have? What changes would you make and why? How would you implement these directions in your home economics career?

3

Teaching and Learning

The teaching and learning process is the keystone of education. In many ways, a good teacher helps students to find meaning in their own lives as well as to gain insight into the lives and feelings of others. This goal is accomplished by arousing curiosity; generating ideas; encouraging student expression through many avenues; giving support, understanding, and affection when needed; and in countless other ways. Furthermore, during the teaching–learning process, teachers and students can develop the capacity to communicate with others, become inspired to seek further learning, and demonstrate independence in learning.

The home economics educator may wish to look at these ideals for practical applications. Teaching–learning is not confined to "telling." Home economics educators in such situations as a day-care center in an impoverished area, a senior-citizen program, 4-H club work, social welfare, or consumer relations in business may need to think about ways to emphasize student needs, to encourage learning, to be supportive, and to implement other facets of teaching and learning.

WHAT IS TEACHING?

A definition of teaching is elusive. The literature provides many interpretations, but none are acceptable to all educators. A clarification of terms is obviously necessary so that teachers may communicate freely about their work and so that researchers may have a guide for their endeavors. One area of confusion is the relation of learning to

Figure 3–1 A teacher assists a student in meeting a specific need. (Photo courtesy of Simplicity Pattern Co., Inc.)

teaching. According to Hyman,[1] a teacher's concept of teaching guides her/his behavior in the classroom. This is a very sobering thought.

A few concepts about teaching will be examined here. Broudy[2] contends that the difficulty in defining teaching stems from the inability to establish any set of behavioral characteristics that make a teacher effective. Broudy gives two loose categories of teaching. Didactic teaching emphasizes the explicit, like the teaching of the measurement of ingredients in home economics, in which instructional goals can be specified and the results may be more-or-less objectively evaluated. Encounter teaching, in contrast, deals with the less tangible. The total interaction of the student with others, including the teacher, is involved, hence the term *encounter teaching*. Because of currently crowded classrooms, the knowledge explosion, the plurality of values, the diversity of student backgrounds, and other facets of contemporary education, it is difficult to combine these two types of teaching. Broudy cautions that the move is toward the didactic, with the emphasis on technological aids, programmed instruction, and self-instruction, but that students need encounter teaching for personal development.

Postman and Weingartner[3] propose that the teacher emphasize stu-

[1] Ronald T. Hyman (ed.), *Teaching* (Philadelphia: Lippincott, 1968), pp. 6–8.
[2] Harry S. Broudy, "Can We Define Good Teaching?" *The Record,* Vol. 70, No. 7 (Apr. 1969), pp. 583–592.
[3] Neil Postman and Charles Weingartner, *Teaching as a Subversive Activity* (New York: Dell, 1969), Ch. 3.

dent inquiry into the questions and meanings that are important to him/her. In most classrooms, according to these authers, students listen to the teacher and are required to remember. Seldom are students asked to make observations, to formulate definitions, to ask substantive questions, or to decide how a textbook author arrived at his/her conclusions. The beliefs, feelings, and assumptions of teachers are the basis of the learning environment, contend Postman and Weingartner. Within this environment, a teacher rarely tells a student what must be learned because then he/she is discouraged from finding out for himself/herself. The teacher's basic mode of discourse is questioning, and single statements by students are seldom adequate to answer a question. Student–student interaction is encouraged. A teacher rarely summarizes because her/his summaries will tend to stifle further thought. Content emerges from the responses of students.

According to Flanders,[4] teaching exists in the social context of reciprocal contacts between teacher and pupils. Special attention should be given to the chain of events along a time continuum. Obviously, the event of the moment will influence what is to follow and, in turn, has been influenced by what preceded. Thus patterns of teaching may be identified through an analysis of the chain of events and teacher behavior. Teachers may discover for themselves which patterns lead to improved instruction.

Raths[5] has established ten major functions for every teacher: informing and explaining; showing how; supplementing the curriculum; providing children with opportunities to think and to share their thoughts with others; helping children to develop values; relating school experiences to the community; creating opportunities for each child to earn status and respect among his/her peers; creating a secure emotional atmosphere to facilitate learning; diagnosing and remedying learning problems; and keeping records and reports that are consistent with the other functions.

This list is not meant to measure the quality of teaching or to rate a teacher but rather to identify teaching tasks. In other words, is the teacher doing those things that are expected of her/him?

The Teacher

What are the ingredients of effective teaching? Combs[6] advances the idea that good teaching is not as much a question of the right

[4] Ned A. Flanders, *Analyzing Teacher Behavior* (Reading, Mass.: Addison-Wesley, 1970), Ch. 1.

[5] Louis E. Raths, *Teaching for Learning* (Columbus, Ohio: Merrill, 1969).

[6] Arthur W. Combs, "Teacher Education: The Person in the Process," *Educational Leadership*, Vol. 35, No. 7 (Apr. 1978), pp. 558–561.

methods of behaviors as it is a problem-solving method related to the unique use of oneself.

Research related to this idea has been done at the Universities of Florida, Northern Colorado, and Massachusetts and substantiates this concept of "self as instrument" in teaching.[7] Results indicated that effective and ineffective teachers can be clearly distinguished on the basis of their belief systems or perceptions in five major areas:

1. *Empathic qualities.* Good teachers have an awareness of the perceptions of other people and use them as a frame of reference in guiding their teaching behavior.
2. *Positive self-concept.* Good teachers see themselves in essentially positive ways.
3. *Beliefs about other people.* Good teachers see other people in positive ways, as able, friendly, and trustworthy.
4. *Open, facilitating purposes.* Good teachers emphasize purposes that are process-oriented, facilitating, and broad.

[7] R. G. Brown, "A Study of the Perceptual Organization of Elementary and Secondary Young Educators." Unpublished dissertation, University of Florida, Gainesville, 1970.

C. Choy, "The Relationship of College Teacher Effectiveness to Conceptual Systems Orientation and Perceptual Orientation." Unpublished doctoral dissertation, University of Northern Colorado, Greeley, 1969.

A. W. Combs, R. A. Blume, A. J. Newman, and H. L. Wass, *The Professional Education of Teachers: A Humanistic Approach to Teacher Education* (Boston: Allyn, 1974).

R. G. Koffman, "A Comparison of the Perceptual Organizations of Outstanding and Randomly Selected Teachers in Open and Traditional Classrooms." Unpublished doctoral dissertation, University of Massachusetts, Amherst, 1975.

Figure 3–2 A teacher selects accessories of various shapes and designs to encourage students to create their own.

5. *Authenticity.* Good teachers are essentially open, genuine, and fair.

If the "self-instrument" concept of a teacher is accepted, then preparation for teaching is a process of "becoming." For a prospective teacher, this may be interpreted as discovering and analyzing how best to use oneself. Using the list of five beliefs above and acting upon them can be rewarding. The teacher then becomes central in facilitating teaching–learning.

Competencies of the Home Economics Teacher

What specific competencies should a home economics teacher have? The American Home Economics Association (AHEA) has had a number of workshops in which leading home economics educators examined this important question. Their role was to identify and establish criteria for assessing educative and subject-matter competencies for home economics teachers. Program accountability in college preparation of home economics teachers and accreditation expectations of the professional organization (AHEA), demand this information. Competency-based professional education in home economics will be discussed first.[8]

The statement of expected competencies and criteria developed in the AHEA workshops will serve as a guideline for nationwide evaluation of home economics teaching, certification standards set by city and state departments of education, and improvement levels encouraged by the profession. The topics selected for the workshops as a frame of reference for the development of the competencies included (1) educational philosophy in home economics; (2) professional role in home economics; (3) program planning for education in home economics; (4) the educative process in home economics; and (5) research in home economics. In relation to each topic, workshop participants defined selected competencies and delineated the criteria to be used to evaluate each specific competency by college home economics education staffs, curriculum committees, administrators, supervisors, and the like, concerned with the professional preparations of home economics teachers.

A model developed in the AHEA workshops for implementing competency-based education of home economics teachers included the following steps: (1) identification of competencies; (2) identification

[8] Arlene Otto et al., *Competency-Based Professional Education in Home Economics, Selected Competencies and Criteria,* (Washington, D.C.: American Home Economics Association, 1974).

of criteria for each competency; (3) identification of instructional strategies; (4) development and selection of assessment measures; (5) implementation of instructional strategies; (6) observation of competency performances; and (7) competency performance.

The competencies and criteria are not intended to represent a perfectly developed program that will fit all situations but are to be appropriately adapted for a particular educationsl setting.

A similar endeavor sponsored by the AHEA was made by outstanding subject-matter specialists and educators in home economics in regard to the preparation of home economics teachers in the various subject-matter areas. The competencies and criteria were directed to the areas of clothing/apparel and textile products, consumer education and management, housing and living environments, human development and the family, and nutrition and food management.[9]

The topics listed under knowledge that home economics teachers should have in order to teach with competence in the area of clothing/apparel and textile products are (1) the functions of clothing/apparel and textile products; (2) the consumption of clothing/apparel and textile products; and (3) occupations in clothing/apparel and textile products. The topics under consumer education and management are (1) consumer education and its effect on the quality of human life; (2) management and its effect on the quality of life; and (3) career opportunities in consumer education and management of resources. The area of housing and living environments is not broken down into subtopics. The topics under human development and family are (1) the human growth and development process; (2) individual development; (3) families; and (4) environmental influences. The topics for nutrition and food management are (1) the significance of food; (2) the nature of food; (3) the provision of food; and (4) occupations related to nutrition and food.

The subject-matter component of the teacher education program used the publication *Concepts and Generalizations: Their Place in High School Curriculum Development*[10] as a basic resource. The information had to be adapted to the college-level preparation of teachers. There is a realization that the criteria and competencies listed may have to be adapted to the goals of a specific program.

The general education, or the third part of the total preparation of a home economics teacher, is generally in the hands of the educational institution and the home economics department, school, or college. It is recommended that students avail themselves of the publications cited here.

[9] Home Economics Teacher Educators, *Competencies for Home Economics Teachers* (Ames: Iowa State U., 1978).

[10] Washington, D.C.: American Home Economics Association, 1967.

WHAT IS LEARNING?

According to Dale[11] the quintessence of learning is to learn how to learn and to develop a taste and an enthusiasm for learning. That is the challenge that faces every home economics teacher.

Theories of Learning

Many theories about learning have emerged from research and experience in the fields of psychology, communications, and anthropology, among others. Combs[12] urges us to distinguish between knowing and learning. He claims that knowing is but a part of learning, that true learning has occurred only when the behavior of the individual has been changed. It is easy to distinguish between the two when one realizes that individuals do not always behave in light of their knowledge. For example, a student may know that protein foods should be cooked at low temperatures but may still cook eggs at a high temperature. At one time, educators placed a high value on knowing; whether knowing effected any changes in behavior was of little concern. Now educators are aware that it is inadequate for students simply to know about family relations and the other areas of home economics; the belief now is that students' behavior should be improved and changed as a result of knowing.

Piaget's concepts[13] on intellectual development are based on a number of stages, each being approximate and flexible. The first stage is sensorimoter, from birth to about eighteen months of age. Here the infant learns about cause-and-effect relationships—if he/she cries he/she receives attention. The second, or preoperational, stage is from eighteen months to six or seven years. In this stage, a child has difficulty in accepting another person's point of view in coping with a change in an object or with a change in her/his own location in relation to an object. The child may not recognize a familiar house, road, or street if he/she sees it from a different perspective. The stage of concrete operations evolves roughly between seven and twelve years of age. Children during this period are concerned with the real world and with what is in front of them.

[11] Edgar Dale, "The Good Society," *The Newsletter,* Vol. 34, No. 8 (May 1969), p. 1.

[12] Arthur W. Combs, *Learning More About Learning* (Washington, D.C.: Association for Supervision and Curriculum Development, NEA, 1959), pamphlet.

[13] Jean Piaget, "How Children Form Mathematical Concepts," in Celia Burns Stendler (ed.), *Readings in Child Behavior and Development* (New York: Harcourt, 1964), pp. 333–334; also, Frank J. Jennings, "Jean Piaget: Notes on Learning," *Saturday Review* May 20, 1967, pp. 81–83; and for home economics applications see Henrietta Fleck and Carolee Nadel, "Applying Piaget's Theories," *Forecast for Home Economics,* Vol. 16, No. 9 (May/June 1971), pp. 77, 98.

Bruner,[14] in contrast, believes that children of any age can learn about an area of subject matter if the organization of operations is appropriate to the age. The challenge is to find the language and the ideas that the child herself/himself would use to explain it. Learning to make certain observations or to perform certain operations that turn out to be regular and predictable is helpful. Young children can observe that the addition of an acid, such as lemon or tomato juice, to pasteurized milk will curdle the milk. Later, with additional knowledge, these children can fathom the reason for this reaction.

B. F. Skinner,[15] as a result of his experiments, believes that learning is enhanced through reinforcement. Rats or pigeons received food or a reward whenever they pressed a lever or learned to use a similar device that presented them with food. Skinner explored the application to the human organism. A human need leads to general exploratory activity. An accidental response may be instrumental in satisfying that need and can become, if reinforced, a learned response. A learned response, in contrast, can be extinguished if the reinforcement is withheld. This theory of learning has been used in the development of programmed instruction.

The Gestalt psychology emphasizes configurations rather than single elements: the health, the self-concept, the cultural milieu of the students, the learning environment, and similar factors are believed to influence learning. Many of the contempory concepts related to learning focus on this theory.

Postman and Weingartner[16] contend that a student has learned to learn when he/she knows how to ask questions that are relevant, appropriate, and substantial. These authors regret that this skill is seldom taught in schools.

Some teachers hold to the notion that if they teach, students will learn. Each pupil must experience learning personally; learning takes place to the degree that an individual can discover a personal meaning in a situation or an idea. The teacher, then, must be certain that activities and ideas are being perceived by the learner in a meaningful manner. The student perceives in many ways—through the senses, through the use of language symbols, through interpretation of the environment through perception, and through the identification of interrelationships.

Individuals tend to repeat behavior that they have found successful

[14] Jerome S. Bruner, *The Process of Education* (Cambridge; Mass.: Harvard U.P., 1960); and Jerome S. Bruner, "On Learning Mathematics," in *On Knowing* (Cambridge, Mass.: Harvard U.P., 1963), pp. 97–111.

[15] B. F. Skinner, *The Behavior of Organisms* (New York: Appleton, 1938).

[16] Neil Postman and Charles Weingartner, *Teaching Is a Subversive Activity* (New York: Dell, 1969), p. 23.

or satisfying in similar situations. Research into the effects of reward and punishment on learning has demonstrated that a reward, called *reinforcement,* is most effective if it follows immediately after the desired behavior. This means, for instance, that a teacher should commend a student promptly. An advantage of programmed instruction is the quick feedback of success. New and exciting classroom experiences act as a kind of reward and encourage learning. Punishment and threats do not have effects precisely opposite to those of rewards, but they are nonetheless usually frustrating and disturbing to the learner. A discouraged student may avoid further effort and may not seek the solution to the problem.

Learning is facilitated if a student's purposes are achieved and if he/she participates in the selection and planning of classroom projects. Excessive direction by the teacher often discourages learning, as does an authoritarian atmosphere. In planning classroom experiences, teachers will do well to select projects that are neither too simple nor too difficult. Students like to anticipate success but do not wish to be too certain of it.

The question of what effect age has on learning is often raised. The most rapid mental growth takes place in infancy and early childhood. During these periods, a child learns to identify familiar faces, spoken words, his/her surroundings, and the routines of daily living. He/she distinguishes between himself/herself and others, comprehends certain aspects of distance and numbers, and recognizes approval and disapproval, all by the time she/he is five years old. In addition, his/her lifelong tendencies to be trusting or mistrusting and his/her self-acceptance and initiative have been implanted and will influence later learning. The ability to learn increases into adulthood and does not appear to decline thereafter unless motivation does. Persons sixty years old and older can learn new languages, skills, and ideas, thereby changing their behavior in many ways.

Watson[17] states that readiness for new learning is complex in nature and depends on an interaction among such factors as the importance of the new learning to the individual, physiological and psychological maturity, mastery of skills and techniques, and the availability of encouragement and confidence.

Forgetting is another concern in the learning process. Forgetting occurs rapidly at first and tapers off slowly. If there is an occasion to recall soon after the learning, then less is forgotten. Relearning takes place more quickly than new learning. Reviewing periodically will aid retention if the individual believes the learning is important. If

[17] Goodwin Watson, *What Psychology Can We Trust?* (New York: Teachers College Press, Columbia University), 1961.

new learning is related to a person's attitudes or values, he/she will remember it longer and more accurately. Generalizations, principles, and concepts are retained to a greater degree than facts.

Learning becomes effective to the extent of its clarity, realism, relevancy, and closeness to desired outcomes. Seeing the target clearly is important to student learning. If the learner sees some organization in the material or skill, learning is easier. Logical subject matter is easier to learn, remember, and use. This logic must become a part of the individual's repertoire of experience so that it may be easily retrieved.

Research emphasizes that learning has many facets. Learning that is related to life is more enduring.

Bloom[18] has researched learning, and his results indicate that under favorable learning conditions, most students can learn. Several variables must be considered when one is planning for mastery learning. *Aptitude* does vary from student to student. The ability of students to learn is frequently categorized as slow, average, and fast. Family members, friends, and individuals in the community may have all judged a student in the same manner. There is a tendency for these labels to become fixed, so that a slow learner may be denied the opportunity to learn to the extent that he or she can. Furthermore, this kind of labeling reduces much of education to a waste of human resources because it implies that only a few can succeed.

Bloom suggests that aptitude be regarded as a student's rate of learning, not the ability to learn. Some students need more time to learn than others. Instruction must be planned to allow for these individual differences.

The *quality of instruction* is critical. Unless students understand what they are trying to learn and how to learn it, they may become discouraged and frustrated. A teacher must be aware of a student's needs and deficiencies, such as reading ability and comprehension, writing ability, skills in mathematics, health problems such as poor hearing or poor sight, and other limitations, and adapt instruction accordingly. Many students have difficulty in learning in large classes. Although a teacher may strive to give equal opportunities to learn, there is a strong tendency to interact more with the bright students than with the slow or average learners. This type of instruction can compound learning errors because students do not have their misunderstandings clarified.

When group instruction is supplemented by frequent feedback and individualized help to provide students with the assistance they

[18] Benjamin S. Bloom, "Favorable Learning Conditions for All," *Teacher*, Vol. 95, No. 1 (Nov. 1977), pp. 22–28.

need, about 80 per cent of all students can learn equally well. Aides may assist in these situations. Group instruction without these supports will reach only 20 per cent of the students.

The home environment can contribute to school instruction if encouragement is given to parents and siblings. Some homes provide for the supplementary help needed by students who have large-group instruction in school. Teachers can promote this additional aid by having closer ties with the parents and the homes of students. As a result, teachers and families support each other.

Other means for improving instruction are to have peers or older students in the classroom act as aides. The use of supplementary instructional materials, particularly if written in simple, easily understood language, is another suggestion. Other useful aids are small-group work, learning kits with pictures, slides, filmstrips, or games.

Learning one step before going on to the next step is important in mastery learning. The use of learning hierarchies[19] is helpful. Here, a student (sometimes with the help of the teacher or others) has to decide what he or she knows and what he or she does not know. For example, in planning some simple refreshments for friends, the student must decide whether she/he can read and understand the recipe; whether he/she has mastered the skills required to measure, prepare, and cook these foods; whether she/he has a knowledge of how to use the range or an appliance, and so on. If these skills have been learned previously, then success is more likely. The time a student is willing to spend on learning, or *perseverance,* is important. Students vary in this trait. Usually a student who is interested is more willing to spend time. Instruction must stimulate motivation. A student in clothing construction who has had little or no experience may become discouraged, but as certain tasks are mastered, perseverance increases. This fact should be borne in mind by a high school home economics teacher or a home economics educator in business who is preparing materials to help the young to sew.

The most important aspect of mastery learning is *time.* Each student should be given the time needed to master an area in home economics. This will require adjustments in methods of instruction, such as the use of some individualized instruction. In some instances, teachers may have to increase the time spent on a unit so that each step will be mastered. Such measures are more supportive of positive development.

Although the emphasis on mastery learning appears to be largely of a cognitive nature, there are contributions to the affective domain: an improved view of oneself, a desire for further learning, the ability to

[19] Rebecca E. Carroll and J. Marvin Cook, "Application of Learning Hierarchies in Curriculum Change in Large Urban School System," *Educational Horizons,* Vol. 55, No. 3 (Spring 1977), pp. 134–139.

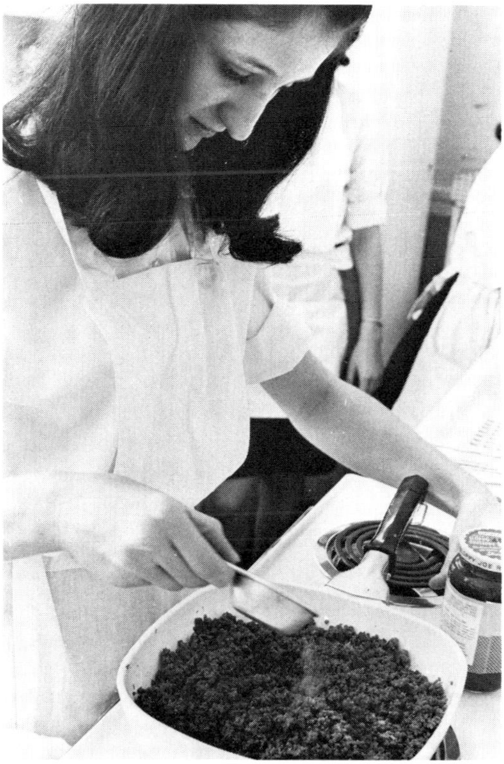

Figure 3–3 If a student wishes to experiment in making a "sloppy Joe," which learning hierarchies are involved?

adapt to change, a feeling of control over the environment, and an increase in self-confidence are examples of positive effects of mastery learning.

Perception and Learning

The learning that occurs in the home economics classroom depends partly upon the perceptions of the teacher and her/his students. Kelley[20] holds that perceptions come not only from the environment through the senses but also from past experiences. The things around a person have meaning only to the extent that he/she attributes meaning to them. People relate themselves to present experiences through their past experiences. No two people bring the same past experiences to a situation, and no two individuals respond to the same situation in quite the same way. For that reason students who view a situation casually may actually gain false perceptions of it, much as witnesses to an accident tell conflicting stories about it.

[20] Earl C. Kelley, *Education for What is Real* (New York: Harper, 1947).

When a person has repeated perceptions about the same object or person, he/she may feel he/she has an absolute perception. This is not necessarily true, however, for one never sees anything in quite the same way twice.

If students can correctly perceive the important elements in their environment, then they will have more successes in their endeavors than failures. However, they cannot separate their environment from themselves, so their perceptions must be tested by action to determine their accuracy.

Motivation

Shaffer[21] states that motivation is manifested in an individual as vigorous activity, deep desire, and an urge to direct energy in one direction to the exclusion of others for the purpose of learning, for the realization of a goal, or for other endeavors. These ideas contrast with the interpretation held by many educators that motivation is some means of getting a student to do something that the teacher considers important. Maslow[22] has formulated a theory of human motivation that is related to an individual's basic human needs. He begins with physiological needs, which he considers the most urgent. A student who is hungry, cold, or beset by any of the many physiological needs will resist motivation in other areas until these needs have been satisfied. In the hierarchy of needs, safety appears to come next. In our culture we are comparatively safe from wild animals, extremes of temperature, tyranny, murder, and the like. However, the sense of safety derives also from such factors as economic security, a familiar environment, and a meaningful philosophy of life.

Maslow recognizes that the emotional needs for affection, belonging, recognition, and achievement are as vital to an individual's well-being as the needs of intellect—to know and to understand. Having friends, belonging to groups, being recognized for an accomplishment in sports or dramatics, and achieving even a minimal goal are examples of conditions that facilitate learning. In addition, a student's environment must encourage learning, not deter it. This includes physical and psychological aspects.

The individual may not be conscious of many of his/her needs; hence they may generate unconscious motivations in him/her. For example, a person may not be aware that his/her motivation to seek friends is a need for affection or recognition. Such interpretation

[21] Laurance T. Shaffer, "Motivation to Learn," in Goodwin Watson (ed.), *No Room at the Bottom: Automation and the Reluctant Learner,* project on the Educational Implications of Automation (Washington, D.C.: N.E.A., 1963), pp. 18–30.

[22] A. H. Maslow, *Motivation and Personality* (New York: Harper, 1954), Ch. 5.

Figure 3–4 Debbie is experimenting with play dough. (*Lincoln Journal and Star*)

gives us an inkling of the difficulty in defining or describing some of the important facets of motivation.

Frymier[23] contends that if motivation gives intensity and direction to behavior, it must be further assumed that a value judgment is involved and that there is a known and purposeful direction reflected in the behavior of students. Five factors in the motivation of learning can be outlined.

First, since an organism thrives on stimulation, the classroom environment should have abundant incentive materials. Frymier emphasizes that the number, quality, intricacy, uniqueness, richness, and complexity of these aids are important. A rich environment is not the only contributing factor. Sometimes stimuli may not match the learner's expectations.

The second factor is perceptual openness. Students who are highly perceptive, self-sufficent, and relatively secure are more likely to be drawn to the new and the unknown. New stimuli tend to be resisted by those who are psychologically "closed."

The way an individual handles dissonance is the third factor that

[23] Jack R. Frymier, "Motivation: The Mainspring and Gyroscope of Learning," in "Motivation, the Desire to Learn," *Theory into Practice-Tip,* Vol. 9, No. 1 (Feb. 1970) (published by the College of Education, Ohio State University), pp. 23–32.

affects the intensity and direction of motivation. Two reactions to dissonance are mentioned. One is the manner in which a student handles the descrepancy between where he/she is and where he/she plans to go. This requires an astute evaluation by the individual of personal resources, knowledge, and capacities. In the second form of dissonance, how a person handles inconsistencies, ambiguities, interpretation of data, and the like is critical. The "open" individual can usually cope more easily with any incongruities.

The physical traits of a learner provide the fourth factor. The intensity of motivation may reflect his/her basal metabolic rate, endurance, cardiovascular and glandular functioning, strength, and general health.

Lastly, anxiety has a decisive effect on intensity of behavior. Although a certain degree of anxiety may lure a student to learning, too much turns him/her off. The interaction of his/her self-concept, the number and type of stimuli, and the amount of dissonance he/she perceives are reflected in the amount of his/her anxiety. Obviously the anxiety-ridden student will encounter deterrents in learning.

Motivation and Learning

According to Shaffer,[24] there are several processes that stimulate motivation. One is development of the natural urge to explore. Small children pronouncedly manifest that urge, but as they grow older, such inquisitiveness may rapidly diminish. In some adults, it barely exists. The development of this behavior depends to a large degree on the opportunities for exploration. Murphy[25] urges teachers to encourage students and provide them with opportunities to explore, to contact, to discover, and to assimilate. Fleming[26] adds that the imperatives of inquiry for learning purposes may be stated as demonstrate, construct, discuss, clarify, investigate, organize, summarize, revise, hypothesize, share, evaluate, create, initiate, and describe.

Educational objectives also have an influence on learning. The work of Bruner[27] and others stresses that the structure of a subject rather than its factual or descriptive content is the key to the encouragement of further learning. Students should be helped to understand the basic concepts and conceptual relationships that

[24] Shaffer, op. cit., pp. 22–23.

[25] Gardner Murphy, *Human Potentialities* (New York: Basic, 1958).

[26] Robert S. Fleming, "Achieving Excellence in the Teacher-Learning Process," a talk presented at the 14th Annual Conference of College Teachers of Textiles and Clothing, New York City, November 4, 1960.

[27] Jerome S. Bruner, "Structures in Learning," *NEA Journal,* Vol. 52, No. 3 (March 1963), p. 26.

serve as tools in the intelligent ordering of new data or in the use of new information. Krathwohl[28] and others believe that emotionally toned assumptions and concepts of students can be examined fruitfully to the child's advantage. Rogers[29] makes a plea that individuals be given the freedom to think their own thoughts, to develop in their own unique way, to be responsible for their choices, and to have the opportunity to explore as many alternatives as possible. The rewards to the student of learning through personal discoveries include increased intellectual potency, satisfactions, useful techniques, and a greater ability to retrieve information from memory.

CHANGING BEHAVIOR

One of the most important processes with which a teacher must be familiar is changing behavior. Benne[30] suggests a number of methods. When problem solving is experimental in contrast to stereotyped and inflexible, change occurs more readily. In consumer education, for instance, instead of a teacher's telling a student how to buy a transistor radio, the student may be encouraged to explore many possibilities, to weigh the impact of personal values and thinking, and to check progress with the teacher and others. Behavior is then hopefully changed from leaning on a single authority and from impulsive buying.

When problem solving is collaborative, change is more likely to occur. When students, for example, decide to tackle the problem of pollution in the home, several courses of action may be possible. Working together, students may analyze the sources of pollution from homes and establish alternative courses of action. These courses of action may then be discussed with parents for their viewpoints. The results may be explored for areas of agreement, disagreement, and suggested changes. This exploration may be followed by a meeting with parents to evolve a workable course of action.

Another suggestion of Benne is that student experiences must be reality-oriented. For example, a teacher who is concerned about the undesirable food habits of students must consider actual experiences to facilitate improvement. Some ideas are for students to categorize the

[28] David Krathwohl, Benjamin S. Bloom, and Bertram B. Masia, *Taxonomy of Educational Objectives: The Classification of Educational Goals,* Handbook 11: Affective Domain (New York: McKay, 1964).

[29] Carl Rogers, *Conflict and Creativity: Control of the Mind* (New York: McGraw-Hill, 1963).

[30] Kenneth D. Benne, "Deliberate Changing as the Facilitation of Growth," in Warren G. Bennis, Kenneth D. Benne, and Robert Chin, *The Planning of Change* (New York: Holt, 1961), pp. 230–234.

foods now eaten into the four basic groups. What are the gaps? Are there foods that students like but eat infrequently that might be consumed to improve their diets? Preparing simple, inexpensive, nutritious foods compatible with their eating styles is another possibility. Students may establish their own goals, such as, "Next week I will eat less of __________ and more of __________." Change is seldom evident from mere discussion; real experiences are vital to change.

Lewin[31] gave some excellent advice about planned change. The following suggestions are offered. The first step is to make a thorough study of the present condition. Next, in order to encourage change, a teacher must be aware of the *adding forces* that will push behavior in the desired direction and the *opposing forces* that may diminish change. For example, some overweight students might come to a teacher for additional information about losing weight. Their doctors have approved a weight loss regime. Students may be helped to see that the possible adding forces might be greater social approval, improved appearance, lower cost of clothes, and wider participation in sports and other activities. The opposing forces might be a fondness for eating, unfamiliarity with the caloric value of foods, lack of willpower, and mothers who are good cooks. Students might use the group decision method to establish their goals and procedures for attaining a more desirable weight. Using this procedure in this situation and in other student experiences will facilitate change.

Sarason, Glaser, and Fargo[32] advance some principles for changing behavior. The first one is that students' behavior is influenced by the consequences they anticipate. For example, a student will probably order carbonated beverages rather than milk or fruit juice for a beverage snack because it is more important to have similar tastes and approval of the peer group than to be concerned about nutrition. It will be difficult to change this behavior unless students and teacher can minimize the consequences of this action.

Another suggestion is the use of positive and negative reinforcers. When a teacher smiles, praises, asks a student for assistance, or commends a student for a finished product prepared in the laboratory, such as a salad or a play suit, then behavior is reinforced. Ignoring, frowning, showing impatience, and criticizing are negative reinforcers that a teacher should avoid because the changing of behavior may be impeded.

It is unwise to overdo one type of positive reinforcer, such as patting on the back, or it will become meaningless. A teacher should

[31] Kurt Lewin, "Group Decision and Social Change," in Theodore N. Newcomb and Eugene L. Hartley, *Readings in Social Psychology* (New York: Holt, 1947), pp. 340–344.

[32] Irwin G. Sarason, Edward M. Glaser, and George A. Fargo, *Reinforcing Productive Classroom Behavior* (New York: Behavioral Publications, 1972).

have a number of reinforcers in mind and vary their use. Once behavior has begun to change, reinforcement should be periodic but not regular.

Another suggestion is to identify the smaller behaviors that comprise an important behavior. In a good grooming unit, small behaviors to be selected might be hair or skin care, choice of clothes, or hand care. If possible, the teacher should capitalize on the help of students in planning action. Peer suggestions are often appropriate and acceptable.

Behavioral control and behavior modification refer to a model of teaching in which an attempt is made to apply the interpretation of behavioral psychology, of which B. F. Skinner is an important proponent, to the classroom. Teaching becomes a method of controlling the behavior of students and the conditions of learning. The principal task of teaching is to manage students so that precisely delineated responses will occur as in programmed instruction. Behavioral objectives are imperative. The chief criticism of this approach is that greater success is attainable in the laboratory than in the classroom, primarily because it is difficult to interpret all educational tasks, such as thinking and appreciation, in simple behavioral terms. When the teacher becomes an experimenter and the students are the experimental subjects, limitations ensue.[33]

The simplicity of implementing behavior modification has been highlighted in popular and professional literature but Kanfer[34] warns that defining the problem situation encompasses more than the simple attachment of reward or punishment to a behavior. A knowledge of theoretical principles, skill, and patience are required in determining appropriate treatment strategy. The behavior modifier must know "when to do what, for which behavior, and with what resources as well as knowing how to monitor and to test treatment effectiveness continuously." The magnitude of this operation implies the need for expertise that many teachers lack.

The changing of behavior rests on many factors. Many techniques discussed here may be used by the students themselves, whenever practicable. This procedure should facilitate changed behavior and encourage independence in the student. Changing the behavior of students is not easy and requires the ultimate in creativity, sensitivity, and know-how.

[33] Graham Nuthall and Ivan Snook, "Contemporary Models of Teaching," in Robert M. W. Travers (ed.), *Second Handbook of Research on Teaching* (Chicago: Rand McNally, 1973), pp. 54–59.

[34] Frederick H. Kanfer, "Behavior Modification—An Overview," in Carl E. Thoresen (ed.), *Behavior Modification in Education,* The Seventy-second Yearbook of the National Society for the Study of Education. Chicago: The U. of Chicago P., 1973, pp. 3–4.

MAKING TEACHING AND LEARNING MORE EFFECTIVE

The true teacher will reach for ever greater insights into the students. Each teacher will bear in mind that her/his students, trainees, customers, clients, patients, and others are infinitely versatile, complex, and varied in perceptions and experiences.[35] An emphasis on total learning rather than on specifics is more enduring.

Characteristics of a Teacher

With the help of a caring person who understands what is to be taught, learning can become satisfying, exciting, and stimulating. The teacher should fulfill the roles of listener, understander, and a humane being.[36] Decision making, giving psychological and other support, being flexible, and keeping up-to-date are other activities of the teacher who wishes to be effective.

Patience and perseverance are often required to help students with learning problems. Teaching styles and instructional materials and devices must be varied to accomplish this end. Encouraging parents to assist in the teaching–learning process and using volunteers and aides in school reinforce learning.

Teachers with the ability to think and feel like their students can facilitate learning. Home economists in extension, or in social service, who work with adults at the poverty level will find it to their advantage to choose examples and suggestions with which this group can identify. Avoiding stereotyped images of individuals in this situation and having an open mind are crucial to effective learning. The kind of sales that supermarkets offer, what can be found in secondhand clothes and furniture shops, protein pairs and equivalents, ways to find more sleeping space in crowded quarters, and how to combat rats, cockroaches, and the like are the kind of information that will be helpful to home economists working with the poor. Throughout teaching, the human dignity of the learners must be protected.

Nurturing and developing communication between teacher and student can enhance learning potential.[37] Questions such as the following may be asked: Do you need help or can you do it alone? How

[35] Louise M. Berman and Jessie A. Roderick, *Feeling, Valuing, and the Art of Growing: Insights into the Affective Domain*, ASCD 1977 Yearbook (Washington D.C.: Association of Supervision and Curriculum Development, 1977.

[36] Linda Ulrich, "Interviewing Gene Hardy of the University of Nebraska—Lincoln Teaching and Learning Center," *Sunday Journal and Star*, Lincoln, Neb., Jan. 16, 1977, p. 5D.

[37] Carolyn J. Girtman, "The Human Element in Teaching," *Illinois Teacher*, Vol. 21, No. 2 (Nov./Dec. 1977), pp. 62–63.

Figure 3–5 Women from developing countries drew plans for and are constructing an improved smokeless mud stove that will be demonstrated to villagers in their respective countries. (USDA Photo)

do you feel about this? What do you suggest? What puzzles you? Can we do this together? What if . . . ? Sometimes a little prompting or clue giving on the part of the teacher will encourage a student.

Teacher and Student Relationships

Teaching and learning may be affected by the person or persons at the center of attention. Some teachers believe that teaching does not take place unless the teacher is in the center. The emphasis in teaching and learning is on learning, so student involvement is critical. The teacher can be more effective if she/he plays the role of facilitator, initiator, guide, planner of a learning environment, and similar roles.[38]

A classroom or teaching situation should not be teacher-centered or student-centered; both students and teacher should contribute to teaching and learning.[39] Teaching styles may vary to accomplish this purpose.

[38] Robert L. Geiser, "If I Am Not in the Center of Things, Where Am I?" *Teacher,* Vol. 91, No. 6 (Feb. 1974), pp. 18–22, 27.
[39] Arlene Silberman, "Is Your Room Child Centered?" *Instructor,* Vol. 86, No. 9 (May 1977), p. 32.

A desirable student–teacher relationship cannot develop without human interactions, such as sharing of life experiences and ideas, and cannot emerge when the focus is entirely on instructional materials. When students feel as though they "belong" and participate in the selection of their learning tasks, teacher–student relations are strengthened.

Teacher and students must understand each other's behavior so that they can undertake trusting working relationships.[40] Often the behavior seemingly manifested by students and teachers is really a reflection of the expectations that they have of each other. If a teacher holds onto an image of students as being limited, they will sense this quickly and may fail to try, lack interest, or give other indications of frustration. If a student believes that a teacher lacks patience, is not humane in personal dealings, and is unfair and cross, his/her response will be negative. The opposite will be true if teacher and students have a genuine concern and a high regard for each other. Teaching and learning will gain when students and teachers prize the relationships they have with each other.

Developing Positive Self-concepts

A student's self-concept is reflected in the way he or she learns. In many ways a teacher can enhance the image a student has of himself or herself. The longings of a student may be highlighted through such devices as responding to "If I were . . . ," "If I could be . . . ," "Five years from now . . . ," "What if . . . ," or "I wish. . . .[41] Each response must be interpreted in the light of its effect on self-concept and what the teacher might do to help or encourage. This information must be treated with great respect.

Information About Vocabulary

Sometimes students' learning may be blocked because they are not familiar with the vocabulary of the area being discussed, such as consumer buying, types of furniture, nutrients, cooking terms, and textiles. One strategy is to stop and discuss the meaning of a word as it is encountered. In addition, writing the word on the board or on a large blank sheet of newsprint taped to the wall may reinforce the meaning. In this way, it is possible to review the word later.

[40] R. P. McDermott, "Social Relations as Contexts for Learning in School," *Harvard Educational Review,* Vol. 47, No. 2 (May 1977), pp. 198–211.

[41] Jack Canfield and Harold C. Wells, *100 Ways to Enhance Self Concept in the Classroom* (Englewood Cliffs, N.J.: Prentice-Hall, 1976), pp. 9, 54, 55, 56, 107, 177.

Making Positive Use of Mistakes

A student's mistake can lead to productive learning.[42] A mistake is evidence that a student "does not know or cannot do." If such errors are not corrected, problems may arise because a certain learning step has been omitted in the hierarchy of learning. Errors that are not detected may be equally serious.

For example, a student may be asked to divide a recipe for fruit punch in half. One of the ingredients is three tablespoons of lemon juice. A fellow student, an aide, or the teacher, in checking, discovers that one student's answer is two tablespoons. How might this situation be handled? One method is to ask the student, "How much is one half of one tablespoon?" When the student gives the right answer, the next question is "How much is one half of two tablespoons?" When that is understood, the final question is "How much is one half of three tablespoons?" With students who may have difficulty with mathematics, this method employs very easy steps to an answer. This detailed process may not be necessary with all students. At no time should the student be criticized, ridiculed, or ignored.

Alternatives in Problem Solving

A teacher may facilitate learning in other ways. One strategy is to encourage students to consider alternative methods in solving a problem[43] One suggestion is to have students become experimental and attempt to predict tentative solutions. With practice, this approach can lead to success and precision if careful consideration is given to all of the factors and their effect on each other, rather than wild guesses. In a simple way, students might be encouraged to ask themselves questions about apparent errors in their laboratory work: "Why doesn't this egg white beat?" "Why does the sleeve of my blouse pucker?" "Why did this sweater shrink?" "Why can't this preschooler button his coat?"

Learning and Decision Making

Teachers and students must be aware that decision making is important in teaching and learning. Are students using the most efficient ways to learn? Assisting them in planning, organization, and ac-

[42] Madeline C. Hunter, "Mistakes Can Be Productive," *Instructor,* Vol. 85, No. 8 (Apr. 1976), p. 62.

[43] Bill Hardin and Bonnie Bernstein, "Monkeying Around, or How to Make Mistakes Pay Off," *Teacher,* Vol. 94, No. 5 (Jan. 1977), pp. 66–67.

tion based on the goals they have established can be helpful. Many students waste time and fail to learn because they do not know what they wish to achieve and how to accomplish this end. Outlining steps is suggested. What comes first, next, and so on. How will progress be identified? Freedom to ask questions, to discuss points, and to assess growth is important.

Teachers, too, must secure feedback frequently and adjust their strategies accordingly. Making decisions about what to include and what to exclude is important. Sometimes students have difficulty in learning because too much is expected of them. Be clear about the intended learning. For example, students may observe the play activities of preschool children in a day-care center for this particular session. The intended learning may be "What did a particular child learn from his or her play?" An analysis of how and what the children ate, for example, is then excluded.

Other Areas of Learning

Certain areas of learning may be slighted in teaching. How long is *learning retained* by a student? If a student, for example, has been taught the importance of milk in his/her diet and then admits to drinking carbonated and other beverages in place of milk, the learning was not retained. However, if a student says three months later, "I began drinking milk every day and so does my father," the learning has been retained, for that time period at least. *Transfer of learning* is another area that demands attention. If a student has learned about aesthetic principles as related to clothing and then gives evidence of discovering them also in foods, such as in braided breads and roll shapes, this evidence points to transfer of learning. Seeing aesthetic principles in home furnishings may be another example.

One of the best demonstrations of the effectiveness of teaching strategies is that the student shows evidence of a desire to continue learning, to be excited by new discoveries, and to be familiar with the uncovering of pertinent resources in the pursuit of learning.

SUGGESTIONS FOR FURTHER LEARNING

1. Analyze some of the most satisfying learning experiences you have had. What made the learning so effective? Are there any implications in these experiences for teaching home economics?
2. Involve yourself in some worthwhile projects that will help you to become a better teacher. First, analyze what kind of experiences you need, such as knowing more about people, trying in informal situations to teach someone about something, clarifying your beliefs about teaching and learning, or strengthening your specialized education.

3. The following reference may be helpful: Home Economics Teacher Educators. *Instruments for Assessing Selected Professional Competencies for Home Economics Teachers.* Ames: Iowa State U.P., 1978.
4. Here are some magazines that you might find helpful:
   American Education
   American Vocational Journal
   Annals of the Academy of Political and Social Science
   Childhood Education
   Daedalus
   Educational Horizons
   Educational Leadership
   Educational Technology
   Education and Urban Society
   Harvard Educational Review
   Instructor
   Journal of Home Economics
   Journal of The American Dietetic Association
   Learning
   Media and Methods
   Phi Delta Kappan
   Teacher
   Teacher's College Record
   Youth and Society
   How many do you know? What is a unique contribution of each magazine?

4

Teaching Children

Childhood is one of the most critical periods in human development. Of all the social influences on the child, home and family are the primary and most fundamental.[1] The major professional focus for home economics delivery systems is the family; included in this focus is a concern for the kind of child rearing that will release the child's greatest potential. Being perceptive of the characteristics and problems of children and families is inadequate without a recognition of the social context in which they live, such as housing, employment, ecology, income, available support systems, and food supplies to provide adequate nutrition.[2]

Most children in the nation grow up in a family, although in recent years family patterns have changed from being strictly nuclear or extended to including divorced mothers or fathers, unmarried mothers, other types of single parents such as a grandmother or other relative, communes, and families with other lifestyles who are responsible for the upbringing of children. Cultural mores and traditions and family sanctity must be respected in any services that are rendered to families at any level of child development.

The need for education for parenting at all stages of child development is obvious if children are to reach their optimum development and to have a high quality of life. There is a movement to make sup-

[1] Wendell H. Pierce et al., *The Role of the Family in Child Development: Implications for State Policies and Programs,* The Fifteenth Report of the Education Commission of the States Early Childhood Project, No. 57, Denver, Colorado, Dec. 1975, p. 1.

[2] Kenneth Keniston and the Carnegie Council on Children, *All Our Children* (New York: Harcourt, 1977), p. xiii.

ports available before a crisis occurs or as soon as a handicap is noted.

For purposes of discussion, this chapter is organized around the following periods of development: infancy, preschool, early elementary grades, and upper elementary grades. The contribution of home economics is discussed for each level.

INFANT AND TODDLER

Child development experts claim that the first three years of life are critical. For that reason, there is a strong movement to educate parents—a child's first teachers. There are several dimensions to parent programs. First is the provision of emotional and social support so that parental anxieties caused by feelings of guilt and inadequacy may be reduced and positive feelings may be generated about parenting. Becoming enlightened about the processes of child development and how these changes manifest themselves and being informed about desirable practices to develop growth are part of a second dimension. A third dimension might be to encourage parents to share ideas and experiences.[3]

The home economics educator may serve parents during these important three years in various capacities: through parent courses in adult education, extension, or agencies; as a nutritionist in a well-baby clinic; as a team member in an infant-care center; or in other situations.

Goals

Probably the most important objective in studying or working with this age span is to appreciate the power that parental love and interest have in producing a sense of physical, emotional, and intellectual security. If this security is not established, the child may find it difficult to relate well to others at a later age.

The consistent expression of parental love leads to what is called *attachment,* or *bonding,* on the part of the child.[4] Bonding is defined as a binding process between two people in a close primary relationship. The attachment is reciprocal; studies now clearly show that the parent is dependent on the baby's responses for the formation of his or her own responses. The close relationship may begin in the womb,

[3] David L. Lillie and Pascal L. Trohanis (ed.), *Teaching Parents to Teach* (New York: Walker, 1976), pp. 3–15.

[4] Nancie Mae Brown, *Bonding: The First Basic in Education* (Bloomington, Ind.: Phi Delta Kappa Educational Foundation, 1978), p. 8.

with the fetus's awareness of the mother's heartbeat and the sound of her voice.

It should be noted that the mother is not automatically the person to whom the attachment is made. Studies have shown that it can be *any* person who serves as an infant's primary caregiver and who has a warm and loving relationship with the infant. In our society this person is usually the mother, but not necessarily.

The following positive practices will not only stimulate the process of bonding—which begins at birth, if not before, and continues through the second year—but will also enhance intellectual, emotional, and social growth. This is a process that includes all family members. A major goal of each family member should be to provide a stimulating home environment and to have sufficient time with the child to facilitate its development.

Promising Practices

Encouragement in the use of the five senses from the day of birth will enhance the process of bonding. Also, later learning will be strengthened by this early sensory education. Touch between parent and child is of paramount importance.[5] This is the only physical

[5] Ibid., pp. 16–17.

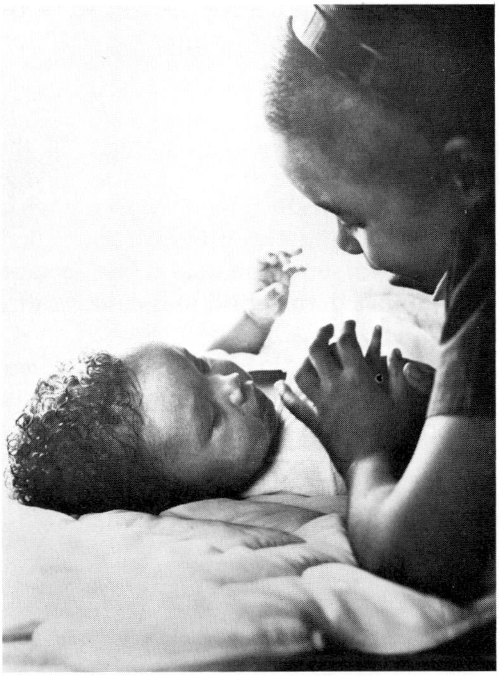

Figure 4–1 The loving attention of an older sister to a baby can strengthen bonding. (Gerber and Co.)

sense that can be experienced in all parts of the body. The newborn, as well as other children, needs to be handled in a loving manner, cuddled, caressed, and gently stroked. Important brain centers are stimulated by the sort of touch that is used for waking the infant or inducing sleep. Touch combined with movement, such as rocking or carrying, aids in the development of a child's sense of movement in space. Most important, affection is transmitted to the child through touch.

Certain toys, such as teething rings or soft rubber toys, are good for stimulating the sense of touch. When a baby is a bit older, let her/him feel the difference between a piece of cord, a thread, or a bit of yarn; a spoon; a small leather purse; and a cotton or silk piece of cloth. Other textures may be cornmeal, dry cereal, water, mud, a flower, grass, leaves, kitchen equipment, and countless other items that provide different touch experiences. Talk about the characteristics of the objects. Talking about differences in texture and about pleasurable touch sensations communicates a positive attitude about this sense even before the words are understood. In toddlerhood, talking about these sensations will reinforce learning. The feel of various items of clothing, such as shoes, socks, bibs, and play clothes, aids in future identification.

The newborn sees more than is often realized. Face-to-face smiling, kissing, caressing, and looking are important for bonding and for stimulating the infant's interest in his/her surroundings. Holding an object and moving it forward and backward gives the baby good visual exercise. Using different patterns, colors, and shapes in the crib bedding is stimulating.[6]

Crib toys may include mobiles strung from an arm that has been clamped to the side of the crib. Objects of various shapes and colors, such as blocks, rings, small replicas of animals, colored photographs of individual members of the family (especially mother and father), or enlarged cardboard drawings of family members, may be hung from this arm at various lengths. These objects should be changed often so that the child may be stimulated more frequently.[7] As the child grows older, household furniture and equipment or other articles may be identified, as well as the people who come into the home. The first books read to a child may contain pictures of articles and activities that are familiar to the child. Children should be helped to distinguish shape, size, color, and even movements, such as walking and running.

Education in sound may demand special attention because parents

[6] T. H. Bell, *Your Child's Intellect, A Guide to Home-Based Preschool Education* (Salt Lake City: Olympus, 1973), Chs. 5, 6, 7, and 8.

[7] Rita Dunn and Kenneth Dunn., *How to Raise Independent and Professionally Successful Daughters* (Englewood Cliffs, N.J.: Prentice-Hall, 1977), Ch. 2.

Figure 4–2 What is the effect of television on a small child? (Richard E. Swartz, *Children Today*)

may not be aware of its importance. Infants respond quickly and learn to identify the voices of their parents, especially the mother, and later of other family members, depending upon who in the family takes care of the baby. Thus communication begins. Having heard the mother's voice in the womb, the baby finds her voice after birth reassuring. Babies respond by their own vocalizations and their body movements.

Singing, humming, and talking to a baby stimulate bonding. In addition, soft sounds from a radio, records, and the playing of a piano or other instrument will add to the knowledge of sounds. A child should be encouraged to become familiar with household sounds, such as a door bell, a vacuum cleaner, an egg beater, and an electric razor, and, in time, to identify the sound with the source. Varying the loudness of the sound can be stimulating. Outside sounds, such as cars and trucks, sirens, airplanes, birds singing, dogs barking, and the sounds of other animals, are intrinsically interesting to the child and should be discussed and identified.

Crib toys may make sounds. Keys, spoons, bottle openers, and other objects that make sounds when they clink together are excellent. Because an infant is immobile in the early stages of life, these experiences must be brought to him/her. Placing beans or other articles in a can and making sounds and ringing a small bell or chimes are other possibilities. In all of these experiences, if family members speak to the child about the sounds, learning will be improved.

Smell has been given little attention in our society, except that we avoid unpleasant odors and accept perfumed and pleasant smells. A conscious effort can be made by mothers, fathers, and other family members to help children experience the smell of various fruits and vegetables and flowers. Unpleasant odors may be brought to their attention because they are important indicators, too.

Infants react quickly to the taste of certain foods. Most infants accept bland foods such as cereals, but fruits and vegetables are more pronounced in taste. A mother or other family feeder may identify the food being tasted so that an association will be made. Making complimentary remarks about a new food may help. A wide variety of tastes will facilitate the eating of a nutritious diet in later life. A sense of taste can be cultivated. If a child is given a small piece of an orange segment and encouraged to run his/her tongue over the cut edge, he/she can taste the sweetness or sourness of the fruit. In time, children will be able to identify many foods by the taste, as well as by their saltiness and other special sensations.

Other ways in which a parent can help a child in the early stages of development are to read to him or her every day, if possible; to speak in complete sentences; and to use acceptable language patterns. Reading or singing can begin immediately after birth. The reassuring voice of a parent who may sing, chant, talk, or repeat lines attracts an infant or small child and is the beginning of an interest in verbal communication.[8] Hearing Mother Goose songs, a baby often responds with smiles and body language. Babies soon recognize pictures in a book and as early as six months may chime in on single words of a verse. By three years of age, a child may retell the story.

Sparkman[9] refers to reading as "talk on paper." An early and major step in the ability to read must be the realization that words are talk written down. This may seem obvious to us, but it is a concept that the child must grasp through repeated experiences, and only then does reading become a comprehensible activity.

Reading to a child has many beneficial effects. It can assist him or her to understand many concepts that may or may not occur very frequently in conversations. Words heard in reading may begin to be used by the child. By looking at the book, the child may begin to see differences and likenesses in designs, pictures, and objects. As the reading is heard, the child may note the differences in the sounds made. The mother, father, or other reader should talk about what is being read, and when the child is able to ask questions, they should be answered clearly. Reading slowly and being dramatic make the reading more interesting. Playing the roles of different characters in

[8] Nancy Larrick, "How to Help the Beginning Reader," *The New York Times*, Jan. 8, 1978, p. 5 ED.

[9] Brandon B. Sparkman, "Johnny Can Read—If You Help," *Parade*, Apr. 23, 1978.

the story helps. Explaining the meanings of words such as *smaller, bigger, more, less, little, under, over, high, low, above, right,* or *left* can be most helpful. Sometimes these words can be dramatized in a simple game. Words that rhyme often please a child, and he or she may learn simple poems. A sensitivity to a child's span of interest is essential. No pressure should be exerted. Reading should be a pleasant experience.

Reaching, kicking, crawling, coordinating, running, and other aspects of physical development may be encouraged in various ways. Placing articles slightly out of reach may entice a child to crawl to them. Outdoor and indoor equipment, if selected carefully, will promote physical well-being.

When a child indicates a readiness, certain basic skills of living can be developed, such as handling a cup or glass and using certain implements for eating. Bathroom chores such as brushing teeth, washing hands, and toileting can give a sense of accomplishment to a child. Learning the various steps in dressing himself or herself can become an exciting game. Self-help clothes are desirable.

Helping to set the table, learning the functions of household equipment, making milk shakes, or preparing fresh fruit or vegetables for snacks are other broadening activities and help to increase the vocabulary and to enhance small-muscle development. At a later age, the child may use beans or buttons for counting or to outline letters or numbers. Number concepts are often difficult, and it helps to make them as concrete as possible. Selected television programs can be educational. Taking a child into the community to a supermarket, a zoo, a museum, a circus, a park, a pet shop, or to other interesting places stimulates growth. Going to a farm is valuable for the city child and to the city for a farm child.

Home economics educators may work with parents to determine the extent to which the growth of their child is progressing. Finding enough time for children can be a problem in the lives of busy family members. This is especially true of the father. Planning time for the children in the day's schedule is important at this critical stage in life.

PRESCHOOL

Preschoolers are children from three to five years of age. Some five-year-olds go to kindergarten for a period of time before entering the first grade. Home economics educators work with children of this age in nursery schools, cooperative nursery schools, day-care centers, or in short-term courses and units for homemaking students in junior or senior high schools. Head Start, business-operated centers, drop-in centers in shopping areas, night-care centers, Montessori schools, and child-care centers for workers in industry, hospitals, or businesses give other opportunities for service. Classes or other educational endeavors may be offered to the parents of these children by schools, colleges, extension, or agency programs. Dietitians may work with children in hospitals, and nutritionists may work with them in clinics.

Goals

Objectives for preschool education vary. Home economics educators may wish to check the answers to the following questions,[10] so that their contribution reflects the purposes of the program. How are individual differences treated? Are all developmental areas—cognitive, affective, and pyschomotor—emphasized? What is the basis for the selection or grouping of the children? How adequate are the facilities and equipment—inside and outside? Is creativity stressed? What is the child–staff ratio? What are the responsibilities of the staff members? Is the center funded privately or publicly? Are you considered a program or nonprogram staff member?

The overall objective is to provide for optimum development in each child. A large number of children of this age do not have access to a program. Even the children who do also have education at home. Home economics educators, through classes, publications, or mass media, may help parents with the total education of their children at this age level. Goals will reflect a continuation and some overlapping of those suggested for the child from birth to preschool, namely, intellectual, emotional, social, and physical development.

Some Promising Practices

In general, parents may need assistance in finding special services, such as diagnostic, financial, and health services or help for a handicapped child. Parents may need to be educated about the various phases or cycles of growth that are related to this period. Some stages are characterized by uncertainties, fears, irritating behavior, or other manifestations in a child. At this period, a parent may need to give extra time and affection in order to understand the child. Parent study groups may become the source of support in these situations, and appropriate literature may be recommended or other strategies

[10] Celia Anita Decker and John R. Decker, *Planning and Administrating Early Childhood Programs* (Columbus, Ohio: Merrill, 1976), p. 11.

Figure 4–3 Some children have learning problems and need special attention. (U.S. Office of Education, Bureau of Education for the Handicapped)

planned. It is especially important for parents to recognize that a problem in one area, such as emotional growth, may effect social or intellectual development.

Intellectual Development

Here are several suggestions for enhancing intellectual development. The development of time concepts may begin at this period. Parents have to be patient because learning about time is not easy and is a long process. Some children begin by identifying times of day, such as morning, afternoon, and evening. Some days of the week may be associated with family routines, such as working, shopping, or free days for family members. The concept of time can be reinforced in the context of different family activities, such as breakfast, the mailman's arrival, or chimes or a siren that sounds at a particular time of day. Family members might observe if a child indicates any idea of present, past, or future, which usually becomes evident around thirty-six months of age. Time concepts are related to the development of a child's memory.

Counting games can be fun. Show a child several objects—not more than three—one at a time. Then take them away or "hide them." Then ask the child which object was shown first, next, and last. Games like this can be fun if there is no pressure to memorize and if they are played within the child's span of interest.

Mathematical concepts are learned by beginning to count actual objects in the home.[11] Many opportunities arise during the day's activities. During food preparation, for example, a child might try to count the potatoes, apples, glasses of milk, pieces of meat, or other items. Concepts of larger, smaller, full, or empty may be developed with these types of experiences.

Other intellectual activities may be related to the anticipation of consequences,[12] such as the amount of milk that a glass will hold or the amount of water to run in a tub for a bath. Stop telling a story just short of the ending and let the child anticipate the end. At the age of four or five, the question might be asked, "What would you have done if you were the child in the story?" Anticipating other activities from those depicted in photographs is challenging. If a girl in a photograph is swinging and there is also a slide nearby, the question might be asked, "What else might the girl do?" Such questions might be carried on to additional activities that are imagined. These are only a few examples of the possibilities for intellectual growth.

Social Development

Social development is enhanced by group activities. Singing together, taking turns in the use of outside equipment, or dancing to music are suggestions. Dramatizing everyday incidents and discussing different approaches to the same behavior can be illuminating to the child. The use of puppets or masks may help to give a child the confidence to speak before others as well as appreciating the feelings and ideas of the character portrayed. Working with others on a project such as planting seeds in an egg carton involves "give and take." When children make up games, taking and weighing the suggestions of others are involved. Visiting and being visited by relatives, neighbors, and friends expand the child's horizons as well. Adults and others may serve as models in social development.

Emotional Development

In the emotional development of children, play has a high priority. Pouring sand or water into containers, for example, teaches children how to control their bodies and gives a sense of power for doing things alone. There is a sense of accomplishment in playing house, doctor, or space man, as well as a feeling of being in charge. Actually

[11] Bell, op. cit., pp. 120–125.
[12] Dunn and Dunn, op. cit., pp. 64–67.

Figure 4–4 Group activities encourage social development. (USDA Photo)

a child learns reality through play. Sometimes feelings and ideas can be displayed in art or other creative activities. Through dramatizations, a child may be helped to see solutions to problems such as a new baby in the home, moving to another home, a mother's being in the hospital, the loss of a pet, the death of a grandparent, or changes in schedule.[13] Understanding and support by parents and teachers can facilitate emotional growth.

Physical Development

Physical growth is facilitated by the development of desirable health habits in sleep, nutrition, exercise, hygiene, care of the teeth, proper clothing, and so on. Parents should strive for less supervision and more independent action by the child. Making these routines pleasant rather than chores is helpful. Measuring their growth periodically, helping with the preparation of their food, and being able to

[13] Lois B. Murphy and Ethel M. Leeper, *Preparing for Change,* DHEW Publication No (OHD) 76-31028 (Washington, D.C.: Superintendent of Documents, 1976).

Figure 4–5 Physical exercise provides for the development of the large and small muscles. (Richard E. Swartz, *Children Today*)

prepare certain nutritious foods on their own may encourage good eating habits in children. Having a small garden will provide exercise and the pleasure of eating their own harvest. Helping to select the clothes to be worn for the day may create an interest in suitable clothes. A story may make the bedtime routine more pleasant. Again, parents can encourage good habits by being good examples.

Physical development is also enhanced by providing activities that use both large and small muscles.

The field of child development is moving rapidly, so home economics educators will wish to keep well informed and to be creative in their dealings with parents and children.

ELEMENTARY SCHOOL

Home economics educators would do well to take advantage of every available opportunity to work with children at the elementary-school age level. These children can profit from home economics offerings because they are so basic to everyday living.

Home economics teachers sometimes serve as consultants to elementary teachers. In some city systems, home economics teachers go from school to school, as an art or music teacher may do, and teach home economics for a designated period of time. In some instances, elementary students may come to the home economics department, especially if the schools are nearby, so that important equipment and facilities may be used. Sometimes home economics teachers have a portable cart with an electric appliance for cooking, plus utensils and the other necessary equipment.

Home economists in business may be invited to an elementary classroom to teach nutrition with a puppet show or some other device; to teach home crafts, clothing selection, or ways to save energy; to show how to prepare simple recipes.

How may other areas of home economics be taught at this age level? The parents of these children may be taught about parenting for this age in adult courses through school, agency, or home economics extension.

Areas of Home Economics

Home economics teaching at this level may focus on one or many areas of content. Sometimes several areas may be integrated, such as food and consumer education. Procedures and content have to be adapted to the particular interests and needs of the group to be taught. Here are some suggestions that may be modified, adapted, or changed to fit the situation.

Food

The emphasis in this area depends upon the information, experience, and ability of the students. In addition, the availability of equipment, supplies, and time must be considered. Much can be accomplished without elaborate facilities. An electric appliance for cooking can be adequate. For individual experiences, students may work at their tables. The teacher may give suggestions about special needs or interests.

Nutritious snacks are usually pertinent, such as apple slices spread with peanut butter, a mixture of puffed or bite-sized unsweetened cereals, or popcorn with grated cheese or celery salt sprinkled on top. Students may compare these snacks as to taste, popularity, cost, ease of preparation, and the possibility of home preparation. Ideas for variations on these snacks will encourage creativity. The cost of these snacks may be compared with the snacks students buy.

Evaporated or dried milk reconstituted with fruit or vegetable juices rather than water are inexpensive, nutritious and easily prepared beverages. Milk shakes with bananas or other ingredients are another suggestion. Preparing fresh fruits and vegetables in interesting ways is appealing.

Concurrent learnings may be measuring, the proper use of utensils, mixing, using fractions, timing, vocabulary, and practicing hygiene, such as washing hands and not sneezing near food. Other learnings are classifying, estimating, counting, reading recipes, and learning about new foods. Students may discuss the contribution of each snack to a daily food selection guide.

In the upper grades, students might compare the flavor, texture, fuel cost, nutritive value, and appearance in the preparation of greens such as spinach, collards, turnip, dandelion, or mustard greens as a cooked vegetable. A small portion of the vegetable may be removed from the pan at three-minute intervals until the last portion is removed at eighteen minutes. Emphasize the importance of scientific procedures and evaluations.

A slice of bread may be used to start a discussion of all its possible uses, as toast, French toast, cold or hot sandwiches, a base for creamed dishes, bread pudding, cheese fondue, and so on. One preparation may be selected to be made in class. A survey of the favorite breads of the children might be made. A chart might be made of the results, with the amounts made into percentages. Breads of different cultures are another possibility.

Children may make a field trip to a nearby supermarket after a discussion of important points about buying food. The class may be divided into committees. Each group might compare prices, types of containers, label information, and other points among popular brands, store brands, and no-brand types of canned tomatoes, evaporated milk, tuna fish, canned green vegetables, canned fruit, or vegetable juices. Other groups may determine the best buy in margarine, fresh milk, and other common foods.

The preparation of nutritious foods low in sugar or fat is a challenging experience for students. In addition, cost is a serious consideration. What is to be done with the final products? Are they to be tasted, sold, or taken home, or are there other possibilities?

Nutrition

Discovering students' food preferences and dislikes may be the first step in planning. Are there basic nutritive lacks? What about the amount of fat and sugar in their diets? Are these children familiar with the basic four food groups? Are ethnic foods important? What kinds of food do the students buy? How much food preparation and buying experiences have the students had?

Vegetables are often disliked. A basket of fresh vegetables, including spinach leaves, carrots, broccoli, romaine or other lettuce (not iceberg), peas, string beans, cucumber, green pepper, or whatever is available, may be discussed with the class. Give each child a small amount to taste. Have the children describe the appearance and the taste of each vegetable. Is it a new vegetable to them? Many children who claim a dislike for a vegetable will enjoy it when it is eaten raw. With younger children, a few vegetables may be introduced at a time. In the same manner, fresh fruit may be the basis of a tasting party. Note the relation of color to nutritive value—especially greenness and yellowness. Discuss effect of the season on selection.

Each of the other basic four food groups, can be presented in an interesting manner. Students may do a twenty-four-hour recall and analyze their diets in terms of the basic food groups recommended. Plans may be made for improvement. Making sensible selections in the school cafeteria or in buying snacks is another possibility for teaching. Food for healthy teeth is timely. Refer to Chapter 16 in nutrition education for other ideas.

Consumer Education

Elementary students spend money and can profit from instruction in wise spending. Information about present buying practices and the problems that students have encountered may be helpful in planning for teaching in this area. One of the first steps with small children is to identify pennies, nickels, dimes, and quarters, and later, small denominations of bills. Playing store at home teaches children how to pay for an item and what change if any to expect from the purchase. Begin with one item at a time for "play buying." A more complicated operation is making two small purchases. Then addition and subtraction are both involved.

Another learning is making choices in a purchase. Which beverage is the best buy when one is thirsty—cola or noncola drinks, fruit juice, milk, or lemonade? Base decisions on criteria established by the class, such as how refreshing the drink is, how much it cost per serving, and how nutritious it is. Might water be a solution?

Satisfying a list of wants with limited funds may be a good problem. Students might compile a list of common needs that could be satisfied if only two dollars, or some other stated sum, is available. Discuss the reasons for the choices and note the wide variation in choices from student to student. How to meet unfilled desires may be explored. The importance of product safety is often ignored in making a purchase. Students might survey the safety features on a variety of tricycles or bicycles and compare results and the implications of buying each item.

Comparative shopping in the purchase of games or other items can be quite illuminating. A consumer advice sheet may emerge from experiences of this kind. Students may share experiences of making faddish or foolish purchases and tell what they learned. The impact of television on student buying can be fruitful to explore, and again, student experiences may be shared. Board games about buying may be made to encourage desirable buying practices. Adult courses for parents may reinforce the consumer education of students. Working with parents can be fruitful. Once students become interested in being better buyers, the need for other types of instruction will emerge.

Clothing Selection

Most elementary students are interested in the clothes they wear and may be taught about line, design, color, and other aesthetic aspects. Exploring the feelings associated with certain clothes can be revealing. Home care of clothing items may be explored. Characteristics of comfort in clothing can be shared by classmates. Students at this age can begin to learn something about the buying of clothes, such as their sizes, suitable fabrics, reasonable cost, and how to judge fit and other criteria. A visit to a clothing store or a clothing department in a store to judge socks, T-shirts, play clothes, and other items

Figure 4–6 The game Bingo Shapes can teach children about forms and shapes, an important element of clothing design. (Gretna Breeze, Gretna, Neb., and Gretna Public Schools)

is an excellent experience. Actual garments may be brought to class for instructional purposes. Throughout these experiences, decision making, value clarification, critical thinking, comparison making, and other learnings may be highlighted.

Being a Family Member

Home economics teachers might have students consider the many roles they assume as family members. The characteristics of competency in these roles are a valid topic for discussion as is consideration of the ways to improve. Often children of this age do not realize that they can make an important contribution to the quality of their family living by learning how to be helpful, supportive, and loving during interaction with family members.

Usually children are assigned to care for the space allotted to them in a home. Can they find new and easier ways to do this? What efforts are they making to help the family save energy, such as turning out lights and turning off the television when no one is looking at it? Innovative ideas may be added to these suggestions and new ones may be explored to make this area especially meaningful. Discussion with parents is desirable.

Other areas of home economics, such as safety in the home, family health measures, and child care, may be added to the list. The important point is to provide students of this age with the help they need and will enjoy.

THE MIDDLE SCHOOL

The middle school is designed for preadolescence and early adolescence. The curriculum is geared to the developmental characteristics of the child of this age. This can be a difficult period, and for that reason, it is considered wise to have the children in a school where their special needs and problems can be met. The program values consistency and generally attempts a balance between active/quiet and concrete/abstract experiences. There are opportunities for clarification of values, for choice making, and for improving basic skills and concepts. An honest, humane, and open relationship is encouraged between students and adults, and counseling is done by the entire staff whenever possible.[14]

The role of home economics in this setting can be challenging and satisfying. The curriculum is planned to reflect the overall goals of

[14] Loren J. Thompson et al., "Benchmarks for the Middle School," in "Early and Middle Years of Schooling," *Theory into Practice* (TIP), Vol. 15, No. 2 (Apr. 1976), pp. 151–171.

this school and may include consumer education (special focus on buying), child care, use of leisure time, preparation and care of food to meet the special needs of this age, personal development, care of clothing, and the construction of simple garments. Low-cost home decoration, personal hygiene, and personal and home management are other areas suitable for these students.

The home economics teacher often has opportunities to integrate learnings with other areas, such as science, the arts, mathematics, and social studies, as well as general studies. Home and community ecology, improved human relations in connection with multicultural education, death and dying, ways to help families with inflation problems, contemplating the future, and career education are suggestions.

Other Considerations

The following topics are receiving attention today. They are not related, but each is a reflection of contemporary times.

Special Education

Mainstreaming or caring for students with special needs, such as the hard of hearing or the deaf, the partially sighted or the blind, and children with other physical handicaps, learning disabilities, and emotional problems is now a legal responsibility as well as a humane one. These students may be in classes in which home economics is offered. Consulting with elementary or special education teachers will be helpful. In any event, every attempt should be made to reach these students.

Figure 4–7 The hard-of-hearing child can be mainstreamed through home economics. (U.S. Office of Education, Bureau of Education for the Handicapped)

Learning is facilitated by activities that emphasize the use of the senses. The use of small-step rather than multi-step directions is desirable. Praising students for accomplishments is important. A few specific suggestions are given here.

The partially sighted or blind child may increase his or her learning by feeling fabrics, food, kitchen utensils, and the like. The hard-of-hearing or deaf child may have limited concepts because he or she has not heard words spoken or discussed, so anything written must be simple and clear. Another student or an aide may translate what is being said by sign language. This is an area in which home economics educators should have special instruction and an opportunity to share ideas.

Death Education

Many students of this age experience dying and death, such as the death of a grandparent, a parent, or a brother or sister. Teacher rapport is vital during these periods. Teachers are encouraged to explore, analyze, and confront their own feelings about death and death education.

Classroom discussions about death may take many avenues. Death rituals associated with religion, personal feelings, beliefs about death, death in literature, handling guilt feelings, and examining myths about death are some possibilities. Considerable information about death education is available to teachers.[15]

One objective is to minimize anxieties about death. Perhaps discussing death will accomplish this purpose. Do not evade questions, but if the answer is not ready, suggest investigating it. What teachers say and how they say it can contribute to wider understanding. This responsibility can be a challenge.

Cultural Pluralism

Multicultural education is an attempt to assimilate certain subcultures in our nation into the dominant culture. Many courses of action have been proposed. In home economics education, there are many ways in which greater understanding of the various backgrounds of children may be facilitated.[16] In addition, a new and stronger appreciation of a child's own culture may emerge. A recognition by children that many cultures exist in our country is important.

[15] Gretchen C. Mills, Raymond Reisler, Alice E. Robinson, and Gretchen Vermilye, *Discussing Death* (Homewood, Ill.: ETC Publications, 1976).

[16] Carl A. Grant (ed.), *Multicultural Education: Commitments, Issues, and Culture Development* (Washington, D.C.: Association for Supervision and Curriculum Development, 1977).

Children reflect the early experiences of their culture. Relationship patterns, methods of communication, and basic values and attitudes are revealed in personal, family, and school behavior. These powerful influences cannot be ignored in dealing with children.

Home economics offers many opportunities to encourage the broadening of this knowledge. For example, students may share interpretations of "family" and what constitutes each of their families. Scrapbooks may be prepared of these various types of families, and their commonalities and differences may be discussed. A next step for the student might be to describe the roles of the various members of her/his family. From this experience, hopefully children will realize that many family patterns are possible and that family roles may vary considerably. Students may role-play family roles for further enlightment.

Through discussion of the cooking, serving, and eating of food; home management practices; holiday celebrations; and child care, students may further enlarge their concepts and appreciation differences in family cultures. Sometimes students express an interest in preparing the food of another culture in their home or adding a new holiday practice to their own celebration.

Figure 4–8 A Chinese girl showing elementary school children Chinese art, cooking, and eating utensils. (*Lincoln Journal and Star*)

Another facet of multicultural education is an examination of sex stereotyping by both teachers and students. The children may want to explore the ways in which boys and girls are identified as playing different roles or having different capacities. Students might examine the desirability of each practice and consider ways to have "cultural pluralism" of the sexes.[17]

Related to cultural pluralism is the trend toward bilingual education. Familiarity with another language may become an asset for home economics educators. This is true not only in the classroom but in the hospital, clinic, agency, or business where home economists work. The challenge is to help this student or person with the English language as well as in home economics instruction. Attention to teaching strategies and teaching materials is critical and a fascinating challenge.

If home economics educators are to meet the needs of individuals throughout the age spectrum, then the teaching of children deserves more attention from the profession.

SUGGESTIONS FOR FURTHER LEARNING

1. Read the following references:
   Decker, Celia Anita, and John R. Decker. *Planning and Administering Childhood Programs.* Columbus, Ohio: Merrill, 1976.
   Eliason, Claudia Fuhriman, and Loa Thomson Jenkins. *A Practical Guide to Early Childhood Curriculum.* St. Louis: Mosby, 1977.
   Elkind, David. "What Makes Kids Tick?" *Instructor,* **87** (Sept. 1977), 78–79, 88–90.
   McCord, Ivalee, et al. *Child Care Handbook.* Washington, D.C.: American Home Economics Association, 1975.
   Spodek, Bernard, and Herbert J. Wahlberg (eds.). *Early Childhood Education, Issues and Insights.* Berkeley, Calif.: McCutchan, 1977.
   Stevens, Harriet A. *Fixing and Eating, Food Activities for Small Children.* Iowa City: U. of Iowa, 1974.
   Williams, C. Ray, et al. "The Early and Middle Childhood Years of Schooling." *Theory into Practice,* **15** (Apr. 1976).
2. Read the following references about children with special needs and consider some innovative ways to teach these children.
   Bowman, Mary, Abigail B. Calkin, and Patrick A. Grant. *Eating with a Spoon: How to Teach Your Multihandicapped Child,* NCEMMH Reprint Series, National Center on Educational Media Publication, No. NC-75.906, Publication Sales Division, Columbus: Ohio State University Press, 1975.
   Granato, Sam, and Elizabeth Krone. "Serving Children with Special

[17] Jean D. Grams and Walter B. Waetjen, *Sex, Does It Make a Difference?* (North Scituate, Mass.: Duxbury Press, 1975).

Needs," DHEW Publication No. (OCD) 73-1063, Office of Child Development, Department of Health, Education and Welfare, 1972.

A Handicapped Child in Your Home, DHEW Publication No. (OCD) 73-29. Washington, D.C.: Superintendent of Documents, 1973.

Jones, Ron. *The Acorn People, A Summer Camp Story About Handicapped Children.* Zephyros, 1201 Stanyan St., San Francisco 94117, 1976.

Levine, Edna S. *Lisa and Her Soundless World.* New York: Human Science Press, 1974.

Metsker, Carol, and Edith King. *Hints and Activities for Mainstreaming.* Dansville, N.Y.: Instructor Publications, 1977.

Moore, Corllie B., and Kathryn Gorham Morton. *A Reader's Guide for Parents of Children with Mental, Physical or Emotional Disabilities,* DHEW Publication No. (HSA) 77-5290. Washington, D.C.: Superintendent of Documents, 1976.

Responding to Individual Needs in Head Start, Head Start series on needs assessment, DHEW Publication No. (OHD) 76-31075. Washington, D.C.: Office of Child Development, Head Start Bureau, U.S. Department of Health, Education, and Welfare, 1976.

What information did you gain that might be applied to home economics instruction?

3. Analyze your own feelings about sex stereotyping and indicate how you would handle it at this age level. Read the following reference.

   Cohen, Monroe D. *Growing Free, Ways to Help Children to Overcome Sex-Role Stereotypes.* Washington, D.C.: Association for Childhood Education International, 1977.

4. If you have not faced your own ideas about death, try to do so before you start reading about it. You might begin your reading with the following references and then find others on your own. Later think about how you would teach about death and dying at this age level.

   Fassler, Joan. *My Grandpa Died Today.* New York: Human Science Press, 1971. A book for a child to read about death.

   LeShan, Eda. *Learning to Say Good-By.* New York: Macmillan 1976. Handling the death of a parent by a child.

   Mills, Gretchen C., et al. *Discussing Death.* Homewood, Ill.: ETC Publications, 1976. This book suggests teaching strategies and has excellent bibliographies.

   Become familiar with the magazine, *Death Education.*

5. Literature can bring understanding to a teacher and to a student. For the would-be teacher or the practicing teacher, this book is helpful:

   Landau, Elliott, D., Sherrie Landau Epstein, and Ann Plaat Stone. *Child Development Through Literature.* Englewood Cliffs, N.J.: Prentice-Hall, 1972.

   These books are for children to read, but if a teacher reads them, a better understanding of children may emerge.

   Berger, Terry. *I Have Feelings.* New York: Human Science Press, 1971. Situations related to seventeen feelings that might be discussed by the child.

   Hazen, Barbara Shook. *Two Homes to Live in.* New York: Human Science

Press, 1978. For small children to read whose parents are divorced or are separated for other reasons.

Zion, Gene. *Harry, the Dirty Dog.* New York: Harper, 1976. A good story for reading to children or for them to read on their own.

A book for older children: Keele, Reba. *Let's Talk, Adults and Children Sharing Feelings.* Provo, Utah: Brigham Young U.P., 1977. An aid in making decisions about some of the conflicts in life.

6. The magazines that a child reads may have a strong influence on his or her thinking, values, and development. The following reference discusses a large number of children's magazines and rates them.

   Larrick, Nancy, "Classroom Magazines, A Critique of 45 Top Sellers." *Learning,* **7** (Oct. 1978), 60, 67–69.

   How many of these magazines are familiar to you? Which ones might be used in home economics?

5

Teaching Youth

For many years home economics has made a unique contribution to the education and development of youth. There is an ever-present challenge to reexamine this stage of life and to evolve new ways of service to this population.

CONFUSION IN THIS AGE STRUCTURE

This stage in life cannot be labeled with precise age limits or definitions of each step within it. Keniston[1] refers to the age of youth as a stage of life that lacks clear definition. Keniston advances the idea that adolescence is preyouth and that youth is the transition to adulthood. Preyouth struggle for identification, but youth has some sense of self and realizes that accommodation to society may be difficult. Even adulthood is not clearly marked. The former bench marks of marriage or holding a regular job are too limited in scope. Clearer classifications would be helpful. In this chapter, for purposes of clarity, youth is approximately identified as the age of twelve through twenty-four. This is one possible interpretation, suggested by Havighurst.[2]

[1] Kenneth Keniston, "Prologue: Youth a Stage in Life," in Robert J. Havighurst and Philip H. Dreyer (eds.), *Youth,* The Seventy-fourth Yearbook of the National Society for the Study of Education (Chicago: U. of Chicago, 1975), p. 3.

[2] Robert J. Havighurst, "Editor's Preface," in Robert J. Havighurst and Philip H. Dreyer (eds.), *Youth,* The Seventy-fourth Yearbook of the National Society for the Study of Education (Chicago: U. of Chicago, 1975), p. viii.

CHARACTERISTICS OF STEPS IN THIS LIFE STAGE

According to Goethals,[3] the first identification of preyouth may be the fact that a boy or girl is no longer considered a child by adults. Physical growth is an important mark of this change. A special rite, such as graduation from middle school, confirmation, or bar mitzvah, is a symbol of entrance into the stage of youth. The second identifying factor is that youth and adults together facilitate this point in growth by acknowledging an emerging change from childhood.

According to the "second step or regulatory theory" of Goethals, there are many patterns of maturation, but in them all, the greatest influence is the family of the youth. The presence of both parents, only one parent, no parents, a nuclear family, or an extended family will make a difference in development. The larger society is also an important influence.

The "third step" is the authority of the family and of society, of which there are many variations, but the existence of authority itself is important.

Lastly, this is the stage when sexuality emerges. All societies make recommendations about the sexual behavior and the sex roles of the young. Depending upon the society or culture, the spectrum may range from liberal to conservative.

Characteristics vary among the individuals in the later stages of youth (approximately at ages seventeen to twenty-four years). Some continue to reflect adolescent rebellion at times and may have difficulty in finding a place in society. Others are married, may have children, and are settled in an occupation. Lifestyles vary, satisfying vocations may or may not have been found, social roles differ, and some resistance may emerge because society has not permitted youth to assume the adult roles of which they consider themselves capable.

Youths, according to Keniston,[4] tend to band together in groups that may or may not be countercultural. At times, any attempts at acculturation are rejected. There appears to be a fear of death, which may be a reflection of the loss of movement so vital to youth. Sometimes loneliness, alienation, or ambivalence about society is evident. Sexual development has an important impact. Youths become interested in family roots, traditions, culture, problems, and accomplishments. Relationships with elders and parents tend to be less tense than during earlier youth.

[3] George W. Goethals, "Adolescence: Variations on a Theme," in Robert J. Havighurst and Philip H. Dreyer (eds.), *Youth,* The Seventy-fourth Yearbook of the National Society for the Study of Education (Chicago: U. of Chicago, 1975), Ch. 3.

[4] Keniston, op. cit., pp. 9–26.

Figure 5–1 Youth band together for many purposes.

The characteristics cited here are general in nature. Home economics teachers will realize that multiformity rather than conformity is prevalent. Each home economics educator will wisely become familiar with the characteristics peculiar to the group that is being serviced in home economics. Even in this situation, there will be diversity. Planning must encompass what is most important to the students, patients, or group members served. Another point is to be aware that there is no closure on development at this stage—it is merely a prologue to future periods of growth, adulthood and old age.

PHYSICAL, INTELLECTUAL, EMOTIONAL, AND SOCIAL TRANSFORMATIONS

Information about the physical, intellectual, emotional, and social maturation of youth is pertinent to curriculum development in home economics.

Physical Development

Young people mature at different ages and at different rates.[5] There are many stages of change during maturation. Heald[6] characterizes this period as one of rapid, interrelated biological changes. Increased body mass, resulting in changes in size, shape, and body composition, is typical. Growth in some parts of the body is greater at times than in other parts, for example, resulting in longer arms and bigger feet. Gonads mature rapidly, affecting secondary sex characteristics. After the onset of early youth, the two sexes are markedly different in terms of body composition and anthropometric measures. A rapid rise in height and weight is indicative of the adolescent growth spurt. Girls do not grow to the same degree as boys, and growth occurs two years earlier than in boys. Body measurements are a more accurate measure of development than chronological age.

Youth have certain special health-care needs. Acne is often a problem, and the impact on feelings about personal appearance can be serious. Obesity is another problem for both sexes and is a matter of concern because of the frequent resistance to treatment. The negative effect of obesity on self-concept can be a deterrent to normal development. Other concerns include increased sexual activity, which sometimes leads to venereal disease. The abuse of drugs, alcohol, and cigarettes is a serious concern. Handicapped youth are confronted with the dual problems of handling their maturation and their handicap as well. Handicaps may be orthopedic, cardiac, neurological, or cosmetic.

Accidents are the leading cause of death in the fifteen- to twenty-four-year-old group. Automobile accidents account for almost half of the deaths, but firearms, private aircraft, snowmobiles, and minibikes also account for a share of the mortality statistics. Dangerous hobbies such as sky diving, motorcycling, and motorboating contribute to the accidental deaths. Homocide, suicide, malignancies, and cardiovascular disease are other causes of death. Overdoses and other complications of drug abuse can be fatal. Marginal nutrition plus serious viral or bacterial infections can also lead to death. Health-care services and education to combat these many dangers are important.

[5] Hilary E. C. Millar, *Approaches to Adolescent Health Care in the 70's* (Rockville, Md.: U.S. Department of Health, Education, and Welfare, Public Health Service, Health Services Administration, Bureau of Community Health Services, 1975). (DHEW) Publication No. (HSA) 76-5014.

[6] Felix P. Heald, "Growth and Development in Adolescence," in Helen M. Wallace, Edwin M. Gold, and Edward F. Lis (eds.), *Maternal and Child Health Practices* (Springfield, Ill.: Thomas, 1973), pp. 827–829.

Figure 5–2 A blind youth is being taught by a scientist ways to identify a bayberry bush. (West Virginia University)

Emotional Development

Emotional development is often related to physical development. During this age, there is a preoccupation with the body, even when the body changes are normal. Youths worry about a big nose or large feet or other physical characteristics. Shenker and Schildkrout[7] state that every pimple may be a tragedy. Imagination may lead a youth to believe that she or he has the same illness as a friend. Depression is common. Severe environmental stress may result in a state of anxiety. Such stress can result from a misunderstanding with a friend or friends, from an athletic disappointment, from the loss of a job, or from similar situations. In the later years of this age, there is a trend toward maturity in emotional growth.

Intellectual Development

Early youth is a time for development of the cognitive skills. Students need to be encouraged to develop the abilities associated with

[7] I. Ronald Shenker and Mollie Schildkrout, "Physical and Emotional Health of Youth," in Robert J. Havighurst and Philip H. Dreyer (eds.), *Youth,* The Seventy-fourth Yearbook of the National Society for the Study of Education (Chicago: U. of Chicago, 1975), Ch. 4.

decision making, reasoning, problem solving, hypothesizing, interpreting, and the like. Raths et al.[8] state that thinking *how,* thinking *of,* thinking *up,* thinking *about,* and thinking *through* are part of the intellectual equipment needed by young people. Education can encourage the development of these attributes. (See Chapter 13 on "Thinking and Research.")

Social Development

Four major tasks confront young people in their reach for adulthood, according to Hofman[9]: (1) release from dependency on parents; (2) establishment of personal and sexual identity; (3) development of a moral and ethical code; and (4) decisions on a career and a lifestyle.

In the early stages of adolescence, some of the dependency on family is transferred to peers and friends. The middle teenager moves to heterosexual relationships. Personal identity tends to be assured between the ages of seventeen and twenty-four years. There is a

[8] Louis E. Raths, Selma Wasserman, Arthur Jones, and Arthur M. Rothstein, *Teaching for Thinking* (Columbus, Ohio: Merrill 1967), p. 113.

[9] Adele D. Hofman, "The Hospitalized Adolescent," *Pediatric Annuals,* Vol. 2, No. 6 (June 1973), pp. 49–64.

Figure 5–3 A teacher will wish to be informed about the magazines that interest youth. (*Lincoln Journal and Star*)

movement at this stage toward giving love and care to others. Focus on a career and strengthening sexual-social relationships are typical of this last stage.[10]

Young people are quite sensitive to social changes and their concomitant values. Material wealth, for example, is not prized by many of the young as in past generations. Expressive living and greater involvement with others in order to improve the quality of life are prized, according to Havighurst.[11]

A very large number of youth are being absorbed into society during the present decade. Forecasts are that this number will decline in the near future. Other factors related to youth are the large number of those unemployed at this age and the postponement of marriage by young women, who consequently spend more time in the labor force.

The family continues to be a viable force in the lives of youth. Both males and females are now learning economic and social roles in the family as well as parental and wife and husband roles. Home economics teachers can reinforce these contributions of families.

TRANSITION TO ADULTHOOD

There is no single blueprint for becoming an adult. Successful coping with prior growth stages is helpful. For some youth, the process goes smoothly, but for most, the adjustment is a matter of steps forward and then some backsliding.

Part of growing up is handling situations such as disappointment in not getting a job, a date, or an honor, and the question of conforming to the group when one is not interested in drinking, smoking, gambling, unrestricted sexual experiences, or cutting class. Often young people do not know where to turn for help. Many communities have "hot lines."[12] Students might survey the various types of help that are available to them and share this information with other students. Sometimes it is difficult to overcome the feelings associated with the generation gap, which are manifested when youth are talking to parents, grandparents, teachers, and others. Youths may judge their progress to the extent that adult privileges are offered and handled well. Comparing oneself in certain situations several years ago and now will lead to the realization that progress has been made; such a realization can be helpful to the student. Being confronted

[10] Shenker and Schildkrout, op. cit., pp. 61–62.

[11] Robert J. Havighurst, "Youth in Social Institutions," in Robert J. Havighurst and Philip H. Dreyer (eds.), *Youth,* the Seventy-fourth Yearbook of the National Society for the Study of Education (Chicago: U. of Chicago, 1975), Ch. 7.

[12] "Finding Help in Your City," *Senior Scholastic,* Vol. 108, No. 1 (Jan. 27, 1976), pp. 32–33.

with questions about identity and the future colors many actions, but striving for answers encourages growing up.

Although being less dependent on parents is a mark of maturity, both parents and youth often have difficulty in severing ties. The time at which a son or daughter is ready to leave home is not easily pinpointed. Some youths and parents sever the ties quickly, which may present problems, too. Again, if parents have tried to facilitate growth, then becoming independent is an accomplishment for all. Who helps parents and youths to make this decision? Home economics education is challenged to help solve this problem.

One drawback to this transition is that society is not ready in many cases to help youth. Gibbons[13] states that there is relatively little contact between youths and adults, that schools have not provided adequate help, and there is insufficient financial aid to prepare for getting jobs or going to college. The unfamiliarity of youth with work and jobs and their lack of participation in the production of society are shortcomings of home, school, and society. Greater consideration needs to be given to alternative programs for youth, better determination of job needs, and better placement to alleviate this situation.

YOUTH EDUCATION IN HOME ECONOMICS

How may home economics assist youths in dealing with family and social problems? Home economics aids in the development of life skills by providing pertinent experiences in family living, child development, home management, consumer education, housing and home furnishings, food, nutrition, and clothing. Interwoven with all of these experiences are opportunities for being involved in making decisions, solving problems, making choices, examining value systems, serving people in the community, thinking critically, exploring the many facets of relations with others, releasing creative talents, and participating in other growth-promoting activities.

Family-Life Education

One of the most important contributions of home economics is through family-life courses or modules and also in extension, social work, and other areas. Here youths have an opportunity to discuss, examine, and evaluate different lifestyles as they pertain to the various stages of youth.

[13] Anne R. Gibbons, "Facilitating the Transition to Adulthood," *American Education*, Vol. 10, No. 5 (June 1974), pp. 35–36.

Relationships with Others

How a youth relates to others is a critical aspect in his or her life. Students in family, personal, or adult living classes may wish to examine their relationships with others as a basis for improvement. This would include family, teachers, friends, and people in the community. Answers to some of the following questions might be helpful. What are the characteristics of a good relationship? Why do I get along with some folks but not with others? Do certain relationships that are desired go unfulfilled? Why? How have my friendships changed with time, and why? What seems to "hold" relationships together? Is it possible to categorize friendships or relationships from close to casual? What might be some desirable plans of action for improvement?

Not only are one-to-one relationships important, but group relationships are assuming a significant role in the lives of the young. Considerable learning occurs in a group. The current trend is for a group to consist of persons of both sexes in all degrees of friendship and love rather than couples' pairing off. Young people study together, go "Dutch" for meals, help each other in the repair of a stereo, wear each other's clothes, and share in many other ways. Support is

Figure 5–4 Relationships with one's peer group members are mutually supportive. (Raleigh Industries of America)

given to each member, and community projects may be planned, and campaigns organized. Group relationships help both sexes to develop friendly relationships and provide a stage for testing ideas and for learning to work and play together day after day. The group members get experience in determining what turns people "off" or "on," in tempering aggressiveness, in receiving helpful impersonal criticism about what they are doing, and in learning to appreciate the different perspectives of others. Students may wish to compare the various benefits of one-to-one relationships and group relationships.

Choosing a Lifestyle

One way to open the subject of lifestyles is to examine the ways in which families and individuals live today. A few ideas to explore in relation to each lifestyle might be the opportunity for the development of each individual in the group, the possibility of growth of the group as a whole, the amount of mutual support, the degree of stability, structured or unstructured relationships, and role in the community.

Students may also wish to explore such facets of living as income sharing, having or not having children, two-career couples or families, role interpretations, means of providing the basics of living, use of space in a home that provides some privacy for each person, cultural space, how a whole person may be developed instead of just a role, sources of love and support, sources of power or authority, and managing the home.[14]

Sex and Sex Roles

Sex stereotyping may be a topic for discussion. Home and family have an especially strong impact on sex-role interpretation. Dunn and Dunn[15] caution parents against making sharp delineations in sex roles, prescribing appropriate dress for boys and girls, or placing sex labels on cooking, carpentering, "fixing," problem solving, or career selection. An open classroom that provides students with the opportunity to discuss their sex roles with understanding is desirable.

Sexual Activity Among Youth

Premarital sexual experiences are increasing rapidly among the young. The estimate is that approximately 12 million teenagers are

[14] *The New Life* (Ottawa, Ontario, Canada: The Vanier Institute of the Family, 1977).
[15] Rita Dunn and Kenneth Dunn, *How to Raise Independent and Professionally Successful Daughters* (Englewood Cliffs, N.J.: Prentice-Hall, 1977).

sexually active. Rebellion against parents is one factor in this increased activity. For boys, sexual relations are a means of proving manhood to their peers. Some cities have opened birth control clinics for girls in spite of complaints that this step breaks down parental authority and gives license for immorality.

Hofman[16] believes that each generation of adolescents defines its own moral code and sexual behavior in light of their times and not in terms of the past or their parents or elders. Early adolescents are especially concerned about the normality of their biological development, especially their sexual maturation. Considerable comparisons of their maleness or femaleness are made among members of the same sex. The curiosity and the experimental nature of this age are other motivations to try sex. Parents and teachers are urged to appreciate adolescent development in a contemporary setting. The messages sent to youth by adults and the mass media and from their observation of community mores, about acceptable sexual behavior are mixed and confusing.

An open forum where youth may explore the alternatives, the consequences, and the responsibilities of sexual behavior is sorely needed. Home economics teachers can be especially effective in this type of education because they are noted for securing student confidence and for giving support to student concerns. In our present society, however, strong parental and community disapproval can be a deterrent. But the price of not doing anything is even greater in light of the high rate of teenage pregnancies.[17]

Teenage Pregnancy

Although the birthrate in the United States has decreased considerably in the last twenty years, over a million teenagers become pregnant each year and over 600,000 of these pregnancies result in births out of wedlock. One in every ten girls fifteen to nineteen years of age becomes pregnant each year. Many preteenagers have become pregnant.

Attempts at birth control are erratic and unenlightened. Information is often taboo and unavailable. Siblings and friends sometimes give information. Middle-income parents, when involved, are quite effective in their advice. Sex education has not been successful because the emphasis in many instances was largely on the reproductive process, when what was needed was an opportunity to get answers to the sex problems young people have. The less informed

[16] Adele D. Hofman, "Adolescents, Sex and Education," *New York University Education Quarterly*, Vol. 8, No. 4 (Summer 1977), pp. 7–14.

[17] Sol Gordon, "Sex Education Is Dead in the Elementary Schools?" *Instructor*, Vol. 86, No. 7 (March 1977), p. 132.

the young are about birth control, the less likely they are to use it. Youths believe many myths about the possibility of pregnancy, such as, "I am too young" or "It can't happen the first time, on Sundays, or standing up." In addition, the lack of communication between the teenage boy and girl about sex or birth control is a real hindrance. The belief in "spontaneity" deters the use of birth control, as does the influence of liquor. Birth control requires planning, and that may interfere with romantic notions.

There is need for additional, objective research in regard to unwed teenagers. Assertion of independence, rebellion, showing love, neurosis, broken home life, loneliness, confusion, or a real desire to be pregnant may be the reasons for sexual activity and pregnancy. Sex has replaced violence as a rating gimmick on television. Strong sex messages are given to youth by TV, as well as by some of their music and the posters they buy.

Teenagers should have an opportunity in home economics classes to examine the consequences of sexual behavior. Information about birth control (if permitted) and realizing that one may say "yes" or "no" when considering sex are alternatives. "Pregnancy roulette" is a dangerous game to play. When pregnancy occurs, there are several options, such as abortion, adoption of the baby, or keeping the baby. Boys as well as girls need to consider the answers. Often the father is ignored, but he may have feelings of anxiety, guilt, and concern.

Keeping a baby may have serious effects on both the mother and the baby. Many teenagers look forward only to the pleasure of loving and caring for a baby. Babies born to teenagers are two to three times more likely to die than babies born to women of twenty years or more. The babies are often of low birth weight and may have other complications. The problems of pregnancy are often more pronounced in teenagers, and their mortality rate is higher than for older women. Youths are lacking in the various aspects of maturity required to bring up a baby. Their babies may not have the care required for optimum cognitive, physical, and emotional development. A teenage mother might ask herself the question, "If I were a baby, would I want myself as a mother?"

Teenage mothers seldom return to high school or complete their education. They are unrealistic about the costs of living and the health care of a baby. A job is often difficult to secure, and then there is the problem of caring for the baby. If the girl marries the father, the burden of support is a worrisome problem, and he usually does not return to school. The picture is not bright,[18] and these marriages often end in divorce.

[18] "Teen Marriage, What Are the Chances?" *CO-ED*, Vol. 23, No. 1, (Sept. 1977), pp. 56–57, 106.

The dimensions of this problem may appear overwhelming to home economics educators. The classroom where pregnant girls are present is one place to begin. They may need special help with nutrition and with developing skills in caring for the baby, and they may be faced with important decisions that can be discussed with the teacher or the 4-H Club leader. Some high schools have special programs taught by a home economics teacher for helping these pregnant girls. As a result, the girls are encouraged to stay in school. Nursery schools or day-care centers are provided by some schools to care for their children. The home economics teacher may assist in the planning of schoolwide programs and community action programs.

Marriage Readiness

When certain criteria are met, a marriage is more likely to occur and to last. Students may wish to discuss these points. The length of acquaintance and particularly of the courtship—at least a year—are important. Certain personal characteristics are critical. Is there a record of alcohol or drug abuse or a jail record? If one partner is a teenager and the other is ten years older, the adjustment to different life interests may be too great. Stress may be caused by differences in religion or ethnic background, especially if the couple's family customs seem strange to each other. Relatives and in-laws may cause wider breaches. Parental attitudes have a strong impact. If the following values are present, marital success is more likely: cooperation, spiritual development, loyalty, a genuine concern for and a feeling of responsibility toward others, expression of a sincere appreciation of others, and the acceptance of responsibility for the consequences of one's own actions.[19]

Students in family-life classes may discuss their own criteria for a lasting marriage and compare them with the points made here. Married teenagers may come to class and share their experiences. Students may develop a questionnaire and survey the opinions of married teenagers in the community. The data can be analyzed in class and the results and implications shared with the entire school. Students in the class who plan to marry may be willing to discuss how they reached the decisions they have made. Critical thinking, value clarification, acceptance of reality, and the potential for development are some of the factors to include in these discussions.

Another important consideration is ability to provide a living. Youths are often quite unrealistic about the cost of establishing and

[19] Nick Stinnet and Mary C. Pyles, "Marriage Readiness Among High School Youth," *Family Perspective*, Vol. 11, No. 1 (Winter 1977), pp. 17–22.

maintaining a home. Before marrying, one or both partners may need full-time employment that appears stable for the future.

Some New Emphases

This section gives a short overview of a few topics that are now an important part of family-life education.

Death education has been under a taboo for many years but is now considered a part of living. Youth are very interested in the subject and welcome an opportunity to examine it. Stanford and Perry[20] offer the rationale that death education is relevant to life needs and not only prepares one for death but can improve the quality of living. A sensitivity to the needs of the dying and the grieving is an important attribute.[21]

The content for this education may include a discussion of feelings and attitudes about death, the language of death, the definition of death, fears related to death, the death of a child, and adjustments by family members to a death. It would also be beneficial to discuss the rights of the terminally ill, care of the dying by family members, personal philosophy of death, stages in dying, death as a part of living, and beliefs about the hereafter.[22] A survey of student interests at the first meeting will be helpful in determining the content of the course.

The current great interest in *cultural heritage or roots* and cross-cultural education has implications for family-life education. A study of the family customs of other cultures provides an opportunity for students to broaden their outlook about people who may differ from them in nationality, in race, in religion, and in other ways. Interpersonal education is recommended by Moyer and Engelbrecht.[23] Having a positive self-concept is a basis for understanding and relating to others and is important in intercultural education. The similarities among cultures as well as their differences are of most interest to students. Students might determine commonalities in family customs related to birth, marriage, child rearing (include toys and games), admission to adulthood, and death. The routines of daily living may indicate common bonds.

An introduction to music and the other arts, recreation, and crafts[24]

[20] Gene Stanford and Deborah Perry, *Death Out of the Closet, A Curriculum Guide to Living with Dying* (New York: Bantam, 1976). Good source of curriculum suggestions, including books, films, and aids.

[21] Polli Howard, "Facing Death, A Way to Celebrate Life," *Teen Times*, Vol. 33, No. 3, pp. 10–11.

[22] Richard O. Ulin, *Death and Dying Education* (Washington, D.C.: N.E.A., 1977).

[23] Joan E. Moyer and Guillermina Engelbrecht, "Multicultural Education, Where Do We Begin," *Childhood Education*, Vol. 53, No. 5 (March 1977), pp. 241–244.

[24] Janet and Alex D'Amato, "African Crafts for You to Make" (New York: Julian Messner, 1975).

of other cultures can be revealing. Reading about the experiences of other youths, especially their feelings, may challenge present attitudes.[25] The examination[26] and debunking of myths and stereotypes about various cultures can be illuminating.

Face-to-face contacts in sports, school, and community activities and working and playing together will help students of diverse backgrounds to become better acquainted and minimize misunderstandings. Students may analyze and research the sources of prejudice as well as ways to counteract this barrier. As a result, students may share their new insights with others and challenge their attitudes about people whom they consider different.

There are many other areas of family-life education to explore. Family-life educators, through surveys of the problems, needs, and interests of youth at various ages, will have ample materials for their curriculum.

Child Development

Many young people have the responsibility of caring for younger brothers and sisters and often have questions about aspects of their care and development. Beginning with their interest in future parenthood, study and observation will lead to a knowledge of human development and what can be done so that a child reaches his or her greatest growth potential. A review of Chapter 4 will be helpful in this respect. Exposure to other sources such as books; observation of children; and working with children in nursery schools, infant and day centers, and church schools for children will all result in a fuller understanding of children. Information, reactions, feelings, and experiences with children can be shared and discussed in the class or in small groups. Examining the ways that a person, especially a parent, can influence a child for life can be sobering.

Parenting

Home economics educators are well prepared to participate in the national movement toward education in parenting for the young. This program presumes that the teacher has a good background in child development and many actual experiences with children of various backgrounds and ages, including infants.

A student in a parenting class may establish criteria for the kind of parent he or she desires to be and may make a plan for securing the

[25] Mildred D. Taylor, *Roll of Thunder, Hear My Cry* (New York: Dial, 1976).
[26] C. Mindel and R. W. Habenstein (eds.), *Ethnic Families in America* (New York: Elsevier, 1976).

Figure 5–5 Having experiences with small children will prepare high school students for parenting. (USDA Photo)

experiences that will ensure this development. The goal and the actions may be scrutinized by the teacher or other students for suggestions and further discussion. In their experiences with children have the following been noted? Are communication abilities; state of independence; physical, intellectual, and emotional development; parent–child relationships; range of experiences available; adaptability; "peer" relationships with other little children; health; and other aspects of development considered? What strong and limiting environmental factors affecting a child have been observed, and how may they be dealt with? Students will periodically wish to check their progress in becoming prepared for parenthood and will hopefully enlarge upon their experiences in weak areas.

Student experiences involving the care of children may be shared with the community through puppet shows, radio programs, participation in TV programs, or as a part of the program for service clubs for men and women.[27]

Consumer Education

The average teenager in the United States spends from $12 to $45 per week. How is this money spent? On food, soft drinks, candy, gum,

[27] "Teen Age Parenting," *Teen Times*, Vol. 32, No. 3 (Jan./Feb. 1977), entire issue.

recreation, hobbies, movies, records, beer and alcohol, gasoline, car accessories, clothes, and gifts. Youth as consumers are an important part of our economy.

Home economics classes may investigate many student needs, such as decision making in regard to making and spending money, credit, budgeting, the legal aspects of consumerism, shopping by mail, making complaints, distinguishing needs from wants, income taxes, social security numbers, checking accounts, interest rates, consumer skills, and values and priorities in spending.

There are many student activities that can help in developing consumer skills. Comparison is important. For instance, students might purchase hamburger, pizza, fried chicken, or fish and chips; attempt to duplicate them in the laboratory; and compare taste, cost, appearance, time of preparation, and other pertinent factors. Conclusions in relation to this experiment might deal with the advantages and disadvantages of eating out or eating at home.[28]

Most youth are interested in the purchase of "wheels" for mobility and other purposes. This transportation includes bicycles, mopeds, cars (usually secondhand), and snowmobiles. Being well informed about the mechanical aspects and ways of testing these vehicles is critical. Care and repair are important. Collecting and testing information about what shops have to offer is part of the decision making. Sharing ideas with friends and others is helpful. Students may collate information, prepare exhibits, or brainstorm other ways to keep this information up-to-date.

Food, clothes, furniture, and other items to be purchased have labels. What is the important information on these labels, and how may it be used? How may goods be tested? Youth are interested in a wide spectrum of recreational activities that require purchases. Sports demand special clothes and equipment. Sometimes student rates are offered on tickets for concerts, plays, games, and other community recreation. The buying of sound equipment, which may include speakers, tape recorders, receiver–amplifiers, turntables, and the like, requires careful consideration and know-how. Students may suggest other areas with which they need assistance in buying.

Students may share ways to save money such as knowing about outlet and other types of stores, buying secondhand items, taping friends' records, and swapping talents, clothes, and other things with friends.[29] A calendar of annual sales of goods should be kept handy, along with information on sources of help, such as the Better Business Bureau, consumer agencies, the library, and magazines or books.

[28] An experiment performed in a laboratory session directed by Anna Marie Warren-Boulton, home economics teacher in Locust Valley, N.Y., High School.

[29] "Cheapskating," *Family Circle* (March 1975), p. 100.

Figure 5–6 An exploration of the cost, safety, care, and benefits of "wheels" is a good study for youth.

Food

Young people have a wide interest in food. Some experiences in this area may be preparation of food for backpacking, snacks, and parties. Buying food for the family from vending machines, take-home food, and making choices in restaurants are other areas in which skills would be helpful. Trying recipes of ethnic foods and discovering the foods in one's own ethnic background are popular activities. Substituting less expensive ingredients for expensive ingredients in a recipe is a good experience. Boys and girls might enjoy developing a particular recipe that carries their name, such as Pirate Sam's Stew or Zelda's Zucchini Bread. Such recipes might lead to a business of preparing the food for interested persons in the community.

These and other food preparation experiences require a knowledge of scientific cooking techniques and preparation. This area provides an opportunity to integrate the basic educational skills such as *reading* recipes, using *mathematics* in measuring and enlarging a recipe, and *writing* in making plans and in judging final products. *Transfer of learning* may be evident when students share home experiences of food preparations.

Nutrition

Young people may be responsible for their own nutrition as well as that of their families. Planning for and buying food for adequate nutrition in times of inflation are serious challenges. What, for example, on any given day is a good buy for a green vegetable or a source of vitamin C? For some families, the cost of meat is almost prohibitive, but lower-priced sources may be found in certain fish, chicken, and beef liver. Inexpensive cheese, milk, and some eggs may have to be included as sources of protein. Pairing of vegetable proteins may be explored. Students may search for other suggestions for good nutrition at low cost.

Students may be familiarized with adaptations that may have to be made in the daily diet because of such factors as age, sex (for example, more iron for young women), weight (overweight or underweight), modifications for special health problems, state of health, and limitations such as inability to chew food. Students may select one or more of these problems and plan and prepare a day's diet that is adequate.

Learning to be discriminating about nutrition information in advertisements, magazine articles, statements made on talk shows, and opinions of neighbors and fellow workers involves separating facts from fallacies. The effects of following such beliefs might be researched. Nutritionists may teach drug users about the effect of drugs on their nutritional status.

Clothing

There are many ways in which clothing might be studied in home economics. Psychologists indicate that clothes are an extension of self. Students may analyze the messages their own clothes are sending, as well as those of other classmates. Sharing these conclusions may lead to other experiences, such as strengthening some messages and subduing others.

The care and repair of clothes is time-consuming, so students may plan unique and clever ways of doing these chores and having an exhibit, a leaflet, or a poster that tells their best ideas to others.

Planning wardrobes and a personal appearance that includes good grooming cannot be neglected. Buying clothes can be an important part of the budget of a young person. Coordinating the wardrobe means that one garment may be used in several ways to provide for more than one purpose. Colors, designs, and textures must be considered, although there is considerable freedom in the kind of clothes that are combined. The study of the effect of color, line, and design in clothes can be stimulating and creative. Clothes related to specific activities are another aspect of wardrobe planning. The person who is interested in sports may have a different wardrobe than the person who is more sedentary in his or her habits. Shopping for clothes requires a number of skills, such as judging workmanship, the care required, and versatility. Some boys and girls may wish to sew their own garments, which may demand the acquisition of new skills. A total look at every aspect of the clothing process is important for young people.

Housing and Home Furnishings

A common need for most youths in this area is a living space that is furnished attractively but with little money. Environment has a strong influence on the person living in it, so planning is important. When completed, it should be a place where the young person likes to be and that his or her friends will enjoy. Drawing a plan of the space and making scaled, flat models of the furniture that can be pushed around on the plan are a good beginning. Looking at magazines and at room arrangements in department and furniture stores, noting unusual uses of space in homes that are visited, and inventing some personal ideas are all helpful.

An analysis of the activities planned for the space is necessary. What kind of storage spaces can be planned? One student had little room for anything but a bed in the space available. Near the ceiling, she built a platform loft bed that was reached by a ladder. It freed the space below for a desk, cupboards, book shelves, a chest, and the like —very compact but interesting. Students will have other suggestions.

Furniture may be family castoffs—even patio or porch furniture has possibilities. Neighbors or friends may contribute furniture or other items, such as a mirror, that are ready to be discarded. Secondhand furniture stores and unpainted furniture have possibilities.

What might be done with kites, baskets, hammocks, portable cabinets, scraps of carpet, a porch chair or swing, fabrics, placemats, or homemade wooden platforms in furnishing a room? What other unique ideas might be shared?[30] This kind of planning challenges

[30] Bobbi Queen, "Low Budget Decorating in a Rented Cottage," *The New York Times,* July 20, 1978, pp. C1, C8.

thinking; leads to clarification of values, decision making, and making comparisons; and encourages creativity.

Older youths may be giving consideration to renting an apartment or buying a house. Choices involved in such a step may be shared with other students, and community resources may be evaluated. Coordination of the inside–outside look of house and furnishings can be a good project. All of these experiences highlight the effect of personal space and environment on the quality of living.

Home and Personal Management

Although management is one of the most important areas of living, to many youths it is a dull subject. The "box" idea[31] might be used fruitfully to enable students to find ways to overcome management problems and to realize their goals. These problems may be a lack of time and money, goals that seem impossible to reach, or difficulty in "breaking out" of old ways of working. Students may place themselves in an imaginary box, cage, or crate that is symbolic of their problem. How do they get out? The Program Action Impact Kit of FHA may be helpful. One approach to getting out of the box may be to take a look at present practices and find keys for improvement. What kind of decisions are being made: planned, deliberative, impulsive, or repetitive? Other approaches are to consider who and what can help. Explode excuses, try brainstorming, plan an experiment, avoid past failures, and analyze the degree of personal perserverance. Students can be encouraged to think of better ideas.

Similar techniques may be considered for dealing with home or personal problems and jobs involving work simplification, task analysis, decision making, or problem solving. The discovery and use of resources can be a game.[32] Resources for finding a job, making more money, or refurnishing a room at home on a very limited budget, as well as new ideas for family recreation or planning additional education, are other possibilities.

The Handicapped

Many families have members who are handicapped in some way. Also some of the handicapped in the community might like help. First, the student has to learn to manage his or her own time and energy in addition to learning ways to assist or to teach the handicapped in their everyday lives. The giving of love and care are satisfying endeavors. Retarded children or adults, muscular dystrophy victims, blind or deaf persons, and individuals in wheelchairs are all

[31] Polli Howard, "The Box Kit," *Teen Times*, Vol. 31, No. 4 (March/Apr. 1976), entire issue.

[32] "The Resource Game," *Teen Times*, Vol. 29, No. 4 (March/Apr. 1974), entire issue.

Figure 5–7 Two blind girls feeling the garment of another girl to identify its characteristics.

persons for whom students can fill a need. One way that students can make the problems of the handicapped real to themselves is to try to get around in a wheelchair, or blindfolded, or to attempt to communicate with their ears covered. Students can become quite ingenious about simplifying tasks or problems for the handicapped, for example, preparing food, dressing, getting help in class and study, learning to participate in sports, adapting cultural experiences, and developing independence in countless other ways. Encouragement, interest, recognition, and assistance are of great value to the handicapped. The student grows in the process and feels that she or he has made a contribution. Helping the aged, who are often handicapped, is another challenge.[33] Students might like to adopt a grandparent or to do volunteer work in a nursing home and plan appropriate activities for the aged.

Ecology

Home activities can be a serious drain on energy, can add to pollution, can waste resources, and therefore can upset ecological balances. Youths might study the energy expenditures of a family, such as the use of appliances or cars, and study ways of reducing the energy consumed. The disposal of garbage and other wastes might be

[33] Sheila Sobell Moramarco, "Teach About the Aging, You Owe It to Yourself," *Learning,* Vol. 6, No. 7 (March 1978), pp. 44–48.

analyzed. How may food, paper, and other waste be reduced? Does a family contribute to noise pollution?

Some of these studies might become community projects in which other students may become involved. Other ways to improve the ecology of the country may occur to students and teachers.

Teaching the Future

Educators believe that youth must deal with the future today and not be past- or present-bound. Youth then will see more readily that what they are doing today is related to the future.[34] Perspective will change because tomorrow will not be considered the same as today. "Future thinking" is necessary because change is so rapid and education is not adequate for the future. Teachers should realize that many of their students will spend most of their lives in the next century.[35]

Here are several teaching strategies to be used in home economics classes. Students are asked to look toward the year 2000. Have them read "Happy Holidays, The Year 2000"[36] and discuss what family life will be like at that time. What do they like and dislike about future family life as they project it? Another strategy is for students to write on a piece of paper five changes that they envision in home and family living in the future.[37] Have them date when these changes will occur, and analyze the results after listing the important categories of the data. What are the implications of the results? Students might suggest newspaper headlines heralding these changes.

SUGGESTIONS FOR FURTHER LEARNING

1. A number of references about youth are cited here. Select one or more of the areas and explore the implications for home economics education.

Death and Dying

Adler, Charles, S., Gene Stanford, and Sheila Morrissy. *We Are But a Moment's Sunlight.* New York: Washington Square Press, Pocket Books, 1976. A book of selected readings on death and dying.

Gunn, Barbara. "What Home Economists Can Do to Prevent Suicides." *Journal of Home Economics,* **70** (Jan. 1978), 50–52.

Klagsbrun, Francine. *Too Young to Die, Youth and Suicide.* Boston: Houghton, 1976.

Levit, Rose. *Ellen.* New York: Bantam, 1974.

See recent issues of *Death Education.*

[34] Alvin Toffler (ed.), *Learning for Tomorrow, The Role of the Future in Education* (New York: Random, 1974).

[35] Draper L. Kaufman, Jr., *Teaching the Future, A Guide to Future-Oriented Education* (Palm Springs, Calif.: ETC Publications, 1976).

[36] *Senior Scholastic,* Vol. 107, No. 8 (Dec. 16, 1975), pp. 3–6.

[37] Toffler, op. cit., p. 6.

Parenting

Chand, Ian P., Donald M. Crider, and Fern Willits. "Parent–Youth Disagreement as Perceived by Youth." *Youth and Society,* **6** (March 1975), 365–375.

Knox, David, and Richard A. Gilman. "The First Year of Fatherhood." *Family Perspective,* **9** (Fall 1974), 31–34.

Lamb, Michael E., and Marguerite B. Stevenson. "Father–Infant Relationships, Their Nature and Importance." *Youth and Society,* **9** (March 1978), 277–294.

McCleery, Judy, and Ruth E. Brasher. "Parent–Youth Conflict—A Solution?" *Family Perspective,* **9** (Fall 1974), 35–41.

Pattison, Deloris J. "Today's Child—Tomorrow's Parent." *Journal of Home Economics,* **69** (May 1977), 30–32.

Phillips, Donna Evans, and Jeannie L. Baker. "Parenthood Education: Meeting the Challenge." *Forecast for Home Economics,* **23** (Oct. 1977), 76.

Porter, Blaine. "The Challenge of Parenting," Editorial. *Family Perspective,* **11** (Spring 1977), 1–2.

Sawin, Douglas B., and Ross D. Parke. "Adolescent Fathers: Some Implications from Recent Research on Parental Roles." *Educational Horizons,* **55** (Fall 1976), 38–43.

Smith, Thomas Ewin. "Push Versus Pull." *Youth and Society,* **8** (Sept. 1976), 5–26.

Teenage Pregnancy

Bruce, John A. "Adolescent Parents: A Special Case of the Unplanned Family." *The Family Coordinator,* **27** (Jan. 1978), 75–78.

"Coping, Teenage Pregnancy by Choice? By Chance? Know the Consequences!" *CO-ED,* **23** (May 1978), 68–69, 78.

Duxbury, Mitzi. "Adolescent Pregnancy, An Interdisciplinary Problem." *Educational Horizons,* **55** (Fall 1976), 34–37.

Walters, James. "Birth Defects and Adolescent Pregnancies." *Journal of Home Economics,* **67** (Nov. 1975), 23–27.

Zackler, Jack, and Wayne Brandstadt. *The Teenage Pregnant Girl.* Springfield, Ill.: Thomas, 1975.

Youth Problems

"A Brush with Juvenile Law, Student and Juvenile Rights and Responsibilities." *Senior Scholastic,* **106** (May 8, 1975), 5–10, 18.

Fooner, Andrea. "Sandy Shoplifted Last Saturday." *CO-ED,* **23** (Dec. 1977), 50–53.

Grams, Jean D., and Walter B. Waetjen. *Sex: Does It Make a Difference?* North Scituate, Mass.: Duxbury, 1975. Stereotypes.

Howard, Polli. *Teen Times,* **31** (Jan.–Feb. 1976), entire issue on youth and alcohol.

Konopka, Gisela. *Young Girls, A Portrait of Adolescence.* Englewood Cliffs, N.J.: Prentice-Hall, 1976.

"Teenage Wanderers, Where Are They Running?" *Senior Scholastic,* **104** (Feb. 7, 1974), 6–8.

Wexler, Henrietta. "Lifeline to the Real World." *American Education,* **14** (Jan.–Feb. 1978), 35. About dropouts.

2. The use of literature to highlight the interests and problems of youth can be an effective teaching strategy because insights may be provided into the reader's personal life. Some suggestions for paperbacks are offered here.

Blume, Judy. *Iggie's House.* New York: Dell, 1970. Prejudice in a neighborhood.

Blume, Judy. *"It's Not the End of the World."* New York: Bantam, 1972. Separation and divorce of parents.

Blume, Judy. *Forever.* New York: Pocket Books, 1976. An idyllic love affair including first sex experience—later separation occurs.

Byars, Betsy. *The Summer of the Swans.* New York: Avon, 1970. A teenager and her retarded brother.

Cleaver, Vera and Bill. *"I Would Rather Be a Turnip."* Philadelphia: Lippincott, 1971. A story of a teenager during a summer's visit of an illegitimate nephew.

Donelson, Kenneth L. (ed.). *Books for You, A Booklist for Senior High Students.* National Council of Teachers of English, 1111 Kenyon Road, Urbana, Ill. 61801, 1976.

Scoppettone, Sandra. *"Trying Hard to Hear You."* New York: Bantam, 1974. A girl who discovers that two of her boyfriends are homosexuals.

Zindel, Paul. *Pardon Me, You're Stepping on My Eyeballs.* New York: Bantam, 1976. The relationship of two teenagers, boy and girl, who are misfits.

6

Teaching Adults

The concept of lifelong learning has unleashed a back-to-school boom. The old American notion that education is only a necessary step from childhood to adulthood is becoming outmoded. Contemporary life, with its complex problems, has brought a surge of adults back to schools or to classes offered at other sites, such as factories, offices, businesses, churches, department stores, and museums. In New York City, courses have been offered on commuter trains. Education by correspondence, with the use of cassettes, slides, games, and other aids, is flourishing.

There are many needs that these types of education meet. Both men and women may update professional or vocational knowledge and skills, some to be retooled for another type of work. Cultural refreshment through learning more about art, music, drama, architecture, culture, and other art forms is satisfying and mind-stretching. Other courses may assist families and family members with estate planning, tax preparation, investments, financial planning, and other problems. An interest in gourmet cooking and in foods of other cultures has produced many types of cooking schools. Some of these courses are conducted by home economists. Parent education is thriving. These and many other possibilities have helped to create education's new popularity.[1]

This upsurge may compensate partially for declining enrollments now and later in schools because of age changes in the nation's popu-

[1] James Cass, "Lifelong Learning, the Back-to-School Boom," *Saturday Review*, Sept. 9, 1975, p. 14.

lation. Hechinger[2] urges high schools and colleges to become more committed to adult education.

HOME ECONOMICS AND ADULT EDUCATION

Home economists have been involved in adult education under many circumstances since the beginning. Some examples have been teaching people to save and to cope with shortages during wartime, helping the poor wherever they are, encouraging better health for children, and advocating consumerism. Whatever the circumstances, past, present, or future, professionals in home economics can make unique contributions that can be applied to everyday living from young adulthood through old age.

Most professional areas make some contribution to adult education. Here are some examples. Among the continuing education courses for adults offered by colleges and high schools may be a course in personal and family nutrition planned according to the Senate Nutrition Subcommittee's dietary guidelines. Extension reaches adults of various age levels and with various needs. Computer programs entitled "Diet-Check," and "Money-Check," are of-

[2] Fred Hechinger, "Education's New Majority," *Saturday Review*, Sept. 9, 1975, p. 14.

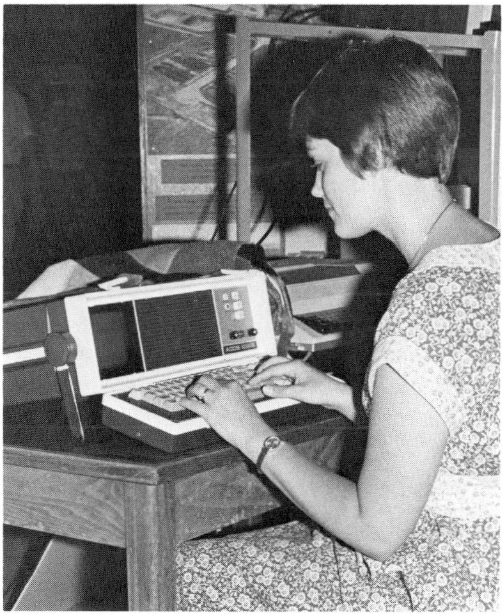

Figure 6–1 A computer program called Diet-Check helps individuals analyze the adequacy of their diets. (University of Nebraska Photo)

fered through extension services at the University of Nebraska—Lincoln.[3]

Home economists associated with welfare make a particular contribution to the education of the poor. Nutritionists in clinics, on television or radio programs, or in government programs such as WIC (U.S. Department of Agriculture child nutrition program [P.L. 96–627] for low-income pregnant women, infants, and children to receive selected, highly nutritious foods to supplement their diet) attempt to teach patients, mothers, and the public about nutrition in innovative ways. Home economists in business may arrange for courses for their employees in areas in which interest has been expressed. In addition, they teach the public through materials, kits, films, filmstrips, slides, and other aids created for use by clubs, in the classroom, in church groups, and at other locations.

SOME BASIC CONSIDERATIONS FOR ADULT EDUCATION

Although the interest in all types of adult education is high, often the provision for this education is haphazard and uncoordinated. There is at the moment a wide diversity of purposes, providers, programs, teachers, sites, and populations served.[4] There are many titles for these programs. This broad spectrum suggests a need for a nationally coordinated delivery system based on adult learning needs. The concept of lifelong learning should be the cornerstone.

General Goals

One of the longtime goals of education has been to provide equality of opportunity among Americans. Present elementary and secondary education has realized this goal only partially. The influence of family background, economic status, and place of residence, such as ghetto or elite suburbs, has made a difference. With adult learning, the doors of educational opportunity are kept open longer.

Education for adults might be tied in some situations to work, thus facilitating movement from education to work and back to education coordinated with work, as the employees require new information, skills, or other types of preparation. This plan could be used at all levels of employment, from entry- to top-level jobs and would encour-

[3] Developed by Harriet Kohn, Nutrition Specialist, and Kathy Prochaska Cue, Extension Specialist in Family Economics and Management, at University of Nebraska—Lincoln.

[4] Norman D. Kurland, "A National Strategy for Lifelong Learning," *Phi Delta Kappan,* Vol. 59, No. 6 (Feb. 1978), pp. 385–389.

age additional education. Cooperation between employers and educators may be a prerequisite.

A wide diversity of options has the advantage of meeting more adult needs and hence is an important goal. An awareness of changing needs is crucial. Wide access to adult education is another consideration. Questions like the following need to be answered. Are families in remote rural areas being reached? What about families whose native language is not English? Are provisions made for the poor, the handicapped, the old, and others with special needs? Are courses offered at convenient hours so that students who work at odd times or have family obligations may attend? Will the type of education that is especially needed be provided? Will education that compensates for failures in elementary and secondary education be offered?

Alternative programs can accommodate the student who lacks motivation as well as the student whose goals are well defined. Older students are often more motivated than the young. Having young and old students mixed in classes may inspire and encourage the young.

Another objective that has strong implications for home economics is parent education. The early years of childhood are critical learning

Figure 6–2 Helping fathers who are responsible for children may be one objective of adult education. (Richard E. Swartz, *Children Today*)

years. In addition, many parents want to learn about routine child care. Adult education courses take the place of the extended family, which once passed on this sort of information. A rich environment is important if the child is to learn. Many parents are uninformed about how to provide such an environment. Teaching parents so that every child has a good start in life is a prime consideration because the entire nation will benefit.

Other goals pertinent to adult education will surface for consideration, such as facing problems associated with the times and the need for outreach and for improving the quality of life in general.

Counseling

Sometimes prospective adult students require counseling to decide what they need. Limited provision is made for this service at the present time. Counselors can suggest possible courses, inform the prospective student of their location, give vocational guidance, and suggest ways to finance going back to school. The setting for this counseling must put the person counseled at ease. Sometimes counseling services are available on the job or in community agencies, libraries, churches, schools, and other places that are convenient.

The Higher Education Amendments of 1976 recognize the need for counseling services and make provisions for them, including an expanded system in "information centers." These opportunities will encourage lifelong learning.

Financing

Another basic consideration is the financing of adult education, according to Kurland.[5] Many questions must be answered. What should be the dimension of public support? What groups, if any, should be favored? How should the financial needs of adults be determined? Should aid cover maintenance and other support costs? Will it be possible for individuals to receive financial aid so that major sacrifice of income is not required? On what basis would aid be allocated to the states?

The Family as Educators

Another basic consideration in home economics is to consider the role of the family as educators. Home economics, with its family-centered emphasis, has become a part of a movement to determine and to facilitate the role of the family and the community as educators.

[5] Ibid., p. 389.

The ramifications of this idea are far-reaching. Leichter[6] suggests a consideration of the many ways in which education occurs within a family, the types of activities, and the family members who are responsible for them, such as mothers, fathers, brothers and sisters, grandparents, and aunts and uncles. Another aspect is the relation of the family to other educational institutions in the community—a potentially fruitful study. The question may also be asked: "During the lifetime of an individual, which institutions had a hand in his or her education?" These might include the family, the school, the neighborhood, peer groups, museums, clubs, hospitals, churches, factories, mass media, and corporations. These concepts might be considered in planning education for adults.

PROFILE OF THE ADULT STUDENT

Adult students represent the broad spectrum of the nation's population. What they have in common is their desire to learn.

Because of these varied backgrounds, the teacher of adults must secure from students information about their experiences, knowledge, needs, attitudes, and objectives as they relate to the course being taught.[7] Birren and Woodruff[8] contend that adult education should use developmental tasks that are characteristic of the age span or spans represented as a guide for learning. Havighurst[9] divides these developmental categories into early adulthood, middle age, and later maturity.

Early Adulthood

According to Havighurst's developmental tasks, the areas important for development at this age are (1) selecting a mate (or a companion); (2) learning to live with a marriage partner or a companion; (3) starting a family (matter of choice); (4) rearing children; (5) managing a home; (6) getting started on an occupation (may involve husband or wife, or husband and wife); (7) taking on civic responsibility; and (8) finding a congenial social group. Finding a compatible philosophy of life or value system and establishing priorities may be other tasks to include.

[6] Hope Jensen Leichter, "Families and Communities as Educators: Some Concepts of Relationships," *Teacher's College Record,* Vol. 79, No. 4 (May 1978), pp. 565–573.

[7] Josephine B. Rudd and Olive A. Hall, *Adult Education for Home and Family Life Education* (New York: Wiley, 1974), p. 13.

[8] James E. Birren and Diana S. Woodruff, "A Life Span Perspective for Education," *New York University Education Quarterly,* Vol. 4, No. 4 (Summer 1973), pp. 25–31.

[9] Robert J. Havighurst, *Human Development and Education* (New York: Longmans, Green, 1953), Chs. 16, 17, and 18.

Figure 6–3 Sharing responsibilities is one way to foster good relationships in marriage. (Bethlehem Steel)

For this age, Sheehy[10] concentrates on "pulling up roots or finding life out there and the urge to love." Next the "trying twenties or taking hold of the adult world" is important. Lastly, there is passage to the thirties, with a desire to expand horizons and to pinpoint what is important in life.

Other characteristics of this age group are an interest in physical activities because energies are usually at a peak. Lifestyles vary from living alone, through living with one or several friends of the same sex or cohabiting with a companion of the opposite sex, to being married. Men are usually working, and so are most women. The household of a couple may have two incomes to live on.

This period of life is one of the most problem- and pressure-filled stages in human and family development.[11] The husband and father and the wife and mother may be committed to being successful in the work world. The child or children are young, demanding, and dependent. The mother may not be working. In many instances, she has severed her job and social contacts, and she may feel guilty about not earning a salary. Much interdependence can place a strain on the marriage, especially if there is an illness, a change in job, or a new baby. Some children can drain their parents of energy.

The more material goods that are consumed, the greater the need for the husband or the wife, or the husband and the wife, to work. The women's movement has created new options and new pressures.

[10] Gail Sheehy, *Passages* (New York: Dutton, 1976), Parts 2, 3, and 4.

[11] Susan S. Golden, "Women and Family," *The University of Michigan News* (Information Services, 6008 Administration Building, Ann Arbor, Mich. 48104), Vol. 41 (Feb. 19, 1976).

Golden suggests that young families take time often to discuss priorities.

Families without children, the single parent with children, and single adults may not have the same pressures, but there may be other problems to be faced.

Middle-aged Adults

Havighurst[12] suggests the following developmental tasks for middle age: (1) achieving adult civic and social responsibility; (2) achieving and maintaining a standard of living; (3) assisting teenage children to become responsible adults; (4) developing leisure-time activities; (5) relating to one's spouse as a person; (6) accepting and adjusting to the physiological changes of middle age; and (7) adjusting to aging parents. Sheehy[13] refers to middle age as the midlife passage in which there are changes in sense of time and sense of aliveness and self. Individuals examine the extent to which goals have been realized. This is a period of maximum influence in politics, in community, at work, and in other areas. For some, this is a period of renewal.

[12] Havighurst, op. cit., Ch. 17.
[13] Sheehy, op. cit., Ch. 17.

Figure 6–4 Including young children in grown-up activities may ease the strain of parenting. (USDA Photo)

Stress[14] at this period can be great, so men and women may turn to various methods of coping with this problem. Meditation, encounter groups, behavior modification, biofeedback, and exercise are some of the techniques. It is suggested that a person check into the degree of success assured in each method because of the expense involved and because of possible undesirable aftereffects.

Middle age is high in divorce problems. Parent-and-child conflicts may be common. The community and national responsibilities at this age level may be heavy because men and women are often at the peak of their capacities and are needed. Income is usually improved, but demands are greater. Assuming the role of grandparents may be part of this age. Planning ahead for retirement is important.

Later Maturity

According to Havighurst,[15] the developmental tasks of later maturity are (1) adjusting to decreasing physical strength and health; (2) adjusting to retirement and reduced income; (3) adjusting to the death of a spouse; (4) establishing an explicit affiliation with one's age group; (5) meeting social and civic obligations; and (6) establishing satisfactory living arrangements. Of all the adult stages, old age is

[14] "Executive Guide to Living with Stress," A Personal Business Supplement, *Business Week,* No. 2446 (Aug. 23, 1976), pp. 75–78.
[15] Havighurst, op. cit., Ch. 18.

Figure 6–5 Old age requires many adjustments. (U.S. Department of Labor)

Figure 6–6 "Caring time" in a day-care center can be satisfying for a senior citizen. (*Lincoln Journal and Star*)

the least desirable for most individuals. De Beauvoir[16] encourages everyone to accept old age because it is a part of total life.

Few Americans really plan for old age. Many cannot plan financially because their income is insufficient. Psychological preparation is also critical. A positive attitude toward old age is helpful.

Retirement does not have to mean the end of activity. Many older Americans continue to do some work as long as they are able. For most, the additional income is helpful. Volunteer work, especially with children, can be invigorating and gives them a sense of responsibility and satisfaction. However, some of the elderly withdraw, become depressed, do not adjust readily, and feel unfit for anything.[17] This condition may be accentuated if a person is unable to adjust to retirement because of a feeling that his or her talents can be expressed only in the occupation that no longer needs him or her. Actually there may be many other ways of using these talents.

Older persons are beginning to have a wider choice of living quarters. Many live in their own homes as long as possible. Special services are available to them, such as transportation, shopping services, homemaking aides, and yard care. Reduced fares for buses and

[16] Simone de Beauvoir, *Coming of Age* (New York: Putnam, 1972), p. 5.
[17] "How Old Is Old?" *The New York Times,* Aug. 8, 1977, p. 12 OP-ED.

discounted tickets to museums, plays, operas, concerts, motion pictures, and other events are often attainable. Because of increasing numbers, this group have greater political power and have been successful in influencing legislation favorable to them. Community centers often have programs that cater to their interests, including the serving of a hot noon meal and snacks. Department and other stores in the community sometimes offer discounts. A telephone organization that checks on elderly persons each day gives a sense of security.

The adequacy of nursing homes and health-care services depends on the locale and other factors. The care of an elderly person can be a serious problem for a family as well as a financial burden. The attitude of younger individuals toward old age requires much improvement. This age group is rapidly increasing in numbers, so that greater attention to their many needs is imperative. The education of their families about old age is equally serious.

These life-cycle theories do not imply that all adults lockstep through certain stages of development. The rate and the change vary according to the personality of the person and the experiences he or she has had, such as health status, death or deaths in the family, presence of devoted family members, financial crises, disabilities, and success on the job. In comparison to child development, the research on adulthood is much more limited and is a challenge to the home economics profession.

Adult Learning

Learning can continue throughout life. Certain attitudes affect the learning of adult students. For example, if individuals believe that they are too old to learn, decide prematurely that the material will be too difficult for them, conclude that their background information is inadequate, or voice other reservations, then learning may be hampered. If their attitude is positive, the reverse is true and learning is enhanced. The amount and kind of previous experiences and background can make a difference. Generally, the greater the previous amount of education, the more motivated students are to learn, although students with limited backgrounds can be highly motivated if the education fits their needs and goals.

The classroom environment is important. An attractive place with freedom to move furniture and other amenities is helpful. If teacher and students are friendly, enthusiastic, and eager to learn from each other, the desire to study becomes contagious. The fact that adult education is a voluntary activity promotes learning.[18]

[18] Rudd and Hall, op. cit., pp. 16–17.

Learning among adults may be self-initiated and self-directed. This fact has implications for self-study materials. Many students who give time to additional learning reap other benefits, such as better jobs, higher incomes, improved health, and greater happiness.[19]

Teaching Adults

Although home economics educators often work with adults, less attention has been given to preparation for teaching at this age level than for teaching children and adolescents. In the future, universities will need to prepare teachers for across-the-life-span education. At present the information about the older adult is incomplete and requires additional research and inquiry.

Here are some points about adults that will be helpful to those who teach them. Capitalize on the students' experience and relate their learning to their lives. The adult is in school with a purpose and hopes that the educational experience will be enjoyable. This person has given up time and money to be a member of the group. The information that the class member hopes to gain will be put to use immediately, not in the distant future. If an elderly man has become a widower and finds that his cooking skills are minimal, he wants to know how to cook now. A teacher must be informed about a student's current needs.

What happens at the first meeting of a group is critical. If a teacher gives a few highlights about herself or himself, students will feel better acquainted. If each class member is encouraged to get acquainted with the others, a sense of belonging to the group should grow quickly. Knowing that personal opinions are regarded as important and that there is freedom to exchange ideas strengthens learning. The teacher should determine quickly why a student is enrolled; various other student needs will eventually surface to be integrated into later sessions. The involvement of students in planning enriches the total experience. Some students may have to be reassured. Having been out of school for a long time, wondering if she or he belongs, and concern about learning ability are common doubts held by enrollees. The most important role of the teacher is to facilitate learning.

DEVELOPMENT OF PROGRAMS

The wide range of adult education possibilities in home economics, the kind of students needing help, and the setting in which the classes

[19] Kurland, op. cit., pp. 385–386.

take place are important determinants of the type of program to be offered.

Sometimes, especially if a program is just being started, there may not be any requests for particular programs. In that event, a survey will have to be made of the community to find potential students and ascertain their interests. An advisory committee may be appointed to make suggestions. Other means may be researched for launching a program.

Once decisions have been made about the adult programs to be offered in home economics, other matters will need attention. A teacher or teachers will have to be found. They may need supervision in working out objectives, content, and instructional procedures. It is a good plan to check how the cognitive, affective, and psychomotor domains will be emphasized so there is some balance among them. Often the affective domain is neglected. Feelings and personal meanings associated with personal experiences, when explored, may enhance cognitive learning. Financing, facilities, equipment, teaching aids, handout materials for students, and promotion of the program must be considered in the plans. The possible contribution of community resources, such as speakers, places for field trips, or businesses that might provide a sample for a consumer education class should be considered. Procedures for evaluation during the course and at the end need to be devised. Usually a report to the administration is given at the end of the course, but the data to be included should be collected during the course. Plans for the future will emerge from these methods of evaluation.

Strategies

The type of adult education envisioned will shape strategies to a large degree. There are many ways to reach adults. A two-year college, Northampton County Area Community College in Bethlehem, Pennsylvania, had a course entitled "Late Start" because it is designed for senior citizens.[20] Information was provided in five categories: social and community services, health care, income protection, leisure-time activities, and cultural outreach. This program was funded under Title 1 of the Social Security Act, so that the students did not pay fees. Transportation was provided, and a free lunch was served as a part of the instruction in nutrition; the students applied the knowledge of nutritional criteria learned as a part of the program. A member of the community safety council challenged the students to examine safety hazards in the room in which they were as-

[20] Daniel M. Larimer, "Carrying on in Late Start," *American Education,* Vol. 10, No. 6 (July 1974), pp. 35–37.

sembled. Examples of student discoveries were a cord for the coffee pot that might trip someone and a thirty-foot cord for the projector that snaked across the room and was equally hazardous. Another part of the program dealt with wills and trusts and getting the most for the dollar in times of inflation. Making friends was another plus in this educational project. One disappointment was the small number of persons on welfare who participated.

A bilingual course, "Compradores Vivarachos/Smart, Lively Shoppers," was a project at Colorado State University[21] in cooperation with Volunteer's Clearing House, a local facility set up to assist low-income families. A desire to help families with legal problems, houseing, money management, door-to-door salesmen, and credit problems was the focus of the project.

An advisory board, composed of English- and Spanish-speaking professionals and nonprofessionals, acted as a steering committee for the project. A plan to prepare consumer education aides evolved. The participants selected had demonstrated community leadership among Spanish-speaking people. Later the trainees had sixteen weeks of experience working in the community as consumer education aides. For example, they made visits, counseled, recruited for the fall class, and reviewed their program at conventions.

The fall class on consumer education included twenty low-income homemakers, largely Spanish-speaking. The group met at the Volunteer's Clearing House. Comparison shopping for food and clothing and other aspects of consumer education were emphasized. Newsletters were prepared by the consumer education aides, and there were requests for additonal copies. Two thirds of the aides improved their employment positions as a result of this experience.

Courses given through newspapers[22] offer many possibilities for home economics. University Extension, University of California—San Diego, made a course entitled "America and the Future of Man" available to 263 newspapers, and 188 colleges gave credit for the course. The enrollment was 4,974 students, and 6,600 others purchased "The Future File," primarily a reader and study guide, but did not ask for credit. At least 15 million persons read all or some of the newspaper lectures. Newspapers in every state except three carried the course. Funding was done by the National Endowment for the Humanities, with supplementary funding from the Exxon Education Foundation.

Each week a 1,400-word lecture, written by one of twenty leading

[21] Janet Reider, Francie Bosche, and Mary Helen Haas, "COMPRADORES VIVARACHOS/Smart, Lively Shoppers," *Illinois Teacher,* Vol. 14, No. 3 (Jan./Feb. 1971), pp. 109–117.

[22] Caleb Lewis, "Courses by Newspapers," *Phi Delta Kappan,* Vol. 56, No. 1 (Sept. 1974), pp. 60–62.

scholar-teachers was presented in the newspapers. Colleges and universities, which can seldom have such "names" on campus, were delighted with this opportunity for their students.

Offering a national course in a local newspaper has much meaning for the future, particularly for offering continuing education to many individuals who are nonparticipants now. One such course may offer individuals their first opportunity to stretch their minds in a pleasurable manner. This type of education is desirable for the homebound and for those who do not have the time for education in a more formal setting. For example, many senior citizens participated in the University of California program. One fifth of the readers had a high school education or less. Almost one third of the enrollees were from rural areas. Obviously many populations were tapped that do not usually involve themselves in adult education. Home economics might experiment with this idea in a county or state area and later, with more expertise, go national. The impact on professional and public relations and image building could be dramatic.

Prisons, mental institutions, reformatories, and other institutions may request courses. Often the need is greatest when inmates are being prepared to return to society. Among their needs may be assistance in finding a place to live, the furnishing of an apartment or a room with inexpensive items, buying and preparing food, planning a nutritious diet, family relations, and renewing relations with children. Students at New York University, in connection with home management projects, have worked with families of prisoners who are living on very low incomes.

Home economics educators may explore ways in which the programs mentioned could be modified to meet their own needs. By reading and talking with others, they may discover new approaches to planning adult education programs. Home economics can have an important role in this surge toward further education.

UNIQUE CONTRIBUTIONS TO ADULT EDUCATION BY AREAS IN HOME ECONOMICS

In home economics, the potential for helping adults with their problems, with their desire for greater outreach, and with improving their quality of life is perhaps greater than in most professions. The possibility of immediate application of learning is a plus. Some ways in which specific areas in home economics can make this contribution are briefly discussed here.

Consumer Education

Consumer education should not be limited to making smart shoppers out of adults; it should also concentrate on how consumer education can contribute to better living.[23] Another emphasis is on an intergenerational approach because consumer problems are common to all ages. If families worked together, their power to combat problems would be more effective and less fragmented.[24] The broad sharing of ideas and solutions to problems can help to make everyone more effective as a consumer. In addition to a consideration of wise shopping for various products, attention should be given to the appraisal of services, such as clothing and rug cleaning, health-care services, schools, and employment agencies.[25] Less attention has been given to this sector of consumer education than to other areas. In Washington, D.C., there is an organization called the Washington Center for the Study of Services, which performs an adult education service through its publication, *Washington Consumer's Checkbook,* in which consumer

[23] Sandra L. Willett, "Consumer Education or Advocacy . . . or Both?" *Social Policy,* Vol. 8, No. 3, Nov./Dec. 1977, pp. 10–17.
[24] Arthur M. Katz, "An Intergenerational Approach," *Social Policy,* Vol. 8, No. 3 (Nov./Dec. 1977), pp. 30–32.
[25] Robert Krughoff, "Checkbook: A Consumer Reports for the Services," *Social Policy,* Vol. 8, No. 3 (Nov./Dec. 1977), pp. 36–38.

Figure 6–7 Smart shopping is helpful in times of inflation. (Cereal Institute, Inc.)

services are rated. Plans are under way to have a series of public-service spot announcements on the radio summarizing their findings. Free pamphlets on the key findings are being disseminated to low-income and elderly consumers. Other towns and cities may follow this example.

These and other points may be considered in planning the underpinnings and bridges of teaching consumer education. A few areas from the broad spectrum of consumer education, as related to adults, are discussed here.

A course on the pros and cons of a cooperative, or interested neighbors' banding together for group buying, may be of interest. Group buying is a help in time of inflation. Some buying groups are restricted to purchasing canned goods and nonperishables. Others may buy clothing, carpeting, home furnishings, tires and batteries, and wines. The kind of organization necessary depends upon the complexity of the plan. Some of the areas that must be investigated are wholesale buying, the evaluation of markets where purchases will be made, the allocation of responsibilities and the willingness of participants to cooperate, financial planning, the legal aspects of the organization, sales taxes, facilities, distribution, and employees. Participants claim that 40 per cent can be saved on food costs through group buying. However, in a cooperative dealing with food, losses from perishable foods can add to costs. This is the type of information that would have to be available to students in such a course. Speakers who have had experience in group buying might serve as speakers for the group.

Consumer education lends itself well to television teaching.[26] In one program, for example, advertising claims made about a paper towel that has greater weight and therefore better quality were tested with two other brands. Weight was compared with and without cores. The brand that made the claim proved to be the heaviest. But other qualities were tested. Another brand had the highest capacity for absorption of liquids and was softer, but it was the weakest because of the type of fiber in it. The point is that judging only one characteristic is insufficient, and the consumer must judge on the basis of the purpose for which the towel is used.

The audience reached on a television program is usually large. If possible, consumers should have an opportunity to ask questions and to give feedback.

Other types of consumer education for adults might focus on "family financial planning," "investments," "credit," or "estate planning." "Homemade money" might highlight ways in which the extra

[26] Sharon King and Royston Lawson, "A Lesson from the Media," *Illinois Teacher*, Vol. 14, No. 5 (May/June 1976), pp. 227–281. (Actual script given.)

Figure 6–8 Food-buying clubs can reduce family expenses. (USDA Photo)

energy of family members might be directed into making things to sell, providing services for pay, writing poetry or short stories and selling them, developing local tours, or countless other activities. "Beating inflation" could be an exciting class, with students exploring many avenues, such as evaluating specials, using coupons, "trash is cash," simple living, and car pools.

Management

Management may be applied to the home, to oneself, to the family, to a job, and to other areas of living. One of the most important aspects of daily living is how it is managed. Many adults, however, are reluctant to examine the role of management in making their lives more effective. Managing a home or oneself can be "big business." Perhaps home economics educators should borrow some of the ideas of business and industry, which have seminars and workshops on various aspects of management—for which high fees are charged.

Seminar titles like the following could make a difference: "Home Economics Needs a New Breed of Managers"; "Bottom-Line Management"; "Participative Management"; "Shirt-sleeve Approach to Long-Range Planning"; "Effective Use of Information Systems"; "Appraisal of Performance"; "Strategic Choices"; "Looking at Pluses and Minuses"; "Who and What Controls You?" "Let's Change Our Ways"; "Unshackle Yourself"; "Cut the Tangles of Time Management"; "How to Shape Decisions." Titles for adult education are important "come-ons." Select one or more of the titles and improve them. Now what would you teach or emphasize on a television program with one of your revised titles? Some of these titles might be adapted for discovery sessions in small groups.

Sometimes management is best taught in connection with other areas, such as management in family living, teaching management to children, managing the clothing dollar, managing for the future, or food marketing tasks in homemaking.[27]

Management might be taught from the standpoint of benefits or particular goals, such as less frustration, working more effectively, having a more satisfying life, or having more time with one's family. A philosophical basis for home management, with an emphasis on values and attitudes, might be explored. Helping working women to manage has great possibilities. If exciting courses can be planned in this area for adults, home economics would add another dimension to its stature.

Foods

The interest of adults in foods ranges from gourmet cooking to "fast fixers." Enthusiasm is high in this area. Sometimes planners of adult programs have a foods course for adults as a kind of leader because reluctant students may enter this course more readily than others. Once they have taken one course, they are more willing to try others in home economics.

Many men and women are interested in the differences between home- and ready-prepared foods. Class activities might include the comparison of various foods, cooked from "scratch" and ready-prepared. For example, vegetables, entrees, desserts, and other categories can be compared with regard to cost, the time involved in preparation, nutritive values, and appearance and taste. Fast foods and restaurant foods might be compared in the same manner. One objection to home-prepared food is the time involved. The use of assembly-line preparation, with the entire family cooperating, might be one answer. Doing some operations ahead of time is another possibility.

The family might decide how the money saved would be spent. In this same vein, compare foods with generic names or no-brand names with popular brands. Shops and food stores with many services, such as twenty-four hour service, delicatessen, check cashing, and delivery, might be compared with those that have "no frills" or with warehouse types of stores that give fewer choices and little service. Often

[27] Rose E. Steidl, "Food Marketing Tasks: Young Women Explain Their Work," *Focus on Food Markets*, Cooperative Extension, New York State, Cornell University, Consumer Education, New York, N.Y., Aug. 7, 1972.

Figure 6–9 Husbands often retire before their wives and assume the family shopping. An adult education course might be helpful. (USDA Photo)

these stores do not stock perishables, but prices are lower.[28] The advantages of this type of adult course are that students will learn much from the experiences of other students and that the course is very current.

For the adult who likes to be experimental in food preparation, a course with this emphasis might have great appeal. This type of course requires a laboratory and food supplies, which would make it more expensive than other courses—a factor to be considered. One suggestion for experimentation is to determine the differences in cost of preparing variations of the same recipe. For example, which beef liver recipe is the least expensive, beef liver with bacon, amandine, or with onions? Take a favorite recipe that is now quite expensive and try to make a less expensive product. Select recipes that may have large amounts of fat or sugar and try to reduce either ingredient, or both, yet have a palatable product. Experiment with a recipe that has ingredients that are difficult to secure by trying one substitute at a time.

Other ideas for adult food courses are cultural foods, quick gour-

[28] Chris McDermott and Ruth Hodgson Klein, "No Frills Shopping," *Focus on the Food Markets,* Cooperative Extension, New York State, Cornell University, New York City Programs, New York, N.Y., Aug. 7, 1978.

met cooking, teaching children how to cook, cooking for men, cooking and buying food for the single person and the working person, and ways to cut the high costs of eating.[29] Families might study ways to examine food waste in the home and how to eliminate it. Also study the food waste for possible nutritive losses to the diet. Other possibilities for food courses for adults may be generated by teachers and former students.

Nutrition

This area of home economics has high interest, and adult courses have appeal. Weight is of special interest. "Food for the Fat" or a similar title may be used. The adult education teacher must be very cautious about prescribing any diets, must emphasize that a doctor's approval is needed before beginning any diet, and must stress that the course is mainly concerned with adequate nutrition and its implementation under a weight-loss plan. The content of the course might include planning and preparing nutritious daily meals by use of a daily food selection guide, analyzing popular reducing diets for adequacy, and highlighting common nutritional deficiencies. Other possibilities are evaluating diet foods in the supermarket and the role of other factors such as exercise, investigating the danger of diet pills and other weight-loss preparations, learning the caloric content of common foods, and considering psychological supports. "Weighing-in" at each session and sharing problems and accomplishments are good techniques.

"Planning Nutritious Meals According to Lifestyle" might focus on the varying schedules of the family and how to maintain nutritional adequacy each day through quick checks or other devices. "What to Believe About Nutrition" might deal with the fads, fallacies, and inaccurate statements that come from the mass media, hearsay, and other sources. The thrust would be to determine the soundness of these ideas and to develop a technique for doing so. The undesirable effects of following such ideas could be explored. Sources of reliable information might be a part of the course.

"Eating Out—Budgetwise and Nutritionwise" is pertinent because the number of families who eat out is rapidly increasing. One idea is for the students to evaluate places to eat by establishing their own criteria. Studying the menus of these restaurants and planning adequate meals might be a preliminary step. The menu does not give insight into the preparation of the food, such as including too much fat, being overcooked, and other shortcomings. In some instances, the

[29] Mimi Sheraton, "25 Ways to Cut the High Costs of Eating," *The New York Times*, June 21, 1978, pp. 19, 21.

group might sample certain restaurants, coffee shops, and fast-food places and evaluate them, as well as checking themselves on their ability to select a nutritious meal. Some families eat certain foods out and then plan how to compensate for dietary lacks when they return home by eating fruit or whatever was deficient in the meal. Comparing the costs of meals selected by various members in the group is a good procedure. Students should consider ways of reducing the cost of their selection without forsaking their criteria. One session might be devoted to "eating out" at home by preparing comparable menus. The difference in cost can be quite impressive.

In all of these courses, emphasis can be placed on making decisions, considering alternatives, learning to make sound comparisons, and developing a realization of the impact of past experiences, food habits, food preferences and dislikes, feelings, values, and attitudes.

Child Development

The family as educators might be reinforced in adult education. Two programs on energy conservation will serve as examples. An interdisciplinary approach was taken by Elaine Wilson, Bonnie Braun, Vicki Ehlers, and Debbie Schaefer, a team at Oklahoma State University, in working with families of young children so that early childhood education at school might be reinforced at home. The project was produced in a kit, with emphasis on a character called Mizer.[30] This puppet or figure is ageless and sexless. Through games, stories, and other devices, children were made aware of the importance of saving energy, such as shutting refrigerator doors, turning off lights and water, and considering trade-offs such as walking upstairs or taking the elevator. The concept of energy was introduced through creative movement—the use of the children's own energy during slow and rapid movements, such as blowing bubbles or running. Students in upper elementary grades might calculate the calories used during these movements and translate them into actual foods, thus integrating mathematics and nutrition.

Letters informed the families of the participating children about the project so that the children were encouraged to practice at home what they had learned in the project. These letters had information about energy awareness for the parents and also included games and other activities for the children, such as making the puppet Mizer.

Jeannie H. James and Peggy Peterson of the University of South Carolina[31] approached an awareness education program in the early

[30] Miniworkshop, American Home Economics Annual Meeting, *Energy: Awareness Education and Use by Child and Family,* American Home Economics Association, On-the-Spot Duplicators, Inc., Washington, D.C., 1978 (cassette).
[31] Ibid.

elementary grades through the use of transportation, heat, power, and other manifestations of energy. The parents of these children were informed and helped with a lending library for themselves and the children. The parents were also encouraged to communicate with their children about the program, to talk about words related to the conservation of energy, and to use visuals or action whenever possible to reinforce the meaning of the word. Talking to children is difficult for some parents. One suggestion was to turn off the light and sit in the dark and consider all the activites that depend upon electricity, such as television and reading. The family might discuss the importance of saving this form of energy.

Some forms of adult education might deal with the types of child care available to working parents and how to evaluate them in terms of specific needs and cost. Other possibilities for enriching a child's experiences through home activities might be explored through a consideration of what the child is gaining from school, church, community, television, and other sources. Leisure-time activities for the family that are also broadening to children might be the basis of a course.

"Parent Readiness Education Project (PREP)" in the Redford Union School District near Detroit[32] is a program for families with handicapped children who have been identified by tests as having learning problems before they enter school. These problems are in language and speech development, difficulty in following directions, inability to identify colors, and poor recounting of detail. The school program and parental involvement emphasized language and conceptualization skills, visual and auditory discrimination, the development of large and small muscles, and strengthening the child's self-concept. Daily home activities included games, puzzles, cooking, shopping, and other valid learning experiences. As one mother related, during preparation of just one meal, her child practiced mathematical concepts by counting the silverware for setting the table, named the colors in the kitchen, and identified the foods being prepared. Parents also kept a journal of their experiences and a list of questions to ask. There was a sense of partnership and satisfaction with the improvement in their child. The program has been so successful that parents whose children do not have problems have asked to be admitted to the program.

Family Life

The keystone of home economics is the family, so a special effort should be made to emphasize this area. A look back at the efforts of

[32] Judith Wagner, "PREP Makes Parents More Intelligenter," *American Education,* Vol. 13, No. 8 (Oct. 1977), pp. 9–12.

the Federal Home Economics Education Service (now a part of the U.S. Office of Education's Bureau of Occupational and Adult Education) in 1939, when four pilot programs were launched—two rural and two urban—is inspirational. The purpose was to discover how schools might work with communities. The goals, briefly stated, were to clarify issues and problems in family life, to work toward optimum family relationships, to implement procedures, to increase the spirit of democratic family living, and to extend family-life education to all people.[33] Only one of these pilot Family Life Education Centers (FLEC) survived, the one in Toledo, Ohio.

This center is the oldest of its kind and, according to authoritative opinions, has one of the most comprehensive and progressive programs of its kind in the nation. Pauline Reulein, the director, has been with the center since its inception, serving first as a preschool education consultant. She stresses a continuing search for "increasingly effective ways to strengthen individuals, to help them become successful, creative, and contributing members of their own homes, their communities, and the world."

FLEC operates under the auspices of the Toledo Board of Education, which provides facilities and a portion of the budget. The major portion of the budget is financed by the State Division of Vocational Home Economics. Additional funds come from cosponsoring organizations, federal or state grants, and various private sources.

Each program that is launched is operated in conjunction with at least one other agency, organization, group, or institution in Toledo. The director and her staff, in turn, work directly with and serve on advisory committees and boards of directors of numerous community agencies. This arrangement is based on the belief that coordination is the key to the wisest use of human resources, money, and facilities.

The development of a nursery school was one of the first objectives, and the Toledo Preschool Center continues to be a model for preschool education today. The programs change with the times. A recent program focused on parent and preparent education, specific homemaking skills, responsible decision making, consumer education, leadership training, human sexuality, and personal growth. Participants in these programs have positive reactions. A mother and her fifth-grade son participated in a sex education program. In evaluating the program, the mother said, "We had never talked about sexuality before but after the first meeting, we talked until well past midnight, talking about lots of things. We continue to talk to each other now that the program is over and we are no longer afraid to discuss our feelings."

[33] Judith Wagner, "Toward Strengthening the Family," *American Education,* Vol. 12, No. 1 (Jan./Feb. 1976), pp. 29–33.

Another example of a specific program is the Parent–Infant Enrichment Program for young families in disadvantaged areas, operated in cooperation with St. Vincent Hospital.

The school administrators in Toledo believe that FLEC is an example of teaching the whole child and recognizing that the child is not only a student but a part of a family. Home economics educators would do well to study this program and to reinforce the ideas of FLEC in their own programs. This program represents the entire spectrum of family-life education.

Other suggestions for adult education in family life might include programs for preparenting and parenting for youth and adults. What are the dynamics that govern the relations between elderly parents and their children, for example? Other fruitful programs might deal with general problems of ordinary family life; drug, spouse, or child abuse; postdivorce; the death of a spouse, parent, or child; runaway and throwaway (children who are ejected from their homes by a parent) children; families with one or more members who are criminals; handicapped family members; poverty; and terminal illness.

"Making Marriage Work," "Nonconventional Family Lifestyles," "Working Parents," "Life as a Single Man, Woman, or Parent," and "The Role of Government in the Family" are other possible titles. Many today have a special interest in fatherhood, and fathers might be interested in examining their roles, especially if they are divorced or widowers with the responsibility of caring for one or more children. The challenge is to be on the alert for innovative ways to strengthen families and family members—that is what home economics is about.

Housing and Home Furnishings

A home, for families, is the environment in which they live, and it can have a profound effect on their development and relations. Adult education in this area has many possibilities. Decisions have to be made and the outlay of money is considerable. One idea is to build a course around experts in this area, such as realtors, apartment rental agents, bankers, and savings-and-loan association representatives, plus the experiences of a couple who have recently rented an apartment or a family that has just bought a home and has ideas on what they would do differently. Having class members define their objectives with regard to a home and the decisions that will have to be made can be illuminating. Selecting a plan for financing that is compatible with income is helpful.

Attitudes, values, and goals about a home may need to be examined and clarified before important decisions are made. How to blend differences of opinion within a family or between a couple may be explored. How much should the suggestions, influence, and experiences of friends, relatives, and neighbors enter into the final decision? Inflation, the energy shortage and smaller families may lead to space- and energy-saving homes on less land, because land may have to be used for food or other purposes. Students may speculate now about the features of such homes because they may be living in them later. For the daring student, imagining living on a platform in space might be exciting.

The decisions required in selecting furnishings may be a suitable topic for adult education. Furnishings must be selected cautiously because the cost is high and the family may have to live with them for years. Also a home should reflect the person or persons who live there. This may be a good frame of reference in planning. What will your home tell others about you?

In working with families in disadvantaged areas or with young couples with limited incomes, home economics educators may highlight sources for purchasing inexpensive furniture and the advantages and disadvantages of each type. An article in the March 1976 issue of *Family Circle,* entitled "Great Living on a Shoestring" (a good title for a course), showed a living room that was furnished for $500. Purchases were made at flea markets, junk shops, and garage sales. Another idea is to use the castoffs of friends, neighbors, and relatives. The recommendation given was "You have to see something as it will become, not as it is."

The search is only the beginning because the "finds" have to be transformed into respectable furnishings. Do-it-yourselfers have a decided asset in this type of venture. The skills of painting, reupholstering, refinishing furniture, doing wall treatments, making curtains and draperies, putting together a screen, framing prints, fixing up old lamps and lamp shades, and making rugs will all contribute to the end product.

Not all adults will be interested in experiences like those already mentioned. They may want information about the selection of upholstery fabrics; furniture styles; the merits of various types of carpeting; buying antiques; judging furniture as to construction, durability, suitability, upholstery, and versatility. Ideas in this area are plentiful, and many adults can be served.

Clothing and Textiles

The clothes that people wear are actually an extension of themselves. With clothes being such an important factor in life, adults may need assistance with their choices. Courses may emphasize such aspects as desirable equipment for sewing and basic construction techniques; making clothes for oneself and others; points to

Figure 6–10 Adult education clothing courses are popular.

consider in clothes for children; selection of clothes related to purpose, durability, and personality; and cost and comparisons of homemade and ready-made clothes.

Other content may include making wise purchases; planning for multiple-purpose clothes, such as year-round use for certain items; importance of line, design, and color; care of clothes; clothes for work, fun, and special occasions, and recycling.

When one is buying clothes, knowledge of textiles is helpful in such areas as cost, care, durability, special qualities, and preferred uses. Keeping informed about trends in clothes and textiles makes shopping easier. These are only a few of the many possibilities for adult courses in clothing and textiles.

Evaluation of Adult Education Classes or Projects

The progress of students, the success of a program (defined in many ways) and the competency of a teacher are usually evaluated on the basis of objectives or expectations.

Student development may be evaluated in several ways. Students may be asked at the beginning of a course or program to indicate what they hope to gain from this course and then to give indications of their progress from time to time during the course. For noncredit courses, students are reluctant to spend much time on evaluation procedures. A progress card on which a few sentences might be written is a good device. A student may demonstrate tangible changes in behavior during class discussions, such as telling about new foods that have been added to his or her diet or about the use of class information in making a purchase. Changed attitudes may be revealed.

Students in courses for credit have to meet requirements that are adequate to determine a grade or other indication of class completion such as pass/fail. The important point is the extent to which student needs and interests were met. At the final meeting of the course, students may form small discussion groups to discuss strengths and possible changes for future classes. The secretary or reporter of the group makes a summary report, which protects the identity of the students who made suggestions. Sometimes students make suggestions for ways to evaluate their own progress.

Evidence of the *success of a program* may be communicated by comments made before, during, and after class meetings. Note may be made by the teacher of positive, neutral, or negative remarks and which predominated. Comments of people in the community who are not in the class can be revealing. When students make inquiries about similar classes for the future, it is a favorable sign. Enrollment is sometimes considered a criterion, but many factors such as interest, the cost of the course and the supplies, transportation, the time of the class, and the needs of the prospective students are important influences on enrollment.

Teacher competency is reflected to an important extent by student evaluations of the program. Student attitudes expressed during the course sessions are additional data. Prior to teaching, the teacher may establish certain objectives to be evaluated, such as knowledge about students, the extent to which students change behavior, the adequacy of the content background, and the effective use of teaching strategies and materials. These may be the basis for an evaluation of the teaching.

The contribution of this project to the total adult education program of the institution or agency may be examined, along with the extent to which adults in the community were served.

Coordination with Other Community Agencies and Availability of Resources

In most adult education programs, community agencies and resources can make contributions to the adult program. Examples are libraries, museums, department and other types of stores or markets, service clubs, and religious organizations. Other resources are welfare and social service agencies, labor unions, and mass media, which may be willing to make announcements and tell the story of the program. City, county, state, and federal agencies may aid with funding, consultants, materials, and other resources. The teacher will wish to consider how the institution or agency where he or she is employed can contribute, so that he or she can reciprocate these favors.

In some programs, many groups may be helped in the same project. In a child development class for adults with access to a nursery school, high school students and senior citizens may volunteer as aides and at the same time learn a great deal about small children. The high school student may become acquainted with the elderly and offer such assistance to them as shopping. The nursery school or child-care center may be a part of one of the social service agencies, so here is another example of cooperation and coordination.

One of the great satisfactions of adult education is the important contribution that home economics can make to the lives of these individuals. Home economics educators who are not in the classroom may wish to consider innovative ways in which they can encourage adult education.

SUGGESTIONS FOR FURTHER LEARNING

1. One way to become a better teacher of adults is to be alert to the promising strategies of other adult teachers. Kenneth Koch, a poetry teacher, has written a book on his experiences in teaching poetry writing to incapacitated, blind, deaf, and ill students in their seventies, eighties, and nineties who were in a nursing home in New York City.

   Koch, Kenneth. *I Never Told Anybody, Teaching Poetry Writing in a Nursing Home.* New York: Random, 1977.

   These students had limited education and had worked in such jobs as dry cleaning, domestic service, or short-order cooking. Most *had* given up on life. Koch began by asking them to write a sentence about something concrete, such as a color, then another sentence, then something again. This had to be done slowly and with patience, encouragement, and empathy. The results were gratifying. As their handling of words was enlarged, the writers gained a sense of power. Later Koch gave his students such projects as imagining themselves as the ocean or to talk to the stars or the moon. These experiences are largely in the affective domain.

   Think of ways in which Koch's ideas might be adapted for an adult course in home economics. Try your ideas with a few adults or even a class. In what other ways than poetry might students express these same thoughts? What do you see as possible outcomes from this activity?

2. Think about your own experiences with adults. What types of new experiences would strengthen your background? How do you envision yourself as an adult education teacher? Can you justify this image? What would you like to teach to adults? How may your ideas be implemented?

7

The Environment for Teaching and Learning

The design of space and facilities for home economics education contribute to the teaching and learning environment, be it a classroom, a television studio, an auditorium for a large group, a clinic, an extension center, or other setup. One's use of space is not only a personal but a professional reflection. Does the place express who you are and what you are like, how you teach and what you teach?[1] What does your space say? What are the silent messages? Actually our setting is a part of us—our outer space reflects our inner space.

For effective teaching and optimum learning, every student must be able to see, hear, interact, experiment, discuss, study, and work singly or in groups. If possible, the physical surroundings should be attractive and adequate, the intellectual environment should be stimulating and adapted to student needs, and the psychological environment should contribute to warm, friendly, permissive, and productive relationships that will foster learning and personal development.

Certain educational and social changes influence the planning of space. Home economics must keep abreast of the times and change the curriculum accordingly. The computer may be used in evaluating dietary intake or the use of family or personal money by many age levels in home economics education. The possibility of working with small children in a high school program may need consideration, so students may learn more about human development. What adapta-

[1] Ellen Barnes, Bill Eyman, and Maddy Bragar Engolz, *Teach and Reach* (Syracuse, N.Y.: Human Policy Press, 1974), pp. 81–85.

tions for space and facilities would be necessary for the study of ecology, family cultural backgrounds, death and dying, or moral development? How might space reflect the wide use of the community or changes in lifestyles?

INFLUENCES ON SPACE

A teacher must be aware of the strong impact that the use of space has on students' learning. The question a home economist must ask when confronted for the first time with the space allotted to the home economics classroom, or if she/he must plan new quarters, is "How will students best learn in this space?"

Personal Space

The personal space allotted to each student bears consideration. Little[2] defines personal space as the area surrounding an individual in which his or her interactions with others occur. Sommer[3] adds another dimension to this definition in pointing out that the territory has no fixed geographic reference points. This space may contract or expand under varying conditions. Lewin[4] referred to this territory as "life space." According to Hall,[5] the human sense of space is a synthesis of inputs from the five senses plus the influence of culture. The output, obviously, varies from individual to individual, according to activities, relationships, environment, and other factors. Hall believes that distorted communication and alienated relationships can be reduced through an examination of these differences in space comprehension and its ramifications.

Individuals have a kind of invisible bubble around them that defines their personal space. The more persons there are in a given area and the closer they are, the more some of them feel an intrusion into their personal bubble.[6] This sensation varies from person to person. What one is prepared to accept is a factor; some persons, for example, will endure a crowd to gain a glimpse of a celebrity. Personal space or territory[7] is a mechanism used to ensure the privacy desired. Indications of personal openness or closeness may be transmitted by one's

[2] Kenneth B. Little, "Personal Space," *Journal of Experimental Social Psychology*, Vol. 1, No. 2 (Apr. 1965), pp. 237–248.

[3] Robert Sommer, *Personal Space* (Englewood Cliffs, N.J.: Prentice-Hall, 1969).

[4] Kurt Lewin, *Dynamic Theory of Personality* (New York: McGraw-Hill, 1935).

[5] Edward T. Hall, *The Hidden Dimension* (Garden City, N.Y.: Doubleday, 1966).

[6] Paul M. Ensel and Henry Clay Ingren, "Too Close for Comfort," *Psychology Today*, Vol. 11, No. 7 (Dec. 1977), pp. 100–106.

[7] Irwin Altman, *The Environment and Social Behavior* (Belmont, Calif.: Brooks-Cole, 1975).

Figure 7–1 Personal and private space is a consideration when students work together in a laboratory.

body language, what one says, or a composite impression that seems to reject or encourage. Home economics educators may wish to examine the methods they employ to demonstrate the levels of their personal space. A sensitivity to the messages that those being taught send out about their personal space limitations is important to effective teaching and learning.

Space and the Senses

Through sight, an individual can identify the physical state of materials, people, foods, and other items of everyday living from a considerable distance. One not only gathers information with one's eyes, but he/she learns to interpret what he/she sees. For example, students who have had meaningful experiences in a clothing laboratory can readily identify a cotton fabric, a buttonhole attachment, or tracing paper. Some students have developed a sense of space in regard to home furnishings—what will fit or be appropriate in the space of a room.

The amount of information gathered by the ears in contrast with the eyes has not been precisely calculated. The relative complexities of the two systems give some clues. The optic nerve contains roughly eighteen times as many neurons as the cochlear nerve, so it is assumed that the optic nerve transmits considerably more information. A two-way conversation that is effective is limited to approximately twenty feet. When distances become greater, auditory clues become less and less potent for human interaction. These facts are important to consider in planning space for home economics classes.

Cultures vary in their perceptual patterns. The Japanese, for example, use visual screens for a variety of purposes but are content with paper walls for acoustical screens. The Germans and the Dutch, in contrast, have thick walls and double doors in their homes to reduce sound.

In America, the sense of smell is quite underdeveloped and has many negative connotations. There is a serious preoccupation with eliminating and disguising many natural odors. Smell, according to Hall[8] evokes deeper memories than either sight or sound. Ignored, too, is the role of the body's chemical communication system. Odor not only distinguishes individuals but often indicates the emotional state of the organism. Excitement, anger, sorrow, happiness, and other emotions apparently give off chemical messages. Failure to use the sense of smell fully is a drawback. In some countries, such as France, people savor the odor of wine, freshly baked bread, newly plucked chicken, coffee from outdoor cafés, garden vegetables, and similar smells of everyday life. How often is smell stressed in a home economics classroom?

Touch has space overtones because it is associated with intimacy. The touch of a child is usually considered desirable, but the touch of a stranger may be resented. If students in a laboratory have to come into close contact with each other and are unfriendly, there may be negative overtones.

If the five senses play such an important role in a student's sense of space, then any contemplation of the arrangement, rearrangement, or planning of new laboratory furnishings must include the possible impact of sensory experiences. What visual sensations do students have when they enter the home economics rooms for the first time, as they work and study, as they consult the teacher for advice on independent projects, or as they attend FHA/HERO meetings? It is apparent that research is needed to determine these reactions. Furthermore it becomes obvious that students should be a part of the planning of the rooms that have such an important impact on their lives. Similar questions may be raised about the other kinds of sensory experiences of students and their relation to the use of space.

[8] Ibid., p. 46.

Figure 7–2 The smell of cosmetics is considered pleasant and is usually not seen as an intrusion on personal space. (Cereal Institute, Inc.)

Space and Culture

Hall[9] encourages us to consider what he calls "fixed-feature" space. Buildings, internally and externally, are expressions of a culture. The layout of villages, towns, cities, and even the intervening countryside change with time and the culture. What are the social overtones of the manner in which space is used in home economics laboratories? This is a dimension that has had little attention in planning.

The traditional classroom, with neatly spaced chairs arranged before a desk or podium, is called "hard architecture" by Sommer.[10] Sometimes the chairs or equipment are bolted to the floor for security reasons. This arrangement is a part of our fixed beliefs on education. Classroom decorations, such as flowers and plants, pictures, murals, and tapestries, are sometimes discouraged by the precepts of this hard architecture.

Many home economics educators have attempted, with the help of students, to make their quarters attractive and livable. Often stu-

[9] Ibid., p. 82.

[10] Robert Sommer, "Movable Chairs, Fixed Beliefs, Hard Classrooms," *Hard Architecture* (Englewood Cliffs, N.J.: Prentice-Hall, 1974), Ch. 6.

Figure 7–3 Crowded living quarters provide limited spatial experiences in the environment.

dents gravitate to this space because of the human atmosphere. But home economists may wish to review what the professional literature has deemed advisable for the best teaching and learning environment. How much hard architecture is advocated, and what steps are in order to remedy these beliefs?

PLANNING PHYSICAL SPACE

The space, to be well used, must, of course, be suitable to a sound home economics program, but it should also reflect the teacher's beliefs about space planning. Strong emotions can be generated by the manner in which space is used. It may spell freedom, comfort, inspiration, constricture, clutter, efficiency, and a host of other meanings. Space is not static. If it is well manipulated, it can actually create many environments and many different effects.

General Considerations

In planning for new space or in using existing space, think about how the space will look in bright sunshine. on dull days, at night, as a busy laboratory, for individual study, and for group activities. Space is generally best used if it is flexible. Will present plans allow for future changes of program? Space should be planned so that it can be contracted for certain purposes and expanded for others.

Barrow[11] suggests that there be space for a lecture–demonstration room. In this area would be concentrated the technological aids as well as facilities for demonstration. Space for activities such as food and meal preparation, clothing construction, laundering, a playschool for small children in connection with child development units, and social activities should be provided. If possible, some space should be available for individualized instruction: space for individual listening, or for looking at filmstrips, or slides, or for laboratory experimentation of a scientific nature. By means of flexible partitions, large spaces can be made into small discussion or conference rooms suitable also for committee meetings and other group activities. Above all, there must be a place with some degree of privacy for the teacher and student to work. Equipment and materials should be stored at or very near the point where they will be used.

Facelifting Space

Select several of the places that need redoing. Make plans for the whole room, but do not attempt to do everything at once. Here are some suggestions. Hide an open clutter-storage cupboard with a Dutch-type door that can be used as a bulletin board space or as a screen for viewing slides and filmstrips. Place large, colorful pillows in a corner where students may talk, study, or read. Paint some of the old furniture in bright colors. Use movable bulletin boards and chalk-

[11] Joseph M. Barrow, "Facilities for Emerging Programs," *Contemporary Issues in Home Economics,* a conference report (Washington, D.C.: Department of Home Economics, NEA, 1965), p. 113.

Figure 7–4 Ideas for "facelift space" that may be used in classrooms.

boards for room dividers. Make places for particular activities, such as sprouting seeds for bean sprouts (high in vitamin C) or doing tie-dye, weaving or macrame, reupholstering, and experiments. Ask students for suggestions. Invite people into your room to give ideas and have them write them on a suggestion sheet for further discussion.

Flowers, green plants,[12] posters, collages, prints of famous paintings that depict family settings or other appropriate themes liven a room. Set up a terrarium. Display garments that have been made on a clothes line, ideas for home storage space on a bulletin board, dioramas to show home safety, and other student accomplishments in

[12] "The Jolly Green Classroom," *Instructor,* Vol. 86, No. 3 (Nov. 1976), pp. 51–54.

various parts of the room. If walls are dull, cover them with murals, fabric (such as tie-dye sheets or burlap), tapestries, rugs, paint, or woven articles. If possible, carpet the floor.

Finally, check your classroom. Does it have spaces for quietness, noisiness, socializing, supporting each other, structured activities, expression of feelings such as anger or joy, being alone, and other activities that facilitate learning?[13]

Planning Nonschool Space

Home economics educators who do not teach in a school have to plan the space that they use so that students, viewers, patients, clients, or customers and the like will enjoy their learning experiences. If an auditorium is used, screens covered with fabrics, patterns, photographs, equipment, or other items related to the content are decorative. Charts about dietary guides and the nutritive density of certain foods or other graphics about what is to be taught will give a softening yet vibrant effect and can be used in teaching and learning as well. Flowers and plants are attractive. Using a small cart for the plants and placing it near the podium, table, or whatever the educator will use for materials and props may help to blot out the dullness of the room.

Each educator can stimulate her/his ingenuity to add some sparkle to the learning environment. This can be quite a challenge if the space is one over which the educator has little control, such as a television studio that is used for an occasional presentation, an auditorium, a city hall room, a department store center, or a church basement. Many businesses, institutions, industries, and clinics have specified areas for instruction. This situation opens possibilities for planning an attractive setting. Another consideration is the seating arrangement for the learners. Can they see and hear, and will they be comfortable?

Planning New Facilities

The most important guideline for planning new facilities is that space must be planned for the functions of the program. In preparation for actual plans, the home economics teacher or the staff will use all available resources. The first step may be to analyze, in great detail, the facilities required for each aspect of their program. In some instances, the program itself may require scrutiny and evaluation for its adequacy and its reflection of student needs and interests before space is even considered.

The next steps may include an examination of the literature, talk-

[13] *Teach and Reach,* op. cit., p. 82.

ing to other teachers who have recently had to plan new facilities, and, if at all possible, visiting new schools that have practical and interesting features. Seeking suggestions from equipment and furnishings companies can be helpful. Often suggested layouts are available for study. An advisory committee consisting of home economics teachers with a special interest in this area, students, knowledgeable persons in the community, and/or home economists associated with architects or equipment companies can be very helpful. Close cooperation with the school administration and the architect is important. They will be particularly helpful if the home economics teacher has clear objectives for the use of space and can communicate them clearly.

The following list of questions may be helpful in the planning of new facilities:

1. What are the projections of future enrollment?
2. Will the proposed surroundings be attractive to the students?
3. Will the proposed facilities require more than a minimum of maintenance?
4. Have the advantages of windowless and windowed classrooms been explored?
5. How flexible are the facilities and the space?
6. Can traffic flow freely?
7. Can all areas of the space be used to a maximum at all times?
8. How is the space to be used efficiently if there are a number of teachers in the department?
9. Do the proposed facilities provide for a wide variety of rich student experiences?
10. Do the facilities adequately demonstrate important aesthetic principles?
11. Has proper consideration been given to such factors as heat, light, safety, comfort, storage, and sanitation?
12. What kind of image will these facilities project?
13. Has consideration been given to the many facets of personal space?
14. Can the space be used for individualized instruction, small-group discussion or work, and large-group activities?
15. Is there adequate space for the teacher?
16. Have priorities in the use of the space been agreed on so that if funds are reduced it will be easier to make adjustments?

These are only a few of the important items that must be thoroughly checked before the remodeling or building of new facilities. In addition, the teacher may wish to decide whether the facilities reflect the economic status of the community. On the other hand, it seems sensible to have equipment that represents a wide range of possibilities to provide richer learning possibilities, because in our mobile society, we cannot assume that any individual will remain forever within a certain social structure.

PLANNING THE INTELLECTUAL OR COGNITIVE ENVIRONMENT

Planning space for intellectual development has been somewhat neglected in spite of the importance of this aspect of learning. Answers to certain questions may be sought. What will be needed in a space planned for students with great variations in ability to learn? Multilevel reading may be one solution. Unfortunately there is a dearth of such materials in home economics. Some of the literacy materials used with adults might be used with high school students, rather than materials for younger children because the content is more appropriate to their interests and needs. Paperbacks on various subjects in easy reading style, cartoon booklets with appropriate content, games, storybooks, books with many illustrations, and other types of visuals, including slides or filmstrips, may be valuable. A study center with these and other instructional materials is a possibility.

What kind of space would be advisable for experimental and creative endeavors? Space and facilities are needed for such experiments as creating a new household gadget for the kitchen, bathroom, or yard; developing unusual nutritious snacks; constructing a new type of garment for teenagers; planning a strategy for improving relations with a friend; finding a scientific answer to a laundry problem; or seeking novel ways to earn extra money. Integrating writing, reading, and math skills (the basics) in a personal or home project may be considered.

Where may self-study or independent study take place? A student may wish to delve more deeply into an area of home economics in which an interest has been sparked. Another student may discover a lack of information about a topic and wish to correct this deficiency. Finding ways to handle a problem may be facilitated by reading a paperback or other literature.[14]

What kind of facilities are needed for a teacher or aide to have one-

[14] Judy Blume, *It's Not the End of the World* (New York: Bantam Books, 1972), about parents divorcing.

Vera and Bill Cleaver, *Where the Lilies Bloom* (Philadelphia: Signet, 1969), about a fourteen-year-old girl who is responsible for caring for her orphaned family.

Paul Zindel, *I Never Loved Your Mind* (New York: Bantam, 1970), about high-school dropouts who live in a commune.

to-one teaching and learning with a student? It is pleasant to have a place with some privacy so that other activities do not impinge on the attention of the teacher and the student. Students profit from this type of high-quality instruction. Here a student can comfortably begin where he or she happens to be and progress at a personal rate. In a short time, considerable learning can take place. The *dialogue* involves and intensifies mental activity related to learning. For example, a student may have difficulty in clarifying a problem that involves values. Assistance from another student or an aide may contribute immeasurably to personal development.

Where will students find space to coordinate their school and community experiences? Perhaps it might be a table for writing observations or exploring tentative hypotheses (for example, about the behavior of children in a day-care center in a poverty area). Or it might be a quiet corner used for outlining the principles of being a good consumer that emerged after an experience in the marketplacc or for summarizing other community experiences to share during a class discussion.

Every day students and teacher should be encouraged to bring, tell, show, demonstrate, exhibit, or ask questions about ideas, problems, tentative solutions, or other cognitive activities. Provisions may have to be made for helping students succeed in their intellectual endeavors.

PLANNING FOR THE PSYCHOLOGICAL AND AFFECTIVE ENVIRONMENT

The psychological and affective environment is less tangible than the physical environment because it is human-centered rather than material-centered. Attractive surroundings can contribute to a favorable climate, but a learning environment that lends itself to the self-enhancement of students must be added. The essential characteristics of such an environment are to offer support, caring, positiveness, growth promotion, and understanding, which can benefit both students and teachers.

One of the prerequisites is a teacher who is "tuned in" to students.[15] Many students of all ages have unmet needs that must be gratified if learning is to be effective and optimum development realized. These needs may be love, achievement, belonging, or self-identity. Freedom to express feelings, attitudes, values, and beliefs is important, and a

[15] Elizabeth Hunter, "Tuning in to Children," *Childhood Education,* Vol. 52, No. 1 (Oct. 1975), pp. 13–19.

recognition of these needs is a part of "tuning in." Home economics is a caring profession. The content of home economics is a means to an end, namely, the release of potentials in human beings. For example, in one facet of home economics, a student who is taught to be a sensible consumer will hopefully become a better manager of herself or himself as one step in the process.

A questionnaire was formulated by Hunter[16] and administered to approximately 275 children between the ages of five and eighteen to determine what children have on their minds. A summary of their comments about what teachers should do included, "Love us, treat us as individuals, compliment us, have fun with us, talk with us, tell us things, and protect our dignity."

To meet these requests, a home economics educator should strive to be natural, open, caring, and democratic.[17] The students must be involved in decision making in areas that affect them, such as the physical setting, the care of facilities, and the planning of learning activities. With the help of the teacher, each student may determine how personal growth can be attained. Students can help each other in reaching this goal, and certainly the teacher will contribute in many ways. When a student realizes that he or she is a unique individual, then learning can bring pride and satisfaction with progress.

Some strategies to reach these goals are

1. Keep a log of ways in which growth has been manifested, such as "I was pleased that I could . . ."
2. Make an analysis of people and other resources that influence the student the most, with desirable or undesirable effects.
3. Does worry about big ears, crooked teeth, birthmarks, and the like interfere with progress? What might be done to solve the problem?
4. Look at personal strengths and think about ways to capitalize on them.
5. Recognize feelings, values, and attitudes that have an impact on growth.
6. How does the future look?

There are many ways to emphasize the importance of the affective part of life. One of the best is to give consideration every day to this part of life's ongoing activities.

[16] Elizabeth Hunter, "Report Cards for Children," *Childhood Education,* Vol. 48, No. 8 (May 1972), pp. 410–411.

[17] Jack Canfield and Harold C. Wells, *100 Ways to Enhance Self Concept in the Classroom* (Englewood Cliffs, N.J.: Prentice-Hall, 1976), Preface.

PLANNING THE PSYCHOMOTOR ENVIRONMENT

Research[18] indicates that recognition of the importance of psychomotor education may obviate school failures. In a study of ten thousand children in Maryland, for example, it was found that when cases of dyslexia (inability to understand the written word) were discovered in the first two grades and proper psychomotor training was initiated, nearly 80 per cent of the children were brought up to normal reading level. Joseph E. Jastak, who developed the Wide Range Achievement Test, has demonstrated that disabled readers are not able to integrate visual, motor, and auditory functions. Piaget made the comment that perception is influenced by motor activity from the outset.

Home economics education has many opportunities to strengthen psychomotor learnings. The first major principle is perception of the qualities of objects and their relationships. Students might be encouraged to see, hear, feel, taste, and smell items of interest in their everyday life. Touch, taste, and smell are used less often than seeing and hearing. Students might take an apple, a bath towel, or a clean comb and test the article with each of the senses. Each student might describe the experience in detail. Tasting may be the most difficult, but passing the tongue over a small surface of the article can be quite revealing and may offer another dimension to the perception of these items. Teacher and students can emphasize the senses in many of their experiences.

Boys and girls may learn to distinguish the meaning in changes in the tone of voice of a small baby, friends, or family members or the sounds made by a car, electrical equipment, or a sewing machine that indicate everything is well or that something is wrong. Another interpretation of cues is reading a pattern for making a pair of pajamas or identifying the feelings portrayed in a piece of music. A game involving geometric shapes strengthens visual perception and eye–hand coordination. Richness of experience in psychomotor education is to be encouraged.

Set refers to a readiness for specific action. To achieve a good mental set, students might be encouraged to consider the kind of tools and ingredients needed and the ability to use them in making a milkshake. If hand shaken, certain muscles can be developed, along with coordination between the hands in holding, stirring, and in other operations related to physical set. Expressing enthusiasm for the task before and during the operation is evidence of the emotional set.

[18] Tom Banville, "The Learning Called Psychomotor," *American Education,* Vol. 12, No. 6 (July 1976), pp. 23–26.

Figure 7–5 Touch experiences strengthen psychomotor skills.

In *guided response,* a more complex operation, a student may watch someone plant tulip bulbs, for example, and then perform the task alone. The extent to which the imitation has succeeded is evaluated. Additional experience under guidance may be needed. Sometimes a student tries by trial and error in such tasks as the best way to shampoo hair, to freeze lima beans, or to clean a bathroom. The number, kind, and sequence of steps are part of the learning. Demonstrations or step-by-step instructions using slides, filmstrips, photographs, or sketches (sometimes accompanied by a cassette) can help students in further development in this principle of psychomotor education.

In *mechanism,* students have learned to act habitually. Sometimes in the school environment, students are taught by guided response and reach mechanism through additional experience at home or elsewhere. Students might think about all the skills they have in which action takes place automatically, such as taking a shower, turning a hamburger over, mowing a lawn, polishing furniture, or running a vacuum. At the same time, they may analyze skills that can be improved or new ones to be learned. Sometimes students may perform a task but do so clumsily—they may need help in determining which muscles to use and coordinate.

The epitome of psychomotor training is the *complex overt response.* Every home economics teacher is challenged to provide a supportive environment for its development. Here a student can go into action without hesitation and gives an automatic performance with minimum effort and time. The preparation of a complete meal with ease, the construction of an entire garment, the management of cleaning a home, or taking care of a child's feeding with expertise are possible examples.

Simpson is of the opinion that a sixth major category is needed, which might be designated as *adapting and originating,* in which students adapt or originate new ways of using psychomotor skills in solving a problem or doing a task. The question raised is "Must an individual have attained a high degree of skill in order to adapt and originate, or can these processes take place at all levels?"[19]

Home economics educators outside of the classroom may consider ways in which they can be supportive and encouraging to their readers, patients, clients, customers, and others. All educators might bear in mind the importance of the many facets of the three types of environments discussed here.

MANAGEMENT OF THE ENVIRONMENT

Whatever the program or the facilities, once the program is under way the teacher will have to define her/his role as manager in relation to the people around her/him, such as paraprofessionals, students, parents, and volunteers, and in relation to other aspects of the management of the department.

In the process of controlling the environment, the teacher is required to make many decisions. Decision making should be considered not a chore but an opportunity. It is imperative that the problems be carefully defined. All too often teachers start looking for the answer before they have defined the problem. Alternative solutions should be considered and the most sensible one chosen. The process should be more rational than intuitive. Every decision that involves unknowns should reduce speculation to a minimum. The timing of decisions is a determinant of their efficacy, for decisions acted on too soon or too late may lose much or all of their effectiveness.

[19] Elizabeth Jane Simpson, "The Classification of Educational Objectives, Psychomotor," *Illinois Teacher,* Vol. 10, No. 4 (Winter 1966–1967), pp. 110–144.

The Teacher as a Manager

One of the most difficult aspects of the environment to control is time. Some kind of comprehensive plan for the best use of time seems imperative. An analysis must be made of what may be called fixed, semifixed, and flexible activities. In the fixed category are the inescapable daily routine activities, such as sleeping, eating, dressing, and meeting classes. Semifixed activities are those tasks the scheduling of which is, at least to some extent, under one's control, for example, the preparation for daily classes. The flexible activities, usually leisure activities, can be scheduled as one pleases.

The time allotted for class and other work preparation should be geared to organizing for the greatest production with the least effort and tension.

Here are a number of time stretchers that may prove helpful:

1. Do not postpone getting started. Much time is wasted by procrastination.

Figure 7–6 Does time seem to go to pieces? (A.T.&T.)

2. Do a job with zest because work is done more quickly when it is enjoyed.
3. Make use of all odd moments. Use little snippets of time here and there for reading, for writing a note, or for similar productive activities. In an average lifespan, ten productive minutes a day will add up to a full year of productivity.
4. Learn to conserve time by estimating how long it takes to do certain jobs. Compete with yourself in an attempt to reduce that time.
5. Keep priorities flexible by analyzing the jobs that require immediate attention. Take care of these first and leave jobs that are not due until later.
6. Delegate as many jobs as possible to other people, to whatever inexpensive services may be available, or to machines.
7. Group similar tasks together, such as doing certain types of paperwork all at once rather than piecemeal.
8. Learn to do two things at once. If a telephone call is delayed, do some job, such as reading mail, making out a market order, or reviewing the schedule for the day.
9. Eliminate jobs or steps in jobs by examining what is actually essential.
10. Simplify jobs by being constantly alert to new and easier ways of doing them.
11. Routinize activities by developing a pattern for carrying out fixed duties and tasks.
12. Meet deadlines. Do not get into the habit of being late, for this in itself can cause tension and frustration.
13. Look ahead in stages, for time seems more manageable if it is considered in units of a week, a month, or a year.
14. Develop a time consciousness by installing an imaginary clock in your mind.

Time is a resource that can be wasted or used well in the fulfillment of your objectives. The future of home economics is in the hands of people who get things done.

Management of People

All too often the home economics teacher does not effectively use the people around her/him as aids in controlling the environment. It behooves the teacher to have a very clear-cut notion of how students, for example, may be of assistance. Students must not be exploited, but they can assist with routine responsibilities, for they are a part of the program. They can help maintain supplies, filing, and bulletin boards, for example, and they can be hostesses or hosts when there are guests. All the items necessary to keep the department in good order might be listed, then specific tasks might be assigned to the custodian, the teacher, and the students. It might also be good to establish standards for maintenance and the way they should be met.

In other ways, students may assist other students who need special attention. In intergrade student tutoring,[20] students who are in upper grades help students who are younger. The tutor's strengthens her/his learning through teaching someone else and also gains a sense of helping. The student who is tutored learns more rapidly in a one-to-one relationship. Research indicates that tutored students frequently improve dramatically in comparison to students who have not been tutored. After giving appropriate preliminary instructions, teachers often use competent peer assistance for tutoring or helping another student in difficulty. These tutors or student aides can also give feedback to the teacher about the student's progress.

Parent aides can be invaluable. In a Brooklyn school, for example, parents[21] accompanied elementary students who were playing the role of inquiring reporters to ask people on the street about community issues. The students had a camera and a tape recorder to record the answers to their questions. This same type of experience could be used in home economics. Questions for interviewing might relate to the need for child-care centers in the community, the ways that individuals and families are saving energy, the consumption of food with a questionable quantity and quality of nutrients, problems related to food buying, or the interpretation of feminine and masculine roles. Results can be analyzed, and a report can be made to the class and also posted on the school bulletin board. Parent aides are especially valuable at elementary- and middle-school levels but are helpful at all levels. Parents can contribute in the daily activities of the program by working with individual students and helping the teacher in many areas.

School volunteerism is widely accepted by schools and communities. At least 5 million volunteers are helping in public schools.[22] Home economists have been slow to take advantage of this trend and should be encouraged to do so. In addition to parents, senior citizens, other members of the community, college dropouts, and others have offered their services. Life insurance companies, industries, and institutions have arranged for their employees to give volunteer service to the schools. Some companies even transport the volunteers to the school.

[20] Ralph J. Melaragno, *Tutoring With Students,* Educational Technology Publications, Englewood Cliffs, N.J. 1976, pp. 3–9.

[21] "Teacher Plus," *Instructor,* Vol. 86, No. 8 (Apr. 1977), p. 16.

[22] Lorna M. Wyckoff, "School Volunteers Face the Issues," *Phi Delta Kappan,* Vol. 58, No. 10 (June 1977), pp. 455–456.

Figure 7–7 School volunteers can contribute to the school program. (USDA Photo)

How may these aides help in home economics? Volunteers may assist students who lack basic skills. Home economics materials lend themselves well to this kind of instruction. Students might be assisted in deciphering patterns for clothing construction, reading recipes, reading labels, or looking up sources of help in the Yellow Pages. Other student experiences may include reading advertisements about leisure-time purchases like recordings and comparing the prices for mathematical improvement.

Other modes of assistance are to set up supplies, equipment, audiovisual devices, exhibits, and other materials for a class. Clerical work, correcting objective tests, helping keep records, making copies of class materials, and preparation of instructional materials are other suggestions.

Success in using volunteers depends on the way that a teacher and an aide decide to work together. The teacher should decide on how an aide may best be prepared to work in a particular classroom with students. Some aides require information about student ways and vernacular. Communication of warmth and support may have to be taught to the aides.

The paraprofessional is usually a paid aide who has had some college preparation in home economics. This arrangement benefits the paraprofessional because he or she can gain experience in the field and benefits the teacher because he or she gains semiprofessional help in the laboratory, for short demonstrations in some areas, or for individualized instruction.[23]

Paraprofessionals are especially helpful with large classes. Teachers must realize that paraprofessionals are not competent to assume all of the responsibilities of the teacher; they should serve as assistants. It is imperative that the teacher work closely with paraprofessionals to prepare them for their responsibilities. The teacher and the aides should determine the areas that are the sole responsibility of the teacher.

One of the benefits of using aides, parents, volunteers, and paraprofessionals is their potential advocacy of the school in the community and the resultant enhancement of public relations. It is especially beneficial that parents learn more about the home economics curriculum. Students gain the most. Extra attention improves their learning and self-concept.[24] The teachers' time is released from the more routine duties so that they can concentrate on teaching and other creative efforts.

Management of the Department

Management of the home economics department includes a number of processes. The first might be called *identification.* A teacher must know all her/his students and something about their backgrounds, their problems, their abilities, and their habits. She/he must, of course, be familiar with other teachers and the school's administrators. Knowing the available resources for the smooth and effective functioning of the department is important.

In the *control* process, authority in various situations is defined, the teacher and students analyzing what roles they are to assume and how. Related to the control process is the process of establishing *standards,* in the course of which students become aware of what is expected of them and what the steps to achievement and the hallmarks of good management are.

In the management of a department, the teacher must give serious consideration to the ways in which she/he will manage communication with students and their parents, other teachers, and interested people in the community. These lines of communication should be kept open and fluid. Reaching people means more than just talking to

[23] Alfred A. Arth and Burton C. Cave, *Teacher Aides, Utilization of Paraprofessionals,* Center for Research Service and Publications, College of Education, University of Wyoming, Laramie, Wyo., 1975.

[24] "Troubled Schools Turn to Volunteer Helpers, *U.S. News and World Report* (Jan. 17, 1978), p. 63.

them; it involves appeals through technological aids, display aids, written memoranda and reports, and the use of mass media.

A number of tasks may be described as the business of the department; all have a bearing on its environment. The major items are the following:

1. Correspondence relating to the activities, program, and equipment of the department.
2. Telephone calls, such as market orders and requests for repair of equipment or the assistance of resource persons in the community.
3. Records of attendance, report cards, and student files.
4. The departmental budget, which includes planning and accounting for expenditures.
5. Reports to school administrators and state, county, and local supervisors.
6. The filing of instructional materials, guides for the use of equipment, and budgetary items.
7. Instructions concerning lesson plans and general organization for the guidance of substitute teachers or a new teacher.
8. Opening the department in the fall and closing it in the spring for the summer.
9. Inventory of equipment and plans for equipment replacement.
10. Planning recruitment and public relations programs for the department.

The least tangible aspect of the classroom environment is frequently called the *climate,* defined as the manner in which teacher and students express their attitudes, their feelings, and their enthusiasm—or lack of it—in the day's work. It behooves the teacher to make a careful analysis of how she/he might produce a desirable climate for learning. The key concept is discipline, a concept that, unfortunately and incorrectly, has come to be equated with punishment. For the purpose of this discussion, let us accept the classic meaning of *discipline,* a word derived from the Latin word *discere,* "to learn." The learner was known as the *discipulus,* a disciple. In the broad sense, *discipline* implies self-control, a product of learning. Each student, by his/her own will, must be able to regulate his/her own behavior. Self-discipline does not emerge as a result of outside force or threats of punishment; rather, the teacher must consider the many ways in which children can be educated so that they will develop this important self-control.

Education cannot proceed without discipline; students need it and they expect it. Youngsters are happier and more productive if they know, understand, and help to establish the regulations governing their situation. Students gain a sense of security when they learn that consistent rules are important for effective group learning. Only when a child has some basis for judging the appropriateness of her/his behavior can she/he really accept the rules of the setting.

First, a home economics educator must decide what kind of behaviors are most desirable for a positive learning environment.[25] Personal convictions and experiences are an important part of final judgments. People give value—positive or negative—to quarreling, loudness, obedience, aggressiveness, quietness, indifference, or moving about, according to their beliefs of what a learning environment should be.[26] Students might help to develop suggestions for a desirable learning environment.

Some Specific Suggestions for Maintaining Discipline

Experiment with various techniques. Get ideas from other teachers, from reading, and from observation. Develop some unique measures. Touching a finger to the lips may stop two students from unnecessary talking. Talking in a whisper or a low tone may attract attention more quickly than shouting. A shake of the head can be very effective at times. A timely humorous remark has saved many a situation. Experiment with the pause.

Having a positive attitude is helpful. Finding something good in the work of a student will encourage him/her, and he/she may become less of a discipline problem, for discouraged students have less interest in self-discipline. Give students the feeling that they are respected and liked. Select interesting activities for students.

The quality of the teacher's voice can be an asset or a detriment in classroom management. If it is pleasing and well-modulated, students enjoy hearing it. The high-pitched, raspy, whiny, or unpleasant voice may cause them to lose interest, even to rebel.

Chamberlain and Weinberger[27] caution teachers to avoid the game of ambiguous rules, in which teacher and students spend needless time interpreting rules that they have previously established. The uncritical enforcement of well-established rules should also be avoided: often rules are perpetuated without an examination of their purpose or aptness. Another pitfall is classwork that is too verbal, too advanced, or in poorly planned sequences. Fatigue or boredom may result. Not recognizing behavior standards that are appropriate for the students in a particular class or group and maintaining standards that are too high or too low can be a hindrance.

Certain classroom logistics must be organized. In foods and cloth-

[25] Mary M. McCarthy, "How Can I Best Manage My Classroom," *Instructor,* Vol. 87, No. 2 (Sept. 1977), pp. 72–73.

[26] *Teach and Reach,* op. cit., p. 87.

[27] Leslie J. Chamberlain and Morris Weinberger, "Games Teachers Play," *Instructor,* Vol. 80, No. 6 (Feb. 1971), p. 69.

ing laboratories, students must secure their supplies by some system. Ranges, sewing machines, and other equipment should be in good working order. Checking supplies and equipment for each class session (either when the teacher arrives at school in the morning or during the afternoon before) is valuable. During any period, students can perform many jobs as assistants. The teacher should think about each lesson, what is needed, how it will be supplied, and who will be responsible for the supplies. If the classroom is shared, the room should be left in order for the next teacher.

The nature of activities in a home economics classroom requires freedom of movement. The use of many pieces of equipment and various supplies for effective teaching offers temptations for fun and sociability. Crowded seating and forced, awkward use of equipment may discourage a student and cause problems.

Certain devices should be avoided. Group punishment is one of them; to punish all for the sake of a few cannot be justified. Using sarcasm or ridiculing a student is unkind. Another questionable procedure is to threaten students with poor grades if they misbehave. Neither tactic encourages self-discipline or learning. Giving afterschool work as a punishment is undesirable, too, for it may lead to a dislike of a particular subject. Furthermore it defies the principles of learning. Urge students to share in the establishment of regulations and the penalty or procedure to be followed when infringement occurs. Group standards become much more workable and promote rapport in the classroom.

Having students write their own reports of misbehavior may be helpful when the teacher later presents the matter to the principal or the parents. Serious problems should, of course, always be discussed with the principal. He/she may be able to assist by giving suggestions that will be useful in the immediate situation and later on in avoiding similar incidents. If possible, the teacher should keep some type of record about students who seem troublesome, for they may have emotional or other problems.

The teacher should have a constant awareness of students. She/he must recognize that they are immature in many ways but are learning to be increasingly responsible. Understanding that their behavior is not static is imperative in good classroom management. The same students may at one time be well behaved, quiet, and industrious, yet a moment later be troublesome, belligerent, talkative, thoughtless, indifferent, or slow—alternating their patterns of behavior within short periods of time. The alert teacher is prepared to meet all these situations. The teacher will be more effective in group reinforcement if she/he knows each student and her/his problems, the groups or cliques within the class, and student capacities for leadership. She/he must be familiar with small-group techniques, such as committee work and the like, so as to aid students in moving at their own pace.

Polls and surveys reveal that discipline is a high-priority problem in many schools. Most discipline problems arise from a complexity of causes. The disruptive student may actually be giving an anguished cry for help because he or she suffers from unmet emotional needs, a negative self-concept, anxiety, despair, or other equally serious problems.[28] A teacher, with the help of experts, must decide if a serious case is normal or pathological and act accordingly. Among the most effective deterrents to discipline problems are competency in teaching, guiding students to alternative behavior, and being positive and supportive in communications. Another suggestion is for teachers to instruct students in self-control.

SUGGESTIONS FOR FURTHER LEARNING

1. Analyze your beliefs about environments for learning in an effective program in your area of specialization, for example, as a middle-school home economics teacher, a home economist in business, a nutritionist in a clinic for obese adolescents, or a home economist in extension. What kind of facilities and equipment would be important? Describe the kind of environment that you would like to create.
2. Decreased enrollment in schools will mean some empty classrooms. How might the home economics department use an extra room for schoolwide purposes? If shared, which other departments might cooperate in program planning with the home economics department? How might a bus ride to and from school be considered another learning environment? The time some children spend riding on a bus during one schoolyear is equal to two months of schooling. How may the library contribute to the learning environment in home economics? What other possibilities do you envision for enriching the home economics environment?
3. Think about a home economics department with which you are very familiar. Consider the kind of aides and the possible ways that they can contribute to the program. Here are some references that might be helpful.

   Barclay, G. John (ed.). *Parent Involvement in the Schools.* Washington, D.C.: NEA, 1977.

   Heffrich, John E., and Mary Jean LeTendre. *Tutoring Resources Handbook for Teachers.* Washington, D.C.: U.S. Office of Education, Department of Health, Education and Welfare, Superintendent of Documents, 1974.

   "How to Put Parents on Your Classroom Team." *Instructor,* **87** (Nov. 1977), 54–62.

   Lippitt, Peggy. *Students Teach Students,* Fastbook 55. Bloomington, Ind.: Phi Delta Kappa Educational Foundation, 1975.

   Masters, Charlotte. *School Volunteers, Who Needs Them,* Fastbook 55. Bloomington, Ind.: Phi Delta Kappa Educational Foundation, 1975.

[28] Richard Kindsvatter, "A New Vision of the Dynamics of Discipline," *Phi Delta Kappan,* Vol. 59, No. 5 (Jan. 1978), pp. 322–325.

8

Teaching Resources Part I

Instructional materials are a key component in the organization of educational experiences for students.

If adroitly utilized, teaching resources may give a student the vicarious experience of living in colonial days or in a family from another country whose lifestyle is quite different from his or her own mode of life. The potential of teaching materials for teaching and learning is almost limitless. For this reason, speculation by a teacher about the way a particular aid will enhance the development of a student is critical.

Dale[1] devised the Cone of Experience (see Figure 8-1), which is an excellent guide to the selection of resources for teaching and learning. In this arrangement of the learning possibilities of different types of teaching aids, there are three categories: direct experience, pictorial experience, and symbolic or highly abstract experience. These three categories may be demonstrated with this simple illustration. A student undergoes a direct experience in making an omelet. If the student sees the steps for making an omelet in drawings, then the experience is pictorial and more abstract. Reading about an omelet in a cookbook is symbolic and highly abstract. Any of these types of resources may be used, depending upon the experience and ability of the student. If a person has had experience in making an omelet and has confidence in his or her ability, then checking certain details in a cookbook may be all that is necessary.

Dale's cone is a practical guide to the selection of teaching re-

[1] Edgar Dale, *Audiovisual Methods of Teaching* (New York: Holt, 1969), Ch. 4.

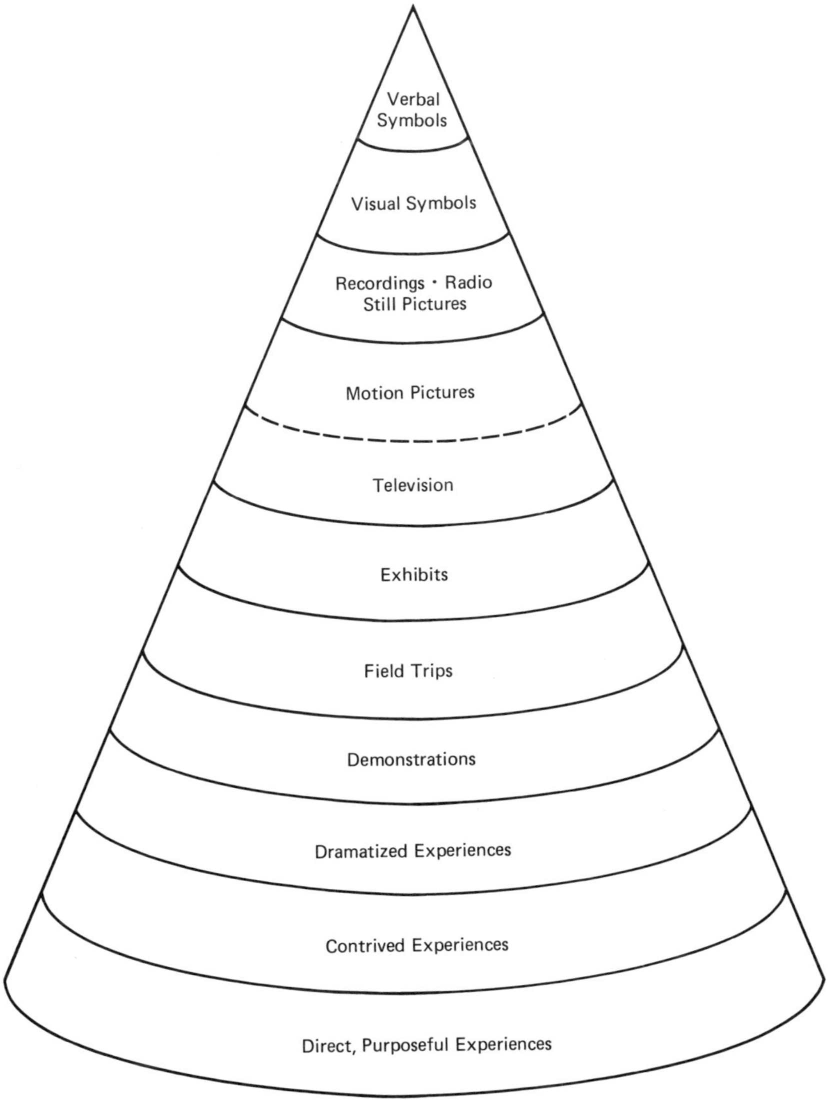

Figure 8–1 Dale's "Cone of Experience" is an excellent guide in selecting teaching resources. (From *Audiovisual Methods in Teaching,* third edition, by Edgar Dale. Copyright 1946, 1954 © 1969 by Holt, Rinehart and Winston, Inc. Reprinted by permission of Holt, Rinehart and Winston and Dr. Edgar Dale.)

sources according to the degree of abstraction or sensory experience necessary; it does not indicate a range of difficulty. The cone suggests the interrelated and interdependent nature of learning and teaching materials. Words or verbal symbols are used in all bands on the cone. The cone may assist a teacher in the choice of the aid most suitable to specific student needs and abilities.

CONTRIBUTIONS OF TEACHING MATERIALS

Teaching resources can make a number of specific contributions to learning.[2] When used appropriately, aids heighten motivation for learning, especially if they are concrete, interesting, illustrated, and well organized for continuity of thought. Acceptance will depend upon the level of learning readiness for this particular material. Instructional materials can add novelty and variety to teaching. Different teaching resources appeal to students of different backgrounds and varying abilities. Some aids stimulate students' participation by encouraging them to reach for new experiences, to seek additional information, or to raise questions about the content presented.

USE OF TEACHING MATERIALS

The use of instructional materials is related directly to objectives. What do teacher and student expect to accomplish? An examination of Dale's Cone of Experience may stimulate choices. In addition to teacher and student goals, certain general objectives of education deal with the total development of the individual, such as critical thinking. A specific goal may be securing summer jobs for high school students. A survey of job possibilities posted on the bulletin board may serve as a teaching resource, for example. Students may bring in want ads or transcriptions of radio announcements, or other items of information and place them on the bulletin board. By the use of a transparency on the overhead projector or the chalkboard, the jobs may be categorized according to the information desired by the students, such as type of work, hours, pay, required qualifications, and length of time (a week, a month, or longer). The absence of certain types of jobs desired by some students may be noted and suggestions made for further inquiry. Each student may summarize his or her own summer job situation through drawings or some other medium and include what he or she hopes to gain from summer work. All this information may be shared with classmates so that all students may profit from the ideas and suggestions. What other aids might be used to explore job possibilities?

Another objective might be to learn to appreciate and to identify with others. Reading the book *Roll of Thunder, Hear My Cry*[3] may lead to a greater understanding of the frustrations arising from prejudice. Stories of other human problems may serve similar purposes.

[2] Ibid., Ch. 5.
[3] Mildred D. Taylor (New York: Dial, 1977).

The concepts associated with becoming a better consumer may be enlarged and built into an orderly and continuous process through the wise use of teaching materials. For example, slides, pictures, and charts may highlight the advantages and disadvantages of buying certain kinds of bicycles prior to actual shopping. Students may assist in the production of these aids.

Teaching materials may lend emotional or intellectual reenforcement in certain circumstances. A film that depicts family and child relationships or child–child relationships may help a student to realize that he or she understands parents or a brother or sister better than he or she assumed.

Students' experience may be widened through the showing of slides about careers in home economics, through a film about the importance of adequate nutrition in the development of an outstanding athlete, or through an illustrated book on child development that results in more effective work with young children.

The teacher needs to evaluate aids to determine the soundness of the material, the skill of presentation, ability to capture and hold interest, and organization. Some aids make a particular contribution, such as introducing a topic; supplying basic information; challenging an idea, attitude, or value; or summarizing. Is the content meaningful, stimulating, and challenging? Does the aid allow the student to think, to examine values, or to make choices? Will it be an aid in making a behavior change? Will a student receive feedback so that he or she is conscious of what was learned? Other points to consider about a material are availability, cost, ease of use, time required, quality, care, portability, and similar items. What other points are important to consider?

VISUAL RESOURCES

Through the use of a wide variety of visual teaching resources, the interest of a student can be stimulated and held to a greater degree. To see a picture, slide, or drawing of an object or an action makes it seem real. A teacher may describe a piece of equipment, a chair, a garment, or a food, and it still may be more difficult for students to understand than if a picture, a slide, or other visual aid is used. If the actual size is much smaller or larger than in the picture, the students should be informed of this fact. Student perceptions of visual aids reveal the extent of their past experiences or the extent to which they are imaginatively involved. The teacher should catch misconceptions so that they may be corrected. Like words, visuals should be read for meaning.

A number of visual aids are described here.

Figure 8–2 A photograph of a boy buying shoes may be used in introducing a lesson. (Cereal Institute, Inc.)

Photographs

Photographs serve an invaluable purpose in communicating ideas more effectively, in dramatizing the points made by words, and in making instruction more vital. Before choosing photographs, the teacher should decide on the purpose they will serve. No matter what the specific use, each photograph should be authentic and large enough and clear enough to be easily seen. Photographs should convey information pertinent to the subject under discussion and should be sufficiently interesting to hold the attention of the students.

Dale[4] suggests the following criteria in judging a photograph or reproduction to be used in the classroom:

1. Will it help to achieve a specific teaching purpose? For example, will large illustrations of how to poach an egg be helpful to students as they are performing this task for the first time?
2. Does the photograph give a true impression? If students are studying homes in different regions of the nation and photographs of Pennsylvania Dutch farm homes are shown, do they represent authentic details, and are they typical? For example, does every barn have a hex sign? To perpetuate such ideas

[4] Dale, op. cit., pp. 432–433.

through photographs as that all Dutch wear wooden shoes, that all Italians eat spaghetti, or that all Alaskans wear snowshoes is not educationally sound.

3. Is an accurate impression of size given? In photographs of fruits and vegetables, are the relative sizes clearly shown? A student unfamiliar with zucchini, for instance, may assume that it is the same size as a string bean.
4. Will a photograph contribute to a student's knowledge? It is pointless to show photographs of well-known articles, such as a chair. However, photographs might be helpful in the identification of chairs of various furniture periods.
5. Is imagination stimulated? If photographs of homemade dress accessories are available will they stimulate original ideas among the students?
6. Is the photograph good from technical and artistic viewpoints? It should be in focus, have at least three gradations of tone, and have a dominant center of interest.
7. Is there a main idea? Is it clear and does it attract prompt attention?
8. Does the photograph have the proper amount of detail? Just a general shape is inadequate if students are to learn from photographs or reproductions.

Students are inclined to explain a photograph in the light of personal influences, such as past experience and cultural background. Thoughtful viewing of photographs should be encouraged. As a teaching tool, photographs can be used in many ways. They can motivate a new interest, supplement reading, demonstrate a process, correct erroneous impressions, evoke emotional responses, and help in the search for facts necessary to critical thinking. Because a photograph's most important function is to communicate, a teacher must be careful in her/his choice of words so that the teacher's comments and the aid complement and supplement each other. It is usually not fruitful to pass photographs around during a class period, for students generally do not examine them closely under these conditions. Learning from photographs calls for detailed study of them. Photographs should be placed on reserve in the library, laid out at a study table in the classroom, projected for the class with the opaque projector, or displayed in some way. One or two good photographs of a subject are better than dozens of indifferent ones.

There are many sources of good photographs. Magazines such as *National Geographic* are especially good. Most women's and teenagers' magazines contain good ideas. Publications geared to the house and home furnishings yield additional possibilities. Travel brochures, publications of city and state chambers of commerce, and house organs of industries and businesses are other sources. Old calendars, such as those of UNICEF, often provide excellent materials. Picture books like *The Family of Man*[5] and *Family*[6] are especially useful. Advertisements frequently contain excellent prints of photographs for all areas of home economics.

Pictures may be used in many ways in home economics. Family living in other countries might be analyzed through magazine illustrations, postcards, or travel brochures. Contrasts and comparisons are recommended, with an emphasis on family values. The influence of other countries on our food, home furnishings, and fashions offers still another interesting picture study.

An appreciation of the influence of time on the home can be fostered through pictures of the artwork of homes, clothes, furnishings, equipment, and even customs at different periods of history. Also provocative as a subject would be the technological changes that have altered our way of living since the advent of the automobile. Photographs of snacks, breakfasts, lunches, or dinners might be evaluated for nutritional adequacy and suitability according to criteria agreed upon by the class and those established by authorities. Illustrations of boy–girl relationships, family situations, parent–child, or child–community relations can provide a springboard for discussion. Photographs may be used for purposes of identification before a field trip, to acquaint students with the important things they are to see. Pictures are also helpful in establishing standards. Photographs may be used of the foods under discussion, of the desirable equipment for a job, and of steps in using time, energy, and other resources to best advantage.

The before-and-after photographs in magazines depicting such subjects as kitchen remodeling, room rearrangement, and good grooming make dramatic illustrations. Students should be challenged not to accept the revised version without careful scrutiny. Are the changes justifiable? Could further improvements be made? Are any gross errors evident? Recognizing the problem or problems involved can be a valuable experience.

Sometimes an interesting illustration of an emotionally toned situation involving several persons depicting anger, affection, sadness, or disgust might be projected so that the class can develop a story progressively. One person starts the story, the second one adds to it, and so on around the class. As each student makes a contribution, the teacher must be aware of its implications. Photographs are excellent, too, when used in the interpretation of past experiences. A teacher might ask, "Have you ever had an experience like this?" "What does

[5] Edward Steichen and Carl Sandburg (New York: Maco Magazine Corporation, 1955).

[6] Margaret Mead and Ken Heyman (New York: Macmillan, 1965).

this remind you of?" "Do you know of someone else who experienced this?"

In work with students who have a reading difficulty or with children who come from foreign backgrounds, pictures are invaluable in teaching about equipment, the steps in a process, the way a finished product looks, and unfamiliar foods or articles of clothing. Photographs may promote interest in a subject and thereby motivate reading. Bilingual captions may be helpful.

This teaching aid can be employed, too, as an evaluation device. Having students describe their reactions to a photograph of an old man or woman may provide an opportunity to challenge stereotyped beliefs about age. Photographs placed around the room can test how well students are able to apply their knowledge. Pictures might include views of a child having a temper tantrum or another behavior problem for a unit in child care; of parent–student problems for a family relations unit; or of various articles of clothing to evaluate proper selection for specific purposes.

After an interesting report on subjects such as roles, the future, or motherhood, a teacher might ask the students to sketch the pictures they have in their minds. Imagination, closeness to reality, points not understood, and so on require the close attention of students and teacher.

Photographs may be available from the audiovisual center in the school or from the community library, but home economics teachers will most probably have to provide their own. A library of good photographs takes a long time to build. Students should be encouraged to help build the collection. By preparing their own photographs, teacher and students can meet precisely their specific class needs or interests. When students have communication problems, their own photographs are helpful in relating their experiences or for reports. Photographs of a baby's christening, a wedding ceremony, unusual markets, foods not found in the community, or a handicapped child playing ball can be stimulating—the possibilities are endless.

Photographs can be used to illustrate good posture, sound eating habits, and appropriate dress. Serial pictures of a growing child at different stages of development will enhance a child-care unit. Photographs of children's clothes help demonstrate such points of design as self-help, easy care, and suitability. Processes can be depicted in a series of illustrations, for example, refurnishing or renovating a room, bathing or feeding an infant, or shopping for groceries.

Photographs should be mounted before they are filed. If a picture is especially valuable, it should be covered with clear plastic or kept in a special envelope. Photographs can be sprayed with a protective transparent plastic. The teacher should examine the picture file periodically and eliminate the pictures that are no longer useful.

Figure 8–3 A family interest in photography will develop skills that will be helpful in school activities.

None should be kept that does not continue to make a positive contribution to teaching.

Students might take photographs to show body language in facial expressions, in posture, in gestures, and in other ways.[7] Students may plan captions for their pictures. How do the captions vary among the

[7] Jerry Griffith, Lynn E. Miner, and Twila E. Strandberg, *Classroom Projects Using Photography,* Part II, Secondary School Level (Rochester, N.Y.: Eastman Kodak Company, 1975), pp. 10–11.

students and why? Another camera project may be to take photographs of different ways for saving energy. These may be displayed in the town library, in a store window, or in another place where the public may view them.

Broomstick Movies

Broomstick movies are *not* made with a camera. This device has been used largely in the lower grades but actually has appeal for all ages. A series of equal-size posters giving related information are fashioned into one long strip. Students may also draw the illustrations on a roll of white shelf paper instead of making individual posters. Each end of the strip is then attached to a dowel or a broomstick stuck vertically through a box. The width between the two dowels is equal to the width of one illustration. The strip is then wound onto one of the dowels. As one student reads a commentary, two others turn the sticks to wind the strip from one dowel to the other, poster by poster, at a pace geared to the commentary. Suggested subjects are managing money or time, the effect of weather on family living, a review of teenage living in various lifestyles, a review of careers in clothing using *Alice in Wonderland* characters to tell the story. Soap operas highlighting family-life situations may be created. The commentary can be written as the script for a narrated story or as a play. Sound effects, staging, and similar devices may be used to enhance the show.

Figure 8–4 Broomstick movies are appropriate for all areas of home economics. Production may be a group project.

Figure 8–5 A relief map and the use of string is helpful in teaching blind students. (West Virginia University)

Maps and Globes

Maps and globes may assist both students and teacher to see important relationships. The relationships of land, water, animals, plants, climate, and other resources to the cultures and products of various countries can, with maps, be explored for implications for the problems of family living in those areas. The same method can be used to determine the effects on housing, eating habits, clothes, the kinds of jobs available for family members, and the like in various sections of the United States.

DISPLAY VISUALS

Displays are a powerful form of visual communication and an excellent teaching tool. Many teaching situations lend themselves to the use of displays. When selected to fit students and learning situations, displays can stimulate creative expression, introduce new ideas, supplement real objects, provide new experiences, and give concrete expression to abstract ideas. They may also lead to individual and group action that promotes decision making, as discussed by Tiemann, Lockridge, and McMurry.[8]

Bulletin boards and posters, chalkboards, flannelboards, magnetic boards, pegboards, flipcharts, exhibits, mobiles, models, mock-ups, and simulations are typical displays. With a modest investment, teachers and students can engage in the creative production of their own class materials.

In the preparation of a design, emphasis must be given to an attractive arrangement that arouses and holds interest. These goals may be satisfied through the application of the principles of balance—formal and informal—unity, emphasis, and clarity. Consideration must be given to color, space, pattern, line, and texture in the selection of materials and their arrangement.

Displays can revitalize an entire classroom and in the process assist students' learning. Opportunities are provided to analyze, challenge, summarize, introduce, review, evaluate, share, create, think, reason, and participate in other activities that promote personal and group development. Displays should not be considered a chore and a bore but a means to effective teaching.

Guidelines for preparing instructional displays are outlined here. Basic to planning is a consideration of the objectives to be reached, the subject matter to be highlighted, the materials to be used, and the resources available. Making an outline that encompasses these points and drawing a rough sketch of the display geared to the space to be used will spare teacher and students many frustrations later.

Attention may be attracted by tricky captions, a strong center of interest, contrasting colors, unusual shapes, and multidimensional materials. Interest must be caught and then held until the message is delivered. A logical sequence, pattern, or arrangement that promotes easy eye movement is one answer.

Those who are making the display should test the rough sketch of the layout by prearranging materials to test balance, space relationships, emphasis, and sequence, and they should experiment, if necessary, until the best arrangement appears to evolve. Captions and titles are a key to successful displays. They focus attention, develop the mood desired, and highlight the purpose of the display. Careless lettering distracts. Many lettering devices are available. Letters may be made from paper strips or gummed tape, or they may be cut out of magazines or newspapers. Commercially prepared letters may be reused.

If the same materials are to be used in other displays, it is wise to make temporary mountings with rubber cement, cellophane tape,

[8] Ernest F. Tiemann, J. Preston Lockridge, and Gerda G. McMurry, *Educational Displays and Exhibits* (Austin, Texas: Instructional Media Center, Division of Extension, The University of Texas, 1966), pp. 1–7.

masking tape, or staples. Some plan must be made for filing materials for future use.

The following criteria might form the basis for evaluating displays:

1. Was the objective simple and workable?
2. Did the display consider the interests, needs, and lifestyles of the viewers?
3. Was attention attracted and held? What was the concrete evidence?
4. Could the display be viewed easily?
5. Was the content informative?
6. Was there evidence that action was generated?
7. Were the time, effort, and cost justified?
8. Did the display contribute to the learning and development of the students?
9. Were enough students involved?
10. Did the display contribute aesthetically to the environment?
11. What should have been done differently?

Teachers may desire to add other criteria appropriate to their situations.

Bulletin Boards and Posters

Bulletin boards can be a prominent part of classroom activities. Bulletin boards may be planned jointly by students and teacher. If there is sufficient bulletin board space in the classroom, several groups of students might work out separate but coordinated ideas on a theme. Finding fresh ideas for a tackboard or a bulletin board is often a great chore for a teacher. Actually ideas are everywhere. Advertisement layouts, magazine article illustrations, commercial posters, window displays, and billboards may suggest ideas adaptable to class purposes. Television commercials frequently show unusual treatments that may spark an idea for a bulletin board display. Brainstorming sessions with students are fruitful. Teachers who develop in themselves and their students an eye for bulletin board material will not lack ideas.

A bulletin board treasure chest of two- and three-dimensional materials might be collected by teacher and students. The materials may be soft, rough, smooth, shiny, colorful, and of irregular and geometric shapes to make the bulletin board more interesting. Rope, yarn, heavy or well-starched string in different colors, split bamboo, twisted aluminum foil, cork, wood, plastic foam, thin sheets of aluminum or copper, buttons, thumbtacks, and a variety of ornamental pins can be used in the lettering of captions. These might also serve to tie parts of the bulletin board together; for example, strings might lead from the captions to the jackets of books, to photographs, to pamphlets, and so on.

Figures can be made from pipecleaners, bent wire, or paper-doll cutouts; stick figures from toothpicks or torn paper; silhouettes from paper or fabric; and figures shaped like spoons from cork, cotton batting, velvet, burlap, fur, leather, wire screening, steel wool, or ribbons.

The background for the display will be more interesting if some or all of the bulletin board is covered with such textured materials as fishnet or other types of netting, wire screening, chicken wire mesh, corrugated cardboard, cheesecloth, burlap, or mesh bags of the kind used for fruits and vegetables. Newspaper want-ad sections or old maps make an interesting background. Students can get novel effects by sprinkling sequins, glitter, sand, or gravel on glue spread over heavy paper or cardboard; by hanging things from a piece of pegboard; or by using moss, sponges, carpet remnants, pieces of bark, excelsior, wallpaper, tinsel, fabric remnants, paper doilies, crepe paper, raffia, balloons, felt, sawdust, foil, crushed cellophane, plastics, blotters, cork, and tile in different ways.

Following are some suggestions for themes upon which to base the main points of displays. All can be adapted, and perhaps they will stimulate other ideas.

1. A clock or a calendar is useful in highlighting a time-management topic.
2. A question—say, "Do You Know?"—may be asked, the body of the display supplying the answer. For example, questions and answers might relate to the correct utensils for certain food preparation techniques, such as a wooden spoon for stirring hot mixtures; to safety rules; to table settings; or to inexpensive food sources of vitamin C or another nutrient.
3. A puzzle or a riddle might be made the setting for a bulletin board theme, for example, matching appropriate fabrics to certain garments; toys to children of different age groups; or suitable clothes to specific occasions.
4. Principles such as those studied in connection with vegetable cookery, for example, the difference in appearance of vegetables cooked for a short period and a long period could be portrayed in colored sketches or photographs.
5. Words common to home economics, such as *recipe* or *pattern,* might be used as theme words for other situations, such as "A Recipe for Avoiding Pollution" or "A Pattern for Good Grooming."
6. Objects such as combs, toothbrushes, empty cartons, fabrics,

Figure 8–6 A preliminary sketch of a bulletin board display.

sewing notions, or small kitchen equipment give a striking emphasis to tackboard messages.

7. The teacher can capitalize on themes that are current with the young. She/he can use the title of the latest record for a caption to highlight a positive slant on the use of organic or health foods, on the latest whim in clothes, or on timely social service.

Most classrooms have bulletin board space available. In a room with little wall space, a bulletin board may have to be suspended from the ceiling. Another possibility is a portable board that may be placed in the chalk tray or propped on a table. If there are more chalkboards than needed, one of them may be covered with burlap or cork and used as a bulletin board.

These suggestions for bulletin board materials, design, and uses apply as well to posters. Materials that can be used for letters are tape measures, rubber bands, colored plastic tape, yarn, braid, ribbons, rickrack, or copper wire. Paper sculpture can produce an interesting effect on a poster.

Students can be very creative in the preparation of posters, which can be signed just as artists sign pictures. This is an excellent way of giving a student recognition. In addition to the materials mentioned, tracing paper can be used to trace designs or ideas from newspapers, magazines, pamphlets, other posters, and so on. Posters can be designed to highlight safety in the home or in the laboratory; to encourage good nutrition among adolescents; to encourage solutions for parent–child conflicts; to advertise opportunities for volunteer work in the community; and so on. Professional magazines list sources of commercial posters. Travel posters are decorative and may be used in the study of cultural foods, leisure time, and other areas of family living. Inexpensive black-and-white posters of the eighteenth and nineteenth centuries about boardinghouse rules, advertisements, restaurant menus, and auction sales may be used for historical highlights and for decorative purposes in the classroom. These posters may be purchased from Pioneer Historical Society, Harriman, Tennessee 37748, or Buck Hill Associates, Dept. MM, Garnet Lake Road, Johnsburg, New York 12843.

Chalkboards

The chalkboard, blackboard, or marking board is probably the most frequently used display device in the classroom and, unfortunately, is the one most taken for granted. What goes on the board becomes important to the learning of students.

The advantages of a chalkboard are that it is instantly available, mistakes can be changed, lists can be revised, quick feedback can occur about differences of opinion and errors, and a high rate of participation by students is encouraged when their ideas are being placed on the board. Questions to consider when listening to a cassette or seeing a film may be listed. House plans or room arrangements may be evaluated. Charts, graphs, and statistics may be displayed for discussion. The development of a topic from introduction to more complex ideas may be explained on the chalkboard.

One disadvantage is that the board is limited to current use. Materials cannot usually be left on the board for the next day. The teacher cannot get student reactions if his/her back is to the students while writing, and students may not be able to hear a teacher's remarks. Writing must be legible, the board has to be clean and without light reflections, and crowding of material must be avoided if students are to read the material easily.

Cartoon effects can liven up chalkboard material. With a few simple lines, a humorous touch can make otherwise dull material memorable. Students in a home management course can summarize some of the basic principles of saving time and energy through the use of stick figures. A teacher may underscore points on unnecessary waste of materials at school and in the home or on the proper use of credit or on teenage marriages, by the use of comic sketches. She/he may give a needed change of pace with a chalk talk in which important points are illustrated with clever drawings. The use of an opaque projector makes blackboard sketching relatively simple. Pictures, cartoons, floor plans, patterns, charts, graphs, and diagrams are projected onto the chalkboard in whatever size is desired, then traced with chalk. Only such details as are necessary for the discussion need to be outlined. Students can help with the drawing. Changes in or additions to the original sketch are easily made as a result of class discussions.

Flannelboards

One of the most dramatic visual aids for the home economics classroom is the flannelboard, or feltboard. The principle is that nappy materials, such as flannel, felt, and velvet, cling. Each symbol, picture, or chart to be used has cloth like the board's covering material pasted on its back, nap side out. Gently pressing a properly prepared article against the board causes the two napped surfaces to stick together until they are pulled apart.

The particular value of this device, in addition to its attention-getting quality, is the opportunity it affords to illustrate immediately, flexibly, and graphically what is being taught or discussed. With it, the teacher can build a complete illustrated story, part by part, point by point. The finished display is a memorable summary of the discussion.

Alert instructors will find many uses for the flannelboard. For example, when a class is exploring the problem of storage space in the home, the teacher might demonstrate very graphically the arrangement of shelves and stored articles in closets for clothing, for linens, for dishes, for packaged foods, for kitchen utensils, for cleaning supplies, and so on. The outline of the closet can be indicated with strips of napped material, and strips representing the shelves can be moved up and down as the most useful shelf arrangements are worked out.

Other possibilities are points in the selection of safe toys for children and the use of a particular food, such as ground meat, in many cultures—Swedish meatballs, stuffed cabbage, or filling for tortillas. Part-time job possibilities may also be depicted.

A set of basic shapes, including a circle, a square, a rectangle, and a triangle, can be used in a discussion of silhouettes in clothes, furniture shapes, and food forms. The letters in the caption may also be of these shapes. Other uses may be found for this basic set of shapes.

An interesting and light touch may come from animated figures made from drawings of fruits, vegetables, sewing and cooking equipment, and other inanimate objects. These can be used in connection with the special use or care of these items.

A flannelboard may be made by the teacher. A fabric with a nap, such as velvet, felt, flannel, or corduroy, may be chosen to cover cardboard, plywood, poster board, or another lightweight material, which may be set in a large picture frame. A clothes or suede brush can be used to keep the nap high so that cutouts will adhere.

Planning and practice are necessary for the successful use of this teaching aid. The first step is to decide on the points to be emphasized in the presentation. Next, symbols, charts, or pictures appropriate to the subject should be collected, backed with flannel, and arranged in sequence on a nearby table so that they can be picked up and placed on the board without delay. Each symbol or picture should be attached to the board at the time it comes into the discussion. If put in place too early or too late, its reinforcement value and the attention of the listeners may both be lost. The teacher should practice placing the required symbols on the board so that she/he will be able to do it easily and without interrupting her/his talk or turning her/his back to the audience.

Because this versatile board is such a valuable teaching aid, the ingenious home economist will want to put it to wide use, in talks or reports to clubs and community groups as well as in schoolwork.

Pegboards

The pegboard is made of Masonite sheets or comparable material that has regularly spaced holes drilled in it. Objects may be displayed on pegs, such as golf tees, hangers, or hooks.[9] Examples of appropriate objects are small kitchen gadgets that may be time savers, authoritative paperback books that are helpful in child rearing or in sewing inexpensive clothes, mounted pictures that highlight the less-known fruits and vegetables, attractive and inexpensive gifts for children, or ideas for inexpensive clothing accessories.

Students may use the pegboard to make committee reports, to summarize a unit of learning, or to arouse interest in FHA/HERO activities. This board is versatile, and its potential offers a challenge to teacher and students.

Flipcharts

Flipcharts are easily made. Material can be pasted on the blank backsides of the pages of wallpaper sample books. Large sheets of paper bearing the illustrations desired can be inserted into a map head on a stand. Sheets of paper or poster board bound with rings

[9] Ernest F. Tiemann and Jerry Mac Linker, *Instructional Display Boards* (Austin, Texas: Instructional Media Center, Division of Extension, The University of Texas, 1968), p. 17.

can be set up like a large looseleaf notebook on an easel. Spiral-bound sketching books are also excellent.

Flipcharts are particularly useful as repositories of information, charts, and diagrams that are used often, for example, patterns; samples of drapery, upholstery, and clothing fabrics; samples of wall coverings; and recipes.

Exhibits

Exhibits are three-dimensional displays of full-sized or simulated articles. Exhibits can be displayed in many ways. They may be placed in the classroom, in the school lobby, in museums, in store windows, in supermarkets, in clinics, in libraries, or in theater lobbies. Many home economics rooms have a large showcase nearby that can be used for exhibits informing the entire school population of home economics activities. The doors of a glass case might be covered except for peepholes at various heights through which people can peek into a well-lighted exhibit. A collection of fabrics, or garments that students have constructed, can be displayed on folding screens. Equipment, books, and other objects can be attached to a pegboard. Plywood or heavy cardboard attached to two poles accordion fashion can save space. Clothes-drying racks and low cupboard are excellent foundations for exhibits.

Students should be encouraged to use a wide variety of materials as props or mounts. Newspapers, enlarged photographs, cartoons, and sketches make good backgrounds. Real objects and models of all kinds are appropriate. Exhibits may be placed on tables, shelves, pegboards, boxes, or on the floor, according to Tiemann, Lockridge, and McMurry.[10] Shoe boxes, gift boxes, and cartons, painted or covered with foil or paper, also work well as display stands, as do bricks, whitewashed stones, glass bricks, cinder blocks, and mailing tubes topped with cards. Dolls, broomsticks, figures cut from newspapers, and colored corrugated paper can be used in exhibits.

Size in itself can be very important as an attention-getting device. Large arrows, big numbers, pennants, broken or dotted lines, and giant letters are suggestions.

Exhibits can be made to appeal to several of the senses at once. The odor of fresh bread or cooked meat will attract viewers. People like to touch fabrics and to handle unusual vegetables or fruits and equipment. A strange sound that excites curiosity can be used as an attention-getting device. Motion attracts attention. A concealed turntable can be used to animate an exhibit; a large mobile might be used to highlight some facet of the exhibit.

[10] Op. cit., pp. 29–36.

Exhibits that require viewers to participate in some way, like one in which a button must be pushed to start some action or in which the viewer participates in some simple experiment, become especially meaningful. A question might appear next to a display and the answer placed under a flap that must be raised.

Handout materials or reference materials should be placed nearby so that the viewers can have additional information about the topic of the display. Pamphlets, books, and flyers related to a pegboard exhibit might be displayed on a table in front of it.

Topics for an exhibit might be clothes for the handicapped, ways to help the elderly in the community, and methods for encouraging the optimum development of retarded children. Literature on death and dying might stimulate discussion. Home and personal applications of the metric system are timely.

Attractive and meaningful displays can be borrowed from many utility companies, mail-order houses, banks, and other private commercial sources, as well as from government agencies. These may be incorporated into class experiences, or they may be used for a school-wide open house.

Mobiles

A mobile not only can be decorative; it can also be used to summarize facts or ideas about a subject with pictures or lightweight objects strung on cord or light wire. The composition of a mobile should be pleasing and well arranged. Mobiles can be hung from light fixtures, beams, doors, or a ceiling hook.

A mobile might be made illustrating the possible careers in a profession. In a nutrition unit, a mobile can be used to illustrate the foods comprising the four essential groups. Toys suitable for a three-year-old child or the kind of sewing equipment needed for a certain project might be made into a mobile by students.

Models

Models are three-dimensional representations of objects, ranging in scale from miniature to larger-than-life. Their primary purpose is to demonstrate the working or the construction of something. For example, the gears of a hand beater might be studied through a large working model.

In the process of building a model, students must be concerned not only with the design, layout, and fabrication of the model, they must do extensive research on the object being modeled, thus acquiring detailed information about it.

In units on housing there are many opportunities to use models.

Anne Greenberg[11] made several models of one type of mobile home. She experimented with stacking several for a two-story house, with making a breezeway between two models, and with using three models to make interesting arrangements of wings. The low cost and the potentials of such arrangements are intriguing.

Mock-ups

The terms *model* and *mock-up* are often used interchangeably. The mock-up is a life-sized model in which a certain element of the original is emphasized so that it will be more meaningful to students. Among the most common examples are the mock-ups used in driver-training courses and the simulations used by the astronauts to prepare them for landing on the moon.

A teacher can make for student use a mock-up of the head of a sewing machine with the parts needed for threading.[12] This aid would be particularly useful where there are few sewing machines and students have limited opportunities for practice. A home-nursing class could make good use of a mock-up of an enlarged fever thermometer with a silver or red ribbon that may be pulled up and down to indicate different temperatures. Other possible mock-ups could show the parts of a light switch or a thermostat and how they work.

REALIA

The word *realia* defines authentic material or real things. The realia of home economics include household appliances and furnishings, food, and clothing. Problems, ideas, and data are dealt with better by the homemaking student through utilitarian contact with related material things. Realia provide students with rich, firsthand experiences and what Dale[13] calls the challenge of distinguishing between *knowing* something and *knowing about* something. He advises teachers to encourage students to use their eyes, ears, noses, hands, and muscles and to enjoy the vitality of firsthand experiences. Following are some suggestions that may inspire the alert teacher to supply his/her students with vivid sensory experiences.

Students in a foods class realized that their knowledge of cheeses was severely limited. The group brought many types of cheese into the laboratory. Here they were tasted, smelled, and examined carefully. The identifying characteristics of each cheese were then tabu-

[11] In a graduate housing course at New York University.
[12] Suggested by Dorothy Moskowitz in one of the author's classes.
[13] Edgar Dale, "Coming to Our Senses," *The Newsletter*, Vol. 25, No. 1 (Oct. 1959), pp. 1–4.

lated. Then the cheeses were used as ingredients in various dishes, and information about the effect cooking had upon each kind of cheese was added to the tabulation. The students even went on to make several kinds of cheese in the laboratory.

Tasting parties are fun and an excellent experience for students at all age levels. Several elementary teachers asked a home economics instructor how they might help their pupils overcome a general dislike of vegetables. The home economics teacher suggested that the problem might be solved with the aid of realia. The elementary teachers asked their pupils to bring in from their home gardens as many kinds of vegetables as possible. Some less familiar vegetables, including zucchini and artichokes, were bought at the market. The young gastronomes washed, scrubbed, and prepared the vegetables for eating. On a plate they put raw carrot strips; turnip slices; string bean slivers; spinach, chard, and cabbage leaves; and rings of green pepper to taste. Some of the vegetables were cooked, and a creamed vegetable soup was prepared. Seeing, smelling, and tasting these vegetables, the children overcame their dislike of many of them.

Blindfold tests with real objects might be performed with small kitchen equipment, with different fruits and vegetables, or with fabrics. Concentrating on the feel of an object may give an entirely new dimension to the students' awareness. One teacher devised a game in which the students sat in a circle, a sheet or cloth was spread over their laps, and the teacher started passing various items around the circle under the sheet—a piece of cotton, some raw rice, a penny, a nail, a piece of velvet, a fiberglass cleaning pad, a nail brush, an unsharpened pencil, and a piece of art gum. By the time the article had returned to the teacher, a discussion was opened about its identification and its outstanding characteristics. Seeing the objects later added to a stronger identification.

In a family relations class, students discussing the legal and economic aspects of family life knew little of the form and content of such documents as marriage certificates, installment payment contracts, life insurance policies, property deeds, leases, and income tax forms until a lawyer, a banker, and several parents supplied specimens. Checks, bank deposit slips, and receipts might be similarly studied. How much more interesting than merely reading about them in books! When students give reports about, say, the newest foods on the market or the best bath towel to buy for the money, they should be encouraged to have specimens to display whenever possible.

The home economics teacher might survey the community for sources of realia. An Italian might be willing to give a demonstration of the making of pizza or a native pasta dish. A grandmother might be willing to teach students how to knit or crochet. Someone else might be willing to bring to class an old patchwork quilt or a few dishes of Englishware that were used in a family in colonial America. Fabrics from Africa that have been handwoven and dyed may be available. A new food, such as green peppercorns, may be examined and used in cooking for a new taste. An old handwritten cookbook may have recipes for testing. The possibilities are endless.

SUGGESTIONS FOR FURTHER LEARNING

1. Consider other ways that teachers and students might use their cameras to provide aids for instruction.
2. Select one of the instructional resources described in this chapter. How might this aid be used to challenge a belief, to apply a principle, or to encourage creativity?
3. Make a special effort to listen to student comments about a poster, an exhibit, or some other display. What are their reactions? Is there a difference between the comments of students who participated in making the display and those of students who are seeing it for the first time? If so, what are the differences, and what is their significance?
4. Experiment with an innovation in the use of displays in home economics. Do some personal brainstorming—as an idea starter, think of the most *unlikely* ways to use displays.
5. Consider ways to use displays materials to keep the community informed about the home economics program.

9

Teaching Resources Part II

Instructional technology has come along with the other technological advances. According to Komoski,[1] a common and limited concept equates technology with machines that promote efficiency and economy. A less constricted concept is that technology manipulates the components of a material environment for the purpose of achieving specific results. Emerging biological and behavioral technologies must not be overlooked. All technologies should contribute to the betterment of the human condition. And the potential of wise use of technology in education should not be underestimated. Snow[2] believes that electronics, automation, and atomic energy are the strongest forces of change that the world has ever experienced. Teachers must understand those forces so that today's students can be educated to master, integrate, and control them tomorrow. Teaching must change to meet innovations.

Teachers must be aware of the many experiences that students have had outside the classroom with television, radio, visits to museums, viewing motion pictures, reading in libraries, listening to records, and visiting art galleries. Outside viewing should be assigned just as outside reading is. Every available resource should be used in the planning of a curriculum.

Each aid should be carefully selected. Teachers and students must clarify their particular needs, problems, or interests. Are certain

[1] P. Kenneth Komoski, "Realizing the Radical Relatedness of Technology and Education," *Educational Technology,* Vol. 12, No. 1 (Jan. 1972), pp. 5–9.

[2] C. P. Snow, *The Two Cultures and the Scientific Revolution* (New York: Cambridge U.P. 1959), p. 31.

values, attitudes, or beliefs to be challenged? Are solutions to certain problems sought? Is an explanation of different patterns of family living in order? Whatever the goal, an appropriate aid, or aids, can be found. Frequently a single aid will not suffice; but the use of many types of materials will enrich the experience of students, and they will be better fortified to tackle their own problems.

PROJECTED TECHNIQUES

Research that has accumulated over a period of years indicates that projected techniques have value for instruction at all grade levels. These instructional aids are no longer on trial.

Television

Television has become firmly established as an educational tool. Today, almost every home has one or more television receivers, and a high proportion of school districts and colleges make regular use of televised instruction. It is predicted that before long public television will reach an audience as large as that reached by commercial television, and that nearly every school will have at least one instructional television system.

Commercial Television

Of the types of television, commercial television is the most familiar. Certain commercial programs may be designated as educational; others, too, do incorporate some educational values. Students may be encouraged to study television programs as an adjunct to their library resources. Programs must be selected for a purpose and with discrimination. Some possibilities are interviews with noted personalities; outstanding drama; reports on social problems, such as the plight of migrant workers, alcoholism, divorce, drugs, and hunger; summaries and analyses of the news; documentaries about life in other countries; political debates; and efforts at community action.

Commercials may be studied for facts and fallacies. Children's programs may be analyzed for content and for the accuracy of the information given in accompanying commercials. Value analysis may be made of the behavior of certain characters in daily or weekly programs. The impact on the family of daily events as depicted in the news may be reviewed. A survey of the television viewing habits of class members may be enlightening to teacher and students alike. Teachers should be concerned about the ways in which television contributes to a change in the perspectives of students.

Public Television

Public television is noncommercial and is operated by nonprofit corporations for the sole purpose of education. In general, the programs focus on instructional courses that may be used in the classroom. Other programs are shown for small children and for adults. The evening programs are dedicated to public affairs and cultural activities.

Public broadcasting has a soaring popularity and a promising future. Programs are produced in a variety of centers in order to represent the country as broadly as possible. One of the serious problems that confronts public television is long-range funding. Public television exists not to compete with commercial television but to provide a unique service that is important to education. Home economics students will find educational or public television a valuable resource for educational purposes as well as for personal improvement.

Cable Television

Cable television is transmitted directly to homes, hospitals and other institutions, libraries, and businesses. In its basic form, according to Hill,[3] cable television consists of an assortment of high-powered television antennas, usually located on a high tower. The television signals from these antennas are amplified and then distributed over coaxial cables to their destinations. Sometimes otherwise unused channels are used. Closed-circuit television as used in schools can often be used successfully with cable transmission.

The advantages of cable television are clear, ghost-free reception even in remote areas; an almost unlimited channel capacity; increased potential for local services; and programming for selective audiences, such as families interested in special theater, sports, or music programs. There is also an opportunity for local groups to plan and produce programs on community concerns.[4]

The possibilities for the educational use of cable television challenge the imagination.[5] Audience participation provides interaction for a variety of purposes, such as reaching homebound or hospitalized students with selected programs, holding a kind of "town meeting of the air," interacting with faculty in other schools in the com-

[3] Roger W. Hill, Jr., "Cable TV," *Today's Education, NEA Journal,* Vol. 59, No. 8 (Nov. 1970), pp. 37–39.

[4] Division of Instruction and Professional Development, Technology Section, NEA, "Special Feature on Cable Television," *Today's Education, NEA Journal,* Vol. 60, No. 8 (Nov. 1971), pp. 52–56.

[5] "Cable TV—Protecting Its Future in Education," *Interpretations: An Occasional Paper* (Washington, D.C.: Association for Supervision and Curriculum Development, Nov. 1971).

munity, and viewing at home programs that encourage professional growth. Computer terminals could be serviced at school or at home. The home economics teachers in a community could plan for creative interaction or plan unusual home and family programs for the community. Home economics teachers will wish to keep alert to the progress of this exciting educational tool, to give consideration to its use, and, if necessary, to participate in community action related to cable television so that educational interests are served.

Instructional Television and Videotape

Television and videotape equipment is becoming an integral part of home economics classes. There are many opportunities for a home economics teacher to use instructional television. Teacher and students may explore the possibilities for its use in class. Television may be used in several rooms in the same building or in several buildings simultaneously. In connection with instructional television, a home economics teacher may play numerous roles: in addition to teaching in her/his own classroom, she/he may be a master or studio teacher for a number of classrooms, a writer, a producer of programs, or a team teacher.

This aid has many potentials. One of the best uses for instructional television is in teaching large groups of students. Videotapes of superior presentations may be reused. A library of superior videotapes might be built. The use of school space may be planned more effectively.

For the student, television is immediate. Every viewer has the equivalent of a front seat. Educational experiences beyond the reach of the classroom may be available to students, such as viewing a sophisticated demonstration, unusual and delicate equipment in operation, rare art, an outstanding teacher, a resource person, or an authority on a subject.

Most methods can be successfully adapted to instructional television. A synchronization of such aids as film clips, slides, magnetic boards or flannelboards, photographs, cartoons, maps, art materials, or real objects is possible. The entire presentation must be dynamic and well organized to attract attention. Visuals should be simple, attract attention, be identifiable to the audience, and be carefully planned ahead of time. Blue, gray, or buff posterboard should be used (white should be avoided). The use of black or India ink is preferred. Sometimes letters become sharper if outlined in chalk, ink, or crayon.

Warch[6] gives a number of excellent suggestions for the use of televi-

[6] Connie Warch, "Learn to Use Television," in a presentation at the annual meeting of the American Home Economics Association, Detroit, Mich., June 28, 1972.

sion. Appropriate programs can be recorded off the air and used when needed. When a field trip is not feasible, the community can be brought into the classroom through videotape. Tapes of techniques may be played again if a student finds it necessary or may be used for review purposes. When teachers share lessons, time is saved. Students should be encouraged to use the camera, to handle the lights, to prepare scripts, and to analyze programs. Use of the camera should not be restricted to boys;[7] girls can be good with cameras, too. The small, portable videotaping units are inexpensive and can be taken into the community, shopping areas, and homes. Again, students can be taught to handle the equipment.

Videotapes in any area of home economics may be prepared by master teachers and shared with others. (This is an excellent in-service device as well.) Videotapes such as field experiences in occupational education by students can interest and challenge other students in home economics. A community project of FHA might be taped and exchanged with other chapters.

Other uses of videotape are (1) a student who has been absent can view the class session; (2) actual shopping experiences can be reviewed; and (3) teacher and students can evaluate student interviews of homemakers or of personnel directors about possible summer or entry-level jobs. Videotapes are excellent for self-evaluation in microteaching and student teaching.

[7] Irene F. Cypher, "Media Memos the Seventies," *Instructor,* Vol. 80, No. 10 (June/July 1971), pp. 33–34.

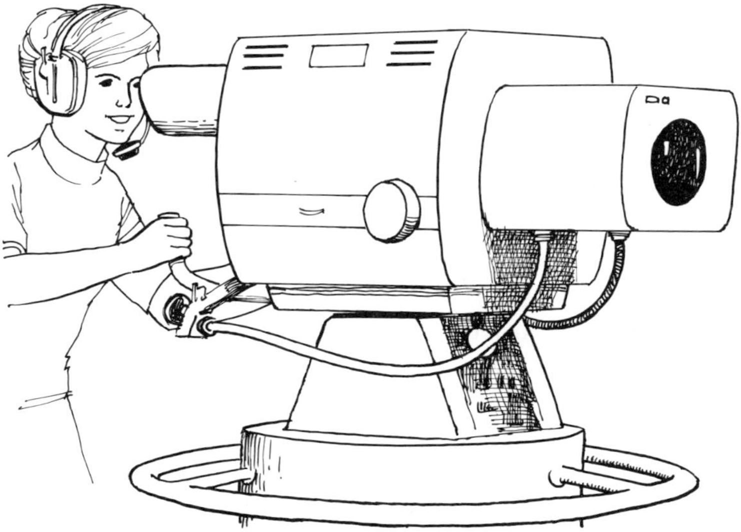

Figure 9–1 A wide range of home economics subjects are available on video tape.

In the psychomotor domain, students have an opportunity to observe themselves in the laboratory to check on their skills, their management decisions, and their ability to work with others. Dramatic techniques, student discussions after a film has been shown, role playing, and other teaching devices are excellent for determining the effectiveness of objectives in the affective and cognitive domains by videotape. One of the most important contributions of videotape is in the development and maintenance of a student's self-concept. To see himself/herself doing something well, to have the support of teacher and other students in analyzing his/her thinking or values and attitudes, to examine his/her performance for possible improvement of further clarification are valuable experiences that television can provide.

Viewing the videotapes from a number of class sessions can be helpful for a teacher's self-evaluation. Seeing oneself in action can be quite revealing. Not only is an appraisal of general effectiveness possible, but mannerisms, innuendos, movements, the handling and appropriateness of teaching aids, and student reactions are equally important. Videotapes of students in action in the classroom and elsewhere have been used in evaluation reports to parents.[8]

Instructional television is not a magical aid, but its contributions to learning can be enhanced when teachers and students work together and experiment with various uses.

Other Types of Television

Satellite television has enormous potential. The possibilities in its use for educational purposes for various sections of the nation and for remote sections of the world are exciting. Legislators, research experts, educators, and others may speak at national conventions through satellite communication. Courses may be taught and broadcast to other parts of the country, such as "Stardate" of the American Dietetic Association (see Chapter 21).

This relay system is being used to link a number of states so that programs can reach classrooms scattered over hundreds of thousands of square miles.[9,10] Education will be lifted into a space-age era.

According to Gabor[11] the video cassette holds promise for combining technology and instruction so that greater stress may be placed

[8] Robert Allender and Jay M. Yanoff, "Using Video for Teacher (and Student)," *Media and Methods,* Vol. 14, No. 2 (Oct. 1977), p. 41.

[9] Walter Coyne, "Education's Rising Star," *American Education,* Vol. 8, No. 9 (Nov. 1972), pp. 16–24.

[10] Kenneth A. Polcyn, "Current Communication Satellite Educational Experimentation: An Overview," *Audiovisual Instruction,* Vol. 18, No. 2 (Feb. 1973), pp. 32–35.

[11] Stanley C. Gabor, "The Video Cassette as an Educational Reality," *Educational Technology.* Vol. 12, No. 4 (Apr. 1972), pp. 35–37.

on self-motivated learning and involvement. The advantages are the elimination of the limitations of space, time, and curriculum. Students can have a structured program of independent study and move through learning sequences at their own pace. Cassettes can be used to supplement regular classroom instruction. By the use of progress tests, a student may be directed into appropriate remedial work or advanced to more appropriate learning sequences. Teachers have more time to give individual attention to students.

Cassettes are portable and can be used in any type of classroom or library. Home use is another possibility. In addition to individualized instruction, the cassette has many uses in group viewing. The potential for preparing homemade cassettes is good. Students and teachers would be spared the winding and rewinding of videotapes. There will be the challenge of aiding industry to prepare effective cassettes for home economics.

Harriet Kohn, Nutrition Specialist in Extension at the University of Nebraska—Lincoln, has developed eight colored video cassettes for use in the preparation of EFNEP (Expanded Food and Nutrition Education Program) aides. Examples of the videotapes are "Mission of the EFNEP Aide," "Nutrition in the Life Cycle," "Cultural Foods of Families," "Recruiting Program Families," and "Working Smarter." The video cassettes are part of a module that includes a guide for the aide and information for the home economist supervisor.

Films

The motion picture offers a means of giving a group a common experience, of appealing to their emotions, of helping them to understand abstract relationships, and of giving them an opportunity to identify themselves with other people, places, and events. Through this medium, the world can literally be brought into the classroom. Educational films are usually 16 mm, one reel taking from twelve to fifteen minutes to show. Films may be secured from a variety of sources, some for a fee but many of them free or costing transportation charges. Films are listed in professional magazines as well as in film catalogues.

Dale[12] lists some important contributions that films can make to teaching. Lessons involving motion are best shown through film. Examples in home economics are laboratory techniques, walking in traffic lanes designed for home furnishings, or the behavior of a child. Films compel sustained attention because outside distractions are removed in a darkened room and the constant movement and change

[12] Edgar Dale, *Audiovisual Methods in Teaching* (New York: The Dryden Press, Holt, 1969), Ch. 14.

in the film hold the viewer's attention. The sense of reality is heightened when students are shown films of family living in other countries, the portrayal of work on an actual job, the building of a house, or incidents in parent–child relationships.

Another contribution of films is the enlargement or reduction of the actual size of objects. Through the use of a camera and a microscope, students can see starch cells, the differences in structure of various fibers used for making fabric, or the structure of vitamins, which cannot be seen by the naked eye. If the camera is at a great distance from the subject, the film can give us a larger view.

The past can be brought into the classroom, for example, through a film about family living in Colonial Williamsburg. A film can highlight the steps of a technique, such as poaching an egg, and may be used again and again.

Motion pictures provide a common experience for all viewers. A film about the problems of an adolescent, an aging man, or a child in the ghetto provides the basis for a discussion that will bring forth personal experiences and ideas about similar situations and hopefully lead to greater understanding.

Films are excellent devices for challenging the values and attitudes of students. Do students hold stereotyped impressions of individuals who differ from them in color, nationality, religion, economic status, age, and so on? Films depicting people of other cultures can be challenging to attitudes.

Films offer an aesthetic experience that can be satisfying. Color, design, music combined with art forms, beautiful homes and furnishings, crafts, unusual table settings, and situations depicting family relationships are possibilities.

Granted that the use of film will be geared to the goals, interests, and needs of the students, each teacher can select and guide the presentation of the film to meet these objectives.

Teachers and students can make their own films. For a report on housing, one student made a film of homes in the slum areas of her community to show the need for federal and community housing projects.

8 mm Films

The 8 mm film has been called the paperback of the audiovisual industry. The 8 mm projecter is lighter to carry and easier to thread and operate than the 16 mm projector. The cartridge film requires no threading or rewinding. It is easily placed in a slot in the machine. This cartridge film lends itself readily to single-concept films. These films range in length from thirty seconds to thirty minutes and are best used where motion is important. Examples are sectioning a grapefruit, dressing an infant, sewing a zipper in a placket, or making a bed. This type of film might be used as a background for class discussions of common problems, such as how to overcome shyness, how to spend money wisely, or how to find a summer job.

Films about the community, experiences while traveling, and home experiences might be adapted for classroom use. These films might be made by the teacher or the students.

Filmstrips

Filmstrips do not have the dramatic appeal of films, but other attributes of this aid make it a valuable teaching device. Brown et al.[13] call filmstrips "a headful in a handful," an apt description of these aids. Compact, simple to use, and requiring little space for storage, filmstrips consist of a series of still pictures and captions arranged in sequence on 35 mm film to tell a complete story. Filmstrips consist of from twenty to fifty frames. Longer filmstrips are more limited in use owing to the time it takes to project them. Filmstrips are available in black-and-white and in color. When a commentary, recorded on discs or tape, accompanies it, the filmstrip is called a *sound slide-film.* In addition to the filmstrip projector, a record player or cassette player is needed.

Filmstrips can be used in home economics in many ways. Show-how filmstrips are effective in teaching the skills of food preparation, clothing construction, buying, home furnishing, and home management. Filmstrips about infant and child feeding, good manners at home, or types of food preparation are also available. Aesthetic appreciation can also be emphasized. Interest in foods of other countries can be stimulated by filmstrips. Relating the importance of equipment to the preparation of food is another area to be explored. Filmstrips can be used for reviewing or reinforcing learning, for highlighting important points in a textbook, or for individual study with a hand viewer.

Many filmstrips are available for use in home economics courses, hence certain criteria for selecting from among them must be used. Is the filmstrip appropriate for the maturity of the students to whom it is to be shown? Will it make a logical contribution to the learning of these students? Is it technically and educationally well produced? Is the subject matter accurate and up-to-date?

Sources of filmstrips are listed in the *Educational Media Index,*[14]

[13] James W. Brown, Richard B. Lewis, and Fred F. Harcleroad, *A-V Instruction Materials and Methods* (New York: McGraw-Hill, 1977), pp. 190–195.

[14] New York: McGraw-Hill, issued since 1964. In addition to filmstrips, includes films, videotapes, kinescopes, recordings, tapes, models, slides, transparencies, cross-media kits, and programmed instruction.

Figure 9–2 A student may use a sound filmstrip in individual study.

the NICEM Indexes,[15] and in special sections of home economics magazines. Many filmstrips are available free from business firms. The U.S. Department of Agriculture and other government agencies offer many excellent filmstrips.[16]

Through the use of frosted film,[17] students may prepare their own filmstrips. Students may use ball-point pens, felt-tip markers, pencils, grease pencils, a common pin, or the typewriter to make their own captions and drawings. A storyboard with the format for each filmstrip must be planned beforehand. A storyboard consists of rough artwork, the message, or other material for each frame in a filmstrip, film, videotape, or television program. A storyboard allows one to check on the sequence of the frames and to be certain that all points

[15] Los Angeles: National Information Center for Educational Media, University Park, University of California. Includes indexes to other aids.

[16] *Filmstrips and Slide Series*, U.S. Department of Agriculture, Agricultural Handbook No. 222 (Washington, D.C.: Superintendent of Documents, U.S. Government Printing Office).

[17] May be purchased from Starex Inc., 655 Schuyler Ave., Kearny, N.J. 07032.

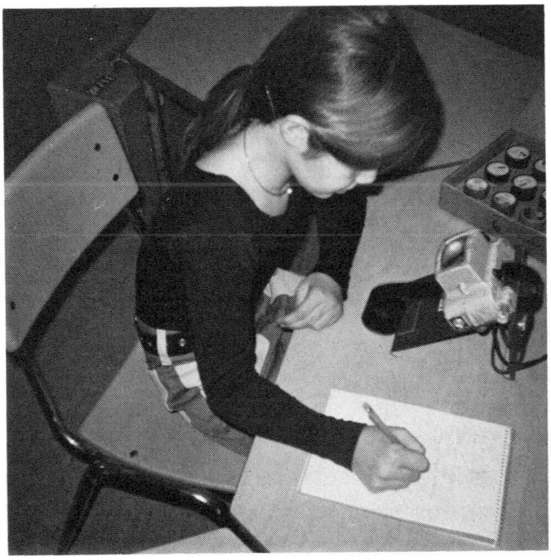

Figure 9–3 A student may use a filmstrip viewer in preparing a committee report. (USDA Photo)

have been covered as desired. Keep the material on each frame to a minimum for strong visual impact. The film may be cleaned and reused. Slides may also be prepared with frosted film.

Slides

Slides are created either photographically or by some art process, usually drawing or painting. Home economists adept in the use of the camera can become proficient in filming slides appropriate to their field. Slides made with a 35 mm camera and color film are most striking, producing 2″ × 2″ color transparencies. Slides are projected by a slide projector suited to their size. A projector for the 2″ × 2″ slides may be attached to a filmstrip projector. A slide projector for 3⅜″ × 4″ slides is sometimes attached to an opaque projector for projection of charts, tables, and drawings.

Inexpensive 2″ × 2″ slides may be made from a filmstrip. Each frame must be cut to a size of 1½″ × 1½″ and sealed in a slide mount for 126 size and 1½″ × 1¼″ for size 136 slide mount. An 8½″ × 11″ transparency can be made into forty-two 2″ × 2″ slides. Before being cut, each square should be marked with soft pencil according to the size of the slide mount. Each slide might have a written or typewritten message or artwork. The slides may be cut and mounted as described above. Other creative techniques have possibilities. A student could prepare a class report, or an entire class may wish to tell the story of a community activity by use of this method.[18]

[18] Frank A. Hollick, "Cheap Graphic Slides," *Media and Methods*, Vol. 8 (Apr. 1972), p. 48.

Silhouettes of opaque paper may be mounted on a glass plate to make interesting slides to depict, say, good and poor posture or the relation of being overweight or underweight to personal appearance. Textiles, yarns, and other opaque substances can be used instead of paper in making effective silhouettes.

Nearly every area of home economics can profit from the intelligent use of slides. The following suggestions serve merely to indicate the scope of the field.

Use of Slides in Home Economics

In nutrition, slides can be designed to show what dietary modifications are necessary in the planning of meals for family members who are allergic to certain foods or are underweight or overweight. Showing slides of nutritious, low-calorie foods, for example, is more dramatic, and therefore more effective, than merely naming and discussing them.

One foods teacher made an interesting collection of slides showing traditional dishes of other countries, which the class found useful in its study of international foods. Slides of attractive snacks, desserts, vegetable dishes, and entrees can be used to establish standards for the appearance of prepared foods.

Some of the many factors to be considered in furnishing a home can be graphically highlighted by the use of slides. One New York University graduate student made slides to show how she furnished a one-room apartment spending a minimal sum. The slides demonstrated vividly just how a clever room arrangement was attained by the ingenious use of secondhand furniture and remnants for draperies, pillows, and upholstery. How color, line, and texture were suited to the interests and personalities of the occupants was highlighted, as was the economy of expenditure.

Slides are valuable, too, in providing permanent records of experiences or occasions; in showing pictorial evidence of the progress students have made in acquiring skills or improving posture or personal appearance; and in giving a comprehensive view of the work done in certain professional areas in home economics. In one school, slides have been made showing many aspects of the home economics program—class activities, highlights of student trips into the community, and field or home experiences. These slides have been reshuffled to suit various occasions, and certain ones have been formed into specific programs. For instance, some slides, with appropriate commentary, have been shown to prospective students invited to visit the home economics department. They may be borrowed by other teachers or schools, shown at PTA meetings, or used at various other community functions. Some have been shown to give beginning home economics students a foretaste of the activities in store for them. To keep the file up-to-date, new slides are added from time to time, ineffective ones discarded, and fresh programs made to suit new purposes. A tape-recorded commentary may accompany the slides.

Slides for Rental or Purchase

Schools can purchase, rent, or borrow slides from the following sources, among many others. The Museum of Modern Art in New York City has slides for sale on housing and home furnishings. The Society for Visual Education in Chicago has many slides for sale, including some of unusual fruits and vegetables. The American Dietetic Association 430 North Michigan Avenue, Chicago, Illnois 60611, and the American Home Economics Association 2010 Massachusetts Avenue, NW, Washington, D.C. 20036, have sets of slides on career possibilities for loan or purchase.

Overhead Projections

The overhead projector offers an unusually versatile and exciting challenge to the imagination of every teacher of home economics. The projector is simple to operate and requires little maintenance. It projects light through black-and-white or color transparencies made on sheets of acetate film, usually 7″ × 7″ or 10″ × 10″. The image is projected onto a screen and is clearly visible in a fully lighted room. The teacher faces her/his class and maintains eye contact with them during the presentation. Looking at the transparency on the stage of the projector makes it unnecessary to look at the screen.

Effective teaching ideas can be preserved for future use, for transparencies can be stored and used again and again. A library of transparencies can be purchased, or the teacher may make her/his own. The teacher can select material, arrange it as she/he desires, and narrate for her/his own visuals rather than depending on someone else's commentary. It is possible to underline key words or to point to parts of a diagram that require special attention.

Step-by-step learning can be provided through the use of overlays (not more than five). The revelation presentation is another technique: all but the first point are covered with a plain piece of paper. After discussing one point, the teacher moves to the next.

The acetate film for transparencies is available in rolls (which provide a continuous surface for writing), in large sheets, and in sheets cut to exact size for use in the projector.

Transparencies may be prepared prior to use, or the teacher can create transparencies while she/he lectures, working much as she/he would at a chalkboard, writing important points with a china marking pencil or a grease pencil. Felt-tip markers in many colors can be used for writing or marking diagrams, charts, or similar visuals. Wide-pointed pens, found in art departments, are especially effective if used with special acetate inks. Varicolored pencils produce fine lines for special detail.

Plain or patterned transparent acetate tape, which is available in a wide variety of colors and widths, is helpful in the preparation of charts and graphs. These tapes can be used as a border for a transparency, to outline an object, and for arrows or other symbols.

Preparing Transparencies

The creation of transparencies is guided by a consideration of the ways light is controlled as it passes to the screen.[19] Opaque materials block out light. In home economics, silhouettes might be made of young children at various ages to indicate important aspects of physical development. In a similar manner, silhouettes might be made of ill-fitting clothes or of the latest fashion silhouettes. Forms of opaque paper may be attached to the transparency or laid on. Real things can be used to cast outlines, such as sewing machine parts, lace or transparent fabrics, a comb, a key, or a pen or pencil. Some of these items might be used for projective techniques, such as "What comes to mind when you see a key?"

Color may be introduced through the use of colored, translucent inks, cellophanes, or foils that color the light. The typewriter may be used for captions, the outlining of steps, or directions. A piece of clear cellophane is sandwiched between two pieces of carbon paper with the carbon-coated face against the plastic. Heavily coated red carbon is recommended. The typing is done directly on the carbon paper. Typing will appear on both sides of the plastic and the image is projected better.

Writing or drawing with a grease pencil produces a black shadow on the screen. It may be used on transparencies prepared before class use. To contribute to interest and effectiveness, the teacher can place a sheet of clear plastic over a prepared transparency and write words or symbols that enhance the presentation: she/he can make a question mark or an exclamation point, encircle a portion of the material, X out a line or a part of the material, or add material as the class members make suggestions.

Another dramatic possibility is to take a carbon-coated plastic film and write or draw with a stylus or ball-point pen while talking. The results are white lines on a black field. A bare outline might be made of a gun or a knife as an introduction to a discussion of the influence

[19] Brown, Lewis, and Harcleroad, op. cit., pp. 128–144.

of crime on the family, a ring to open the question of marriage or non-marriage, or a cigarette to discuss the effect of smoking or drugs on an individual. The date of a class meeting might be written to start a discussion along these lines: "What has happened to you today that enables you to characterize the day?" "What were your positive and negative feelings and why?" "Over which portions did you have control?" "Over which ones did you not have control?" "Who did control them?" "What would you have done differently and why?" "What were your relations with people? Discuss them." "Were any beliefs strengthened or weakened today?"

Suggestions for Use

In home furnishings classes, floor plans can be projected and cut-outs of furniture arranged on the screen by a student for other students to evaluate or suggest rearrangements. Full-color transparencies of attractive room settings or storage facilities may be made and projected for discussion and evaluation. Students can present their own room designs on transparencies. Overlays can be used to develop the furnishing of a room as a step-by-step process.

In clothing classes, colored plastic film can be used to demonstrate various color schemes. Silhouettes can be drawn on a transparency, and with the use of overlays, harmonies of line, mass, and color can be demonstrated. Accessories, such as scarves, jewelry, and handbags, can be projected on basic silhouettes to dramatize their effects.

In nutrition, interesting charts can be made of colored tapes to highlight the nutritive values of foods within a food group, such as fruits and vegetables. Cost comparisons of foods that yield similar nutritive values can also be dramatically presented. The analysis of a student's diet in front of the class, just as the English teacher corrects a paper, can be valuable. Studying the foods of others countries through sketches or colored reproductions is another possibility.

In studies of family life, a transparency may be made of an emotionally charged picture. Students can then write a paragraph about it, develop a story, or evaluate the action that appears to be taking place. This procedure may yield insights into students' values, attitudes, and beliefs. Statistics about various aspects of family living can be graphically projected at appropriate times.

In food classes, a map of the United States or the world can be made on a transparency. Students can prepare overlays to illustrate sources of important family foods, sections of the world that lack certain nutritious foods, the effects of various social factors on food habits, and so on.

Recipes, steps in food preparation and clothing constuction, stages of maturity in child development, the preparation of family budgets, and the steps in decision making lend themselves to creative interpretations on transparencies.

The following idea was borrowed from an animal husbandry class. Eggs of different grades are broken individually into clear glass dishes and projected. The two types of translucent albumen are easily distinguishable, and distinction among grades can be discerned.

A kind of programmed instruction can be effected with the overhead projector. First, a test with the answers covered is projected. Students write their answers on a sheet of paper. Next, the teacher uncovers the answers on the transparency and students correct their mistakes immediately. This procedure saves time and reinforces learning.

Opaque Projections

An opaque projector is a versatile instrument that can project almost any kind of two-dimensional, nontransparent material, such as pictures, photographs, and diagrams; book pages; newspaper clippings; magazine color plates showing table settings, fashion designs, foods, room arrangements, and the like; textiles, the textures of which are accentuated by the projector; cartoons, maps, postcards, and drawings; flat objects or specimens; handwritten data; and typed information. Some machines have a pointer arrangement so that a teacher may pinpoint items on the material being shown. A number of pictures hinged together in an order sequence permit the examination of a step-by-step process, such as how to modify the behavior of a small child. Drawings with captions can be prepared by students on a strip of paper that can be pushed through the projector.

The primary advantages of this type of projection are low cost, ease of use, suitability to a wide range of materials, and dramatic appeal. Materials for projection are easily prepared. The chief disadvantage is that the room must be very dark for good projection.

AUDIO AIDS

Listening aids add another dimension to the learning of students, and the use of tapes, recordings, and similar devices is receiving more emphasis in education.

Listening

If students are to realize the greatest benefit from audio aids, they may have to be taught how to listen. Research indicates that the average person spends 42 per cent of his time listening, 32 per cent speaking, and 16 per cent reading. Listening is closely correlated with thinking and speaking and with reading and writing skills. There are a number of factors that influence the efficacy of listening, according to Taylor.[20] When the message is challenging, the environment conducive, the health of the listener good, and her/his attitude toward learning positive, then listening is beneficial. Other factors include the ability of the individual to understand the meaning of spoken words or to identify associations with them. In addition, the listener must organize the ideas conveyed in some meaningful manner and be sensitive to the moods or nuances of the speaker or the source of communication. Dale[21] suggests that people stop listening when too many ideas are being fired at them too fast. When speakers do not suggest an action, listeners' attentions drifts. Persons who are involved hear accurately; a keen listener has questions in mind that he/she hopes will be answered.

Classroom activities that can demonstrate the importance of listening carefully are recommended. Myers[22] has suggested an experience that has been adapted for home economics. Students are each asked to bring to class a single-panel cartoon that is appropriate to the topic being studied; then each student is supplied with paper, pencil, and crayons. One student at a time, without allowing the others to see his/her cartoon, reads the caption, just once, so that everyone can hear it. The other students write the caption as recalled, then draw a cartoon appropriate to the caption. In graphic terms, this activity shows how students differ in the interpretation of short messages as well as the degree of their failure in listening.

Two students may be selected as interviewer and interviewee. The rest of the students act as observers. The interviewer should be limited to eight or nine questions on a topic that is of high interest selected by teacher and students. Later, the observers may ask questions of the interviewer and determine how adequately the interviewer has listened. The interviewee may be questioned about the clarity of the questions asked to determine his/her listening acuity.

Tape Recordings and Cassettes

Tape recordings are becoming widening avenues of communication. Schools trade tapes with one another, as do students and teach-

[20] Sandford E. Taylor, *Listening, What Research Says to the Teacher,* No. 29 (Washington, D.C.: Department of Classroom Teachers and American Educational Research Association of the National Education Association, 1964).

[21] Edgar Dale, "Why Don't We Listen?" *The Newsletter,* Vol. 28, No. 6 (March 1963), pp. 1–4.

[22] R. E. Myers, "Climb on an Empty Bandwagon: Learning and Listening," *Instructor,* Vol. 81, No. 3 (Nov. 1971), pp. 99–102.

ers throughout the world. A class might correspond by tape with students in Armed Forces Dependents Schools or in schools founded by American firms for the children of their employees stationed abroad.

For class use, short, original plays depicting situations appropriate to child development or family-life classes can be taped. Interviews with young homemakers about the problems of food buying or with an elderly person about her/his nutrition problems are other possibilities. Imaginative teachers will think of many ways to use excellent teaching tool.

The "gossip clinic," a variant of the old game of "rumor," is an effective method of emphasizing the difficulties of communication, and here, too, the tape recorder can be used. Have one student tell another about a simple classroom incident or other suitable situation, recording his tale. The recording is continued as the second student relates the incident to a third, who has not overheard the previous conversation, and so on. This can be done with five or more students, who ultimately analyze the recording to discover where communications broke down and to speculate about the possible reasons for whatever misinterpretation cropped up in the retellings.

Cypher[23] makes other suggestions for the use of the tape recorder. On field trips, a recorder can be used to tape the comments of guides or leaders, student commentaries as the trip progresses, and any special sound effects. The tape may be synchronized with photographs that have been taken of the trip. Instead of a written report, students should be permitted to record their ideas. Some students like the freedom and may be more creative. A tape of a discussion in family life can be used to evaluate student thinking, analysis, contribution, soundness, and other criteria that have been established by teacher and students.

Tapes may be prepared for use on reels or as cassettes. The latter are more compact than reels and are especially handy if a portable tape recorder is used. Students should be encouraged to make creative recordings of ideas, experiences, original drama, and poetry. With music and other effects, students may enhance the presentation of a topic such as "Living in a Commune," "Taking a Trip" (drugs), or "Generation Gap."

Recordings

One of the promising practices in teaching home economics is the use of popular phonograph records. This auditory aid is particularly helpful in the highlighting of certain aspects of personal, social, and family living as experienced by individuals in the group.

[23] Op. cit., p. 33.

Recordings demand a minimum of effort in setup and operation. If the school does not have a phonograph, one can usually be borrowed. Only a small portion of the class period need be devoted to the playing of recordings, yet in that interval, an appeal can be made to the emotions and intellects of the listeners, providing a background for lively discussion.

The methods for using recordings will vary with the particular needs of the group. Playing a recording should not be an extraneous experience but should be incorporated into the plans and purposes of a program. Recordings can be used in practically every area of home economics and at all levels.

Youth's music[24] points to a distinctive culture. Teachers might broaden their awareness of rock music because it is an expression of youth's frustrations, beliefs, and hopes. Through this medium the young sometimes depict values that seem counter to the power orientation, materialism, and alienation that they feel is typical of the adult world. In contrast, their focus appears to be on human beings.

Folk and rock music may be effectively used in family-life classes. Teachers may listen to disc jockeys to hear the latest records and especially the message given by the lyrics. Students may suggest some of their favorite recordings. Recordings reveal many feelings about family relationships that could spur discussion in the classroom. Students might be asked what the song communicates to them. A section describing the attributes of many cities from the recording "Manhattan Tower"[25] provides a good background for a discussion of the intangibles that make an individual or a family like or dislike where they live.

The enterprising teacher might profitably make a survey of recordings suitable for other areas of home economics. An examination of record catalog should furnish ideas, and radio programs of recorded music offer preview possibilities. Students themselves frequently suggest records that come to their attention. Available on newstands are anthologies of lyrics of popular songs.

Telephone

Courses may be taught by telephone when there are insufficient students or if students in various locations desire the same course. For example, a high school found that some of its students needed a course in applied chemistry in order to secure a certain position. Ar-

[24] Ideas on use of rock music excerpted from Henrietta Fleck and Kristina Markle, "Learning from Rock," *Forecast for Home Economics,* Vol. 16, No. 2 (Oct. 1970), pp. 57, 82.

[25] "Manhattan Tower," composer, Gordon Jenkins; artist, Beverly Mahr, Decca recording 40087, Side 3, 78 rpm.

rangements were made to take the course by telephone with teachers in another town. In another high school, the number of students who desired a course in ecology far exceeded the supply of qualified teachers. The problem was solved by the use of a portable conference telephone. The telephone has a loudspeaker built in for listening and two microphones for asking questions. Push buttons keep the microphones always under the teacher's control. Students who have to be away from school for lengthy periods can keep up-to-date with a telephone system called Tele-Class. The teacher assembles her/his class by telephone. Conversation is possible with the teacher and with other students. If the teacher wishes to speak to a child privately, she/he touches a button.

Through an amplified telephone system called Telelecture, students can hear guest speakers talk to them at a time in their learning when such a resource is helpful. For instance, students in a discussion on various aspects of family finances could hear a banker outline a bank's services; the head of the credit department in a department store describe the operation of a charge account; or a stock broker explain investment plans. Two or more classes in distant cities can be linked together by telephone so that their students can share experiences, or several home economics departments could be linked by Telelecture to profit from the ideas of an outstanding consultant. A supervisor or college professor could lecture to hundreds of teachers miles away from the speaker and from each other. The Telelecture can be enhanced by the use of slides or transparencies shown concurrently to give a feeling of personal contact with the speaker.

The telephonic Electrowriter enables one to transmit written messages over the telephone wires to an audience while talking to that audience by telephone. The material must be written or drawn. The lecturer uses a special stylus and writes on a roll of paper. What he/she writes is transmitted almost instantly from one telephone to another equipped with a receiver, the stylus of which reproduces the sender's message on a screen. The stylus can also be made to point to parts of the written message that the speaker wishes to emphasize. When a member of the audience questions the speaker and figures or drawings are needed to amplify the answer, the speaker may use the Electrowriter for illustrative purposes.

Radio

Radio is more than ever a powerful medium of communication, and the home economics teacher should make every use of it. Radio's ability to call up mental imagery is great. On shortwave receivers, programs from other countries may be heard; the reception from many nations is usually good. Practically every home in the United

Figure 9–4 Students might listen to a disc jockey program on radio to discover lyrics that have meaning for personal and family living.

States has one or more radio sets. Nearly every car has a radio, and portable radios accompany many people almost every place they go.

If there is a local radio station that cooperates with the school, students might participate in programs that are an extension of their classroom activities. Students might offer hints about homemaking, child care, family relations, or consumer education, selecting topics that require only a few seconds to outline nicely. Such short items, only twenty-five to one hundred words in length, could be prepared in connection with a topic they are studying.

Listening to a disc jockey's program to identify personal and family values or problems highlighted in the recordings might be an interesting homework assignment. The teacher or the students could tape-record outstanding radio programs for use later in the classroom.

USE OF MULTIPLE MEDIA

Interest is increased and better sustained when students are presented with several effectively combined media. Bizarre or exotic effects should be avoided.

Students can assist in planning and presenting shows combining slides with tape-recorded sound effects. For example, many students do not eat an adequate breakfast. To develop enthusiasm for breakfast, a short program to be given during an assembly period or to club or home room groups could combine attractive slides of breakfast foods with the sounds of foods being prepared—bacon sizzling, toast popping, a milk shake being prepared in a blender, juice being poured, or the crackle of milk being poured on dry cereal. A cartoon effect on some or all of the slides might add extra appeal. In addition to the sound effects, students might give a running commentary on the importance of breakfast. The sounds should be synchronized with a storyboard of slides in sequence.

Projected materials can be used with nonprojected demonstrations. For a fashion show backdrop, a slide of a department store window or a street in Paris or New York might be projected on a rear projection screen on the back wall. For role playing or short dramatic sketches, a slide of a living room or kitchen wall can simulate the background and lend realism. Slides with captions may be flashed on the wall, and students might pantomime action to accompany the ideas. The teacher might consider how to use a flannelboard and a tape, a recording and a minute drama, or a print of a famous painting and a recording of a poem.

RESOURCES IN THE GRAPHIC ARTS

Among the basic teaching materials are textbooks, reference books, newspapers, pamphlets, magazines, business-sponsored aids, and photographs. It is important that students learn to use these resources wisely.

Textbooks and Reference Books

What makes a good textbook? A textbook is good to the extent that it helps to accomplish educational goals. Cronbach and his associates believe that a textbook should permit the learner to "perceive new relationships, new patterns, and new forces as bearing a positive significance to his/her activities."[26] Educators feel that a good textbook builds on a student's past experiences and does so in such a way as to prepare him/her for subsequent work in a given area. A good textbook is also adapted to students' readiness—their reading readiness, of course, and their emotional, experiential, and intellectual readiness as well. Many textbooks neglect the social and family roles of blacks and other minority groups in the content and the illustrations. Teachers are charged to select texts that are appropriate and acceptable for *all* students.[27]

The home economics teacher might review textbooks and reference books against the following criteria. The books should have accurate, up-to-date information in the economic, psychological, sociological, and scientific aspects of every area of home economics education; principles, concepts, and generalizations should be emphasized. Students should be able to find their textbooks' answers to questions they may have about their physical, emotional, intellectual, and social development. Are the cognitive, affective, and psychomotor domains emphasized? The books should include comparisons of family life in other lands as well as comparisons of cultural differences within the United States. Textbooks should also suggest to students ways to apply the knowledge they gain to their particular needs, interests, problems, style of living, family organization, and the like, perhaps by suggesting activities or posing questions. Textbook explanations should be readable and easy to understand.

A textbook must be supplemented with many references so that students have access to a wealth of information, different points of view, and various approaches to the same topic. These books must be selected as carefully as a text is. Here is an opportunity for a teacher to recognize individual differences. The available references books may vary in reading difficulty and in presentation and may be useful to students of varying backgrounds and abilities. Some reference books give general background information, for example, a textile dictionary, cookbooks, and encyclopedias on homemaking. Occupational education demand books pertinent to that area. Some reference books should be available in the school library; others will have to be searched out elsewhere. Some advanced courses do not have an available textbook, so that students must do their background reading by using many references.

[26] Lee J. Cronbach (ed.), *Text Materials in Modern Education* (Urbana, Ill.: U. Illinois Press, 1955), p. 90.

[27] Max Rosenberg, "Textbooks: Do They Meet Fair Minority Group Standards?" *Educational Leadership*, Vol. 30, No. 2 (Nov. 1972), pp. 141–143.

Paperback Books

The wide range of paperbacks, which vary in content, length, complexity, and readability, has stimulated students to more independent and individualized study.[28] The distribution of these low-cost books has not only led to a kind of educational revolution in the schools but has developed a mass culture that has an impact in and out of schools. The ready availability of books with timely information should encourage students to develop desirable reading habits that will be reflected in later life.

The home economics teacher will find it profitable—and fun—to browse through the paperback offerings of bookstores, supermarkets, drug stores, and other shops for books that might be of use in her/his classroom. Available are books on nutrition, child development, housing, and consumer education; cookbooks, many of them specializing in the recipes of nations around the world; how-to-do-it books on such subjects as how to refinish furniture or make toys; books geared to the problems and interests of the teenager; and fiction that might be used in discussions of family life. The teacher may also discover books that would be helpful in the planning of the curriculum, such as works on sociology, education, or psychology.

Students should be encouraged to find paperbacks appropriate to home economics. Fiction paperbacks may give students insights into the problems of their concern, such as drugs, death, morals, unmarried mothers, divorced parents, and getting a job. (See Chapter 5.) Many schools have their own paperback bookstores, and the home economics teacher may suggest appropriate titles to stock for his/her students' use. FHA, PTA, and service clubs may be willing to furnish paperbacks for the home economics department library. Paperback trading posts have been established in some schools so that students may exchange paperbacks. (Stronger covers can be made for the paperbacks that are read frequently.) If school policies permit, students may wish to join the paperback book club of a reputable publisher in order to buy books at lower cost.

Newspapers

Most people take newspapers for granted, but they are among the most versatile teaching aids available to the home economics instructor. Newspapers can be used to advantage in every phase of the subject.

The news section is almost certain to contain human interest

[28] Vivienne Anderson, *Paperbacks in Education* (New York: Teachers College Press, Columbia University, 1966), p. xiii.

stories about individuals and families. A story about a family that has found a unique approach to a universal problem is an example. A newspaper clipping, particularly if it contains something controversial, can be a good opener for a discussion on family relations, consumer education, child care, or home management. Students might

Figure 9–5 Teachers and students might browse through paperbacks displayed in bookstores, supermarkets, and drug stores for appropriate related to home economics. (Educational Facilities, Inc.)

be asked to clip news stories relating to the subject being studied. A classroom bulletin board with a daily change of such clippings could add much to the students' understanding of the subject.

The classified advertisements can be used in a number of ways. An appreciation of the wide range of skills required to produce clothing for a family can be gained through an examination of the help-wanted listings for various jobs in the clothing industry—models, fitters, textile experts, factory workers, department store clerks, and so on. The food or furniture industries can be examined in the same way. Rents and housing facilities in different section of the community may be compared through a study of the real estate listings. Finding livable, inexpensive housing for a newly married couple can be a challenge to students concerned about this problem. Students may also be interested in analyzing the available jobs from the standpoint of the skills required and the wages, the benefits, and other special inducements.

Display advertisements give the teacher innumerable suggestions for teaching materials. A classroom study of the advertised prices of the goods offered by different stores could be followed by a field trip to the stores to validate the information in and the accuracy of the advertisements. Comparisons might be made of the same article, such as a coat, pants, or a dress, as advertised by various stores—stores of the same size or in the same location; stores in different locations, such as a suburban shopping center and a store in the city; or a department store with a specialty shop or a boutique. Students may find it enlightening to analyze the clientele to which an advertisement is geared: the age, the economic or social level, or the interest of the buyer.

Students may be encouraged to use the advertising technique to write their own advertisements for eating nutritious snacks, for avoiding crash reducing diets, or for examining carefully the merchandise they buy.

The woman's page of a newspaper offers timely pictures and stories about new products and equipment; foods, recipes, and menu planning; fashions, trends in home furnishings, and new developments in textiles; beauty hints; articles on marriage and child care; and suggestions for family finances. Also to be found on the woman's page are articles about timely topics such as the effects on family life of drug addiction and women's liberation, making things to sell, unusual careers, and profiles of outstanding women. All of the articles on the woman's page can be criticized for accuracy by students in the course of their study of the various aspects of home economics. Students might also provide their own answers to the problems posed in the advice columns.

From newspaper listings, students might study a week's schedule of radio or television programs to decide which would be worthwhile for a whole family to watch. The motion pictures to be seen on television or in the local theater can be evaluated through the reviews and the advertisements. Book reviews can be helpful to one selecting books for personal and family libraries.

It behooves a teacher to be a newspaper reader. The classroom cannot shut out the problems of the world, and the teacher has an obligation to point out to her/his students the role that newspapers play in their lives. The newspaper that comes into the home day after day through the years is bound to be a powerful force in the development of attitudes and values in parents and their children.

The class might profitably establish criteria for judging a newspaper. How do different family members rate the paper? Which sections are most popular? To what extent are the special services, rendered by a paper—the advertisements, the amusement section, the book reviews, and so on—used? Is there something in the paper for every member of the family? What are its editorial policies?

Local newspapers are an excellent source of information about the community, the students, and their families, and the local newspapers available in one's community might be evaluated in terms of the criteria the students establish. A local editor could be invited to talk to the class. A supervised trip through a newspaper plant is always interesting. Students might write news stories for the local newspaper that describe interesting class activities or that grow out of the current unit of study, for example, an article on the cost of health foods. Students may also want to write letters to the editor about problems in the community that have a personal or family impact.

Newspapers from different sections of the country and different parts of the world might be brought into the classroom. Single copies of the same date of a few newspapers from various regions can be purchased for a small sum. *The Ayers Newspaper Guide* gives the addresses of American newspapers. Newspapers with wide circulation and many news sources include *The Baltimore Sun, The Miami Herald, The New York Times, The Christian Science Monitor, The Cleveland Plain Dealer, The Des Moines Register, The St. Louis Post-Dispatch, The Chicago Tribune, The New York Daily News, The Atlanta Constitution, The Washington (D.C.) Post, The New Orleans Times-Picayune,* and *The Los Angeles Times.* Any of several others might be selected. Copies of *The London Times* or papers from other parts of the world would be of interest. *The Wall Street Journal* provides excellent coverage of new products, new trends in housing and education, and consumer information. If a student examines these newspapers, he/she can pinpoint local influences on family life, such as climate, the type of industry, the apparent goals of the city, the leisure-time activities available, the types of jobs open, and the emphasis in major local news stories. Students might make a project of imagining themselves residents of different localities for a day.

Magazines

Magazines bring a wealth of valuable material to a teacher. Obviously the home economics teacher will be familiar with her/his own professional magazines: *Journal of Home Economics, Journal of the American Dietetic Association, Journal of Marriage and Family Living, Home Economics Research Journal, Forecast for Home Economics, Food Technology, Illinois Teacher,* and *VocEd.* Some of the other magazines that may help the teacher keep up-to-date in education are *Educational Leadership, The Harvard Educational Review, The Clearinghouse, Instructor, Teacher, AudioVisual Instruction, Childhood Education, Learning, Today's Education, American Education,* and *Media and Methods.* Among the many other magazines that will be challenging and broadening for the teacher are *Daedalus, Social Policy, Signs, Saturday Review, Annals of the American Academy of Political and Social Science, The Gerontologist, Harpers, Atlantic, Psychology Today,* and *The Futurist.* Information about national and

Figure 9–6 Magazines have valuable information and resources for both students and teacher. (*New Yorker Magazine*)

international problems may be secured from such magazines as *Time, Fortune, Newsweek, Business Week,* and *U.S. News and World Report.*

The many magazines geared to the home contain articles that students might evaluate for accuracy, information, and new trends. The illustrations in these magazines provide bulletin board material and other teaching aids. Some well-known magazines in this field are *Good Housekeeping, McCalls, Ladies' Home Journal, Better Homes and Gardens, Redbook, Woman's Day, Family Circle,* and *Parents' Magazine.*

Magazines for teenagers and young adults can provide information and classroom material for the home economics teacher. Such magazines include *Seventeen, CO-ED, Ingenue, Glamour, Mademoiselle,* and *Redbook.* Some of the ideas found in sophisticated magazines such as *Vogue, Harper's Bazaar, House and Garden,* and *House Beautiful* might be adapted for class use. Magazines for young students include *CO-ED, American Girl,* and *Boy's Life.*

A home economics teacher cannot be expected to read all of the magazines listed here as well as the many others. She/he must choose the magazines that suit her/his purposes best. Picking up an unfamiliar magazine occasionally from a newsstand can prove stimulating. Exchanging magazines with friends and fellow teachers will widen resources. The chief advantages of any magazine are its up-to-date materials, its articles by authorities, and its wealth of illustrative materials.

Students might bring favorite magazines to class and report on their appeal. This information can be revealing to a teacher. What do her/his students consider important? What appear to be omissions of interest? How may she/he amend the curriculum to broaden the students interests? How may reading be stimulated?

Pamphlets

Among the most authoritative sources of teaching materials are government pamphlets. Teachers may secure these pamphlets from the U.S. Department of Agriculture, the Children's Bureau, and other agencies. Every home economics teacher should be on the mailing list for the publications catalog of the U.S. Government Printing Office.[29] On this comprehensive list are many bulletins appropriate for classroom use. Pamphlets are also available from social institutions, community organizations, state and county government agencies, magazines, industry, life insurance companies, and so on. The

[29] *Selected United States Government Publications,* issued biweekly by the Superintendent of Documents, U.S. Government Printing Office, Washington, D.C. 20402. Free.

teacher must select carefully so that accurate and interesting materials can be placed in the hands of her/his students. Many of these publications are free or very inexpensive.

Cartoons

Among the most effective yet inexpensive teaching aids is the cartoon; its succinct, humorous message is highly memorable to the reader. There are limitless ways in which cartoons can be used. Cartoons may be found in daily newspapers and in magazines such as the *New Yorker.*

The cartoon can be used to highlight students' beliefs about a family issue or problem; students' social sensitivities might be aroused and challenged when they examine their responses to cartoons about national and international situations that have an impact on family living. Students often read newspapers and listen to radio reports with greater discernment as a result of such an experience. They can be asked to write their responses, indicating what they favor or disapprove of in the cartoon. The teacher can use these reactions for further discussion. Personal problems or questions can be detected in their responses, which also reveal the extent to which students use good judgment and sound understanding of the problem depicted in a cartoon. One teacher who successfully used cartoons as a means of evaluating student progress in a consumer education unit distributed cartoons depicting the principles and various problems of buying, accompanied by specific questions. In their answers, students revealed information about their own buying practices as well as the depth of their consumer knowledge.

To stimulate interest in a forthcoming unit on clothing selection, a teacher posted on a bulletin board cartoons that emphasized such points as family attitudes toward clothing, unwise spending for clothes, extreme fashions, the relation of clothes to personality, and the impact of peer approval on clothes selection. To give a spark to housekeeping responsibilities in the laboratory, an enterprising student committee illustrated the task list with cartoons. Humor was added to the performance of tasks, and the posted list was pictorially attractive. To promote the social graces and to improve the food selection of students buying lunches in a school cafeteria, a student committee planned a series of posters. Cartoons were used to make fun of the line-pusher, students who hold up the line because they can't find their money, the gulper who doesn't take time to eat, the noisy eater, and the food faddist.

Students can make good use of cartoons as illustrations for individual reports. One senior, for example, created cartoons to illustrate her home-experience report on keeping house for a week. The following events were highlighted: the unexpected dinner guest who made a sixth diner when there were only five desserts; her consternation at discovering the imprints of tiny, grimy hands on towels freshly hung in the bathroom; and the necessity of juggling the budget.

In the selection of cartoons, a teacher must recognize that many are very timely and cannot be filed for future use, whereas others have a timeless quality. Cartoons as a teaching device require skillful use, according to Dale.[30] Teachers must be cautious about oversimplification, stereotyping, bias, misrepresentation, and the strong emotional charge. Students may study cartoons individually, or they may be projected by an overhead or opaque projector. Other uses are bulletin board displays or incorporation into a mural. The photocopy process may be used if the teacher wishes each student to have a copy of an individual cartoon to study relationships, decision making, or consumer practices. Cartoons may be mounted or placed in a cellophane envelope.

Comics and Comic Books

The comic strip is a sequential story depicted through a series of drawings. Some are humorous, others are serious, and some are educational. Most are entertaining or have some other form of appeal. The characteristics of the comic strip, according to Steinlein,[31] are rapid action, colloquial language, clear-cut values, crude humor, obvious outcomes, and simple psychology and morality.

Before using them, the teacher should evaluate both comics and comic books carefully, considering the following points, according to Dale:[32]

1. Does the material have value in relation to classroom objectives?
2. Will the experience be uplifting or maturing?
3. Is a respect and regard for others fostered?
4. Is empathy with others illustrated?
5. Is a desire to help others encouraged?
6. Is thinking encouraged?
7. Is the way of life depicted compatible with democratic ideals?

A teacher may wish to establish other criteria that are pertinent to the situation.

[30] Edgar Dale, *Audiovisual Methods in Teaching,* 3rd ed. (New York: Dryden, 1969), p. 515.
[31] Leo J. Steinlein, "What We Can Learn from Comic Books," *English Quarterly* (Spring 1950), pp. 9–11.
[32] Op. cit., p. 517.

Comic books may be a means of encouraging the nonreader or the slow reader to read and to comprehend material about home economics more readily. Their use should be only a step, however, toward more difficult materials. Because this medium has a strong entertainment value, it may be difficult to encourage students to assume a responsible attitude toward learning. This will depend upon the student and the teacher. Obviously, this technique has merit in describing the operation of equipment, scientific phenomena, and room arrangements. Because of the simplicity and the drawings, the imagination of students may be blunted.

Students may consider ways of using comics and comic books in giving reports, in describing a process, in depicting personal relationships, and in highlighting the pros and cons of a question. Using characters from *Peanuts, Blondie, Mary Worth,* or *Gasoline Alley* in problem-solving situations adds interest. If, when, and how to use comics must be decided by the teacher and the students.

SUGGESTIONS FOR FURTHER LEARNING

1. Consider ways in which teaching resources may aid a student specifically in the following:
   a. To extend the range of vicarious experience.
   b. To give experience in the use of the senses.
   c. To appreciate one's heritage.
   d. To clarify a value.
   e. To cope with a problem.
2. Consider ways in which teaching resources may be found in giveaways, castoffs, nature, or other sources that do not cost anything. Examples might be paperbacks, old magazines, posters, fruits and vegetables from home gardens, or fabrics. Are there any teaching resources in the classroom that seem ready to be discarded but might be recycled? Brainstorm with students about ideas and specific uses for them.
3. Examine magazines, paperbacks, and recordings prized by boys and girls or adults of the age that you plan to teach. Consider ways in which they might serve as teaching resources.
4. Think about specific teaching resources that would require student involvement, challenge thinking, apply principles, or provide an opportunity to analyze feelings.

10

Teaching Strategies

Most teachers want to be effective. Often discussions of teaching strategies have emphasized the role of the teacher. However, the involvement of the learner is equally or more significant. When student involvement is low, educational effectiveness is reduced. In choosing appropriate methods, teachers must bring to bear their knowledge of human behavior, group processes, motivation, communications, and human relationships. Not only is knowledge, skill, understanding, and appreciation of home and family living of great importance, but creative teachers must also recognize their influence on the minds, human qualities, actions, attitudes, and personalities of students. This is an almost overwhelming responsibility, and teaching strategies cannot be taken lightly.

Every time a teacher makes a lesson plan, an important step is to select appropriate techniques for implementing this plan. The process is multifaceted. The objective of a lesson may be to help youth become better consumers in their buying of a radio, a recording, or some other item. In addition, whenever expedient, a teacher is encouraged to give consideration to the following emphases believed to be important in the total development of an individual.[1] Among them are (1) democratic values; (2) an appreciation of heritage; (3) insights into reality and the future; (4) preparation for jobs and further education; (5) family life; (6) leisure time; and (7) encouragement of lifelong learning.

[1] Mildred G. McCloskey, *Teaching Strategies and Classroom Realities* (Englewood Cliffs, N.J.: Prentice-Hall, 1971), p. xxiii in Preface.

Figure 10–1 A teacher may wish to assist students in becoming better consumers in buying records. (Cereal Institute, Inc.)

Other foci of attention for the choice of strategies are the diverse backgrounds of various types of students, social impacts on their behavior, their stage of development in life and in education, and a familiarity with student needs, interests, problems, values, and the like. A practical question is the accommodation of students who are restless, indifferent, rebellious, alienated, and in some instances violent. Another question is the handling of students who lack basics, such as communication skills. These pressures in certain elementary and secondary schools are not easy for a teacher to face. It is not hopeless, however, because some teachers have found strategies that are successful with these problems.

CHARACTERISTICS OF STRATEGIES

Berliner and Gage[2] define *methods* as recurrent, instructional processes used by many teachers in the teaching of various subject-matter areas, for example, the discussion method. These authors categorize teaching strategies according to patterned teacher behavior that includes lecturing, discussion, or recitation. Delivery systems for the

[2] David C. Berliner and N. L. Gage, "The Psychology of Teaching Methods," in N. L. Gage (ed.), *The Psychology of Methods, The Seventy-fifth Yearbook of the National Society for the Study of Education,* Part 1 (New York: U. of Chicago, 1976), p. 5.

curriculum, such as textbooks, technological aids, games, programmed instruction, and computer-assisted instruction, are a second type of strategy. Methods may also be organizational structures, such as tutoring and independent studies.

Approaches to teaching may be influenced by the size of the class, the available space and equipment, and the aptitudes of the students. The cost of materials, such as food and textiles, is usually important. The time allowed for a class period establishes certain parameters. Often the time of day—such as first class in the morning, when students may be sleepy, or last class in the afternoon, when students may be weary and eager to leave—can offer additional challenges. Friday afternoons, especially before a game or other big event, may require special treatment.

In addition to these practical aspects of selection, teaching strategies should stimulate, excite, and interest the students; enhance their self-concept; and be enjoyable. When the strategies employed help the students to find the answers to their problems, then the selections have been wise ones.

SELECTION OF STRATEGIES

A home economics teacher may choose a strategy or strategies from many types. No one strategy should be considered the only one. The teaching of foods need not be confined to the laboratory method. A variety of approaches gives interest, challenge, enjoyment, and benefit to students.

Here are some questions that appear logical in the selection of a method appropriate for a specific teaching situation:

Preliminary Considerations

1. How may cognitive, affective, and psychomotor domains be emphasized?
2. Is there an opportunity to implement democratic values?
3. Can the criteria for effective learning be implemented?
4. Is stimulation of sensory experiences included?
5. Is there an opportunity for students to share in goal setting, learning experiences, and evaluation?
6. Will students' needs, problems, interests, and maturity fit with this method?
7. Are students given an opportunity to inquire, to analyze, to explore, to experiment, to create, to clarify, to initiate, to manipulate, to observe, to organize, to test, to search, to think, to make, to choose, or to be exposed to other creative processes?

Figure 10–2 Planning a simple breakfast would be relevant in the lives of many students. (Cereal Institute, Inc.)

8. Are students helped to experience success, pleasure, and ego involvement?

Actual Selection

9. Which approach is most suitable to the particular content and objective?
10. Is it relevant to the lives of students?
11. Does it lead to a high degree of student involvement?
12. Will encouragement be given to the self-direction and independence of the student?
13. Can provision be made for cooperative effort?
14. Are students involved significantly in their own instruction?
15. Can the teacher use the strategy with confidence?
16. Can provision be made for individual differences among students in background, in learning, and in other capacities?

Obviously, all of these criteria cannot be included in one session, but more are likely to be included if the list is consulted during planning. The teacher should review the list from time to time to see whether the cognitive domain has been emphasized more than the affective domain, to what extent students are involved, and what the emphasis is on other criteria.

USE OF STRATEGIES

A teacher should feel free to be experimental and innovative in choosing and using teaching techniques. A newspaper story appropriate to family life, such as one about living in a commune, might be read, followed by a "rap" session and concluded by drawing or using another art form to portray the feelings or ideas generated in a student by this experience. An expert on job interviews may talk to students on occupational education. This talk may be followed by role playing in interviews, or the expert may interview certain students in front of the class. A discussion and evaluation may ensue.

Suggestions for new teaching techniques may be found in professional magazines, during professional meetings or workshops, and by interaction with fellow teachers. A teacher may invent some methods on her/his own. The development of a large repertoire of successful strategies can facilitate successful teaching. A strategy that has been thoroughly tested by a teacher in many circumstances can enhance confidence.

AN OVERVIEW OF METHODS

A creative home economics teacher will study and experiment with methods. Familiarity with many strategies and a clear notion of the circumstances in which they have been effective will strengthen choices.

Demonstration

The primary function of a demonstration is to show something—anything from sewing a button on a boy's shirt to a flannelboard illustration of the steps in buying a house. A demonstration generally involves working with objects, but it can also be used for an exploration of such intangibles as the effect on others of one's moods, facial expressions, or postures. Since the advent of videotapes, interest in this method has increased considerably.

The subject of the demonstration must be linked to the concerns of the audience, which may consist of students in the classroom, an adult class, parents and visitors at an open house, or members of a club in the community. Demonstrations might include a comparison of flameproof fabrics and untreated fabrics; introducing one's friends to one's parents; registering in a hotel; shortcuts in food preparation and clothing construction; novel ways to use mixes; and simple refreshments to serve friends. Everyday problems can be dramatized through a demonstration. If the preparation of an adequate breakfast appears to be a problem, the demonstration might be of how to prepare a tricky breakfast in ten minutes. Or a teacher might capitalize on the latest fad by showing some worthwhile adaptations of it to personal or family life. Catchy titles such as "Super Space Savers," "Big Ideas for Little Cash," "Fun Foods," "Matchmates," "Are You Recycling?" or "When Mother Works" spur interest in demonstrations.

Demonstrations require careful planning. The steps in the procedure are outlined in detail, and the equipment and actions suited to each step. The demonstration is arranged so that all will be able to see it. Lighting and seating should be checked to that end. Practice of the demonstration may be desirable. Timing is important; the demonstration may last five minutes or an hour, but the demonstrator will know in advance the time that each step requires. A good beginning will capture interest promptly. The demonstrator will present a logical, step-by-step presentation and be sure that the audience understands the points being made. She/he may or may not encourage questions and summarize from time to time. Standards are encouraged to be high, so that students will have good guidelines for their own performance.

Students can often assist the teacher with her or his demonstration and can plan and give demonstrations of their own. Sometimes a team is effective, one group doing the demonstrating, the other providing the commentary, arranging the props, or manipulating the technological aids.

Demonstrations in the classroom can be especially valuable to students in explaining the how and why of processes, as well as in motivating them to develop certain skills. When the teacher uses the same materials, equipment, and processes as the students will employ later in the laboratory, as in making a sandwich or putting in a zipper, the potential for success of beginning students is enhanced. Displaying the steps in the process and explaining each step accurately, clearly, and definitively while demonstrating expedites learning. Having visuals such as charts, pictures of other uses of the product that is demonstrated, and samples stimulates interest.

If the teacher asks questions about the process, leads students to anticipate the next step, offers suggestions that will facilitate doing a step in the process, and summarizes periodically, the demonstration becomes more valuable to the students. Leaving the finished product or products on display encourages the students to compare and to evaluate their own product. Practice by students should follow as soon as possible, especially for manipulative skills, while motivation is high and the demonstration is still clearly in mind.

Spot demonstrations in the laboratory are desirable. When several students are having the same difficulty, such as in some aspect of operating a sewing machine, the teacher may gather these students around a sewing machine and show them how to overcome the difficulty. The teacher may capitalize on these situations for teaching points that appear to be unclear to the students.

The following questions may be considered in evaluating a demonstration:

1. To what degree were the students able to follow the steps of the demonstration?
2. Were standards established for the final product, for work habits, and for practical applications?
3. To what degree did the students demonstrate knowledge of the content, processes, and definitions during the follow-up experience?
4. Did the teacher demonstrate good preparation, organization of time, acceptable techniques, and desirable end-products, and did she/he hold the interest of the students?

A good overall question for a teacher to ask is "What would I do differently if I repeated this demonstration, and why?"

Students' personal development is encouraged when their own demonstrations contribute to poise, knowledge, and the ability to think logically. This result in turn will depend upon the degree to which a teacher involves the students in this teaching technique.

Lectures

The teacher may occasionally wish to present in lecture form an overview of a topic for which there is little material available for students to do research on their own. This method requires careful preparation by the teacher.[3] The purpose must be well defined. How does this lecture fit into the rest of the program? Will the material be new to all students, or will some of them be acquainted with some of the information? Will there be an element of persuasion in the talk? What kind of action should emerge from the lecture?

Select an interesting approach that highlights who, what, when, why, or how. Plan a sequence or outline of what is to be said. Will visual or auditory aids be employed? Attempt to support the main points with facts, statistics, quotations, comparisons, or questions. Have a strong conclusion. These points might be considered not only for classroom lectures but also for talks given in the community or at professional meetings.

[3] John McLeish, "The Lecture Method," in N. L. Gage (ed.), *The Psychology of Teaching Methods, The Seventy-fifth Yearbook of the National Society for the Study of Education,* Part 1 (Chicago: U. of Chicago, 1976), Ch. 8.

The lecture is frequently used when a resource person is brought into the classroom. A lecture is generally followed by questions from students, so that some interaction takes place. Two dangers of lectures are that the subject may not be of equal interest to all students and that the opportunity for interaction is limited.

Readings and Storytelling

As a modification of the lecture method, the teacher may read to the class.[4] To be of value, the reading must be well done. A teacher may read a short newspaper item—for example, on prices or a family situation—an article from a "little magazine" published by students, such as *Foxfire,* or a reading suggested by class members. One teacher read short excerpts of poetry highlighting mother–child relations, and students were asked to select from among the ideas presented those that were most in agreement with their own. Telling or reading short stories about child development, family life, and decision making can be effective. Resource persons with unusual competence might be asked to assist.

Reading unfinished stories can provide high interest to students. Stories of this type are appropriate for discussing typical ethical problems that students may encounter, and they may lead to thoughtful and forceful expression by students. Teachers and students may produce their own unfinished stories.

Many teachers have become good storytellers, according to Hodges.[5] The techniques are simple. The setting is orderly, with a minimum of noise and distraction. The students are comfortable. The teacher is at an easy eye level with the students. The story may be told with feeling and with belief. Students relate more quickly to feelings than to words. If possible, a story time will have special meaning: a time when storyteller and listeners share mutual pleasure. Students may be encouraged to tell stories, because this experience is not only enjoyable but enhances personal development in many ways.

An occasional story hour can become a part of any area of home economics. Teachers and students alike can search for appropriate stories. The librarian can be helpful. Many of the stories in *CO-ED Magazine* have appeal. Classics in poetry, fiction, and drama may be adapted. The lyrics of some popular songs may be recited while the music is played softly in the background. Sometimes there are illustrations from a book or magazine to show while the story is being told. Students may develop original stories to tell.

[4] Betty L. Broman, "Storytelling: The Frosting on the Cake," *Childhood Education,* Vol. 51, No. 6 (Apr./May 1975), p. 323.

[5] Margaret Hodges, "Telling Stories to Young Children," *Instructor,* Vol. 77, No. 3 (Nov. 1968), pp. 57–60.

Interviews

For a change of pace, the teacher might interview two students who hold differing opinions on a topic of interest to the entire class; for instance, in a senior class studying a unit on preparation for marriage, selected students might be asked their views on a family lifestyle that has developed in recent times; on childless marriages; or on wives who earn more than their husbands. Such an interview might serve as a prelude to a planning session on the topics to be covered in the unit.

Instead of having a resource person or an expert in some area of home economics lecture to the class, it might be more interesting to have the teacher and several students interview this person. They might simulate a radio or television panel interview, first studying such programs to see how they are conducted.

DRAMATIC METHODS

The dramatic methods include role playing, pantomime, playlets, and skits. They are performed by live actors, perhaps with masks, or by puppets or marionettes. The dramatic presentation is an appealing method that can be very helpful to the busy home economics teacher. Most important, students enjoy learning by this method. Students may suggest the situations to be dramatized.

Role of Observers

Dramatics of any kind are of little avail unless the audience, too, feels that it has a part. Students should be prepared to give constructive criticism of the actors and the action. Certainly the group will want to discuss the presentation in the light of their own problems and interests, and they may want to offer other approaches or solutions to the situations presented.

Plays and Skits

The situation is best when appropriate to the age and the interests of the students. Some suggestions are offered here. Review questions can be dramatized: pairs of students could be given one question each to answer in a dramatization of their own invention, using any of the dramatic methods. Minute dramas highlighting important points in home economics, such as home safety, planning home furnishings, or getting along with younger brothers and sisters, might be enacted by couples selected from the class. Many stage plays include excellent scenes highlighting some aspect of personal or family relations. Giles and Cadigan[6] have selected appropriate excerpts from plays by Maxwell Anderson, Eugene O'Neill, Moss Hart and George Kaufman, Henrik Ibsen, John Steinbeck, Alvin Childress, Robert Sherwood, and others. In addition to the excerpts, the authors have compiled provocative questions for discussion, additional readings, thoughts for reflection, and suggested activities. Although many of the plays are not of the contemporary period, the problems are still timely and can be used in the home economics classroom. Students are assigned to read parts. Discussion of possible personal applications follows. Other appropriate plays may be adapted in the same manner.

Directions for dramatic presentations, whether original or from a play, must be adequate, but spontaneity and creativity of production should be encouraged. Rehearsing may be eliminated or kept to a minimum. The teacher can terminate the performance when the action seems to lag. Only a few students should act at the same time. If the use of dramatics is new to the group, select the more poised, adaptable students for the first few sessions, then work in the more retiring ones in minor roles until they have gained confidence. All students should eventually be given a chance to participate if this method is to be truly helpful.

Props for Playacting

Props highlight a character or a setting. Hats, a shawl, a cane, an apron, a toy telephone, spectacle rims, a toy, a letter, and similar articles can be used with imagination. Roles can be assumed more realistically when students can wear something appropriate or hold an article in their hands. Laboratory equipment may also be used effectively.

Chairs as Stage Settings

By an arrangement of chairs, various settings can be suggested: the corner hangout, the school cafeteria, a bus, a car, or an athletic event. Two girls might pretend to discuss their parents' being too strict, their lack of interesting boyfriends, or ways to earn money. Another situation might dramatize a boy and a girl who are not having a good time at a school party. A mock telephone conversation can be portrayed by the placing of two chairs back to back, a small distance apart. A high school girl might be calling her mother to ask if she can buy a sweater she saw in a shop window, or a boy might be telephoning home to explain why he lost his part-time job.

[6] H. H. Giles and Robert J. Cadigan, *Playwrights Present* (New York: Harper, 1942).

Pantomime

The ability of students to express themselves can be broadened when they must act without talking. Some suggestions are asking a small child to be quiet while his father is sleeping; showing displeasure and disappointment when a mail order for goods is opened; asking a member of the family for something to read when a sore throat prevents speaking; and showing a deaf homemaker a more efficient way to open a carton of milk. Other appropriate situations may be suggested by students. Students might evaluate the clarity of the message as depicted and suggest other methods. A discussion of the feelings of students while they are pantomiming can be revealing.

Pantomime is used as an aid in understanding nonverbal communication and body language.[7] Students may be asked to portray common emotions, such as gladness, sadness, shock, and annoyance. The students who observe may relate the reactions that these pantomimes produced in them. Another point for discussion is to share personal experiences in which nonverbal communication was pleasant, unpleasant, threatening, frustrating, or disturbing. What are the implications for personal and family living?

Masks

Masks have many possibilities. One of the more important values of this device is that the shy student seems to have more confidence when he or she wears a mask. Making them is a good creative activity. Masks can be made of papier-mâché or cloth. Wigs of yarn or string mops can be made to suggest a young or old man or woman. Situations can be built around a family's activities or relations. Masks representing various gradations of skin tones from very light to very dark might be used in a clothing class in a study of color, or in human relations discussions as a way to examine prejudices. When a white student dons a mask of a skin color different from his or her own and does some role playing, the experience can be enlightening.

Puppets

Puppetry has been used to great advantage with all age groups to dramatize situations of many types. This dramatic device allows a forceful presentation of ideas and feelings without undue labor on the part of the teacher or students. It offers unique possibilities for stimulating creative activities, for gaining new insights into students, and for animating group discussions. One of the outstanding values of using puppets is the freedom it gives students, for talking through a

[7] Julius Fast, *Body Language* (New York: Pocketbooks, 1971).

Figure 10–3 Students may reveal feelings and problems through the use of puppets.

puppet gives a freedom to express thoughts and feelings that might be stifled in class discussions. Not only do the students who participate in the presentation profit, but the other members of the class respond to the action.

Puppets can be very simple or highly elaborate. They may be hand, stick, fist, or finger puppets, or marionettes, which are manipulated by means of strings. Shadow puppets are managed behind a screen that is lighted from behind, the puppets appearing as silhouettes.

Puppets can be made from simple materials. Heads can be constructed of papier-mâché, modeling clay, rubber or plastic balls that fit the index finger loosely mounted over a strong cardboard cylinder, paper bags, and even vegetables—carrots, apples, or potatoes with holes bored in them to fit the index finger. Hair can be made of rope, yarn, fur, steel wool, or pot scrapers. Facial features can be indicated with buttons, fake jewels, or pipe cleaners, or they can be painted on. Dresses or blouses are usually cut kimono style and may be decorated according to student fancies. A hat, a special ornament, or a coat can be made the highlight of a characterization. Galdston[8] offers many suggestions for the making of puppets.

Create a Puppet Community

If possible, students should make their own puppets. Every home economics department might well boast a puppet family of parents, grandparents, and children of various ages, even puppets depicting such community characters as a supermarket checker, a department store clerk, and a police officer. Some puppets representing individuals from other cultures might be interesting. Students will suggest other characters.

With such a puppet stock company, an extensive repertoire of puppet plays could be developed.

Use of Puppets

In connection with a discussion of family situations, student puppeteers might wish to portray incidents relative to the sharing of homemaking responsibilities among family members, a grandparent's coming to live with the family, or the entertainment of difficult guests. In connection with a study of consumer education, the dramatic action might develop around the return of merchandise to a store, an unwise purchase of clothes, the temptation of bargain basements, or a bride's planning of home furnishings. Similar situations may be developed around the harassed adolescent who never has time to spend with his family or mother–daughter conflicts over homemaking standards. In a unit on clothing selection, the problem of a mother reluctant to let her daughter choose her own clothes could be acted out. In nutrition classes, puppets might be used to dramatize the effects of undesirable eating habits, the choices in a fast-food restaurant, or the planning of a meal for a family with many food dislikes. Sometimes a visiting puppet show is brought into a school by an outside agency. Students have an opportunity to see how puppets are made and manipulated.[9]

[8] Olive Galdston, *Play with Puppets* (New York: Play Schools Association, 1971).

[9] "No Strings Attached," *American Education*, Vol. 13, No. 5 (June 1977), p. 4. Story of a university puppet show taken to schools.

Role Playing

Role playing[10] is a dramatic method that seems to have unusual possibilities in home and family-life education. Role playing does not mean playacting or impersonating in the sense of acting in a stage production. It is, rather, a free situation in which the role player spontaneously performs what she/he feels and thinks about a given role under specific conditions. The action should never be rehearsed. The action should be terminated before it becomes tedious, when the possibilities of the role seem to have been exhausted by the role player. Students differ considerably in the ability to take on roles. The interrelationships that various individuals of the household assume in personal, social, and family living can be examined deeply through this technique. For example, those who hold the roles of husband and wife, father and mother, child and parent may also hold the roles of host and hostess, nurse, manager, buyer, provider, homemaker, consumer, and companion, among many, many others. Almost any role can be explored by students.

There are a number of important steps involved. The interest of students is aroused and their desire to participate is stimulated by a warming-up process. To illustrate: for a home situation, a student may be asked to describe a room she imagines herself to be in, its furniture, and its relation to the remainder of the house. Next, role players go into action.

The class may appraise one another's role playing, suggesting alternative responses. There should be opportunities for role reversal or exchange, in which participants take the opposite part in a similar situation. A deeper appreciation of the other fellow may result, particularly when an adolescent plays a parent or a student plays the role of teacher.

Role playing can be pertinent to various units of study. In connection with a study of home management, "a brother and a sister" could discuss ways to improve their use of time; in consumer education, "a young couple" might analyze the leaks in their budget; in a clothing course, several boys and girls might generate ideas for recycling T-shirts; in a health unit, students may talk about ways to stop using drugs; and in a food unit, a girl may show a boy how to cook out-of-doors. After the role playing, the other students may offer differences of opinion, questions about the soundness of an approach to the problem, or give other suggestions than those portrayed during the role playing.

[10] Howard Lamb, "Role Playing," *Today's Education,* Vol. 59, No. 1 (Jan. 1969), pp. 67–68.

Through role playing, students are brought into close relationship with life situations and are thereby at least somewhat prepared to meet real problems with realistic solutions. They are helped to overcome self-consciousness and learn to adapt themselves gracefully to various situations. A broader understanding of roles should emerge: roles are not static, and they vary from person to person, place to place, and circumstance to circumstance. Through role playing, students have an opportunity to evaluate their adequacy, and the teacher gains valuable insights into the students' range of information, resourcefulness, and ability to adapt what they know to new situations.

TEACHING STRATEGIES WITH GROUP INVOLVEMENT

Group methods promote a high degree of group participation. Students and teachers can pool experiences, knowledge, feelings, and ideas, and group decisions can be reached. A teacher will wish to become skillful in the use of these techniques.

The Discussion Method

Many teachers have found the discussion method unpredictable. Sometimes it is very rewarding, at other times it is exasperating. Understanding what is meant by *discussion* may make success in using it more certain. One of the most naive of notions is that anyone is competent to lead or participate in a discussion. Discussion is a skill that must be learned, and the only way to learn it is by doing it. The discussion method must not be confused with recitation, nor is it debating or wrangling. It is a technique whereby a group or class, under the guidance of a leader, examines its views of a problem through group interaction, then attempts to reach the best solution possible. Therefore it should be used only in appropriate situations and not in every class period.

Selection of a Problem

Discussion cannot be effective unless it revolves around a problem that is of significance to the group; in fact, it should be so vital to the group that the members deem an early solution necessary, for problems of the remote future seldom stimulate discussion. The teacher might evaluate the immediacy of a problem by asking herself or himself some questions: Did the problem arise in the group? Does it recur often? Does it affect many of the members? Will a discussion of the problem be helpful to the group? Is the group competent to discuss the problem? The trouble with many poor discussions is that the problem is too trivial.

Role of the Teacher

The emotional climate of the group often reflects the temperament of the teacher. If the teacher is permissive, humorous, kind, encouraging, and warm, the response is usually good. A teacher must clearly understand her/his role, or else there will be chaos. During discussion, the teacher should not remain absolutely quiet in the mistaken belief that only students should participate, but neither should he or she do all the talking. The function of a leader is to inaugurate and then to guide the discussion.

Role of the Student Participant

Every student participant must feel a responsibility for helping the group. A discussion can be successful only if everyone contributes what he/she can. From time to time, individuals may raise questions, clarify statements, give illustrations, cite authorities, agree or disagree with the ideas of others, listen carefully, summarize, add humor, nod, smile, or give other indications of interest. All students should examine the role they played in a discussion to determine how they might improve their participation.

Steps in a Good Discussion

To give a discussion a good start, a number of warm-up devices may be used. Problems or quotations written on cards, or newspaper clippings, pictures, or cartoons related to the subject matter of the discussion problem are each cut into two pieces, the halves then distributed randomly among the students, who enjoy finding their partners by matching up pieces. Each pair of students then discusses the implications of their message on their cards. This procedure is especially effective in family life, child development, and consumer education units. The paired students then return and share ideas with the entire group.

Another method is to have students write on cards a few sentences indicating their reactions to a given word. The teacher collects the cards and reads them. In one nutrition class, students had the following reaction to the word *nibble:* "Makes me think of calories," "That's what I do when I watch TV," "I nibble when I am lonesome." The

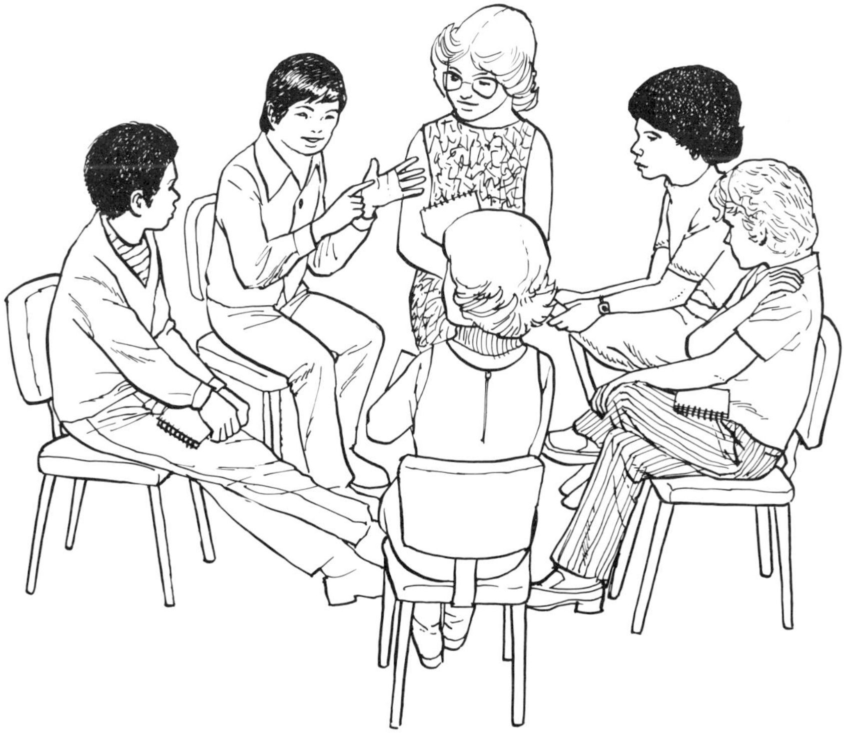

Figure 10–4 The buzz group is a good warm-up technique.

reactions provided material for a discussion of between-meal eating habits. Words that are stimulating include *borrow,* for discussions about money; *quarrel,* for discussions about relations with brothers and sisters; *holiday foods,* for a discussion of meal preparation; and so on. The reactions stimulate group discussion.

Another warm-up device is the incomplete sentence written on the board. Students are asked to complete it as they wish. Such sentences might include "I think a father should __________," "When someone you know uses drugs __________," "When you do not have the money for something you want very much, you __________."

The buzz group is especially effective in starting discussion or stimulating a lagging discussion. The class is asked to gather in small groups to talk about the problem. This is sometimes known as "Discussion 66," so called because groups of six persons get together and talk for six minutes. These sessions can be varied in format, for instance, "Discussion 45"—four persons talk for five minutes. Or they may be called different names, such as "Party Line" and "Chatter Sessions." Students can help in creating names for these groups.

Some Variations

Sometimes several students may be designated "listening posts" in a discussion group. They are charged with spotting specific ideas brought out by the group. If the cost of a date is the topic, one listening post may be on guard for all low-expenditure ideas, another for the high-expenditure ideas.

In junior-high-school classes, where the span of interest is short and it is difficult for students to sit still for long, the "pop-up" technique may be used. Students sit in a circle and pop up when they have something to say—but not more than one student at a time may hold the floor. This method is good, too, for a review session.

These are only a few suggestions for making discussions lively by stimulating the dynamics of the group. The important things are to use imagination and to have students participate in planning.

The next step in discussion is to define the problem clearly and then to explain and analyze the possible causes for the situation. Then possible solutions may be examined. Finally, the best solution should be selected and means of implementing it outlined. This includes deciding when the action will be taken, where it will occur, and who will be responsible.

Influences on the Thinking of Students

Every teacher must be aware of the complexity of the influences on the way individuals think in a discussion situation. Their traditions, their religion, their ethnic backgrounds, the part of the world in which they live, and the dominant people in their lives are all reflected in their ideas. Lack of the needed language skills may be a potent deterrent to satisfactory discussion. If students cannot adequately express their ideas and feelings or are unfamiliar with the meanings of certain words, they are in a poor position to make valid contributions.

Thinking is encouraged when students are given an opportunity to test their ideas and to discover many angles of a problem, a belief, or an attitude. Discussion helps students to respect the ideas of others and to increase their appreciation of other students.

Dialogues

According to Decker,[11] understanding is reached through dialogue, a form of discussion with high personal involvement. The crux of a

[11] Fred Decker, "M/C Publisher's View," *Marketing/Communications*, Vol. 299, No. 1 (Jan. 1971), p. 2.

dialogue is earning the right to be heard by listening to what others have to say. This method leads to self-understanding and to an understanding of others through an awareness of nonverbal forms of expression, attitudes, ideas, and tones of voice. This cannot be accomplished through monologues.

There are a number of ways in which dialogue can be used in the classroom. Small groups may have dialogues about questions that seem vital to the participants. This is a good technique for FHA. If there is considerable empathy among the students in a class, it may be worthwhile for a small group of students to have a dialogue before the remainder of the class as a warm-up to a discussion by the total class.

Topics should be freely chosen and talked out or acted out, and feelings should be disclosed, with the primary guideline to "tell it like it is." Students of all ages have a desire to be understood, to communicate, to belong, and to establish themselves as personalities.

Figure 10–5 Rap, dig, and similar types of discussion need to be in comfortable surroundings.

Possible topics for talk sessions in the home economics classroom might include: what it means to be a member of an ethnic group, dress, school discipline, adjustments to junior or senior high school, alcohol addiction, money, or dieting. These and other problems of a personal nature and of current interest are appropriate.

Benefits that are derived from this technique are that students are heard, respected for what is said, make decisions that become more mature, separate fact from fiction, and enhance their intergroup understanding.

Laboratory Method

The problems presented to students in the laboratory should be confined to unusual or complex problems that cannot be worked out with simpler techniques.

Almost every area of home economics can provide opportunities for laboratory experiences. In a laboratory session, students can work individually, perhaps experimenting with some locally plentiful food

Figure 10–6 Laboratory experiments in consumer buying of foods are useful.

or testing an original recipe. In a clothing class, students can experiment with ways to use inexpensive fabric. In a consumer project, each student could select an article of clothing, a food product, a school supply, or a household article, then do comparative shopping for it in different stores, comparing brands and packages. The student might then do some type of testing on the article for usability, performance, unit cost, and safety. Similar projects might be carried out on household equipment—the comparing and testing of small kitchen utensils or appliances for use of energy. Students then share results and formulate generalizations.

Laboratory experiences should be planned so that students will work with materials, ideas, people, or processes. In addition, this method provides excellent practice in the application of principles and generalizations and the execution of plans. It also strengthens managerial abilities.

A well-done laboratory lesson requires careful supervision and coordination. In planning laboratory work, the teacher and the student first clarify the problem to be solved and the goals associated with it, then explore specific procedures to be used to accomplish their objectives. Careful planning of work schedules is important, for class periods are short and there will be much to do. Committees for cleanup, the replacement of supplies and equipment, and other laboratory tasks are appointed. Students will require some instruction in ways to guard against accidents and other hazards. A period for evaluating the laboratory experience in relation to accomplishment, for formulating generalizations, and for discussing the application of principles is necessary.

The advantages of the laboratory method are several. Students are generally enthusiastic about it, for it provides opportunities for decision making, problem solving, experimentation, and research. Students can see the results of their errors. They develop the ability to work with others, to plan effectively, and to apply objectively the principles and generalizations they have learned, and the teacher can observe which skills and what knowledge of the use of equipment need strengthening. Spitze[12] summarizes the strengths of the laboratory technique by suggesting that it is especially useful in learning management skills and in developing human relations skills through working with others.

Unfortunately laboratory work is usually expensive, owing to the relatively high costs of the equipment and supplies required, and often it is difficult to supervise. Moreover it is difficult to allocate work so that all students have equally challenging jobs and experiences. Unless well organized, a laboratory period can result in much wasted time.

[12] Op. cit., pp. 23–24.

Games

Considerable interest has been engendered in games as a learning device since business executives began using them to simulate actual business problems and situations.

Historically there are four basic types of games modeled after the four types of human decision-making. *Puzzles* are games in which the player can manipulate the environment rather than its manipulating him. Puzzles might relate to the grade of canned tomatoes to use in a casserole, a good choice of fabric for a dress to be worn in active dancing, or the best type of shoes to wear on a hike. Games of *chance* are the opposite of puzzles because the environment manipulates the player. Laws of probability and so-called systems can be examined. Games might relate to the probability of certain home accidents' occurring under specified conditions, of certain physical characteristics that might be inherited by the future children of a student, or of the profit-making possibilities of a home-based business.

The *aesthetic* game involves an application of a set of rules to someone's behavior—it may be the student's or someone else's. Judgment is involved. For example, students might judge the degree to which rules for the school cafeteria or a school dance are upheld and the possible reasons for deviations.

In a game of *strategy,* the essential is the opponent. Students might analyze how strategies are employed by themselves or family members to gain certain ends, such as allocation of limited funds for many wants, or how to gain social action in the community on a youth problem.

Abt[13] classified educational games in slightly different categories. Games of skill are those in which the outcome depends upon the capabilities of the players, such as in tennis and chess. These games reward achievement, encourage individual responsibility and initiative, and discourage passivity. Games of chance, already discussed, are included in Abt's classification. Here the outcome is independent of the player, particularly in games involving dice and the like. The value of these games is the dramatization of the limitations of effort and skill. Games of chance minimize personal responsibility, effort, and skill and may foster passivity.

Games of *reality* can help a student comprehend structural relationships and the problems, methods, and motives of others. These games create a high degree of motivation because adolescents can have a taste of adult reality through vicarious experiences that are not available directly. Examples of such games are simulations of

[13] Clark C. Abt, "Games for Learning," in Sarane S. Boocock and E. O. Schild (eds.), *Simulation Games in Learning* (Beverly Hills, Calif.: Sage, 1968), pp. 65–92.

buying a house, parent–child relationships, and confrontation with crises. One danger is that students may be inclined to overrate their ability to predict events.

Games of *fantasy* have little cognitive content but do challenge the imagination through abandonment of conventional perceptions and inhibitions, such as playing the role of a historical figure.

Abt also includes *strategy* games, which have already been described.

General Characteristics

Games are one kind of simulation as distinguished from other simulations, such as motion pictures, computer simulations, and dramatic plays, according to Abt.[14] There are a number of advantages in the use of games in the classroom. Students are highly motivated to participate in problem analysis. Solutions for problems are both required and rewarded; more than one winning strategy is available, although some strategies are superior to others. Learning is encouraged through a strong focus on attention. Most games are an abstraction of simple elements from a complex confusion of reality, and the goals and the means of achieving them are governed by rules.

Games for Home Economics

Teachers and students can make their own games. Feldmiller[15] and students at Youngstown University developed games for learning about home management and the use, care, and selection of household equipment. *Sally States* is a board game with a pathway of slots for pieces of paper containing questions about the use and care of household equipment. A spinner determines how far a player may move on the pathway. Obstacles and bonuses introduce an element of chance into the game. *Spinning* involves decisions about owning and choosing household equipment and involves the use of time and money. Winning and losing depend upon chance. Small models of equipment, a plastic board, a spinner, and symbols for time and money (peas and beans) are used, and the game stimulates thinking about alternatives in choosing appliances economically.

Common games may be adapted by students. Rummy, for example, has been made into a game entitled *Menu Rummy* by the Extension Service of the University of Minnesota. The purpose of the game is for a player to collect the cards for two menus—one for dinner and

[14] Clark C. Abt, "Why Educational Games Win Converts," *Nation's Schools*, Vol. 80, No. 4 (Oct. 1967), p. 92.

[15] Ilajean Feldmiller, "Youngstown Develops Its Own Set of Home Economics Games," *Nation's Schools*, Vol. 80, No. 4 (Oct. 1967), p. 95.

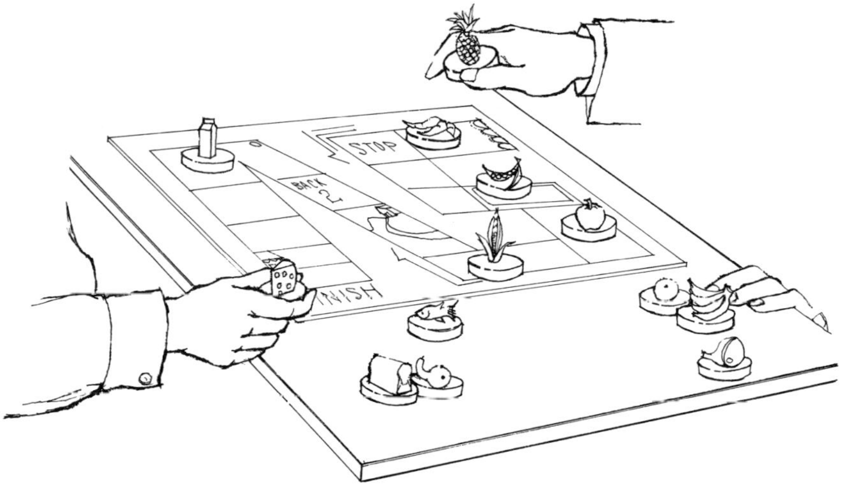

Figure 10–7 Games may be adapted for purposes of learning.

one for lunch or breakfast. When a player has two complete menus, they are placed on the table and the group discusses them in terms of nutrition, color, flavor, and texture. Other factors might be introduced, such as cost, time of preparation, family likes and dislikes, and ethnic or other preferences. Bingo can be adapted for the identification of sewing and kitchen equipment. Each number on the bingo card must correspond with a picture or an actual item of equipment that has been numbered on a sheet of paper held by each player or is listed on the overhead projector or on the chalkboard. Games by computer, games that use the television screen, and other modern games may be adapted for home economics.

An adaptation of charades is to place a piece of tulle or other very sheer material over the head of a student and pretend that it is a "magic story-telling net." The stories to be told can be related to any phase of home economics. Even introverted students can be encouraged to talk.

In-Basket Technique.

The in-basket technique is a simulation of the in-basket and out-basket on an administrator's desk that can be adapted for curriculum purposes. The in-basket deals with such matters as inquiries, requests for assistance with the solution of a problem, information about new products and equipment, and so on. The out-basket depicts the answers, suggestions, requests for additional information, or ordering of equipment, supplies, and other needs. The point of this game is that decisions have to be made.

There are a number of possibilies for the use of the in-basket, according to Spitze.[16] It may be used with a few students or with an entire class.

This method can be employed in every area of home economics. Here are a few in-basket items that can be used:

1. A telephone bill that is especially large.
2. A letter from a friend who is having boyfriend problems.
3. A note reminding a student of a sweater he borrowed.
4. A letter that describes a contest with a vacation as a prize.
5. An invitation to a party that does not appeal to the student.
6. A request for a donation to help flood victims.
7. A flyer about a sale of costume jewelry.
8. A letter inviting a student to secure a charge plate.
9. A circular letter inviting a student to offer his/her services to campaign for a local official.
10. A letter from the student's grandmother asking him for suggestions for his birthday present.
11. A letter describing a plan that allows a student to live with a family abroad for a month.
12. A letter from someone in West Africa asking the student to be a pen pal or to exchange recordings.

All students may be given the same communication, and then the student reactions that are put in the out-basket might be discussed with the entire class. Another possibility is to give each student a different in-basket item that relates to present class activities and for the class to discuss each reply.

Students will be required to make up other information pertinent to the item, such as more details about the situation. The critical point is the analysis of the solutions that students have suggested in their out-basket replies and the possible consequences of such solutions.

INDEPENDENT STUDY, PERSONALIZED INSTRUCTION, AND COMPUTER-ASSISTED INSTRUCTION

Independent Study

Independent study is supervised study in which the student has maximum freedom with a minimum of teacher guidance. One of the

[16] Op. cit., p. 25.

basic concepts related to this type of instruction is the recognition given to individual differences in such areas as problem solving, skills in language, visual and auditory acuity, dexterity, readiness to learn, motivation, ability to work alone, and many other personal, intellectual, and academic characteristics. Individualized learning depends on educational procedures that have the right amount of flexibility to maximize the use of human potential.

One objective may be enrichment. For example, a student in a family-life unit might search for works of fiction, poetry, or other art forms that portray family behavior and problems or other aspects of family interaction that particularly interest him/her. Enrichment tends to enlarge interests and to broaden study activities.

Individual programs may encourage exploration and discovery. Inquiry can be real and meaningful. A student in a clothing construction unit, for example, may select the best shops and stores for buying fabrics, based on cost, range of choice, and location.

In preliminary planning, a student may draft an outline of a project, stating the ways that his/her personal needs or problems are to be met, performance objectives, the procedures already tentatively explored, the resources available, and the proposed methods of evaluation, including progress reports. Teacher conferences, the possible use of a paraprofessional, the time schedule, the equipment required, and the place of work are all points that are considered.

Supervision may be minimal, so that student independence is encouraged. Students study alone or in groups of two or three. Books, pamphlets, magazines, journals, maps, charts, posters, pictures, photographs, and cartoons are all potential resources. Laboratory materials and equipment also encourage inquiry. A listening and viewing center for use with tapes, radio, television, slides, or transparencies should be available. Models, materials for expression —such as crayons, paints, and different kinds of paper—and programmed texts are other desirable aids.

Mobile equipment, such as portable sewing machines, electric skillets, or a kit of stain removers, is valuable. Fabrics, small household appliances, preserved foods of various kinds for testing, clothes, blueprints, floor plans, and other resources could be made available. A student may be given a package of a recently marketed frozen food to research thoroughly. The same might be done for new fibers, children's toys, small kitchen appliances, detergents, and snack foods.

Writing, experimenting, creating, visiting, interviewing, seeing, analyzing data, evaluating progress, and making reports—in short, using every available resource to solve problems—are characteristic of independent study.

The space in the classroom must be flexible so that the equipment and materials associated with an independent project do not interfere with other activities. For students who work alone, a work space that is relatively free from distraction and interruption is desirable. If the study is prolonged, there must be storage space for the materials being used. Many classrooms and laboratories are limited in space and require careful planning for maximum use. The atmosphere must be permissive, encouraging, and challenging. The room might be arranged to permit a casual atmosphere in which students can gather in small conversational groups and in which teacher and students can talk easily with parents, visitors, or community consultants.

Students engaged in independent study have unlimited opportunities to explore problems on their own. Stewart[17] offers these topics for independent study: food fads and fallacies, drugs and their abuse, the adoption of children, teaching the handicapped, outstanding contributions of women, and clothing styles for men.

Students may give their reports to the class individually or, if studies are related, as a committee. Reports should be lively and dramatic and include the use of aids, such as transparencies, pictures, photographs, charts and graphs, films, filmstrips, slides, tapes, or demonstrations. Also helpful are bulletin boards, pegboards, easels, and other display devices for sharing results, for highlighting progress, or for illuminating important concepts associated with individual projects. The other students may participate in the evaluation of independent study projects.

Learning Packages

Packages of various types are also available for use in individual learning. Well-designed packages are built on broad concepts that have been organized into manageable, coordinated modules. Well-defined objectives convey the quality of learning that is expected from each student. Multimedia learning materials of various types are included so that each student may make a choice among them according to his/her inclinations. Built-in self-evaluation devices assist a student in determining progress. The principal role of the teacher is to guide the students in the use of these materials.

Shear and Ray[18] have developed learning packages entitled HELP. The components are (1) a concept that connotes the major idea, such as "Impact of Advertising on Buying Practices," "Purchasing Fruits and Vegetables," and "Human Development and the Family"; (2) instructional or behavioral objectives; (3) multidimensional learning materials; (4) diversified learning activities; (5) evaluation; and (6) suggestions for student-initiated and self-directed activity for the

[17] Marjorie S. Stewart, "Another Look at Independent Study," *What's New in Home Economics,* Vol. 35, No. 2 (Feb. 1971), p. 20.

[18] Twyla Shear and Elizabeth Ray, "Home Economics Learning Packages," *Journal of Home Economics,* Vol. 61, No. 10 (Dec. 1969), pp. 768–770.

purpose of problem resolution or further study related to the learning package concept, to home experiences, or to FHA activities.

In addition to the many learning packages that are available, teachers may wish to develop some of their own packages. Kapfer[19] suggests a strategy for the development of learning packages like those of HELP. Students may assist in the preparation. Learning packages, according to Shear and Ray,[20] make a unique contribution in meeting the different needs of students and in locating resources for this purpose.

Computer-Assisted Instruction (CAI)

This strategy for teaching and learning has educational promise, according to Magidson.[21] Teaching by computer personalizes the instructional process and simulates experience that is not available elsewhere. This instruction can serve as "text, test, and tutor." For students to work at their own pace, it is an advantage. More advanced instruction is not forthcoming unless students have demonstrated mastery of previous learning. There is constant feedback of student progress, providing excellent reenforcement. Other advantages are the opportunities for students to review previous instruction, to ask for help, or to continue other activities that are enriching. Instruction for the computer may be systemically prepared, sequenced, tested, and revised.

Modes of Computer-Assisted Instruction

There are three modes of instruction. The *drill and practice mode* is the least complex, is easily prepared, and is the most widely used. In this mode, students are given a series of related questions to answer and have immediate feedback about the accuracy of their answers. In home-economics–related occupational education, for example, information about certain skills that are essential could be developed for this mode.

In the *tutorial mode,* students are given actual instruction in a field, such as nutrition, some phase of home management, or textiles. Questions are asked in the format of matching, fill-in, or multiple choice. In some programs, students may ask questions of the computer. This system is quite sophisticated because allowances can be made for synonyms, misspellings, various phrases, and other complex answers.

The *simulation mode* has greater flexibility and permits the student

[19] P. G. Kapfer, "An Instructional Management Strategy for Individualized Learning," *Phi Delta Kappan,* Vol. 41, No. 5 (Jan. 1968), pp. 260–263.

[20] Op. cit., p. 770.

[21] Errol M. Magidson, "Issue Overview: Trends in Computer Assisted Instruction," *Educational Technology,* Vol. 18, No. 4 (Apr. 1978), pp. 5–8.

to discover and generate new information, such as conducting laboratory experiments or research projects. Students might plan family menus by examining all the possible combinations of food items, based on such factors as nutritive value, cost, availability, and age-level nutritive requirements. The same might be done for planning budgets or developing original recipes.[22] Setting up time schedules, choosing color schemes for room decoration or personal wardrobes, and making appropriate career choices are other possibilities. One caution is that the quality of the computer input will be reflected in computer output.

Published studies indicate that learning takes less time with computer instruction. Note that programs usually emphasize the cognitive domain rather than the affective domain, although programs in that area can be developed.

Use in Home Economics

The use of this technological strategy is a challenge to home economics educators. Present uses include such examples as ranked nutrient research, as in finding foods rich in iron or another nutrient and ranking them in order; food intake analysis; energy and nutritional requirements; and nutritious food shopping. These programs have been developed by the Extension Service at the University of Minnesota. At the University of Nebraska, extension specialists have developed "Money Check" and "Diet Check." These programs evaluate financial planning and diet. Many other universities have developed programs in consumer education and in other areas. Programs for use in the home, the library, and the community bear consideration.

SUGGESTIONS FOR FURTHER LEARNING

1. Observe a class session in home economics. List statements, actions, and other evidence of the following:
   a. The students were encouraged to present viewpoints differing or in conflict with the ideas under discussion.
   b. Many opportunities were afforded for group involvement.
   c. The topic was related to the outside world and the social scene.
   d. The teacher identified the students having difficulties.
   e. Questions came up that challenged student thinking or values.
   f. The class activities were related to student problems, interests, and needs.
2. Choose at least four of the strategies discussed in this chapter. Through reading, discussion with others, and thinking, identify the theories and research that are the basis for the use of these methods.

[22] Alison Lauber, "Math Can Be Fun!" *American Girl*, Vol. 54, No. 6 (Apr. 1971), p. 37.

11

Planning

The home economics teacher plays an important role in home economics curriculum development and in implementing the curriculum. This task is not easy for a number of reasons. There may be a wide chasm between the interests of students[1] and the expectations of curriculum experts, state departments of education, and the board of education.

Discussion among teachers occurs frequently on the topic of the proper focus of education. Community and state *emphasis* may be on the "basics" as well as a strong interest in a cognitively oriented curriculum. Mass media reflect this value, as indicated in a recent Paul Greenberg article, in which he stated, "I submit that the gutsiest challenge a teacher can accept is to teach kids to read and write, to figure, and think."[2]

Many people in the community, members of the state departments, and mass media personnel do not realize that the curriculum that they experienced as children is not appropriate for the present-day student. The curriculum of today must be varied, stimulating, and geared to the ever-changing needs of students who are looking toward the twenty-first century.

Curriculum designers must recognize that the school has to compete with or, preferably, integrate with the impact of mass media, especially television; the great mobility of individuals and families,

[1] Elliott D. Landau, Shirley Epstein, and Ann P. Stone, "The Curriculum," in *The Teaching Experience* (Englewood Cliffs, N.J.: Prentice-Hall, 1976), pp. 228–229.

[2] "Education's New Frill: Death Studies," *Lincoln Sunday Journal and Star*, Sept. 10, 1978, p. 5A.

which brings exposure to a wide range of experiences; and the great variety of present-day lifestyles. The broad offerings of curriculum materials make it necessary for the home economics teacher to make many decisions about the kinds of experiences to offer students to best meet their needs. The teacher's freedom of decision is strained by the school in such areas as time schedules and facilities and by the community in its demands for inclusion (example, education for citizenship) and exclusion (example, sex education) of certain areas of study.

The community and often the state or federal agencies ask for accountability. This dictum requires that a teacher diagnose the strengths and weaknesses of each student and teach accordingly but, in addition, prepare students to do well on standardized tests when they are required or to succeed in fulfilling behavioral competency-based objectives. A teacher is expected to assimilate the latest research in learning, educational processes, methodology, and other areas pertinent to the curriculum and to apply it in her/his teaching. The development of a curriculum is a challenge in light of the diversity of thought about what and how students should be taught.

WHO PLANS THE CURRICULUM?

Comphehensive or total curriculum planning, which could involve many experts and agencies, is expensive in time and money, according to Brandt.[3] Teachers and schools cannot undertake this kind of planning because of a lack of resources, such as a lack of necessary research projects and the funds they provide, lack of personnel qualified to acquire necessary data, and lack of money. Ideally the public, the states, the federal government, the intermediate agencies, the voluntary consortia, the regional laboratories, the school districts, the schools, and the teachers might be orchestrated to develop curricula. But who and what would provide for this undertaking and its administration?

Working with the public, for example, is desirable in the determination of goals. But working with large groups of people is difficult, especially if one is trying to secure ideas from all sectors and not be dominated by one vociferous group. Brandt suggests two questions: What are students expected to learn, and what do individual students choose to learn? The public might have more input in answering the first question.

In the planning of the home economics curriculum, professional

[3] Ronald Brandt, "Who Shall Be Involved in Curriculum Development?" Editorial, *Educational Leadership,* Vol. 34, No. 1 (Oct. 1976), pp. 10–11.

home economics educators with various skills, including subject-matter specializations, are needed. In the planning of the broad scope and sequence of the curriculum, such skills as clarifying and selecting aims, analyzing appropriate content, selecting teaching and learning strategies, and placing curriculum plans in desirable sequence require both curriculum experts and home economics teachers (who will be especially responsible for applicability to the school and life situations of the students).

A curriculum plan is best tested in the classroom and revised according to results. Feedback from teachers, students, and parents is invaluable. The difficult task of a school board is to determine if a state plan for the total curriculum or the home economics curriculum is compatible with local needs. Drawing upon the expertise of administrators and faculty seems necessary in order to make these decisions. Curriculum planners need to make allowances for flexibility, choices, alternative programs, and other adjustments that the local situation may require.

A home economics teacher may participate in the planning of the total curriculum for students, of the total curriculum of home economics, and as a specialist in a level or subject-matter area, such as consumer education or nutrition. The curriculum should represent the best and the most progressive thinking of the home economics profession.

BACKGROUND FOR CURRICULUM PLANNING

Prior to designing a curriculum, planners must review and consider the need for change and trends in society, education, and home and family living. The last three categories are discussed in Chapter 1.

Need for Change

The curriculum planner must be a catalyst who influences and encourages change that reflects current research and experimentation, the basic values of education, and insight into the changing social condition. The strategy for change includes the creation of a social, political, and educational climate by the people who are influential or who control decision making, such as administrators, teachers, parents, and state department of education personnel. These persons must direct their efforts so that change will occur at all levels at which decisions about making curriculum changes are made—the community level, the school level, and the classroom level.

Strategies for Curriculum Development

Some specific and pragmatic approaches to curriculum change are suggested here. Many state and city departments write new courses of study or curriculum bulletins, to which teachers usually contribute. The assumption is that the changes recommended will be made. More teachers can be involved efficiently if the curriculum is changed at the school level. The in-service education of teachers helps to develop new perceptions and skills and is especially fruitful if principals and other administrators are included or have their own in-service education. Supplying teachers with consultants to assist them with innovation, or with new materials of instruction, has been tried successfully in curriculum development.

Another approach is provided by workshops in which key teachers participate and then serve as resource persons and leaders for other members of the teaching staff. This approach has been useful when there is focus on a specific area, such as human relations, family finance, or occupational education. Another way to facilitate change is to have teachers visit new programs that are operating in situations similar to their own.

All of these processes have been tried in changing home economics curriculums. The more opportunities for the involvement of the per-

Figure 11–1 Workshops are valuable for planning the curriculum and for communicating ideas to others.

sons affected by curriculum change, the greater the likelihood that change will take place. A recognition that curriculums must constantly be open to change may encourage the creation of mechanisms for bringing about change.

The informal communication system must not be ignored. Sometimes the formal organization is not the real power, so the innovator must rely on communicating informally for acceptance of change. Teachers will try an innovation more readily if it is advocated by someone whose reputation or authority they respect, or if a notable organization or institution is associated with the change. Providing assistance to teachers as they begin to implement curriculum changes fosters successful innovation. A continuous program of in-service education is necessary because many changes occur in teaching personnel, and each new teacher must become acquainted with the plans for instruction.

PREPLANNING THE CURRICULUM

The design for preplanning a specific curriculum generally includes the following: a democratic philosophy of education, the available resources, the community, the school, the students, the content, and the scope and sequence.

A Philosophy of Education

Philosophy, to many, is an abstraction. Although it may be difficult to articulate, teachers, need a philosophy for guidance. A philosophy attempts to define and systematize ideas, values, and beliefs about the nature of the good life and the good society. A philosophy gives criteria and guidelines for what is considered desirable and undesirable. From personal and social philosophies will evolve an educational philosophy—what teachers value and believe about education. Classrooms are segments of the social environment. What happens to students in this environment is a reflection of the educational philosophy.

Philosophy will be founded on the democratic ideals[4] that our country has always valued so highly—respect for the worth and dignity of the individual, cooperation for common purposes, and the application of intelligence to the improvement of the human lot. These democratic values guide people in adapting social institutions, eco-

[4] Harry S. Broudy, "Democratic Values and Educational Goals," in Robert M. McClure (ed.), *The Curriculum: Retrospect and Prospect.* The Seventieth Yearbook of the National Society for the Study of Education (Chicago: U. of Chicago, 1971), pp. 113–152.

nomic programs, and moral and ethical standards to the ever-changing circumstances of their lives. One of America's greatest and most constant needs is for teachers and students to reaffirm their allegiance to these democratic ideals.

Resources

There are many planning aids to which a teacher may turn, including curriculum guides; books, periodicals, and pamphlets on curriculum development, some with special emphasis on home economics; workshops, institutions, and refresher courses in curriculum development; and lectures by authorities at professional meetings. Surveys of student and parent interests in home economics can be useful. An advisory council composed of outstanding leaders in the community and/or alumnae of the home economics program might be formed. Analysis of the current research in the various aspects of curriculum development is also worthwhile. Other teachers may also offer good suggestions.

The Community

Through observation, surveys, information from local authorities, and discussions with students, a teacher can inform herself/himself about the community in which her/his students live.

The following questions may serve as a guide for such an inquiry:

1. Families

What are the ethnic, racial, religious, and social family backgrounds in the community?

How do family members interpret their roles?

What are the evidences of family instability, divorce, separation, and delinquency?

What are the family lifestyles?

What family customs and traditions prevail?

What family values prevail?

Is there evidence of extended family ties?

2. Housing

What kind of homes are found in the community?

What is the ratio of multiple-unit housing to single-family dwellings?

Is there a housing improvement program?

What appliances and conveniences are used?

Figure 11–2 A study of family lifestyles is basic to curriculum planning.

How much space is allocated to children?
What are the opportunities for privacy in the home?
What are the most serious housing problems?
In which room or rooms does the family congregate?

3. Community Economics
What are the sources of family income?
What percentage of the mothers work? In what kinds of work?

What are the principal industries in the community?

Economically how does the community compare with the nation as a whole?

What are the shopping facilities?

To what extent do residents use shopping and other facilities outside the community?

What opportunities are there for students to earn money? What spending allowance arrangements prevail?

What problems confront deprived families?

What is the family welfare situation?

4. Recreation

What are the preferred forms of recreation?

What are the facilities for recreation?

To what extent is recreation family-centered?

What kinds of recreation take place in the home?

Are there any recreation problems?

Are there museums and theaters and centers for arts and crafts, music, and other aesthetic activities?

5. Community Values

What are the values of the people in the community with regard to money, culture, education, homes, sports, human relations, sociability?

What is the attitude of the community toward its schools?

How is the home economics program viewed?

How is education for personal and family living rated?

In which areas is social action in evidence?

6. Community Organization

Who are the leaders in the community?

Who are the power groups?

What service clubs exist?

What is the role of the churches?

What are the important community projects?

Are there serious conflicts within the community?

Is there evidence of class stratification, and what are its implications?

Is the community a part of a larger urban, suburban, or other type of organizational complex, and what are the influences of the larger complex?

Answers to these questions and similar information will be invaluable in the planning of a program that reflects the needs and problems of the community and its students. Additional information may be gained from school records and direct observation of the students and the citizens in a variety of situations. Reading the local newspapers, talking to the citizens, and discussing the community and the students with teachers who have been on the staff for some time, as well as securing the reactions of recently appointed staff, are other possibilities. Walking or driving through shopping and residential areas can be illuminating. Attendance at community functions may be helpful. All of this information will have to be analyzed, and tentative hypotheses about families, students, and community will have to be tested.

The School

To know the goals of the total school program is important, for the home economics program must be integrated into the overall program. The teacher must determine what objectives of the school can be met through home economics. In addition, the teacher should become familiar with any emphasis given to personal and family living in other courses, such as English or social studies, so that he or she can reinforce, enrich, and utilize what is taught in other subjects.

Schools are a subsystem of the general social system and consequently reflect society, according to Macdonald.[5] Reflected within the school are many of the human values that have developed in Western civilization. Not only are radical leftist and rightist values present but also a broad spectrum of middle positions. Schools should not be dedicated to having students select a position but rather to acquainting them with the total range of values.

The Students

If a program in home economics is to be functional, then the interests, problems, and values of students must be determined, understood, and incorporated into the curriculum. Information concerning their home experiences and background is important. The influence of their age, sex, socioeconomic status, level of ability, previous experiences, and personal purposes in taking the course may prove enlightening. If possible, the teacher should learn something about the students' interests outside of school—their participation in commu-

[5] James B. Macdonald, "The High School in Human Terms: Curriculum Design," in Norman K. Hamilton and Galem Saylor (eds.), *Humanizing the Secondary School,* (Washington, D.C.: Association for Supervision and Curriculum Development, 1969), pp. 45–48.

nity activities, their jobs, their family and civic responsibilities, and their hobbies. This information may be secured through checklists, autobiographies, logs, and teacher observation.

SPECIFIC PREPLANNING IN HOME ECONOMICS

The definitions and concerns of home economics in Chapter 2 give a historical review of the thinking of home economists. More effective service to individuals and families continues to be a primary concern, and the home economics teacher is challenged to interpret this concern in a meaningful manner to students and their families. Every day in the classroom, the home economics teacher must help each student to cope with life a little more easily, to solve an important problem, to begin to formulate a goal, or to look at a value more objectively.

The Content of Home Economics

What is usually considered content—information about nutrition, clothing, housing, and all the other areas of home economics—is a means to an end. Unless this content helps a student to release potential and to maximize development, it is of little use. So if a teacher has students memorize the names of vitamins, sew a straight seam, and shine the pots and pans or never has them experiment with the ingredients of a recipe, what are the objectives? The point is that a teacher will select and help students to determine the content of home economics that is appropriate to their problems, needs, and interests. The means is the subject matter, and the ends are students and their development.

This does not mean that home economics content does not have a structure. Home economics curriculum experts, specialists, teacher educators, supervisors, teachers, and students, through many meetings and workshops, have utilized concepts as a basis for curriculum development.

In 1961, the U.S. Office of Education initiated a national project for curriculum development in home economics.[6] This step reflected a general movement to improve the curriculum of secondary schools and particularly to reexamine basic questions related to home eco-

[6] Edna Amidon, *Concepts and Generalizations: Their Place in High School Home Economics Curriculum Development* (Washington, D.C.: American Home Economics Association, 1967).

nomics curriculums. The Home Economics Seminar[7] held in French Lick, Indiana, attempted to examine the problems of articulation and differentiation of home economics subject matter at various teaching levels—secondary, college and university, and adult. The strong focus on the role of concepts in the planning of home economics curriculums had considerable influence on later workshops that worked on curriculum in home economics at the secondary level. Seven workshops sponsored by the Office of Education and various institutions of higher learning concentrated on the development of basic concepts and generalizations.

The five content areas of home economics selected for emphasis in curriculum were

Human development and the family.

Home management and family economics.

Foods and nutrition.

Textiles and clothing.

Housing.

Subject-matter specialists, high school teachers, and home economics educators and supervisors were actively involved in these workshops.

Concepts in the Five Areas

The workshop participants believed that the concepts included in the five areas of home economics subject matter could serve as a guide for local and state groups to develop curriculum resource materials. Following are examples of one concept and a supporting generalization from each of the five subject-matter areas.[8]

Content Category: Human Development and the Family
Concept: Universality of individuals and families
Generalization: There are more similarities in family patterns within a culture than there are in family patterns of different cultures.

Content Category: Home Management and Family Economics
Concept: Environmental influences on individual and family management

[7] Home Economics Division, *Home Economics Seminar,* July 24–28, 1961, French Lick, Indiana (Washington, D.C.: Association of State Universities and Land Grant Colleges, 1961).

[8] Amidon, op. cit., pp. 25, 29, 32, 39, 45.

Subconcept: Economic
Generalization: The family economy affects and is affected by the larger economy.

Content Category: Food and Nutrition
Concept: Significance of food
Subconcept: As related to nutrition
Generalization: Adequate nutrition can be attained from many combinations of food commonly available throughout the world. No single food pattern is essential to health.

Content Category: Housing
Concept: Influences of housing on people
Subconcept: Social
Generalization: Housing and its surroundings are status-defining for individuals and families.

Content Category: Textiles and Clothing
Concept: Significance of textiles and clothing
Subconcept: Social and psychological aspects of clothing
Generalization: As an individual matures, his or her clothing perceptions and values change.

It must be emphasized that concepts and generalizations, as used in planning, are not given to a class; rather, students should be encouraged to develop and state their own concepts and generalizations. These will vary in complexity according to individual maturity and abilities and can run the gamut from the very simple to the very sophisticated. The teacher will find that the identification of concepts and of supporting generalizations provides a framework for what is to be taught. These, in turn, will be related to the solving of student problems and the expansion of students' interests.

Taxonomies

Improved selection of objectives, content, and learning experiences occur if a teacher is well informed about the taxonomy of educational objectives. Taxonomies are patterned after the biological taxonomies, but the categories are terms that are descriptive of the kinds of behavior that are sought from students in the teaching–learning process, according to Krathwohl.[9] From these descriptions of desired behavior and the selections of subject matter, objectives can evolve.

[9] David R. Krathwohl, "The Taxonomy of Educational Objectives—Its Uses in Curriculum Building," in James R. Gress (ed.), with the assistance of David E. Purpel, *Curriculum, An Introduction to the Field* (Berkeley, Calif., McCutchan, 1978), pp. 341–358.

Taxonomies have been developed for three domains in human functioning: the cognitive, the affective, and the psychomotor.

The broad categories for the cognitive domain are[10]

1. *Knowledge:* the recall and recognition of specifics, principles, processes, methods, and the like.
2. *Comprehension:* understanding and making some use of specifics, principles, facts, and the like.
3. *Application:* the learner is able to make use of her or his knowledge of specifics, principles, and facts in a particular situation.
4. *Analysis:* the learner is able to break down a problem into its elements and to see the organization of those elements.
5. *Synthesis:* the learner is able to integrate the elements of fact, principles, and the like into a meaningful communication.
6. *Evaluation:* the use of judgment concerning the value of a communication, a theory, a generalization, or the like, based on internal and/or external criteria set by the individual. Note the increasing complexity of these operations.

Krathwohl[11] and others developed the following taxonomy of objectives in the affective domain, which is concerned with changes in interests, attitudes, values, appreciation, and personal social adjustments. The major categories are

1. *Receiving,* in which the concern is to sensitize the learner to the existence of certain phenomena and stimuli.
2. *Responding,* which deals with interest—the desire that leads to involvement or seeking out.
3. *Valuing,* a concern that certain beliefs, attitudes, values, and ideals have been internalized sufficiently to be manifested consistently in the learner's behavior.
4. *Organization,* in which internalized values are conceptualized and organized into a hierarchical system.
5. *Characterization by a value or a value complex,* in which values have not only been internalized into a consistent hierarchy, but the behavior of an individual is controlled by these values, and evocation of the behavior is no longer accompanied by emotion or affect.

[10] Benjamin S. Bloom, *Taxonomies of Educational Objectives: The Classification of Educational Objectives, Handbook I: Cognitive Domain* (New York: Longmans, Green, 1956).

[11] David R. Krathwohl, Benjamin S. Bloom, and Bertram B. Masia, *Taxonomy of Educational Objectives: The Classification of Educational Goals, Handbook II: Affective Domain* (New York: McKay, 1964).

Simpson[12] suggests a tentative system for a classification of educational objectives for the psychomotor domain. The major categories are

1. *Perception,* an awareness of objects, qualities, or relations through sensory stimulation, such as hearing, seeing, touching, smelling, tasting, and muscle (kinesthesis).
2. *Set,* which involves a preparatory adjustment or readiness for a specific type of action. The three aspects of set are mental, physical, and emotional.
3. *Guided response,* in which the early steps in the development of a skill emphasize the components of a more complex skill. A subcategory is *imitation,* in which an individual attempts to execute an act from a demonstration of another person.
4. *Mechanism,* in which a learned response becomes habitual and denotes skill and confidence in performance.
5. *Complex response,* indicating a high degree of skill, so that acts can be carried out with ease and efficiency. Finely coordinated motor skill and muscle control are evident.

All these domains are interrelated. In curriculum development, a teacher may consider the cognitive, affective, and psychomotor objectives that seem necessary to develop a successful family member, for example. In addition, the three domains challenge home economics educators to look at the total person. All in all, they give direction to teaching.

Background for Objectives

Educational objectives are conceived along a broad spectrum of expectations from the wider society to the individual classroom.[13] The wide range of thought associated with the development of objectives is examined here.

Objectives give direction to education, so a distinction must be made between *ideals,* such as ethical character or mental health, and *aims,* such as the ability to become a wise consumer, the ability to think critically in life situations, or the ability to appreciate beauty in nature and in home surroundings. In addition, a home economics teacher will identify how an objective, as stated may be evaluated. In

[12] Elizabeth Jane Simpson, *The Classification of Educational Objectives, Psychomotor Domain,* Vocational and Technical Education Grant, Contract No. OE–5–85–104, Vocational Education Act of 1963, Section 4(c) (Urbana: U. of Illinois, 1966).

[13] Daniel Tanner and Laurel N. Tanner, *Curriculum Development, Theory into Practice* (New York: Macmillan, 1975), Ch. 3.

these aims, there may be an even more specific reference to measure expectations, namely, the ability of students to identify and define problems, their ability to make relevant hypotheses, their ability to select and analyze data pertinent to the solution of problems, and their ability to formulate valid conclusions, solutions, and generalizations.

Smith and Tyler[14] contend that the first and most important step in curriculum planning is the formulating of objectives. These objectives become the criteria, according to Tyler,[15] by which materials are selected, content is specified, instructional procedures are developed, and evaluative techniques are prepared. In the final analysis, objectives reflect the personal preferences or ends desired by the curriculum developers or the teacher. The major goal in home economics programs is to prepare students for effective personal and family living.

Popham and Baker[16] contend that most objectives written by teachers are ambiguous. According to these authors, objectives should be stated in terms of *how* the learners *behave* and *what* they *can do* after instruction. This type of objective provides guidance for the teacher. Furthermore it is stated that this method of writing objectives makes it simple for a teacher to select relevant learning experiences for students and to evaluate whether the learner has acquired the intended behavior. Preassessment of present behaviors before instruction allows teachers to revise upward or to develop new goals if many students already possess the behaviors sought. Behaviors that a teacher has assumed that students have, may be lacking, which means objectives will have to be altered accordingly. In planning instructional sequences, there is a preference for "What behavioral changes do I desire?" to "What shall I do?" The ability to write these kinds of objectives shows that the teacher is a technically skilled expert and consequently very systematic in educational procedures.

There are a number of suggestions offered by Popham and Baker about the writing of objectives. If an objective is too broad, it can be interpreted in a variety of ways, and consequently it may lack direction. Vagueness is another problem, such as "A student will have a greater appreciation of his/her environment." Popham and Baker disapprove of objectives that are written in terms of topics, concepts, or generalizations.

[14] Eugene R. Smith and Ralph W. Tyler, *Appraising and Recording Student Progress* (New York: Harper, 1942), pp. 15–21.

[15] Ralph W. Tyler, *Basic Principles of Curriculum and Instruction* (Chicago: U. Chicago, 1950), pp. 3–4.

[16] W. James Popham and Eva I. Baker, *Establishing Instructional Goals* (Englewood Cliffs, N.J.: Prentice-Hall, 1970).

To avoid these problems, recommendations for writing objectives, according to Popham and Baker, include writing objectives in terms of observable student behaviors; avoiding the use of such words as *knowledge* or *insight;* and clearly communicating an educational intent, such as "describe an adequate diet". Some priority of learning behaviors is indicated in objectives. The cognitive level of presentation of an objective should be appropriate to the learning ability of a student. The achievement desired of a student is indicated in the objective.

Tyler objects to the current type of behavioral objectives because they are patterned after the industrial and military world of training and management by objectives. The most serious shortcoming is that the objectives are so narrowly specific that the purpose of education and the nature of learning are not reflected adequately.[17] Tyler states his criticism as the failure to distinguish between the (1) learning of highly specific skills for limited performance and (2) the more generalized understanding of problem-solving skills and other kinds of behavior that thoughtful educators seek to help students develop.

Combs, like Tyler, is noted for being an advocate of humanistic objectives in education.[18] He feels that educational objectives can no longer be written in precise behavioral terms but must be humane and holistic. Examples of humanistic objectives are the development of intelligent behavior and the production of self-directed, creative, problem-solving, humane, and caring citizens who can deal with and contribute to the betterment of our complex society.

Humanists believe that the human personality is not static. Behavior is broadly interpreted not only as external action but as internal processes. Ignored by some experts on objectives is the point that the dominant influences on behavior are found in the feelings, attitudes, beliefs, values, hopes, aspirations, and perceptions of persons.

According to Combs, new concepts of learning should be recognized in the writing of objectives, such as the basic principle that any information must be personally relevant and close to the self to be meaningful. Concentrating on processes rather than behaviors in learning is more effective. Processes include facilitating, encouraging, providing opportunities, helping, and creating the need to know something. Combs believes that this focus in education results in superior achievement, and excellence is not sacrificed.

A realization that self-concept is a major determinant of every be-

[17] June Grant Shane and Harold G. Shane, "Ralph W. Tyler, The Father of Behavioral Objectives Criticizes Them, An Interview," *Phi Delta Kappan,* Vol. 55, No. 4 (Dec. 1973), p. 57.

[18] Arthur W. Combs, "Humanism, Education and the Future," *Educational Leadership,* Vol. 35, No. 4 (Jan. 1978), pp. 300–303.

havior is important in writing objectives. What happens to a student's self-concept may be the most important emphasis in teaching. Students with a low self-concept usually have difficulty in learning.

Humanistic objectives have been a part of American education since its beginning. Some examples are "a healthy mind in a healthy body," "concern for democratic values," "worthy home membership," and "good citizenship." This type of objective is largely ignored now with the swing to an emphasis on subject matter and skills that can be easily measured.

A home economics teacher may raise the question, "Which type of objective is most suitable to what I wish to accomplish with students?" Granted, a home economics teacher may not have a choice, because the type of objectives to be used in the home economics curriculum may have been decided elsewhere. If there is a choice, the objectives to be formulated will reflect the educational philosophy of the teacher. Critical to the development of objectives is the position of the teacher on how effective learning takes place and how the potentials of each student are best released.

Scope and Sequence

In planning a total program in home economics, it is helpful to develop an outline of the scope and sequence of the work to be accomplished in different subject-matter areas and at the various grade levels—in short, a developmental progression of tasks and learnings. Needless repetition can thereby be avoided, and plans can be geared to learnings appropriate to the type of student involved.

Tracy and Walsh[19] suggest that among the considerations the teacher should bear in mind when deciding the scope and sequence of a home economics program are the socioeconomic status, the stage of the life cycle, the vocational needs, and the geographic and cultural backgrounds of the students to be taught. In addition, the ability of the students, the degree of need for the information, the possibility of suitable learning experiences, the extent to which learning can be extended, and the resulting omissions when certain selections are made may be considered.

DEVELOPING THE PROGRAM

Planning must involve the students concerned; it should be centered on their vital interests and meaningful problems. This planning

[19] Jane Tracy and Letitia Walsh, "Improved Teaching Through Essay Tests," *Illinois Teacher of Home Economics*, Vol. 3, No. 5 (1960), p. 208.

involves teacher and students making choices, examining all viewpoints critically, accepting and adjusting to changes, and exploring pertinent resources. Planning should promote continuity, thereby giving teacher and students a feeling of security.

Kinds of Planning

A teacher must examine the total program to determine what kind of planning is required and what choices are open. What are the offerings for which he/she is responsible? Are they as well planned as is possible, or should changes be made?

Another facet of planning involves distilling all the informational input collected about the community, the school, family lifestyles, the students, and the available facilities and evaluating them in terms of assets, limitations, resources, and tentative hypotheses that will give direction to the program. A few examples are cited here. In regard to facilities, a teacher may realize that some of the equipment is not well placed or well stored. Could this problem be incorporated into one of the units? How much is the budget for the year? It may be lower than anticipated, so what is expendable? Can something equally exciting be substituted for that minicourse in gourmet cookery? The neighborhood is changing, and the number of disadvantaged students has increased. Present materials may have to be checked and new ones prepared. Articles in professional magazines, pamphlets, and other sources of information may have to be surveyed for suggestions for working with these students. How may additional students be recruited for the department?

These hypothetical problems are offered as instances of the preliminary planning a teacher must do so that she/he is in a better position to work with an advisory committee, with students, with other home economics teachers, and with the administration in further planning. In a notebook or folder a teacher may wish to assemble facts that are pertinent to planning, questions that must be answered, and some tentative ideas for the year's plans.

Advisory Committees

Ideally, the home economics department should have an advisory committee that serves in a consultant capacity. Members should be selected on the basis of the unique contributions they might make to the department. Individuals from department stores, industry, food service establishments, and other community businesses would be helpful in planning community endeavors, such as work–study programs, field trips, and part-time summer jobs for students in home-economics–related areas. Members that represent social agencies

Figure 11–3 The input of an advisory committee can be stimulating and helpful.

and civic organizations would be helpful in giving information about the community and how to work with students and parents. A retired home economics teacher can be very helpful.

For some departments, it may be feasible to have a number of committees available for advisory purposes as needs arise. Included might be committees to assist in planning new or remodeling old facilities; in planning community projects, such as home ecology; or in utilizing community resources. Inviting parents for the sole purpose of discussing the home economics program, and keeping the occasion and refreshments as simple as possible, may produce helpful suggestions. Groups should be kept as small as possible to promote wide participation. Students and parents may be divided into discussion groups, and then each group may report back to the entire group. Questions to be discussed might be "What are your feelings about this program? What suggestions do you have to offer? What do you think should be done differently?" Parents and students cannot be expected to agree on all points, but disagreement stimulates thinking. Some concrete plans for implementing suggestions must be considered, so that parents and students can feel that they have not advised in vain.

Sometimes a professional or service club may be encouraged to adopt the department or to act in an advisory capacity. It behooves the teacher to consider all the possibilities for sources of advisory assistance.

Teacher–Pupil Planning

Pupils in the home economics department can be helpful in planning to the extent that they are interested and competent to make decisions. In some instances, it is important to inform students about the possible contributions of home economics in the broader world. With this information, students, formed into committees or into small groups, might consider their particular needs and how home economics might be helpful to them. Teacher and students might match the needs to possible adaptations of the teacher's plans. There is no doubt that having students involved in the planning process contributes immeasurably to their sense of responsibility, their interest, and their satisfaction with class activities; perhaps most important, they become more adept at decision making. The teacher, however, must never forget that she/he is the key to the planning process. Frequently students have ideas for modules, minicourses, or special clubs that may lead to more ambitious endeavors.

Each teacher must face realistically the extent to which she/he can be comfortable with student suggestions. If student assistance is solicited, it cannot be ignored. Some criteria for the feasibility of ideas may be cooperatively established. Planning is facilitated when teacher and students have good rapport.

Components of Planning

Tyler suggests four major tasks in the preparation of a curriculum: (1) the selection and definition of learning objectives; (2) the selection and creation of appropriate learning experiences; (3) the organization of learning experiences to achieve a maximum cumulative effect; and (4) the evaluation of the curriculum to furnish a continuing basis for necessary revisions and desirable improvements. The home economics teacher may use these tasks as guidelines in planning.[20]

Sequential Planning

After deciding which aspects of the program to emphasize, the teacher should schedule the program in terms of the whole year. The school calendar is often divided into semesters or some other time segments that influences planning. Courses should be divided into areas or units of interest. If the teacher is responsible for more than one grade level, it may be advisable to arrange a scope and sequence chart. Planning should be broad so that new needs, interests, and problems may be recognized. From this yearly outline, a home economics teacher should organize the units or areas of concern in considerable detail, and from these will emerge the daily lesson plan. The teacher should consult the school calendar in order to locate units in the best time slot as well as giving consideration to other determinants, such as availability of community resources, seasonal supplies for the laboratory, space commitments, and teaching schedules. If possible, a unit should be planned for an unbroken time period. Interest may lag when a long holiday period divides a unit.

[20] Ralph W. Tyler, "Specific Approaches to Curriculum Development," in Jon Schaffarzick and David Hampson (eds.), *Strategies for Curriculum Development* (Berkeley, Calif.: McCutchan, 1975), Ch. 2.

Although each teacher will wish to develop a personal format for writing units, here are some ideas that may be helpful. Possible approaches should be considered in terms of pupil interests. These approaches are more effective if incorporated naturally as part of ongoing school or out-of-school activities. An outline of possible content, related to probable questions and problems of students, is important. Suggestions for possible student experiences take into consideration how students learn, indicate opportunities for them to make decisions, and allow for student growth.

The unit plan generally includes sources of teaching aids—books, magazines, pamphlets, audiovisual aids, and community resources. The evaluation procedures, such as written devices, observation, and consultation with parents, should be suited to the objectives of the program.

Some teachers may desire to make their unit plans very detailed, whereas others may prefer them very brief. In any case, it is wise to put something on paper as a guide, for writing serves as a discipline in thinking through the planning more concisely and comprehensively.

Modules, minicourses, and other types of classroom organization will require the same type of planning. In some instances, plans will include provision for independent study and individualized instruction.

Objectives

To be prepared for the writing of objectives, a home economics teacher will wish to review the "Background for Curriculum Planning," "Taxonomies," and "Concepts in Five Areas" sections that appear earlier in this chapter. A few key objectives may be written about the entire year's program and for each unit to be taught at certain levels. These objectives should be tentative in nature, yet sufficiently clear and definite to serve as guides for the ultimate selection of what is to be used in the weekly or daily lesson plan. When students participate in planning, then the objectives may be cooperatively selected as those most pertinent to student needs and interests. Related to objectives are the development of concepts and generalizations, which is reviewed next.

Concepts and Generalizations

Prior to examining specific concepts in relation to these five areas of subject matter, it seems appropriate to examine some general ideas about concepts and generalizations.

The building of concepts emerges from attempts to classify experiences. A child recognizes bread, for example, then discovers that there are many kinds of bread and that bread is made into toast and even pudding. When something new is learned, a student is building or rebuilding a concept. Education is vitally concerned with this classification of a student's experiences.

Dale[21] defines a concept as a summarization of past experiences or as a general idea that is formed about several experiences. There are two interacting parts to this definition. First, specific vivid experiences provide the foundation upon which an individual constructs usable concepts. Second, the individual must have the ability to combine and recombine these experiences in many ways. Concept building is an essential goal in all teaching because by building concepts, students learn to shape general ideas about life and to arrange their lives into meaningful patterns. Because education is open-ended, teachers and students must recognize that concepts are fluid, flexible, and growing. Conceptual development is influenced by the quality and quantity of experiences, so the teacher must be challenged to enrich a student's concepts by extending and deepening her or his experiences.

Vocabulary is one key to concept building. Students give names not only to things but to thoughts and to ideas. As the individual develops intellectually, this naming becomes increasingly complex and abstract. Words do have limitations. Sometimes thoughts and understanding cannot be expressed in words. Nonverbal thought may be expressed in art or music. Some experiences are so personal that they cannot be transferred to others.

The use of concrete objects when possible in teaching will facilitate word meaning. If a child is unfamiliar with a word, such as *avocado,* he/she may be given this fruit to feel, taste, smell, and examine. In the future, the child will be able to match the word *avocado* with experience of the fruit. With an abstract idea such as love, there may be greater difficulty. Photographs of expressions of love may be helpful, but love is not something that can be tasted. Words such as *democracy, citizen,* and *value* are even more difficult to grasp. Through the discriminating use of films, recordings, dramatizations, and class discussions, an understanding of abstract words will develop.

Generalizations may be made from concepts. Dale suggests that a generalization may be defined as a short sentence that condenses long experience. The concrete and the abstract interact in the process of concept development. Generalizations lend understanding to new concrete experiences, and concrete experiences enlarge or refine generalizations.

[21] Edgar Dale, *Audiovisual Methods in Teaching* (New York: Holt, 1969), pp. 70–102.

Selection, Creation, and Organization of Learning Experiences

An important part of effective teaching is mastering the large repertoire of approaches to teaching. Competence in teaching can be expanded by increasing the *range* of teaching strategies that might be used in the classroom and by becoming more *skillful* in the use of these strategies.[22]

Learning experiences are based on theories of how students learn, grow, and develop. Some learning experiences are designed to strengthen self-concept, to improve human relationships, to clarify values, or to master certain subject matter.

Tyler[23] believes that less progress has been made in the organization of learning experiences than in any other aspect of the curriculum, particularly in theoretical frames of reference. One distinction between the informal and incidental learnings that take place on the street, in the playground, or in places other than the classroom is the conscious effort by educators to organize the learning experiences of the curriculum. Organization is preferred to haphazard, isolated, and undisciplined learning.

To achieve changes in thinking, values, habits, skills, or interests requires considerable time, continuous attention, and many learning experiences that focus on the same outcomes. Furthermore learning in one area must graduate from simple to more complex learnings as the student progresses. Also, many of the general learnings, such as those already mentioned, are being reinforced in other areas such as in English and science classes.

Tyler recommends that all of the learning experiences in the curriculum be organized to produce a maximum cumulative effect in the attainment of objectives. An effective organization of learning experiences centers on the development of students and *not on the organization of subject matter.* In organizing learning experiences, educators must be aware that many experiences of students are outside the control of the school.

Certain commonalities in elements might be used as a basis for organization. *Concepts* are one example. For instance, the concept of interdependence is learned at an early age and is broadened in meaning as the child grows. Certain *skills,* such as reading and social skills, are another commonality. *Values* are another type of common element.

Another challenge is to consider the linkage of one level with the

[22] Bruce R. Joyce, *Selecting Learning Experiences* (Washington, D.C.: Association for Supervision and Curriculum Development, 1978).

[23] Ralph W. Tyler, "The Organization of Learning Experiences," in Arno A. Bellack and Herbert M. Kliebard (eds.), *Curriculum and Evaluation* (Berkeley, Calif.: McCutchan, 1977), Ch. 4.

Figure 11–4 The learning of a student comes from many sources.

next. *Generalizations* may serve as stepping stones. Another organizing principle is chronological, such as studying human development from birth to death. Moving from concrete experiences to abstractions is another suggestion. Tyler recommends that serious study be given to possible organizing principles for the curriculum. All too often the organization proceeds on a mere "rule of the thumb."

Suggestions for learning experiences are included in many chapters of this book. Teachers are encouraged to create their own strategies, which may be especially appropriate for the students being taught.

The Daily Lesson Plan

No planning is complete until a teacher decides what is to be accomplished each day. Some teachers, especially inexperienced ones, prefer to chart this in detail, whereas others write only a brief outline. Taba[24] suggests a structure that begins with the concepts, skills, or pattern of ideas that serve as a framework for the development of objectives. *Objectives* should be stated in terms of the behavior manifested by the learner or in other concrete terms. *Supportive learnings* cite the important facts, generalizations, and skills related to the objectives. *Pupil experiences* provide the opportunity to realize the objectives of the day's lesson and to bring satisfaction to the learner. *Evaluation* includes the means to determine the extent to which the objectives were realized. *Critical suggestions* adapt the day's lesson to the needs, interests, abilities, and problems of the disadvantaged, handicapped, gifted, and other types of learners. Market orders and the teaching aids to be used might be listed. Emphasis on the community, particular social problems, family applications, or recent changes that might increase the value of the class session, may be added. Teachers may adapt this format to various purposes, including laboratory sessions, team teaching, open-school arrangement, or individualized instruction. It is assumed that the teacher has an understanding of the content, of the skills needed, and of individual student needs. The lesson plan serves merely as a guide—the alert teacher will keep tuned in to new interests or problems of the students and will weave in their ideas and suggestions as the lesson evolves, and she/he will take advantage, too, of her/his own second thoughts.

Creative use of teaching aids helps to make a lesson more interesting. The teacher may begin the class session with a newspaper clipping, an interesting photograph or cartoon, a filmstrip, or a game that has been adapted to the purpose of the lesson. Later the teacher may resort to a chart, a flannelboard presentation, or a demonstration that further develops the important ideas of the lesson and will incorporate student contributions. If a laboratory or experimental period is part of the plan, the teacher can supervise individuals or small groups. At the close of the session, there could be an evaluation of the progress made; a determination of the extent to which criteria

[24] Hilda Taba, *Curriculum Development: Theory and Practice* (New York: Harcourt, 1962), p. 425.

were met, concepts were enlarged, and objectives were achieved; an enumeration of learnings; the development of a generalization or generalizations; and a consideration of the next steps. In addition, both teacher and students should appraise the growth and development of individuals and the group as a whole.

Hamilton et al.[25] suggest a format for a lesson plan that is especially suitable for certain aspects of home-economics–related occupational education. There are three major categories: lesson approach, lesson development, and lesson summary.

Certain general information is put at the top of the lesson plan so that this information may be used by a substitute teacher in the event that the regular teacher is absent. Subject, date, title of lesson, grade level, and hour or period that the class meets are suggested for inclusion. If the plan is for team teaching, the part that is the responsibility of each teacher should be indicated. Including the time alloted for each segment of the lesson plan is helpful.

The *lesson approach* highlights the specific objectives, aims, or goals that are pertinent to this lesson. These objectives have been drawn from the broader objectives of the unit plan, for example, "Your Clothes." In the introduction, a teacher may wish to include acquainting the students with the ways that the lesson is related to previous learnings and the ways that the lesson is related to them personally.

The *lesson development* includes the selection of an appropriate method, such as discussion, laboratory, or role playing, plus the instructional materials or media to be used. Learning experiences that enable the student to apply, integrate, experiment with, or be creative with the instructional materials are included. The subject matter, concepts, or content of the lesson is determined by the objectives.

The *lesson summary* is the time for citing generalizations, considering individual or group action that may grow out of the lesson, and evaluating whether the objectives were attained.

A lesson plan has to reflect the teacher's philosophy, teaching style, and personal manner of managing a lesson. Few educators agree on a format for a lesson plan. Teachers are urged to develop their own formats unless the situation demands following a prescribed form.

Assignments

The role of assignments in the planning process is a neglected area in educational literature, but educators agree that assignments that are vague, uninteresting, indefinite, or unrelated to the class activity

[25] James B. Hamilton et al., *Develop a Lesson Plan* (Atlanta: American Association for Vocational Instructional Materials, 1977).

contribute to students' failure to learn. A stimulating assignment, however, is recognized as an integral step in the realization of educational objectives.

The purpose of an assignment is determined largely by the goals a teacher has in mind. She/he must decide if the emphasis is to be on a mastery of facts, on memorization, or on a stimulation of thought about concepts, generalizations, principles, or interrelationships. For example, will students be expected to memorize the foods in a daily food selection guide, or will the teacher provide experiences for them to determine the adequacy of their own diets according to this guide?

One far-reaching purpose of assignments is the release of the creative potential of teacher and students alike. An assignment may be related to ongoing class activities with special emphasis on student interests, needs, and concerns. A good guideline is "Will this assignment contribute to student growth and development?" Students might be challenged to gather information about something in which they are interested, for instance, the best way to buy a secondhand car or the principle that explains a chemical reaction. Other projects might include studies of how to gain peer approval, how to arouse interest in a community project, or how to solve some problem involving money management. Assignments can be planned to plumb students' social sensitivity. Are they aware of the impact their activities and ideas have in their homes, in their community, and in the world at large? Does a student realize how her desire for a costly stereo set may affect her family's finances? If a student is college-bound, is he concerned about those who do not go to college? Are students aware of the possible influence on their own lives of the traditions, values, and ideals of adolescents in the developing countries of Africa?

Planning the Assignment

The goal of assignment planning is the determination of ways and means of realizing the desired objectives. Continuity of assignments with ongoing coursework is important, and students should be aware of the bearing each assignment has on the realization of class goals.

One of the most serious complaints about assignments is that they are dull and similar. Must they be confined to "reading" and "writing"? How much more exciting it is to survey, interpret, analyze, interview, visit, look, make, solve, categorize, listen, experiment, explain, imagine, select, plan, develop, prepare, outline, think, serve, help, dramatize, or display!

Different levels of student achievement must be considered: Will the same assignment suffice for all, or should an effort be made to meet the needs and interests of students of differing talents and abilities? Some teachers accomplish this goal by indicating the range of scope and depth of an assignment so that students can estimate the degree of their accomplishments. Does an assignment take into consideration the diversity of social, economic, and cultural backgrounds represented in the class? If students are encouraged to assist in planning assignments, there is a greater likelihood that these distinctions will be recognized and accommodated. Offering students a choice of approaches to meeting an assignment is a good way to accommodate individual differences. On an assigned study of parent–student relations, for example, one student may read about the recommendations made by authorities concerning adolescent–parent relations, whereas another might prefer to interview a number of parents and students, presenting the results in a report to the class. Others might paint pictures, draw cartoons, write songs, or use other creative ways to highlight feelings and thoughts about parents. For the ambitious or bright student, supplementary experiences may be suggested, such as additional reading for a purpose, preparing certain aids such as charts, tables, or slides that illustrate principles or concepts, or exploring in depth a particular facet of the assigned problem.

Some teachers find it helpful to indicate to their students the difficulty of the assigned books and other reading materials, rating them on some scale ranging from the simple to the complex. Sometimes students themselves may be asked to rate the difficulty of their reading sources. The teacher should use an abundance of resources to enrich learning; the availability of resources is highly important in the planning of assignments. An inventory of the resources of the school and the community is helpful, as is an assessment of those within the student group.

Assignments must be planned so that there will be evidence of achievement. The teacher should note in advance the kind of behavior she/he expects to observe as indicative of progress; students might well assist in this process. If planning has been careless, neither the teacher nor the student may be able to demonstrate clearly what has been accomplished.

Making the Assignment

The teacher making an assignment should keep a number of points in mind:

1. Clarity and conciseness are imperative. Students should be given limits and bounds within which to work, for overpermissiveness often leads to frustration.
2. Sufficient time should be allowed to resolve questions, to ar-

range necessary committee work, and to explain the assignment so that all students understand it and the performance standards expected of them.

3. Consideration for the students should be shown. Assignments should not interfere with major school events.
4. Whenever feasible, the work should be integrated with that of other courses, such as English, social studies, or science.
5. Students should not be overloaded for the sake of making the teacher feel important.
6. Many small, fragmentary assignments should be avoided. Periodic summaries of progress may indicate a need to reorganize plans.
7. Assignments may be made at any point in a lesson, according to need or student interest.
8. Students should be encouraged to devise some plan for keeping track of their assignments; notebooks are excellent for the purpose.

Resources for Assignments

Ideas for assignments can be derived from a variety of sources, including state and local curriculum guides, professional magazines, professional meetings, educational books and other types of literature, guidebooks accompanying textbooks, films, and filmstrips. Elementary education magazines often give creative ideas that can be adapted to higher levels of student maturity. An exchange of ideas with other teachers and students is also helpful.

SUGGESTIONS FOR FURTHER LEARNING

1. In the following book, read these references on "Teaching Styles," pp. 27–44, and "The Curriculum," pp. 228–239.

   Landau, Elliott D., Sherrie Epstein, and Ann P. Stone, *The Teaching Experience,* Englewood Cliffs, N.J.: Prentice-Hall, 1976.

   Discuss possible answers to the questions cited with several of your classmates.
2. If someone asked you to describe your philosophy of education, what would your answer be? Give an example of your philosophy in action.

12

Evaluation

Evaluation, in simplified terms, is a comparison of hoped for changes or developments with actual accomplishments.[1] Feedback will reveal the extent of student growth, the degree of success of the teaching strategies and resources used, and the impact of the environment and the information given in areas of home economics. This feedback will provide insight for further steps. Education is complex, and to secure total evaluation is difficult. The teacher who is tuned in for evidence every moment can facilitate the evaluation of a curriculum and of the students. In addition, a teacher is challenged to determine the ways that home economics may be applied to the unmet needs of personal development.

Evaluation is an integral part of the ongoing process of home economics education. Assessment is not confined to testing, statistics, inventory of before-and-after status, study of cause and effect, or prediction of future achievements.[2] All of these, plus many other means, contribute to a continuous understanding of what is worthwhile and what needs to be changed. A sensitive, accurate, and sensible interpretation is essential for future planning.

This educational procedure covers a wide spectrum. A teacher may evaluate the degree to which social and family problems may be incorporated into the curriculum. Several teachers may discuss ways

[1] Arlene Fink and Jacqueline Kosecoff, *An Evaluation Primer* (Washington, D.C.: Capitol Publications, 1978), p. vii.

[2] Robert E. Stake and Terry Denny, "Needed Concepts and Techniques for Utilizing More Fully the Potential of Evaluation," in Ralph W. Tyler (ed.), *Educational Evaluation: New Roles, New Means,* National Society for the Study of Education Yearbook (Chicago: U. of Chicago, 1969), Ch. 16.

to encourage the progress of a particular student. An analysis of the extent to which the goals of a group session, a workshop, or a national home economics convention have been realized is another possibility. There are other areas of professional concern, such as career opportunities for students or new areas in which the profession may be of service.

PURPOSES OF EVALUATION

Broadly speaking, in an evaluation one attempts to determine whether specified objectives have been accomplished. An evaluation will include the information to be stressed; theories, concepts, principles, or applications; and decisions about the teaching–learning process.

Objectives should include the type of evaluation process that will be used, such as essay, open-book examinations, observation of student behavior, evidence of the cognitive or affective responses of students, frequent tests or a comprehensive examination, student contracts, and other procedures. Some decision must be made about the weight and importance to be given to various types of objectives and their evaluation. Bloom[3] warns that unplanned-for results will occur and should be regarded as valuable for further study. Of course, undesirable results, such as dislike of the subject or negative attitudes toward learning, become a matter of concern. The point is that the teacher need not adhere solely to the objectives that have been stated if there is strong evidence that valuable nonspecified goals are emerging in a quantitative and qualitative manner.

One of the common pitfalls in evaluation is that teachers fail to realize that their evaluation is geared to facts or emphases that are unrelated to their objectives. Students quickly tend to select those learnings about which they are examined. According to Taba,[4] the method of evaluating what is learned will dictate the way in which learning takes place.

Another purpose of evaluation is to determine the program's adaptability to students of various backgrounds and environmental conditions. These and other kinds of data will be helpful in the process of accountability, which has taken on new and challenging dimensions for teachers and administrators. Constituents to which departments and school must justify their performance include themselves, the

[3] Benjamin S. Bloom, "Some Theoretical Issues Relating to Educational Evaluation," in Tyler, ibid., Ch. 3.

[4] Hilda Taba, *Curriculum Development, Theory and Practice* (New York: Harcourt, 1962).

community, the board of education, the state department of education, and, at times, federal agencies and concerned publics.

Smith and Tyler[5] list five purposes of evaluation. The first is to evaluate the effectiveness of the total home economics program. Second, the hypotheses on which the program operates must be tested. A sample hypothesis might be to determine the extent to which a home economics program contributes to improving the family living of its students. A third purpose is to secure sufficient information about students to permit effective guidance. Fourth, evaluation tends to give a psychological security to teachers, parents, and students. If a new curriculum is launched or attempts are made to create closer parent–school relationships or more use of community resources, it is reassuring to have tangible proof of progress and success. Students, particularly, are anxious about their achievements and feel more secure when given evidence of their progress.

Last, evaluation can provide a means of strengthening a school's public image. Parents are impressed with concrete data concerning the achievements of their children in any undertaking. The home economics teacher can strengthen public relations for the department by citing actual examples of the ways in which the community is being used to amplify certain class projects, of contributions made by members of the community to classes, or of the results of wage-earning courses and other departmental activities.

The purposes of evaluation in any department of home economics or school should be determined by the teachers, with the involvement of students whenever possible, for as partners in the evaluative process, the students will be more interested in realizing the goals.

CHARACTERISTICS OF EVALUATION

Teachers should envision curriculum planning, guidance, and evaluation as integral parts of the educational process, for as independently operating processes, they are much less effective. This is particularly true of evaluation, the primary objective of which is to facilitate growth and improve development among students.

Evaluation facilitates self-evaluation. The single most important outcome of evaluation is what happens within the learner.[6] Evaluation must help him/her toward a healthy and valid self-concept, self-insight, self-acceptance, and respect for his/her uniqueness, and

[5] Eugene R. Smith and Ralph W. Tyler, *Appraising and Recording Student Progress* (New York: Harper, 1942).

[6] Frances R. Link, "Humanizing the Curriculum and Evaluation at the Crossroads," *Proceedings of the Twenty-Fifth Biennial Council Pi Lambda Theta,* 1971.

Figure 12–1 One source of evidence for evaluation is the observation of children in a group situation at school. (USDA Photo)

toward the ability to examine the composition of his/her thoughts, feelings, and concerns, according to Schwartz.[7] Traditionally educators have not been concerned about this facet of evaluation.

Self-evaluation can give students a sense of strength and encourage them to use all the available resources and opportunities to achieve greater self-insight. Often students emerge with a sense of failure as a result of the evaluation procedures that are used and consequently never become good diagnosticians of themselves.

Evaluation is concerned with means and ends. It is not sufficient to appraise end results alone, the teacher must be equally concerned with the processes by which those results evolve.

Do the evaluative means used frighten, discourage, or frustrate students? Do they facilitate learning? Evaluation, then, begins to operate as soon as purposes are planned and defined and continues until they are realized. Purposes must not be accepted without critical examination for consistency and controlling values.

[7] Sheila Schwartz, "Self-insight and the Student," *Educational Leadership,* Vol. 24, No. 2 (Oct. 1967), pp. 45–50.

Evaluation is a continuous process. Appraisal is not a periodic phenomenon with spasmodic exposure to tests and other evaluative measures. Some authorities question whether an ongoing program should be halted for tests. Evaluation is concerned with the whole range of students' learning; it is not limited to students' personalities, attitudes, and interests. The teacher must continuously collect evidence of the students' growth in democratic living as a basis for effectively directing their efforts.

Evaluation emphasizes the importance of the individual. The teacher must have equal concern for every student in the classroom, regardless of their backgrounds or abilities. She/he must make every effort to keep well informed about students in order to help them become increasingly self-directive.

Evaluation is an integral part of the teaching–learning process. Teaching and learning are greatly influenced by the kind of evaluation that takes place in the classroom. Evaluation can be carried on concurrently with teaching. For example, a discussion of some social problem, such as inadequate housing, may involve an appraisal of students' awareness of this social problem and a review of their behavior relating to it. In the context of the teaching–learning situation, evaluation is both individual-centered and group-centered.

Evaluation is a cooperative procedure. Evaluation is not a function reserved for experts; it is the concern of all individuals who are associated with an educational activity or who are affected by its results. Each should contribute to the extent of his/her interests and ability. The areas of common understanding are thus widened, and evaluation becomes something shared and vital.

Evaluation involves reconstruction. There is little necessity for having evaluation as an important part of education unless something positive results, and improvements should be made following an appraisal effort. Revisions, refinements, corrections, or enrichments may affect not only the home economics program but the entire school, even the community itself.

PLANNING EVALUATION

Basic to the planning of evaluation is a determination of the goals to be evaluated. The specific goals of home economics are ramifications of the general one of concentration on improved family living and relate to the feeding, clothing, and housing of the family; child care; health; the management of time, money, and other resources; human relations; and allied subjects. But the home economics teacher is equally concerned with the broad purpose of all education, namely, the personal and social development of students. Goals relating to this end include the development in students of the ability to think critically; the clarification and examination of values, attitudes, and beliefs; the solution of problems; the stimulation of interests; the development of appreciation; the satisfaction of emotional and other human needs; and the fulfillment of other aspects of personality. (See Chapter 11 for a discussion of objectives.)

In a realistic sense, a distinction must be made, warn Stake and Denny,[8] between what a teacher proposes to do, what the teacher sees herself/himself doing, and what in fact is actually being done. To evaluate all objectives is no small task. It is sensible to indicate the relative importance of goals; that is, which have priority and which are less desirable. These priorities can be elusive and complex and so are subject to change as students reveal new requirements in developmental needs. Evaluation is thus facilitated if the teacher judges the relative importance of each objective.

Another consideration in the evaluation of objectives that is generally slighted is the allocation of the resources needed to realize each objective. If a home economics teacher, for example, wishes to encourage and broaden the interests of the students, some pertinent questions might be: Are there adequate evaluative techniques to appraise outcomes? Is the teacher's own background in this area adequate? Are there experts to help? Are there materials and facilities that allow the students to express, execute, and display their interests? Do teacher and students have time for these activities? What can be done with the students who are unresponsive?

The next step is to explore all of the possible ways of securing the evidence needed for evaluation.[9] Of the methods commonly used, personal observation can be most revealing. A teacher might start with the students' appearance. Do facial expressions connote tension, happiness, moodiness, or relaxation? What do grooming, posture, and health tell? From all this, a teacher may establish certain tentative hypotheses for later verification. Observation will also reveal the number of friends a student has and the extent to which he/she has mastered certain skills; developed an appreciation of line, color, and texture, has the ability to work with others; and countless other aspects of growth.

Listening carefully is another way of gathering evidence. If the teacher provides a permissive atmosphere, the students may talk freely, but she/he must be fair-minded in evaluating this kind of evi-

[8] Robert E. Stake and Terry Denny, "Needed Concepts and Techniques for Utilizing More Fully the Potential of Evaluation," in Ralph W. Tyler (ed.), *Educational Evaluation: New Roles, New Means,* National Society for the Study of Education Yearbook (Chicago: U. of Chicago, 1969), pp. 375–377.

[9] Jeanette Miccinati, "Watch, Listen, and Record," *Educational Leadership,* Vol. 34, No. 4 (Jan. 1977), pp. 252–256.

dence. What does a student say during a class discussion? What are his/her favorite topics of conversation? What do students say about each other? What are the opinions of other teachers? What kinds of information do parents occasionally venture? What insights are revealed by the remarks of townspeople?

In a similar manner, students' written work—logs, diaries, autobiographies, reactions to readings or experiences, essays—can be helpful in evaluation. The ingenious use of certain teaching methods and materials—films, photographs, filmstrips, and recordings—is particularly noteworthy for challenging thinking, values, attitudes, and beliefs. Also valuable are student records on file in the school office, particularly personality and intelligence tests. The counsel of guidance personnel can be helpful, too. Conferences with individual students are very worthwhile. It is particularly important that they be held in a relaxed, unhurried, and comfortable atmosphere and that the discussion center on something specific.

There will be occasions when a teacher will find it most effective to use evaluative checklists, inventories, questionnaires, such sociometric devices as sociograms and social distance scales, rating scales, anecdotal records, interpretation of data tests, and other such devices.

Teachers will bear in mind that these records are confidential. Parents and a student may have access to the student's records according to law. These will include any recommendations that the home economics teacher or departmental chairperson may write.

EVALUATIVE TECHNIQUES AND DEVICES

Any device or procedure used in the evaluative process should have the properties of validity, reliability, and objectivity. *Validity* refers to the soundness of evidence and its relevance to what is being evaluated. *Reliability* stresses the consistency with which a procedure or device can be applied: a reliable procedure is as effective with Mary as it is with Susan, with this year's class as it was with last year's class. *Objectivity* emphasizes an intrinsic freedom from bias in the design and applicability of a device or procedure; but more, a truly objective device should afford little or no opportunity for a teacher to exercise bias in the application of the device or in the analysis of the evidence it produces. In the limited time afforded to the teaching of some classes, unfortunately, it is often difficult for a teacher to verify beforehand that an evaluative device or procedure she/he proposes to use will meet these important criteria of evaluation.

Evaluation, particularly as it concerns human measurement, is still an inexact science. So a teacher must be aware of the limitations and potentials of evaluative techniques. If used wisely, they can help to diagnose student achievements, needs, and other areas of development. Classroom teaching can be made more effective through the highlighting of the strengths and weaknesses of curricular objectives, content, and method. Evaluation should give students a sense of what is important in learning, help them in the process of self-evaluation, and encourage them to develop worthwhile study habits. Students should also learn to support their results with personal judgment and observation.

Achievement Tests

Standardized achievement tests are usually used by a school to determine where its students stand in a particular area in comparison with their counterparts in other schools. For home economics, few tests of this nature are available, hence teachers must devise their own. Following are some general suggestions to bear in mind in the construction of tests in general.

1. Tests should assess students' progress in reaching the educational objectives that have been stressed in teaching. A well-planned test will reflect the relative importance that each objective has received in actual teaching.
2. The format of a test can be essay, multiple-choice, completion, true–false, matching, or a combination of these. Using a combination tends to expand the scope of measurement.
3. Carefully plan test questions according to what purpose the test will serve; what skills, information, content, and other areas are to be measured; and what the relative weights are to be. Check the test for fairness. Some teachers find it helpful to write each test item on a card so that it is easy to arrange the items in the order desired. If the test is to be used again in the future, test items that failed in some manner can be easily deleted and others added.
4. It is best to group together similar items to facilitate scoring and to determine the areas in which the entire class did well or poorly. It also encourages better thinking on the part of the student, because all of his/her knowledge on a particular facet is brought to bear at one time. Skipping from one area to another without good rcason may do nothing but confuse.
5. Use simple, yet adequate and clearly stated directions. Many tests do not accomplish their purposes because students do not understand what they are supposed to do.
6. In tests that call for write-in answers, permit plenty of room for

the write-ins. For objective types of tests, answers may be arranged at either the left or the right side of the page. If there is to be a free response, allow sufficient space for the student to write the answer.

7. Consider the length of the test and be certain that all students can complete it in the time allotted. Remember that they will work at different speeds.
8. Clarify unusual terms in the test.
9. Word the test in language familiar to the students. Do not try to trick students with sly wording. Content is the important thing. Proofread carefully for ambiguities.
10. Be certain that clues to the answers do not appear in the questions.
11. Avoid test items that are too easy, too difficult, superficial, or obvious; encourage bluffing; are partly true or partly false; may have different meanings; or use the exact language of the textbook, because this places a premium on rote memory.
12. It is psychologically sound to progress from the easiest items to the more difficult. As a result of such an arrangement, a student gains a certain satisfaction, and the test itself gives reinforcement.
13. Prepare an answer key for the test beforehand and be certain of the correct answers. Some kind of plan should be made for scoring. If one section of the test is more important than others, it should have greater weight.

The atmosphere of the testing situation is very important. When tests are used as a threat or punishment, they tend to cause fear, and students cannot learn in a climate of fear. The teacher must be careful that a student is not penalized because she or he works slowly. If a test places high value on unimportant details or rote memory, students may become discouraged.

Popham[10] recommends customized criterion-reference tests as an alternative to achievement tests. The emphasis in these tests is on a clearly defined class of behaviors, such as behaviors associated with certain occupations, personal nutrition, or mastery of principles related to home furnishings.

The teacher must make definite plans for using the results of the test to discover the strengths and weaknesses of individual students and of the group as a whole. Scores will give some idea of the ranking of students, indicating those who are obviously in need of further study.

[10] W. James Popham, "Customized Criterion-Reference Tests," *Educational Leadership*, Vol. 34, No. 4 (Jan. 1977), pp. 258–259.

Essay Tests

The essay test is used frequently in home economics, particularly when a teacher wishes to measure functional information, certain aspects of thinking, or study skills and habits. Other purposes are to gain some indication of a student's ability to organize ideas logically, clearly, and quickly and of his/her social philosophy. An essay test, if effective, taps high levels of reasoning because it usually requires students to make inferences, comparisons, and contrasts from their experiences. Effective use of knowledge is emphasized also. Students must have some skill in English to write an essay test well. Following are some specific uses and suggestions for essay tests.

1. To analyze possible causes and effects, means and ends, or omissions in a process.
   a. Analyze spending to determine the cause and effect of financial problems.
   b. Read the labels on some common household drugs for omissions or ambiguity in directions and possible effects.
2. To apply principles, knowledge, or skills.
   a. What principles of food preparation would be applied in the making of a cheese omelet?
   b. What would you have to know in order to select suitable fabric for a school outfit for yourself?
   c. If a boy complains about the length of time it takes to prepare a certain meal for his family, what information would you need to secure in order to help him plan more efficiently?
3. To compare two or more items, ideas, or situations.
   a. Compare the feasibility for a young couple of renting an apartment as against renting a house.
   b. Compare the advantages and disadvantages of several leisure-time activities available in the community.
   c. List the major differences between a family that is organized democratically and one that is organized autocratically.
4. To describe characteristics, a process, or an experience.
   a. What were the steps you took when making your most important decision of the past summer?
   b. Describe your favorite food.
   c. Describe what you would do if you were given a thousand dollars.
5. To appraise what is desirable or undesirable in terms of certain standards or goals.
   a. A woman found a pizza recipe in two different cookbooks. She tried both of them. One recipe was very successful, the

other was a failure. The woman wondered why there was such a difference. Discuss what you must know before you can tell her the reason.

6. To exemplify or to illustrate.
   a. Discuss an example of what you believe cooperation among family members means.
   b. Discuss, with examples, what you believe a junior high school student should be able to buy by himself/herself.
7. To explain meanings or operations.
   a. Write the directions for the use of some small kitchen gadget.
   b. Explain a tradition of your family to a pen pal in another part of the world.
8. To interpret data, trends, comments, or information.
   a. Listen to your favorite radio or television news commentator. Analyze the newscast for evidence that he/she may be going beyond the data or is being overcautious.
   b. Read the content and nutritional labels on a can of tomatoes and interpret the information on it in terms of the uses to which this product might be put in your family menus.
   c. Find in a newspaper or a magazine a graph dealing with something pertinent to family living, such as the consumption of certain foods, the use of credit, or teenage spending, and interpret the meaning for you as a student. Do any trends have special meaning?
9. To organize in logical steps.
   a. Describe the steps in putting a simple nightshirt together.
   b. Plan the class division of labor for the preparation and service of nutritious refreshments for an FHA party.
10. To summarize major points, ideas, or conclusions.
    a. Summarize the main points to consider in the selection of a bicycle or cassette player.
    b. Summarize what you learned in a visit to a nursing home.

These suggestions should stimulate other ideas. The essay question can be quite versatile and does help a student to express himself/herself more fluently. The areas to be discussed should be as specific as possible.

Before grading a class's essay tests, the teacher may wish to read all of the papers to get a general idea of what the whole class did and how well they did it. In reading each question, she/he should note errors, omissions, and inadequate discussions. If students have been previously warned, it might be well to deduct for rambling and gratuitous material. If pertinent points that were not originally considered by the teacher are included, the student should receive extra credit for them. Such factors as neatness, the general appearance of the paper, spelling, grammar, and other aspects of English might be taken into consideration.

Essay questions have decided limitations. Their validity and reliability are frequently low, owing to the inevitability of subjectivity in scoring by the teacher and the difficulty of applying rigorous standards of scoring. Time might be well spent in teaching students how to write essay tests. Choices of topic should be avoided, for they only compound the difficulties of judging and scoring.

Objective Tests

A number of purportedly objective tests are used by home economics teachers. Actually all tests should be objective, and the only unique claim to objectivity that these tests have is that there is generally only one correct answer per question. Students do not react as unfavorably to objective tests as to essay tests, because there is less opportunity for subjectivity in grading. Objective tests tend to be exercises in recall or to put more emphasis on facts than on eliciting beliefs and attitudes. These tests are easy to construct and take only a short time to administer and score. Their great limitation is that the teacher cannot know for certain if correct answers are the products of knowledge or good guesswork.

Of the various kinds of objective tests, *true–false tests* are often used if a quick general survey of a field is desired. This form has a number of serious shortcomings: the student is offered only two possibilities to which he/she can react; there is a greater opportunity for guessing; it is very difficult to construct statements that are absolutely true or absolutely false; and teachers too often use words such as *all* and *everyone* (as in "All mothers work" or "Everyone likes to eat"), which generally make a statement false by implication. Another serious disadvantage is that it is extremely difficult to construct test items that actually test for important generalizations, principles, and concepts. One of the best uses for true–false test items is in the teaching of principles in food preparation, such as cooking protein foods; in clothing, such as principles of line or design; or in budget planning.

Modified true–false tests have been developed to reduce guessing. Students might be asked to do something in addition to choosing *true, false, yes,* or *no.* One possibility is to have students strike out a word or words to make a statement true or false; another is to ask them to defend their choice in a brief essay. Students might be asked to rephrase a statement so that it will be true or false; generally speaking, to make a false statement true is educationally the wiser choice.

Multiple-choice tests are difficult to construct, but they are adaptable, easy to administer, and easy to score. A multiple-choice item consists of two parts. The first part is sometimes referred to as the *stem* and consists of a statement, an incomplete sentence, or a description of a situation. This is followed by a series of at least three, but usually not more than four, alternative responses from which the student is expected to select the correct or most suitable response. The difficulty in constructing these tests is to make the alternatives as plausible as the correct response. Teachers might use essay tests that they have given previously and select from them incorrect answers made by students as the basis for alternatives. Several safeguards are needed in the construction of these tests. It is wise to avoid any pattern, such as having the second response consistently the correct one, and to avoid textbook or ambiguous language. The stem should be framed as a question rather than a statement, if that seems more appropriate. If they are well constructed, multiple-choice tests are generally valid, reliable, and discriminative.

Here are a few suggestions. Multiple-choice might be used for purposes of identification. At the left side of the paper there might be a sketch of a piece of kitchen equipment, a part of a sewing machine, or a cut of meat. On the right there might be a statement such as "this is" followed by a list of three or four items. Students could be asked to cross out the incorrect responses to make the statement true, to circle the correct response, or to place an *X* before the correct choice. A short description might precede the alternatives to which a student may respond.

Mary is helping her mother plan the family meals. The doctor has recommended that her brother John have a diet that includes iron-rich foods. Which of the following foods would be her first choice:

1. Carrots
2. Apples
3. Milk
4. Whole-grain cereals

This type is sometimes called reverse multiple choice, because it calls for a process of elimination rather than selection.

A matching test is composed of a list of items in the form of words, phrases, statements, or diagrams that are to be matched with correlative items in another list, which Arny[11] calls the *stimulus list.* The stimulus list can be longer, but the list of items to be matched with it should include no more than ten to fifteen items. Care must be taken that the lists are consistent, and it is important that there be only one correct pairing of items. Both lists should be complete on one and the

[11] Clara Brown Arny, *Evaluation in Home Economics* (New York: Appleton, 1953).

same page, so that students need not turn pages back and forth to match them up. Matching tests are generally more economical of space than multiple-choice tests are. They contribute to the recognition of relationships, and they have been found to be highly reliable and quite discriminating if they are carefully constructed.

The following is an example of a matching test.

Directions: Place the number of each dish after the nation with which it is associated.

1. Antipasto	England	( )
2. Rice cakes	France	( )
3. Fish and chips	Russia	( )
4. Borscht	Germany	( )
	Sweden	( )
	Japan	( )
	Italy	( )

Matching tests might be used to emphasize the application of principles, such as democratic principles to family life situations; cause and effect, such as identifying the causes of pollution and its effect on environment; meanings, such as the names of fabrics with the suitable uses of those fabrics; problems and solutions, such as management of time, energy, or money; and relationships, such as reactions of a mother to a small child's behavior.

Another type of objective test is the *completion test,* which is actually a form of recall test. It is of value only when it must be determined whether or not a student has accurately memorized information. In the construction of this test, not too many words should be omitted from each question, otherwise it will be too confusing to answer. The following are typical completion-test items.

1. An inexpensive meat for a family dinner is __________.
2. One of the best sources for Vitamin C in the diet is __________.

Performance Tests

Performance tests are frequently given in the laboratory so that a teacher may gain some idea of a student's information and skills, as well as ability to apply what he/she has learned. Having students prepare a very simple meal, for instance, gives the teacher an opportunity to observe the performance of the students individually or as a group. In a unit on home nursing, a number of stations might be set up, each with the necessary equipment and supplies to demonstrate a specific home-nursing procedure. Students work in groups of twos, one of each pair acting as patient for the other, alternately from station to station. The problems may include treating a fainting person, a burn, or a cut; taking a patient's temperature; assisting a patient from a bed to a chair; and other similarly simple procedures. In a study of textiles, students might be given a number of swatches to identify and perhaps suggest the most suitable uses. A simple construction project can help a teacher to test certain clothing construction skills as well as the students' knowledge of the use of the sewing machine. An actual function, such as a cultural fair, in which traditions and family practices are highlighted, may serve as a performance test for organizational ability, application of principles, ability to present ideas to the public, and other capabilities.

Performance evaluation is necessary for determining the adequacy of a person on a job and is important in occupational education as well as in student part-time work. Performance tests may be developed according to the elements of performance pertinent to the job, such as skill, accuracy, or productivity, or according to the tasks of a job, such as how to make a sandwich in a short-order restaurant or how to feed a bed patient.

Checklists and Inventories

Checklists and inventories are substantially similiar and efficiently gather comprehensive data. For instance, students can be asked to indicate on a checklist of leisure-time activities those in which they participate frequently, occasionally, and never. Similarly students can be asked to indicate on an inventory list what foods they have prepared and how frequently they have prepared them; what they spend their money on; or how familiar they are with home appliances and equipment.

Projective Techniques

A teacher may learn about a student by exploring her or his world of fantasy and make-believe, according to Hill.[12] A vague stimulus provides an opportunity for an individual to project himself/herself into a situation suggested. The procedure is to present a single stimulus or a series of weakly structured stimuli, such as a vague picture, a cartoon, or a word or two of a sentence for the student to project himself/herself into the picture; to emphasize freedom of response in the instructions given; and to analyze reactions for possible problems, values, hopes, plans, and other data that may be significant in helping a student to develop. If the stimulus is too specific or too clear, the fantasy will not be evoked as readily. In some instances, class discussion may follow the use of a projective technique.

[12] Ruby Hill, "Projective Teaching," *Illinois Teacher*, Vol. 11, No. 1 (Sept. 1967), pp. 9–26.

The *open-end sentence* has possibilities. Examples are

1. I want to know more about __________.
2. I wish __________.
3. If I had __________.
4. I like __________.
5. I get along best with __________.
6. I want __________.
7. I try to avoid __________.
8. The job I would like to have __________.

This technique may be used individually, in groups, or in class discussion. The *unfinished story* has similar possibilities.

Word association can be challenging in a number of ways. Saying the first word or words that come to mind can be quite revealing. In food preparation, students might be asked to list the preparation that comes to mind when the following foods are listed: eggs, potatoes, chicken, corn, ground beef, or bread. In consumer education, responses to such words as *borrow, debt, credit card, down payment,* or *interest* give insights into student feelings and needs.

Sometimes a word or several words clipped from an advertisement or the title of a timely article or story in a newspaper or magazine can be used as an evaluation device. Examples are "Starting at," "Give up," "Come see," or "We're moving."

Projective techniques are useful in the evaluation of affective education. This domain is more difficult to assess than the cognitive area. Feelings, senses, emotions, values, and other affective characteristics are elusive of discernment and to interpretation. Teachers are encouraged to secure what evidence they can because of the importance of this domain in student development.[13]

Evaluation of Problems

Students' problems can be quite disturbing to them, and it is important for a teacher to evaluate the kinds of problems the students in her/his classes have. Checklists have proved helpful for the purpose. Mooney[14] has developed problem checklists to be used at the junior high school, high school, and college levels. They cover the areas of health and physical development, school, home and family, boy–girl relationships, relations to people in general, self-centered concerns related to moods, morality, and a miscellaneous group related to money, the future, religion, educational–vocational plans, and so on. Students are asked to draw a line under the problems they

[13] Arthur L. Costa, "Affective Education: The State of the Art," *Educational Leadership,* Vol. 34, No. 4 (Jan. 1977), pp. 260–263.

[14] Ross L. Mooney, *Problem Check List: Junior High School Form* (Columbus: Bureau of Educational Research, Ohio State University, 1942).

believe are important, then are asked to reread the whole list and check those that are bothering them the most. Miller and Morgan[15] have developed a checklist called "Are You a Worry Wart?" which can be used in whole or in part.

Role playing is an effective device for evaluating problems. Selecting a problem that is common to a group, the teacher might have students act out possible solutions through role playing. The teacher can observe what aspects of the problem seem to the students to be particularly acute and how the students react to them.

Projective methods are especially valuable in the securing of evidence of students' problems. The teacher can show the group an emotionally charged picture, cartoon, or story and ask them how to solve the problems depicted. A similar use can be made of wishes. Students may be asked to jot down their three most important wishes of the moment. To encourage freedom of expression, their papers should be unsigned. The teacher can rapidly categorize the areas with which these wishes are concerned and speculate about what problems may be associated with them. During the discussion, note evidences of values, critical thinking, practical approaches, signs of maturity or immaturity, use of resources, and other indications of growth and development. These problems might also be presented in a checklist headed "What Would You Do If ___________?"

Evaluation of Social Sensitivity

Devices that evaluate social sensitivity gauge a student's concern for the people and the world in which she/he lives. This characteristic is generally evaluated through teaching materials and methods, but occasionally a teacher may wish to get the reactions of the entire class recorded on paper. One such device takes the form of an opinion poll.

Read the following statements and check below to indicate about how many people you think agree with it: *Slum housing is a problem in our country. Many people are living in inadequate homes. We should not have to pay taxes to build suitable homes for them. If these people would work as they should, they would be able to build their own homes.*

Nobody ___________

Only a few ___________

Much less than half ___________

About half ___________

Much more than half ___________

Almost everybody ___________

[15] May Miller and June Morgan, *Projects with Penny* (Danville, Ill.: Interstate Printers and Publishers, 1961).

The results might be shared with students for the purpose of discussing possible personal and community implications. A similar technique is to read a news item that highlights a social problem relating to, say, the aged or the unemployed. Students are asked to write anonymous opinions about the article or reactions to the problems. The teacher might profitably open the topic for discussion.

Sensitizing or *sensitivity modules* are relatively brief experiences for students that enable them to become more sensitive to the issues and the people around them, according to Simon.[16] To discuss poverty, problems of minority groups, welfare, the fact that the poor pay more, and similar topics as related to families in a vacuum becomes an irrelevant pastime. In a program using sensitivity modules, a list of twenty to thirty modules is submitted to a class. Teams of two or three students select their first module and then make their own arrangements for the experience. No effort is made to prescribe a sequence of modules. The number of modules undertaken is related to student needs and program emphasis. If possible, teams should report back in groups of no more than fifteen to eighteen students in a feedback session. The purpose is for the teacher to encourage discussion and to be concerned about value clarification and indications of greater social sensitivity without attempting to label "right" or "wrong" ideas. Students usually keep logs or journals of their experiences.

Some of the modules suggested by Simon have been adapted here for use with home economics students.

1. Go to a community health center or clinic. What are the common problems? Talk to some of the patients, if possible, to learn more about why they are there. Would you like to work in such a setting?
2. Attend the services of a religion that is very different from your own. What are your impressions? Perhaps you do not attend services. Talk to some students who do. Why have they selected their particular belief and what are the benefits to them?
3. At election time, work in the office of a candidate or go on some campaign rounds. Which groups of people are important targets? What are the issues that touch you or your family?
4. Interview some elderly citizens about their interests and problems and the suggestions they offer to the young. If they are willing, make tape recordings of your conversations. If possible, have representatives of different social classes and ethnic groups, or make your own decisions about how to proceed. Visiting a home for the aged might be interesting.

[16] Sidney B. Simon, "Sensitivity Modules," *Scholastic Teacher*, Vol. 97, No. 2, supplement (Sept. 21, 1970), pp. 29, 42.

5. Volunteer to work in a children's ward in which the children are handicapped. Talk to parents, relatives, nurses, and others about them.
6. If you can, do volunteer work in a hospital, and talk to charity patients about their problems.
7. Ask to help in a day-care center. Become friendly with a child of a color different from your own.
8. Talk to some men or women who have lost their jobs.
9. In the school cafeteria, arrange to sit next to a student whose background you believe is quite different from your own.
10. Write letters to the editor of your newspaper, to your Congressman, or to your Senator about some of the insights you have gained from your module experiences.

Teachers can adapt these suggestions according to their situation or develop others suitable to their students. A warning must be given that sensitivity experiences may only reinforce some of the original stereotype ideas held by students. The degree of insight gained may vary greatly. Some students will be charged with enthusiasm to "do something."

Books, motion pictures, field trips, visits to museums, and other experiences can become sensitivity modules if the experience is new to the student and there is an opportunity for genuine involvement, according to Kirschenbaum.[17] There is a wide variety of devices that encourage social sensitivity and increase human understanding.

Evaluation of Interests

Interests are among the most potent drives that an individual can possess. The interested student is oblivious of time, has boundless energy for marshaling resources or executing a project, and in general gives indications of satisfaction. Interests connote likes and dislikes, pleasure and concern, satisfactions, and dissatisfactions. A student's personality may be revealed in many ways through her/his preferences and choices and the decisions she/he makes or the solutions she/he finds in the pursuit of her/his interests. Students' interests are not static; they change from time to time—some endure, others are fleeting.

To discover his/her students' interests, the teacher should observe and listen, but a checklist is certainly one of the most efficient devices. A checklist may ask students to disclose their vocational, cultural, leisure, home and family, school, and community interests. Students' preferences in books, magazines, and newspapers are very

[17] Howard Kirschenbaum, "Sensitivity Modules," *Media and Methods,* Vol. 7, No. 6 (Feb. 1970), pp. 36–39.

revealing. An examination of a student's responses should disclose the range and intensity of his/her interests. Do they cluster around one area, or are they diversified? Is there any evidence about the length of time particular interests have endured? Which seem ephemeral? Are there any unique qualities in the interest patterns? Are the interests self-centered? Is the family involved? Are altruistic motivations apparent? If a student reveals few or no interests, this should be a matter of grave concern. Information gained about student interests has curriculum implications.

Evaluation of Appreciation

Appreciation is one of the most difficult student qualities for a teacher to evaluate. An expression of appreciation generally shows that a value is placed on something and reflects feelings, background, or experience that is usually positive in tone. Often appreciation is closely associated with interest. Interests emphasize liking, but appreciation includes insight with interest. Do students express sensitivity to their reading, to artwork, or to their surroundings in general? The quality of the words used in writing, the selection of attire, and the time spent in aesthetic expression are all evidence of appreciation.

Practical situations appear to offer one of the best means of evaluating appreciation. Students may be given fabrics from which to choose a suitable combination for a costume or for decorating a room. They might be asked to respond to photographs of different rooms and to analyze their likes and dislikes. The teacher must be careful to guard against injecting personal appreciation in so overpowering a manner that students do not feel free to make their own judgments. Appreciation of personal qualities in other people is another example.

The Student Log

A student log or diary is a kind of all-encompassing evaluation device, offering material for tentative hypotheses about a students' interests, values, problems, knowledge, and social adjustment that may be further explored or tested during teaching and counseling. The teacher must decide what kind of information she/he wishes to elicit before constructing a log form. Is there an interest in the kinds of experiences a student is having in school, at home, or in the community? Would it be helpful to know how significant these experiences are to a student and the values revealed as he/she pinpoints important aspects of his/her activities? Is use of time a vital consideration? For slow learners, for younger students, or at the initiation of the

Figure 12–2 Students might write in their logs about plans for nutritious snacks at home. (Cereal Institute, Inc.)

devicc, it might be well to confine it to a few significant points. Logs can be changed in format during the course or from one course to another; their flexibility is an important point in their favor. Following is a sample log suitable for use with high school or college students. Experiences should be listed on the left, and on the right space should be allowed for the student to describe the significance of each experience.

WEEKLY LOG
Name
Week Ending
I participated in the following activities (not classes):
I did the following things outside of school this week (such as rapped; worked; looked at TV; went to parties, movies, or concerts; listened to recordings):
Although I did many things in and out of school, there were three or four cxperiences that stand out as being successful, happy, unsuccessful, perplexing, new, strange, or different:

Experiences:	*Significance:*
1st experience	
2nd experience	
3rd experience	

I did the following reading this week:
Newspapers:
Magazines:
Books:
Other reading:
Reactions and comments:
I had the following home and family responsibilities this week:
If I had more time, I would like to:
Here are some attitudes, ideas, issues, or views that I like, with which I agree, about which I have strong convictions: (Be very specific.)
Here are some ideas, attitudes, issues, or views that I dislike, with which I disagree, about which I have strong convictions: (Be very specific.)
Here are some problems, topics, questions, ideas, feelings with which I need help, need more time to think about, and the like:

Some of the areas emphasized in the foregoing sample log may not be of value in a particular teaching situation. Other types of statements that may be used are as follows:

I made progress in . . .
I was blocked or kept from doing something I wanted to do by . . .
The thought occurred to me that I might solve a problem, further develop an idea, or improve a situation by . . .
If I did . . . again, I would make the following changes:
I observed the behavior of a person in a situation; I would have behaved like this . . .
A new method or technique I tried this week was . . .
As a result of this course, I . . .
This week you may have intended to do certain things but you did not. If this was your experience tell what and why.
I found my previous experience, education, or training inadequate in doing . . .
I had some difficulty, success, or bewilderment in getting along with a certain person this week . . .
I felt good about . . .

What do students write in their logs? Here are some typical entries. Regarding problems:

"I disagree with the idea that I have to account for every penny of my allowance."
"My mother is a problem to me."
"If we move away I will miss a certain fellow."
"I can talk with my friends but I have trouble talking in class."

Regarding experiences:

"I was eighteen this summer and feel that I should be my own boss now."
"I worked with my mother in a flower garden along the road. Neighbors seemed to enjoy it."
"I helped my seven-year-old brother practice the piano."
"It was fun last week when the blizzard kept all of us at home. We cleaned closets, baked our favorite cake, watched the storm from the windows, and just talked."

Regarding reflections:

"One of our neighbors is planning to marry a widower with a five-year-old child. I think she will have trouble."
"I disagree that quarrels can be avoided in marriage."
"What can *family* mean to someone from a broken home?"
"Are table manners so important? My father is a good man but he talks with his mouth full of food."

Regarding the social scene:

"A computer cannot tell us what to do about unemployment or people on relief."
"Can a married woman work and not neglect her family?"
"I met one of our neighbors in the supermarket on Saturday morning. She was upset because her son had been caught stealing from the drugstore."

Administration of Logs

The administration of logs is a delicate responsibility. Students must be assured that what they write will be held in strict confidence by the teacher and that other persons will not be permitted to read the log. This device cannot be associated with grading or students will not respond in the manner desired. Logs should be given to the teacher directly, never collected by other students.

The best results are achieved if the device is continued for only a short period of time—say, two or three weeks—or is at least collected at intervals of no more than several weeks. If asked to maintain logs for longer periods, students generally lose enthusiasm for the project. If they request specific assistance, then some response by the teacher is in order. If many students indicate the same problem or need, the material can be discussed in class without the identity of the individuals being revealed. Sometimes information in logs will reveal lacks, lags, or errors in information. This can also provide material for class discussions or experiences.

Logs are most helpful as an evaluative device if a teacher actively capitalizes on the information gained, either through class discussion or in conferences with the individual.

Logs may be kept by students in connection with home experiences, a part-time job, or a class project to identify problems, progress, feelings, and satisfactions or frustrations. Techet[18] uses a type of student log in some of her classes. The last few minutes of a class period, each student writes something in a personal notebook. It may be a contribution that was not made during class, a note of disagreement or agreement concerning the discussion or class activity, a further thought, feelings, an insight, or an activity that may grow out of the class. Students turn in their books periodically or at the end of the course to be read by the teacher and returned.

GRADING

The grading of students is being scrutinized by educators. Kirschenbaum, Simon, and Napier[19] give an overview of alternative grading systems. A distinction must be made between private and public evaluation. In private evaluation, teacher and student work together to identify strengths and weaknesses. Feedback and other pertinent information are shared. In many instances, parents may become a part of the process.

Public evaluation, in contrast, is not a part of the teaching–learning process but consists of the summary data about a student that are made available to employers, colleges and other educational institutions, and to others with similar concerns. This information is used in making decisions about the student.

Although there are a number of alternative grading systems, all of them share four basic components. They are, first, a clear statement of behavioral or other objectives and the procedures for measuring them. Second, there are written or oral communications or a combination of both by the teacher to the student that include information about his/her strengths and weaknesses and suggested directions for improvement for each objective. The third ingredient centers on a student's self-evaluation on the same points as in the second stage, plus meaning for the student's own educational goals. Last, time is planned for student and teacher to consider each other's evaluations and to share and discuss their reactions.

Grading systems are in a state of flux. In some schools, only a few teachers use grades. In other schools, students have a choice of several systems. Some schools have combined several systems.

[18] Mabel Techet, a former home economics teacher at Rye Neck, N.Y. High School, in a conversation with the author.

[19] Howard Kirschenbaum, Sidney B. Simon, and Rodney W. Napier, *Wad-Ja-Get, The Grading Game in American Education* (New York: Hart Publishing, 1971), Appendix B.

One alternative to traditional grading is the use of a *written form.* This may be a form that has spaces for a discussion of strengths, weaknesses, statements with examples, and recommendations for improvement, or there may be a detailed form related to a specific subject. Discussion and suggestions for next steps and improvements are an important aspect. A copy is sent to parents and another filed for future reference. Parents' comments are sometimes added, as well as students' self-evaluations. Another type is *self-evaluation.* A student may grade himself/herself after prior self-evaluation. In some schools, students write their own evaluations each term, the teacher adds his/her comments and reactions, and then the evaluations are sent to parents and included in permanent records.

In the contract system, grading criteria established by teachers, committees, or other groups may apply to a whole class. For example, if each student's work reflects a stated quantity and quality or a variation thereof, he/she is graded accordingly. In some schools, a student draws up his/her own contract for a grade and makes an agreement with the teacher about the terms for fulfillment.

In the performance curriculum, the teacher determines the operational objectives for her/his students. These objectives are organized into segments or units in a logical sequence, and the teacher decides the extent to which a student has mastered or fulfilled the objectives. Levels of mastery or proficiency are carefully designated. Students are provided with this necessary information.

There are several variations of the pass/fail grading system. At the beginning of a course, a teacher will state the criteria for a passing grade, or the decision may be made jointly with the students. Students who meet the criteria pass; students who do not, fail. A modification is the credit/no credit grading. Here the "no credit" is not a failure but indicates that the student did not receive credit for the course.

Most of these systems are attempts to relieve the tension and competition that grades may foster. The learning atmosphere is freer, and students are willing to take more risks and to be more innovative in their approach to learning. When the student evaluates himself/herself and when he/she participates in establishing goals and criteria, important learnings take place. For some students, tension is not relieved by any type of grading system. Some teachers have difficulty in adjusting to alternative grading systems. Home economics teachers must be informed about these systems to perform adequately in the schools that may use them.

In schools where the traditional grading system remains, a teacher must be prepared to meet criteria developed by the school or department. First a teacher must determine on what basis a grade is to be made. Areas that are commonly included are class participation—discussion, committee work, panels, oral reports, and individual work; tests—short quizzes, midterm examinations, and final examinations; assignments—written work, surveys, reports, and similar matter; and whatever special responsibilities may be peculiar to the nature of the class. Teachers will have to decide whether and to what degree such matters as attitudes, lateness of assignments, class behavior, or absenteeism shall influence the grade.

It is also difficult to assign a weight for each of the items that have been decided upon as the components for a grade. Within each integral part—for example, tests that vary in difficulty and importance—a decision may have to be made concerning the contribution of each item to the total. What arc the minimum standards to which the teacher shall hold the class? Shall higher standards be required of superior students than of slower ones? Are the standards to be flexible relative to student and situation, or will they be absolute? Shall a grade accordingly represent a student's progress relative to a class norm, or shall it represent improvement or individual development? In what context is a grade determined?

Conflicts and tensions quickly arise if students are not aware of the standards on which they are graded, so it seems logical that they should be informed and, if possible, should participate in establishing those standards. Letter grades appear to be much fairer than numbers, because a student is classified in a broader range.

Marks should never be used as a threat, nor should they be based on meaningless assignments. The primary intent of a grade is to stimulate a student to greater development and to inform his/her parents of progress. Grades are necessary, too, as the basis for eligibility for schools of higher education. In spite of the deficiencies claimed for them, grades have proved to be quite valid and reliable in predicting future achievement.

Teachers must realize that the evaluation of students goes on in the day-by-day teaching and that it should be an integral part of, and contribute to, the comprehensive evaluation program of the entire school.

SUGGESTIONS FOR FURTHER LEARNING

1. Look through the table of contents of the *Journal of Home Economics* or *Home Economics Research Journal* or an educational magazine such as *Educational Leadership, Childhood Education,* or *Today's Education* for the last three years for articles on evaluation. Select one article to analyze critically. Which ideas can be adapted to your situation? What kind of objectives did the author have in mind? What is emphasized—evaluation of

students, subject matter, the teaching process, or other ideas? In which areas were you in agreement or in disagreement with the author?

2. Consider a possible use for each of the following in the development of an evaluative device in home economics. Indicate types of students, objectives, study area, and other factors that would influence its use.
   a. A newspaper clipping.
   b. An advertisement.
   c. A movie that students are likely to see.
   d. An illustration in a magazine or newspaper.
   e. A taped conversation between two students.
   f. Asking students to make a sketch of a child or a mother.

13

Thinking and Research

The development of a good mind is a basic task of the home economics educator. Dale[1] asks the question, "What is a good mind?" The ability to conceptualize is paramount. Drawing conclusions, grouping and making classifications from experiences, and applying them to new experiences become a continuous process for an individual with a good mind. In this way, words, symbols, and other forms of communication develop meaning.

A teacher or a student with a first-rate mind is eager for new and enriching experiences; explores and searches for new and additional data; classifies readily; is aware of alternatives; gauges the relevance of data; is well stocked with information; labels, rearranges, reviews, revises, and retrieves information easily; and makes discriminating decisions.

The quality of thinking enhances or limits the decisions of a consumer, the contributions of a worker, the analysis of human relationships, and all other areas of living. Every educator in home economics must ask the question, "What kind of strategies, materials, experiences, assessments, or other aspects of teaching will help to develop a good mind?"

WHAT IS THINKING?

Thinking is so complex that it is difficult to define. The following is an adaptation of Dewey's[2] definition.

[1] Edgar Dale, "A Good Mind," *The Newsletter* (Apr. 1968) pp. 1–4.
[2] John Dewey, *How We think* (Boston: Heath, 1933), pp. 9, 12.

Figure 13–1 How did the sculptor Rodin interpret thinking? (Metropolitan Museum of Art)

1. *The survey.* First the thinker becomes familiar with the problem area and forms a mental image of its ramifications. This involves recognition and definition of the problem.
2. *Extracting the essentials.* Next he/she examines the mass of detail comprising the problem and identifies the key factors that hold it together. The statement of a hypothesis comes next, and the resulting inquiry into all of the relevant evidence, including previous research or authoritative opinion, observation, and experience.
3. *Testing the hypothesis.* When possible solutions have been identified, one is judged to be the best. It must be tested in as many situations as possible and summarized, reexamined, and reconstructed, if feasible.

This definition emphasizes the problem-solving approach to thinking.

Other forms of thinking are imagining, making judgments, forming opinions, reasoning, meditation, reaching a conclusion, formulating a viewpoint, originating mental pictures, considering something, or reflecting. To generalize from the particular is defined as *inductive thinking,* from the general to the particular as *deductive thinking. Creative thinking,* also called *productive* or *autonomous thinking,* takes place when concepts and generalizations are independently produced and then used to create or build new knowledge. If personal meanings or images are involved, the thinking is called *perceptual thinking. Cognitive* or *categorical thinking* involves the sorting of ideas, beliefs, and objects.

Divergent thinking refers to generating various types of information from given information. A simple example is that sheets are used on beds (known information); divergent thinking occurs when other possible uses of sheets are considered, such as for draperies or clothes. *Convergent thinking* involves taking general information and generating specific information, for example, giving consideration to possible careers for an individual and then selecting the career cluster deemed most suitable for that person. *Logical thinking* is a disciplined process, not guessing or groping, in which inquiry is controlled and objective and leads to the discovery of proof or the solution to a problem. These are some of the important types of thinking.

Raths, Wasserman, Jonas, and Rothstein[3] advance the idea that thinking is not a simple act but consists of several mental processes that are not always orderly and may overlap or intertwine. An emphasis on the operations associated with thinking, such as coding, comparing, classifying, observing and reporting, summarizing, interpreting, analyzing assumptions, problem solving, criticizing and evaluating, and imagining and creating, are suggested as being helpful in the teaching of thinking. This listing is not considered complete, so a teacher is free to add or to adapt.

Influences on Thinking

The quality of students' thinking is influenced by the quality and kinds of experiences they have or have had; generally, rich thinking is the product of a wealth of varied experiences. Values, attitudes, and beliefs color thinking. People tend to be uncritically protective of values they cherish, with the result that they may avoid thinking about them. Students' backgrounds and the cultures in which they have lived also have an important bearing on the way they think as they do. The attitude toward thinking of the key people in students' lives also has a strong impact.

Emotions and feelings also play an important role. For example, if students have strong prejudices about race, religion, economic or social status, or politics, they will have more difficulty in thinking objectively in these areas. It is never easy to change a prejudice, but it is easier to change one intellectually than emotionally. Other influences include health, age, economic status, attitudes toward life, environment, and the challenges to think that are afforded to students.

[3] Louis E. Raths, Selma Wasserman, Arthur Jonas, and Arnold M. Rothstein, *Teaching for Thinking, Theory and Application* (Columbus, Ohio: Merrill, 1967).

Students must be given opportunities to think. If parents, teachers, or others have made most of the decisions for students, their opportunities have been limited.

Taba[4] believes that we must take into consideration our very rapidly changing and expanding world, which involves constant adaptation of the images we use to interpret our experiences. Furthermore she contends that we must prepare individuals to think in a transcultural environment. It will no longer be adequate to think only in terms of our community and its people; we must encompass an understanding of the cultures of the world. In so doing, we must be objective about our own culture.

The Role of the Teacher

The teacher is responsible for creating a climate for thinking so that students feel free to think, are encouraged to think, and are chal-

[4] Hilda Taba, "Education for Independent Valuing," in Alexander Fraxier (ed.), *New Insights into the Curriculum,* Yearbook of the Association for Supervision and Curriculum Development (Washington, D.C.: NEA, 1963), Ch. 10.

Figure 13–2 How is a father's thinking influenced when he has the sole responsibility for his young child? (Richard E. Swartz, *Children Today*)

lenged to think. In addition to the creation of a climate for thinking, Raths and his colleagues[5] recommend to the teacher three steps in teaching for thinking. First, the teacher must point the students toward thinking operations in a period of explaining, demonstrating, and answering questions. Next, she/he must handle the responses of students in such ways as to encourage thinking. The educator must avoid pressure and insistence. There may be experimenting with questions or comments that are thought-provoking or that help a student to reflect. Many questions can be raised by teacher and student in order to gauge the quality of thinking, as well as salient influences on thinking. Here are a few points to consider: What were the sources of evidence? Were there gaps? Were there errors of thinking? How did the emotions, feelings, or other influences color the situation? What would you have said or done? What are your reactions to the solution offered? Were there any evidences of creative thinking, of deductive or inductive thinking, of analysis, of synthesis, or of organization? In contrast, a teacher must be alert to questions or methods that appear to discourage thinking.

Last, a teacher will give the students continuous feedback on the quality, creativity, and depth of their thought. The beginning attempts of students in thinking operations may be timid. This is a time when it is especially important to encourage them and to cite some evidences of progress. Thinking skills do take time to develop. Students will learn at varying rates of speed.

Students can be assisted to think more critically if they are taught to recognize some of the common errors. A frequent error is to *go beyond the data*—drawing inferences from data that the data cannot support. We see a single cloud in the sky and say, "It is going to rain." When we look at a graph we may be guilty of making unjustifiable extrapolations or interpolations. *Inconsistency* is evidence that a student's ideas have not crystallized. *Failure to apply principles* is evidence that a student does not relate abstract principles to the solution of practical problems. *Dependence on a single authority* indicates a disinclination to weigh alternatives. Adherence to the fallacy of *single causation* results in another error of thinking. In our complex way of life, effects generally have mutiple causes. *Semantics* may cause difficulties in class discussions because words do not have the same meaning for all students; semantic difficulties may be due to ignorance or to limited experience, but they can also arise when people have similar backgrounds and experience.

Students display overcaution when they are reluctant to draw the conclusion that the evidence obviously forces. Students are often overcautious because they have been ridiculed in the past, they fear loss of face, or they lack experience in making decisions.

[5] Op. cit., pp. 107–110.

Students should look for assumptions related to their thinking operations. In lieu of facts, which may not be available, assumptions may be considered. Assumptions are probably true, probably false, or uncertain. For example, a student may be selling costume jewelry at a very low price. Here are some possible assumptions that potential buyers may be making about the reasons for his selling the jewelry: the jewelry was stolen; the jewelry consisted of family castoffs; the student bought it even more cheaply from another student or a neighbor; it was obtained at an auction at a low cost. Assumptions are important and do illuminate the processes of discrimination and decision making.

The examination of means and ends is appropriate in the thinking process. That the ends justify the means is often stated, but there is a failure to consider ethical justifications. For example, a man may have great wealth as a goal. In gaining this end, he uses alien labor at low wages; sells shoddy merchandise that does not meet standards; and witholds profits from his partners. If students ask, "Why not?" the question may be raised, "Suppose you were a partner, a worker, or a buyer of his goods?" The democratic principle of respect for others has been violated. From a different viewpoint, individuals do not always select the most efficient, the least costly, or the most appropriate means to gain their ends. A young homemaker, for example, is anxious to have attractive furnishings in her home, so she purchases only the most expensive of items on her limited budget. She has spent too little time in considering the means to gain her ends.

Moffett[6] believes that too little attention has been given to the affective domain in the emphasis on thinking in teaching. There need not be a dichotomy between the cognitive and affective domains. For example, if students are looking at photographs of malnourished children, they can be analytical (cognitive domain) about signs of malnutrition but at the same time may express compassion (affective domain) for these children. These deliberations may lead to possible solutions to the problem and what individuals in the group might do to help.

Moffett further emphasizes his point by referring to the recent research on the two hemispheres of the brain. In a right-handed person, the left hemisphere (which governs the right side of the body) is digital like a computer, verbal, and linear and is sometimes designated as analytical/intellectual. The right hemisphere (which governs the left side of the body) is spatial, visual, and non-verbal and is sometimes called the holistic/metaphorical hemisphere. Moffett contends that the thinking related to the left hemisphere is emphasized much more than that of the right hemisphere. The alert teacher may wish to con-

[6] David Sohn, "A Talk with James Moffett," *Media and Methods,* Vol. 11, No. 6 (Feb. 1975), pp. 22–24, 60–61.

sider how products of the affective domain and the right hemisphere, such as feelings, art, music, or poetry, might be used to stimulate thinking.

Home economics educators may wish to ask themselves, "Are there certain competences, skills, or cautions that will facilitate the process of thinking?" Teachers may use the following list to check on their own thinking habits as well as those of their students. This list is only suggestive in nature. It should be used only if helpful in a specific situation.

Students might find a *model* or *blueprint* helpful for a sequential order in their thinking. Many plans are offered in the literature. The definition of thinking at the beginning of this chapter may stimulate ideas for personal guidelines. Some students will have established ways of thinking, but for students who have not, an ordered method may be an aid.

A skill in *securing pertinent information* that bears on problems, plans, questions, or the like is valuable. Are students familiar with ways to secure information from competent persons; from libraries, such as from card catalogues; from available books and publications, guides and indexes to a specific type of literature, encyclopedias, dictionaries, yearbooks, atlases, almanacs, biographical dictionaries,

Figure 13–3 Competency in securing pertinent information facilitates thinking. (Barry Busbiber, Ohio State University)

magazines, newspapers, the Yellow Pages of the telephone directory, and others; personnel in public and private agencies and institutions and museums; and the like. Students may consider ways to pass on the information they have gained for the use of other students.

One competence is in the discriminating selection of reliable authorities in the field under investigation. Certain criteria may be helpful. Information from a person, book, magazine, lecture, or other source may require scrutiny for soundness. Information from a professional magazine or person is more likely to be accurate than that from a magazine picked up from a newsstand. What is the background of the author or the person in the field? Do other professional persons have a high regard for the individual? These and other questions must be asked. Sound information is often difficult to obtain, but students should be encouraged to find and to evaluate data.

The *development of an adequate vocabulary,* sometimes termed *expressive fluency,* is an important aid in sharpening and defining one's thoughts, as well as communicating them to others. Be careful with the use of words such as *all, everyone, equal,* and *always* to avoid giving the impression that what is said applies to everyone in the entire population or that two or more items or persons are identical.

Another aid to thinking is the ability to make *generalizations.* Generalizing occurs when an individual makes a statement or a kind of conclusion based on a wide array of concrete experiences, materials, or ideas. The statement should be based on adequate and sound data. For example, a simple generalization made by someone who has visited a number of home economics departments might be "All home economics departments have nursery schools." Actually this generalization must be confined to the departments visited.

The skill of *distinguishing opinion from fact* is important. Opinion is usually an idea that may not have been tested; in fact, it may be a tentative hypothesis to be tested. A fact is based on research, statistics, or scientific evidence of some kind. Facts commonly used may be the nutrient content of foods as found in a government publication, census figures, or data from local survery. Facts may relate to what one actually sees or hears, but they still need to be checked. An opinion is a guess.

Avoiding *common errors* in thinking described at the beginning of this section can facilitate thinking. Other personal attributes on which teachers and students may wish to check themselves are *ability to adapt and to be flexible, fluency of ideas, use of associations,* and *quantity and quality of thinking.*

Teaching Strategies

The teaching of thinking cannot be done in a vacuum but must become a vital part of the teaching–learning process every day in every area of home economics. Thinking becomes vital when it relates to the unique aspects in the lives of the individuals being taught. Gross[7] says that the only subject matter in education is "life in all of its manifestations." The challenge to home economics educators is to help young and old to use critical thinking when dealing with their problems, interests, needs, goals, and other life concerns.

It is important that all subject-matter areas of home economics be involved. The entire age specturm, from an infant or child to the aged, must be included. All home economists, in whatever position they hold, would do well to consider ways in which critical thinking might be emphasized. There are many opportunities in the classroom; in teaching employees; in preparing educational materials for industry; in counseling persons in a clinic or an agency; in working with youth in 4-H clubs or in FHA/HERO; and in many other situations.

Some teaching strategies for helping students to be familiar with and to use the various aspects of thinking are suggested here. Once students have a firm basis for making judgments, then the further development of critical thinking is enhanced.

Adaptations from thinking operations listed by Raths and his coauthors[8] for use with home economics students are described here.

Observing or Perceiving

Sensitive observing or perceiving can enhance thinking. Observations or perceptions may involve all of the senses. The objective of this thinking operation is not to concentrate on isolated observations but to accumulate pertinent points and formulate an intellectual conclusion.

Some activities for students are

1. Blindfolded, identify (by touch) such foods as an apple, a leaf of lettuce, a stalk of celery, a stick of spaghetti, a walnut in a shell, and a cookie. This activity is especially appropriate for children and junior-high-school students, but other age levels might enjoy it as well. Additional experiences of this nature might be provided for students who have difficulty in identification. Encourage students to think of similar activities, for example, an experiment with spices in which odor and taste might be included as identifying factors. Eating other foods while blindfolded, such as fruitcake, tossed salad, or a casserole, and identifying the ingredients is a good exercise. These activities may

[7] Dorothy Gross, "Encouraging the Curious Mind Through the Curriculum," *Childhood Education,* Vol. 51, No. 1 (Oct. 1974), p. 5.
[8] Op. cit., pp. 164–174.

Figure 13–4 Critical observation through the use of the senses can strengthen identification. These students are using their sense of smell to identify spices.

take place in the classroom or at a club meeting or may be used as a party game. One gain will be increased perceptive ability.

2. Listen to a cassette of various sounds made by a baby. Analyze the messages the baby is trying to convey. This activity may be useful in encouraging observation among students in a classroom, for a study group of young mothers in a well-baby clinic, or in a family-life or preparation-for-marriage course. Home economists in business or extension workers may wish to adapt this activity for the materials they distribute.
3. Touch various types of fabrics and list several words that are sharply descriptive of each. In a study of clothing or textiles, this activity is appropriate. Students may consider the appropriate use of certain "feels." How might warm, cool, stiff, smooth, soft, downy, clingy, or other feels be best used? Home economists in the clothing industry may adapt this activity for their materials, and other home economics educators might find other uses.
4. Walk in the neighborhood and identify types of houses and building materials. Observation may also concentrate on the advantages and disadvantages of living in certain houses, and the effect of these houses on a neighborhood or the families living in these houses. This housing activity is excellent for the development of sharpness of perception at most age levels.
5. Observe a number of shoppers in a supermarket. What selection problems are they encountering? Is there any reason for these

problems? This consumer problem may be modified in many ways to develop the power of observation. Try to select consumer problems that are pertinent to the students involved.

Classifying

In classifying, or taxonomy, students are asked to group or to categorize a variety of items that appear to have a relationship to each other. The challenge to thinking is greater if the students must identify their own categories. The creating of criteria by students should not be ruled out but encouraged. Determining if the groupings are purposeful and having students defend their classifications are worthwhile experiences. Categories may be based on function, use, size, effect, form, rank, or other criteria. In the process, students discern likes and unlikes. Here is a single device that may be given to students during the study of foods.

How's Your Listing?

Our thinking is helped if we can identify things or ideas and place them in the proper category. Here is a simple example. Read the words carefully, decide what the headings are, and place each word under the heading to which it belongs.

ant	cactus	dog
ivy	bee	mosquito
walrus	bear	grass

One answer is

Insects	*Plants*	*Animals*
ant	ivy	walrus
bee	cactus	bear
mosquito	grass	dog

Now let us apply this idea to home economics. Assume that you have been reading in your reference books about planning and preparing breakfasts. Read the following words carefully, and decide in which categories each belongs. Place it under its correct heading.

eggs	minerals	eggbeater
vitamins	spoon	carbohydrate
orange squeezer	cereal	butter
milk	protein	toaster
toast	knife	orange juice

NOTE: The teacher will examine the lists completed by students to determine how they have categorized the words. Here is an example:

Foods	*Nutrients*	*Equipment*
eggs	vitamins	orange squeezer
milk	minerals	spoon
toast	protein	knife
cereal	carbohydrate	eggbeater
butter		toaster
orange juice		

If the students make many errors in categorization, the teacher should look for possible causes. The students may be unfamiliar with certain words or their relationships to each other, or they may lack experience in this process.

Another food categorization device is offered here:

Group the following foods under headings in appropriate columns:

Baked apple, pineapple juice, pizza, custard, milk shake, bread, omelet, roast chicken, French-fried potatoes, tossed green salad, cherry pie, waffles, broccoli, melon, vegetable soup, crackers, roast beef, macaroni and cheese, cocoa, steak, string beans, orange juice, tuna-salad sandwich, jellied salad mold, lollypop, bananas, salmon.

Some possible student responses:

1. Four food groups—daily food guide or other dietary guide.
2. Cooked and uncooked foods.
3. Food preferences and dislikes.
4. Foods known and unknown.
5. Solids and liquids.
6. Foods for meals and snacks.
7. Breads, meats, vegetables, fruits, desserts.
8. Starches, fats, proteins, vitamins.
9. Low-calorie and high-calorie foods.
10. Expensive and inexpensive foods.

Students might analyze the above groupings for underlying principles. Consider ways of grouping the ten groups. Consider groupings that were omitted.

Similar devices might be developed in other phases of home economics, such as textiles, equipment, scheduling, consumer education, and family relations.

Comparing

There are many opportunities for comparisons for students in home economics classes. Learning to look for similarities and dissimilarities involves thinking and perceptive observation. Attempting to compare things, ideas, or persons that appear to have no apparent relationship can be demanding; students' abilities to make valid comparisons depend on the variety of their experiences. When the experience in comparing is limited, a teacher may assist a student through skillful questioning by pointing to possible areas of difference or similarity. When students become more experienced, a teacher may determine if a student can pick out specific evidence to support her/his points and assumptions. Through many acts of comparison, students learn discrimination.

Students must not confuse *equate* and *compare: equate* implies similarities; *compare* implies both similarities and differences. *Contrast* implies differences only.

Some suggestions for comparisons in the home economics classroom are offered here:

1. Compare the work of your mother with the work of your father.
2. Compare living in the city with living in a small town.
3. Compare the costs of one serving of various foods with a high vitamin C content.
4. Compare the costs of educational toys for a preschool child.
5. Select a common stain on clothes and compare various spot removers.
6. Compare Puerto Rican food with Italian food.
7. Compare the home of a Mexican with the home of a Swede.
8. Compare an eggbeater with a large spoon.
9. Compare the peel of an onion with the peel of an apple.
10. Compare poor people with rich people.

Teachers are cautioned not to make the comparisons for their students but to encourage them to develop this skill so that they have the ability to make their own judgments.

Interpreting

Everyone is confronted frequently with the necessity of interpreting data, either from newspaper stories and other reading materials or from the comments made by family members, neighbors, and others. Some ordinary examples may relate to the cost of living, to the number of teenage marriages, or to the unemployment rate.

The following exercise may be presented to students to determine if they are inclined to make judgments on insufficient data, if they are overcautious, or if they go beyond the data.

Recycling

Last winter Bill and Cindy were looking at some of their old clothes for possibilities of recycling. They looked at some of their old T-shirts and decided that some had possibilities. Ideas were discussed with their mother. Cindy decided to decorate the worn spots with washable ribbon, lace, or an unused doily. Bill selected some "eye-catching" press-ons for his T-shirts.

Instructions: Read the story carefully and take for granted that every statement is true. Then read each statement below and decide whether you consider it true or false, or whether you are uncertain about it. Mark your answer *T, F,* or *U.* Do not go back to change any of your answers.

______1. In brief, this story is about recycling T-shirts.
______2. The time was last spring.
______3. Cindy and Bill were brother and sister.
______4. The 4-H Club encouraged recycling.
______5. Cindy decided on press-ons for worn spots.
______6. Sally was the girl in the story.
______7. The recycling cost a total of $3.00.
______8. The story does not tell how many T-shirts Bill and Cindy each recycled.

NOTE: Here is the key:

1. True.
2. False—the time was last winter.
3. True—the story mentions their mother, not their mothers.
4. Uncertain—insufficient evidence.
5. False—Bill decided on press-ons.
6. False—Cindy was the girl.
7. Uncertain—insufficient evidence.
8. True.

In examining student results, a teacher should be concerned about the students who mark *T* statements *F* or *F* statements *T.* This is a very crude error to make in thinking. An equally important observation is to identify those students who mark *U* before statements that are obviously *T* or *F.* This indicates overcaution, and a teacher should watch for this characteristic in other situations. The tendency to go beyond the data will be indicated if students mark *U* statements with an *F* or a *T.*

The teacher will use this information to improve a student's understanding of thinking in general and, specifically, his/her own thinking. In every situation, a teacher will encourage thinking by challenging students to consider such points as: Do you have adequate evidence for such a statement? Who is your authority? How did you reach this conclusion? What is the basis for your generalization? Is this information relevant? Is such a prediction sound? To help a student to practice sound thinking can be a great satisfaction for a teacher and a far-reaching contribution to the student's preparation for life.

Interpretation focuses on inferences and generalizations that may be drawn from reports of various types: literary, artistic, numerical, pictorial, or graphic. The interpreter is not confined to the mere translation of facts but must understand, look for gaps, and develop an ability to interpolate and to extrapolate with judgment. Questions like the following might be asked by the teacher: What do the data tell you? What can you predict with certainty? With probability? What additional data would have been helpful? What questions might be raised? Are there any practical applications?

There are many occasions when interpretation is important in every area of home economics, such as interpreting directions for operating household equipment; interpreting a physician's diet order for a patient; interpreting instructions for feeding a baby for a young mother; customer interpretation of telephone or utility bills; and welfare families' interpretation of information about where to go for help. Analyzing different interpretations can provide the content to enforce critical thinking.

Summarizing

In order to summarize, students must focus on the essential and significant facts; synthesize the salient points; decide what is to be included and what is to be omitted; and organize the summary to fit a specified purpose. Students may be asked to justify the basis upon which they decided upon the essentials. During the class discussion, the teacher may ask several students to give their summaries and may ask other students such questions as: How would you summarize differently, or would you have included the same points?

Here are some suggestions for summaries for home economics students:

1. Prepare a summary of the important points to consider in losing weight.
2. Summarize a newspaper article about buying meat.
3. Select an advertisement of an article that you are interested in buying. Summarize its important points.

Home economists and their students can profit from a facility to summarize. For example, summaries might be made of the remarks made by a panel of experts on a particular subject, or departmental accomplishments, of annual reports to administrators, of field experiences by students, or of an interview of an expert reported by a student to a class or group.

Hypothesizing

As the first step in hypothesizing, students must become acquainted with the nature of a hypothesis. (Students in junior high school are not too young to learn this concept.) Suggested definitions

Figure 13–5 Hypothesizing may be related to securing sources of help in a crisis. (A.T.&T.)

of a hypothesis are that it is an educated guess, a reasonable possibility, or a statement that is to be tested. Initially the class may work together in the development of hypotheses about a certain idea or situation that concerns them. For example, some questions that can be explored are What is the best diet for a football player? What are ways to save money when buying recordings? How may littering be stopped in our neighborhood?

The teacher can ascertain whether the students understand the concept and which students may require additional help. The teacher must stress that many hypotheses may emerge from a single problem. Each must be tested for appropriateness to the problem.

Students can be helped to see that hypothesizing goes on in everyday life and that one does not have to be a research specialist to handle it. Assistance may be necessary to help students to sharpen their hypothesis so that it states their problem clearly. Next, steps should be taken to find information, collect data, analyze data, and reach a conclusion.

Analyzing Assumptions

In analyzing assumptions, students must find out if a statement is a fact or if they are guessing that something is true. It is recommended that teachers plan experiences so as to give students an opportunity to name assumptions that support a given conclusion; to identify and distinguish between fact and assumption; and to determine whether the assumption is a guess, an inference, or a judgment based on previous experiences.

Here are some techniques to use with home economics students to test their ability to analyze assumptions:

1. There are two boxes of wheat cereal on the table. One is larger than the other, so it weighs more.
   What assumptions are necessary to support the conclusion?
   Possible assumptions (for teacher use):
   a. Both boxes contain the same cereal.
   b. Both boxes are made of material that weighs the same.
   A question that might be asked is "What if one of the boxes is empty?"
2. Helen sees two glass pitchers of milk in the refrigerator. One is low and squatty and the other is tall and cylindrical.
   What assumptions might be made about the pitcher that holds the most milk?
   Some students will assume that height is a good criterion of volume and assume that the tall pitcher has the larger volume of milk, or they may make other assumptions. In this case, the only accurate method is to measure the milk in each pitcher.
3. From a collection of magazine and newspaper pictures of individuals at work, ask students to identify the jobs being performed. With each identification, have a student list the assumptions she/he made.

In addition, students may be encouraged to identify the assumptions made by commentators on radio and television; by politicians as they are quoted in newspapers or magazine articles; by characters in a television drama, in a play, or in fiction; or concepts of editorial writers. Discovering the assumptions in the conversation of another will help to illuminate the arguments made by him or her.

Application of Principles

Applying principles during class work has many potentials for home economics. The goal is to be able to apply principles learned from previous experiences to new situations. The ability to see relationships is necessary to this goal.

Some exercises in the application of principles in the home economics curriculum are offered here:

1. If you had only three colors of paint and wished to create some color schemes for a family room, what might you do? How can you predict the results?
2. What do you think would happen if:
   a. You cut up fresh apples and pears for fruit cup an hour before serving.
   b. You cooked broccoli for fifty minutes.
   c. You prepared the orange juice for breakfast the night before and forgot to put it in the refrigerator.
   d. You waited thirty minutes before serving a baked cheese soufflé.

Other experiences in the application of principles may be developed by the teacher and students.

Critical Reading

Critical reading, according to Johnson, Lackman, and Reisboard,[9] can stimulate critical thinking. Critical reading may be applied to fiction, advertisments, newspaper and magazine articles, drama, and other reading matter. Determining the purpose, mood, and intent of the author or the creator can be challenging. Students might ask questions such as: What is the author's purpose? Is he or she trying to convince the reader of a certain viewpoint? In what ways? Is only one side highlighted? What biases, if any, are evident? What evidence is there of the strength of the biases? For example, if the author of a book on strict vegetarianism indicates that he or she is an advocate of the movement and tries to convince readers that this is the only diet for health, that author has a strong bias. Selecting the words and phrases that enforce this bias is revealing. What is the mood of the author and how is it indicated—positively, negatively, neutrally, or in some other manner? Does the author seem well informed and competent? Are there any discrepancies? If the reading material is a story, are the characters real for the type and age depicted?

Distinguishing fact from opinion, fiction, fantasy, or fallacy is important. Advertisements offer a good study in this area. A health spa may offer a regimen that takes off ten pounds in a week. That may be a fact, but what are the consequences? Read advertisements for CB radios, hearing aids, freckle removers, mopeds, microwave ovens, records, cassettes, and other items that may appeal to the students

[9] Marjorie Seddon Johnson, Thomas W. Lackman, and Richard J. Reisboard, *Critical Reading* (Dansville, N.Y.: Instructor Publications, 1977).

according to age and interest. Determine what is factual and what is nonfactual.

Analyze reading for cause–effect relationships and note if an answer is based on a single or a multiple cause. Make inferences from the data offered, be alert to propaganda devices, note points that are relevant or irrelevant, and check on the validity and reliability of the content.

The professional reading of students and educators should be equally critical. Although these materials are more likely to be credible, errors have been made and even experts occasionally go beyond the data. Read letters to the editor in a professional magazine and then read the original article. Is the criticism sound? Where do you stand?

Evaluation

Evaluation of thinking is an integral part of teaching–learning strategies, as indicated previously. Educators must bear in mind that individuals will be more inclined to think critically in the areas that are important to them. Later these personal concerns may be related to broader social concerns. And the perennial question is "How may individuals steer their thinking to matters of the most importance?" There is no ready answer for that.

Students' ability to think must be nurtured, encouraged, and stimulated. Treating the ideas and questions of students with respect is essential. The teacher should share problems with them. What can you do to save energy? What responsibilities do you have for world hunger? She/he may ask questions that dig—"Are there other possibilities?"—bring up problems that are pertinent to students, encourage the solution to a problem that is unusual, and mitigate students' frustration when answers are slow in coming by building students' confidence in their thinking skills and capacities. Above all, a teacher's enthusiasm and her/his role as a model of clear thinking are paramount.

RESEARCH

Research workers are not by any means isolated from the problems of the world. Understanding the techniques of and participating in research should be a responsibility of everyone in home economics, students and teachers alike. A firsthand acquaintance with research techniques will open a new world to one, sharpen his/her methods of solving problems, broaden his/her fund of knowledge, and enhance his/her appreciation of the important role that research plays in everyday living.

What Is Research?

Van Dalen[10] defines research as "a careful, critical search for solutions to the problems that plague and puzzle mankind." Research, he continues, is born of curiosity and nourished by an intense yearning to learn the truth and to improve our ways of doing things. Research as an activity is characterized by truthfulness and an emphasis on definiteness and completeness. The objective of research is to determine exactly what ideas and things are and how they work. Researchers distrust the easy, the plausible, or the customary in seeking positive knowledge that can systematically explain a whole and its parts.

Need for Research in Home Economics

Research in home economics is needed, according to Montgomery and Ritchie,[11] to emphasize that "home economics is grounded in science, not in myth, common sense, or traditional wisdom." These authors further challenge us to consider how the research that we might have done would have greatly enhanced home and family living and what can be done in the future.

It is discouraging to note that home economics carries only a minimal share of the research in our subject-matter fields as reported by professional journals—not only home economics journals but other professional journals that carry research reports on nutrition, human development, and other areas, according to these writers. A revolution to correct these shortcomings should be encouraged by members of our profession. How can we be considered professional unless we emphasize research?

Home economics has made some progress, with the publication of a research journal, *Home Economics Research Journal;* annual research reports in the various subject-matter areas; and some research articles in the *Journal of Home Economics.* The findings of research are the voice of authority, and progressive professions foster research as a vital part of their development programs. An effort was begun in 1976 by the American Home Economics Association to secure grants and contracts. This effort has been successful and may provide the necessary impetus to further research.

[10] Deobold B. Van Dalen, *Understanding Educational Research* (New York: McGraw-Hill, 1966), p. 1.

[11] James E. Montgomery and S. J. Ritchie, "Home Economics Research: Are We Doing All We Can?" *Journal of Home Economics,* Vol. 67, No. 1 (Jan. 1975), pp. 35–39.

Research Process

Research proceeds in a sequence of operations: the selection of a problem, the survey of related literature, the establishment of an investigative procedure, the collection of data, the analysis of data, and the presentation of findings and their implication.

The researcher should select a problem that is of great interest to him/her, to which his/her competences are suited, and that he/she can reasonably expect to pursue fruitfully within whatever limitations in facilities, time, equipment, and money are imposed. Above all, the problem should have professional and social significance.

The successful conduct of research depends largely on the efficiency of the investigative procedure, which should be spelled out in detail. How to establish suitable criteria of accuracy, identify independent and dependent variables, maintain objectivity, and test for reliability and validity are explained in standard textbooks on research methods. Many a study has failed because an important step was not properly defined. Time and effort in the planning stage will eliminate errors and give confidence.

Research in the Classroon

There are limitless opportunities to make research a part of daily class activities. Research can prove an interesting and intellectually stimulating challenge to students and will interest parents, too. Research can be done in groups or by individuals. Following are a few suggestions for research projects:

1. Survey the ways in which selected families are saving water.
2. Compare the cost and adequacy of the dry cleaning of a certain type of garment at home, in a self-service dry-cleaning machine, and by professional cleaners.
3. Analyze the snack habits of peers according to the types of foods eaten, their nutritional value, or the amounts of money spent.
4. Survey the leisure-time spending habits of a sample group of students.
5. Survey a sample of families that own hand calculators and how they put them to use.

These problems for student research are only suggestions. More enthusiasm will be expressed if problems emerge from the students' own interests and concerns. The problem may be worked on by individual students as an independent project or in relation to a subject-matter unit of study. An entire class may work on a problem, or a committee of students may report their results to the entire class.

It is sensible for students to develop an outline before launching on their research. The problem should be stated clearly: list the steps necessary to gain the information (sometimes called subproblems), and detail how the investigation will proceed, how the data will be collected and analyzed, and how conclusions may be drawn. More mature students may wish to indicate underlying assumptions, state a hypothesis, and consider the implications of their results.

Attention may be given to how to write a research report, and how to make charts and graphs for illustrations. Even photographs can be made of experimental results, for example, the use of various types of equipment in the beating of eggs for scrambled eggs, such as a fork, an electric mixer, or a hand eggbeater. A report of the research may be built into an exhibit for others to see, or an abstract might be distributed.

An evaluation of the research project by the students is important. What were the shortcomings? What were the possible contributions? Were the conclusions justified? Did the procedures have certain weaknesses, such as the persons interviewed being reluctant to give information or failing to give complete information, or implications for further research? An examination of the contributions made by the students' research and their satisfactions or dissatisfactions in doing this project is a good experience. Students may wish to make suggestions for improving their research projects and to consider other areas of study in which research may enhance their learning.

Teacher Research

There are many kinds of research that could benefit teaching: a systematic study of the problems and interests of students, a survey of the home economics department's graduates to evaluate the adequacy of the curriculum, or an analysis of student plans for future careers.

SUGGESTIONS FOR FURTHER LEARNING

1. Make an analysis of your own thinking patterns. What are your strengths and weaknesses? What improvements are in order?
2. Collect evidence of uncritical or careless thinking by listening to friends in rap sessions. What might be the consequences of such thinking?
3. Select an article on research related to teaching in the *Home Economics Research Journal.* Establish criteria and evaluate the research project critically. How would you have done the research project differently?

14

Creativity

Creativity may be encouraged at every level and in every area of home economics. The home economist in extension, for example, may encourage homemakers to imagine new or different ways to save energy. The nutritionist in a clinic may help an obese patient to find creative ways to stop or to do less raiding of the refrigerator. In home economics occupational education, new opportunities for service and jobs may be explored for entry-level positions. The home economist in business may induce customers to experiment with novel uses of products, and the home economics teacher in the classroom may encourage students to explore the impact of their heritage on their lives.

THE NATURE OF CREATIVITY

The word *creativity,* according to Andrews,[1] connotes movement or action; such words as *searching, testing, experimenting, thinking, making, organizing, changing, identifying, probing, manipulating, observing, choosing, appraising, extending, constituting,* and *synthesizing* describe creative processes. Imaginative students try new ways rather than sticking to the old ones; they substitute, reverse, subtract, modify, add, and adapt; they are aware, intuitive, discriminating, and resourceful; they go beyond the usual and the ordinary. Creative people experience intensely a gamut of feelings—spontaneity, satis-

[1] Gladys Andrews, "Releasing Creativity—Extending Curriculum Opportunities," in Robert S. Fleming (ed.), *Curriculum for Today's Boys and Girls.* (Columbus, Ohio: Merrill Books, 1979), Ch. 13.

Figure 14-1 Early sensory experiences encourages creativity. (Courtesy of Will Kyselka, University of Hawaii)

faction, elation, frustration, discouragement, perseverance, excitement, and so on. It is essential for home economics teachers to have some concept of the nature of creativity so that they can recognize and encourage it.

Definition

Ghiselin[2] defines creativity as a process of change, development, and evolution in an individual's subjective life. He states that creative talent is not easy to identify, that productivity is the final proof of creativity. Foshay[3] lists four major ingredients in the creative process. The first is an attitude of openness and a willingness to try new experiences, to suspend the usual judgments, and to be flexible in the examination of data. The second is having perspective on one's experiences. There is, Foshay believes, a time when one sees all her/his ideas or plans in focus, and at that time the creative person is able to

[2] Brewster Ghiselin, *The Creative Process* (New York: New American Library, 1955).
[3] Arthur Foshay, "The Creative Process Described," in Alice Miel (ed.), *Creativity in Teaching* (Belmont, Calif.: Wadsworth, 1961), Ch. 2.

transform her/his ideas into action. The third ingredient in the process is discipline, the ordering of one's experiences in such a way that methodical production can come about. The word *discipline* connotes responsibility, devotion, rigor, the imposition of the necessary limitations, and planning. Artists, scientists, and other talented persons may be disturbed from time to time by frustrations and confusions within themselves, but they pay scant attention to external distractions. The fourth ingredient is *closure,* the ability to identify the point at which a creative work is completed. Foshay contends that creative persons generally stop when their criteria have been met. Closure should bring a feeling of pride and satisfaction.

One of the problems facing us in the recognition of creativity, according to Getzels and Jackson,[4] is that current intelligence tests measure only certain forms of cognition and do not identify the unique qualities of individuals. Intelligence tests measure the ability to achieve but not the ability to create.

Identification

Research, according to MacKinnon,[5] has demonstrated that creative people seldom have the characteristics of a stereotype. On the whole, highly creative persons have above-average intelligence. The relationship is not clear-cut, however, because intelligence has many facets. For example, creative architects have a highly developed sense of space, whereas creative writers have a highly developed sense of language. Apart from various intellectual gifts, it is apparent that creative persons have an unusual capacity to record, retain, and have readily available their life experiences. Their other capacities include discernment; high concentration of attention; the retention of a wide range of facts and experiences, which can be used singly or in combination, depending on the need; and an openness to experience. Theory and aesthetics are the philosophical values that predominate in a creative person. MacKinnon warns that there is no single path to creativity.

Arieti[6] identifies creativity as a unique phenomenon. Creativity may be manifested in a wide spectrum, including the arts, jokes, games, religious beliefs, and philosophical studies.

The following suggestions are designed for the ferreting out of students' creative talents and may be adapted to any content area of home economics. Many of these suggestions have been adapted from

[4] Jacob W. Getzels and Philip W. Jackson, *Creativity and Intelligence.* (New York: Wiley, 1962).

[5] Donald W. MacKinnon, "What Makes a Person Creative?" *Theory into Practice,* Vol. 5, No. 4 (Oct., 1966), pp. 152–156.

[6] Silvano Arieti, *Creativity, The Magic Synthesis* (New York: Basic, 1976).

tests for creativity devised by Guilford, Torrance, and Barron in Parnes and Harding[7] and others.

A sensitivity to problems may be uncovered when students are asked to consider ways to improve a telephone, lighting for bedtime reading, a refrigerator, shopping practices, mail services, or the use of space in a room. The quantity and quality of ideas and unusual approaches may indicate creative thinking. Giving students sketches entitled "What's wrong?" and asking them to find errors quickly is another way to test creativity. The sketches can be of apparatus from which an essential part is missing; a kitchen arrangement without, say, a sink; a table set without flatware; and so on.

The teacher can uncover originality by giving students a short story about a family situation and asking them to give it a clever title or by asking them to tell or write a story suggested by an emotionally charged picture. Or the teacher may suggest that students use unusual materials, such as colored leaves, whole or ground spices, flower petals, steel wool, or pot cleaners, to make a poster or collage.

The teacher can assess students' spontaneity by asking them to seek novel uses for a scarf, a wire clothes hanger, a wastebasket, kitchen sponges, or a bottle. One teacher asked students to consider the decorative uses of the cockleburs found on weeds in the school yard. One student made a monogram by sticking burrs on her coat.

Adaptiveness may be revealed when students are asked to adjust to a fanciful situation: What adaptations would a family have to make to a vacation home on the bottom of the ocean? How might certain frequently encountered directions be reduced to symbols—for example, what symbols might be used for "use a buttonhole attachment," "keep refrigerated," or "bake for thirty-five minutes"?

The teacher may judge students' fluency of ideas by having them react to ink or watercolor blots that they make themselves, to incomplete drawings, or to odd sounds from a tape recording. Students may be given a number of circles, triangles, squares, or other geometric figures and asked to use them as a basis for designing a new kitchen tool, a chest, a dress, or a labor-saving device. Finding new ways of using old things (a brass umbrella stand as a vase for leaves and tall flowers) or using color in unexpected places (a mosaic for the kitchen, made of pieces of dyed cork) is another possibility. They might also work with space in finding new uses for a chest, bookshelves, or closet gadgets—such as hanging place mats or gloves on a skirt hanger. Asking students to write in one minute all the words they associate with home and family life, such as *mortgage, wedding, mother-in-law, divorce, bread,* and *birthday cake,* may be stimulating.

[7] Sidney J. Parnes and H. F. Harding, *A Source Book for Creative Thinking* (New York: Scribner's, 1962), Guilford, Ch. 14; Torrance, Ch. 4; and Barron, Ch. 19.

Figure 14–2 What creative changes in family living might take place in a vacation home at the bottom of the ocean? (Courtesy Investor-Owned Electric Light and Power Companies)

Development of Creativity

The realistic home economics teacher knows that she or he cannot make of every student a creative genius but should endeavor to encourage the creative potential in each student. Maslow[8] stresses that creativity is not confined to artists, writers, inventors, and other professionals. He uses as an illustration a poor, uneducated woman who expressed originality, inventiveness, and ingenuity in her homemaking. "I learned from her, and others like her," he states, "that a first-rate soup is more creative than a second-rate painting."

Thelen[9] believes that education for creativity is a continuous inquiry and that teachers must continually urge students to think of new ideas and new ways of doing things and to probe for answers and new meanings. In this way, practical and unusual substitutions in such problems as pollution, waste, and inflation may be sought.

[8] Abraham Maslow, "Creativity in Self-Actualizing People," in Anderson, op. cit., p. 84.

[9] Herbert K. Thelen, "Teaching for the Development of Creativity," *Creativity and College Teaching,* Vol. 35, No. 4 (June 1963), pp. 62–76.

Creativity thrives best in the classroom that offers rich experiences, permissiveness, security and encouragement, and freedom from threats. There must be respect for the unusual question or the novel solution. Credit must be given for self-initiated learning or thinking and for ideas that have value or potential.

Toynbee[10] gives a single directive to teachers that might well supersede all others: "Give each child the feeling that he or she has inherent capabilities that belong to no one else."

The creative urge may be very vague. Help students to recognize and nurture it. Assignments that demand original work, experimentation, and exploration are desirable. Acquainting students with the nature of creative thinking done by eminent persons can be helpful; brainstorming sessions can be rewarding. Helping students to be constructively critical tends to elicit original solutions and ideas.

The teacher has a responsibility to bring rich experiences to students, including the active use of all the senses in savoring movement, color, sound, form, flavor, texture, temperature, light and shadow, and space. Fruits, vegetables, and cheeses can be examined for texture, color, form, odor, and flavor. The teacher will have to be patient with student responses and not rush in with personal ideas, descriptions, and reactions. Students can be encouraged to express feelings freely, to imagine, and to show interest. Even the halfhearted attempts, the fumblings, and the experiments should not be ignored.

There should be many allowances for individual differences. Encourage students to bring in things that please them; to relate treasured experiences; to see special qualities in the materials with which they work in the home economics classroom (the feel of wood in furniture, the draping and molding qualities of fabrics, and forms and color in foods); observe line, color, form, and space in the world and to listen to its sounds; and to realize that the way things feel, smell, taste, and sound are important. Individual experiences may be compared. No one should be forced into these activities. Rather, stimulate students to study the qualities of their own work, plan additional steps, and give technical assistance when necessary—supplying information about the rudiments of color, line, and design; giving guidance in the selection of materials; explaining procedures; and smoothing out fumbles.

Arouse students to the stimuli and resources in their environment. In education, unfortunately, as well as in life generally, teachers and students alike frequently neglect the rich and vivid experiences commonly available to them. In the fast tempo of the present day, take the time to admire the handiwork of neighbors and friends, appreciate the emotions aroused by a beautiful poem, recognize the feelings

[10] Arnold Toynbee, as interviewed by Margaret Mason, "Creativity in Our Schools," *Instructor,* Vol. 77, No. 8 (Apr. 1968), pp. 132–134.

Figure 14–3 Can students be creative with common shapes, such as the square and circle, plus materials such as string, board, and thumbtacks?

Figure 14–4 A solar hot-dog cooker developed by a student for a science fair. (Courtesy Gretna Breeze, Gretna, Neb., and Gretna Public Schools)

of gladness, sadness, surprise, or sympathy expressed by others. The ability to laugh, to imagine, to play, and to have fun is characteristic of the creative person, according to many authorities, and should be encouraged.

Deterrents

According to Torrance[11] the most common blocks to creativity are tradition, social approval, and habit. Students fear ridicule by their peers, and their creativity may be inhibited by a fear of being so original that their judgment will be questioned. Some students do well for the first step or two in a creative process but cannot proceed further without help; others need only an initial suggestion or warm-up. Original ideas or images are not easy to describe, in words or in any other medium. If a creative student were asked to draw an image of her/his idea, communication might be facilitated.

Worry, poor health, and frustrations in other areas dampen creativity. An unusual child may be able to produce in a bleak and dispiriting environment, but few children learn to make sensible decisions or to develop homemaking competences in a home where such efforts are belittled or discouraged. Almost everyone can be creative if some materials and inspiration are available. An elaborate, expensive setup is not essential, but good use of the available resources is.

Research

Cross-cultural studies give evidence of the nurture of creative development. In the United States, research indicates that after the age of ten, girls perform better than boys on verbal tests for creative thinking.[12] In India,[13] investigators using independently collected data in different parts of the country discovered that boys excelled over girls. Children in India performed much better on verbal than on figural tests of creativity. But children in Western Samoa,[14] black children in Georgia,[15] and lower-class children in Pittsburgh[16] per-

[11] E. Paul Torrance, *Creativity* (Washington, D.C.: NEA, Department of Classroom Teachers and American Educational Research Association, 1963), pamphlet.

[12] E. Paul Torrance, *Education and the Creative Potential* (Minneapolis: U. of Minnesota, 1963).

[13] A. O. Prakash, *Understanding the Fourth Grade Slump: A Study of the Creative Thinking Abilities of Indian Children.* Unpublished master's thesis, University of Minnesota, 1966.

[14] R. T. Johnson, *The Growth of Creative Thinking Abilities in Western Samoa.* Unpublished doctoral dissertation, University of Minnesota, 1963.

[15] E. P. Torrance and R. J. Goldman, *Creative Development in a Segregated Negro School* (Minneapolis: U. of Minnesota, 1966).

[16] E. Paul Torrance, "Nurture of Creative Talents," *Theory into Practice,* Vol. 5, No. 4 (Oct. 1966), p. 169.

formed better on figural tests than on verbal ones. It is not plausible that Indian children are born with superior verbal abilities from a creative standpoint or that children in Georgia, Samoa, and Pittsburgh have inherited creative capacities in figural tests. Torrance believes that the nurturing influences of these various cultures are responsible.

Certain cultural influences seem to be important in the development of creativity. Historical evidence shows that the child who begins creative efforts early has the best chance of reaching the heights in her/his field of interest, according to Reynolds.[17] When a student's questioning is discouraged, creative progress is hindered, according to Torrance.[18] Forty-three per cent of the potential dropouts in a seventh grade indicated that they were afraid to ask questions, and 95 per cent reported a lack of interest in any of their ideas and suggestions. Torrance points out that when the American success orientation is overemphasized, creative thinking is inhibited because experimenting, taking risks, and making mistakes and correcting them are vital to creative learning. Strong peer influence that values conformity can be detrimental. Strong emphasis on sex roles eliminates many areas of rich experiences for both boys and girls and consequently limits creative behavior. Concentration on a limited number of talents rather than on a diversity is deplored by many of these researchers.

Creative Teaching

Guilford[19] thinks that education can encourage creative performance and perhaps creative abilities themselves. When there is an overemphasis on the memorization of facts, a too-closely-prescribed curriculum, and an overreliance on textbooks, creativity will be stifled. Creativity is more likely to flourish if the teacher places the greater value on helping students to make independent judgments that they can defend. Students should be stimulated to have the courage to share new ideas—an innovation begins with one person, it is said, and to be a minority of one requires courage.

Creativity may depend on the way a teacher responds to students. This interaction has another dimension in the mutual sentiments expressed among students: the extent to which students help each other, respect each other's ideas, and recognize that they are learning together. Creativity is more likely to bloom in an atmosphere of reciprocity.

[17] M. C. Reynolds, "Nurturing Talents," paper presented at Elementary Leaders Conference, Iowa State Teachers College, Jan. 31, 1958.
[18] Torrance, "Nurture of Creative Talents," p. 170.
[19] J. L. Guilford, "Traits of Creativity," in Anderson, op. cit., Ch. 10.

Figure 14–5 Encourage students to be creative in the display of kitchen equipment. This Chinese God of the Kitchen adds an aesthetic note. (Gas Appliances Manufacturers Association [GAMA])

Certain situations lend themselves to the challenge of creative teaching. One way is to take advantage of available resources. For example, using the talents of an *amateur radio operator*[20] who may be a student in a home economics or other class, or may be someone from the community, is a possibility for opening new vistas to students. Students may talk to radio amateurs in many parts of the world and learn about their personal and family lifestyles and compare these with their own life patterns. *Science fiction*[21] is excellent for helping students to imagine the unimaginable. What kind of foods might be grown on the moon? One boy planted beans in a simulated moon soil,

[20] Louis Hoestra Jr., "Kids on the 'Ham' Band," *Instructor,* Vol. 86, No. 6 (Oct. 1976), pp. 74–75.

[21] "Close Encounters of the Classroom Kind," *Instructor,* Vol. 87, No. 5 (Apr. 1978), pp. 54–57.

and the beans did grow. What kind of recreation would be suitable for family members living on a platform in space? What would be a new source of energy? Students might discuss possible solutions. These activities highlight the emphasis on teaching for the future. Use of the *telephone*[22] in daily living may be facilitated by planning innovative uses.

Mainstreaming demands creative teaching. How may a home economics teacher handle a *blind*[23] student in class? The special-education teacher is responsible for teaching braille and meeting special needs. The home economics teacher, with the help of other students, can help the child to become self-reliant in living skills, such as preparing foods with a nutritional emphasis, becoming acquainted with the community, and assisting in the care of younger brothers and sisters. Students may help a blind student to feel or to hear in place of seeing during cooking, in keeping house, and in other activities.

In some schools, students are learning sign language so that they may communicate with *deaf*[24] students. Placing a small lead weight on the forearm of a student with *cerebral palsy*[25] helped her to write. In a similar manner, teacher and students may assist all types of special students.

Teaching the gifted[26] is another creative teaching problem. Gifted students may be helped to overcome the feeling of being different and to avoid undue pressures. These students may be offered some individualized instruction that requires additional reading; experimentation; testing their talents in art, writing, and other creative endeavors; or teaching other students. Opportunities to grow are important.

Kohl[27] describes a creative approach to a lunchroom problem. In one school, students threw their food, left the tables dirty, fought each other, and in general created bedlam. Supervisors were unable to cope with the situation, and there was discussion of seeking help from the police. Kohl involved the faculty and helped them to see that order in the lunchroom appeared to be their only goal.

A start toward making a change was to think about all of the characteristics of an ideal lunchroom, such as the type of tables and

[22] "Telephone, Uncommon Explorations with Common Objects," *Instructor,* Vol. 86, No. 6 (Feb. 1977), p. 127.

[23] Mary Lou Alson, "He's Blind, He's in Our Class, Everybody's Learning," *Instructor,* Vol. 87, No. 2 (Sept. 1977), pp. 222–224.

[24] B. Charles Dorsey, "Sign Language in a Hearing Classroom," *Teacher,* Vol. 95, No. 9 (June 1978) pp. 75–77.

[25] "Teacher Plus," *Instructor,* Vol. 87, No. 5 (Dec. 1977), p. 12.

[26] Suzanne Ramos, "Don't Forget the Gifted," *Teacher,* Vol. 93, No. 4 (Dec. 1975), pp. 46–48.

[27] Herbert Kohl, "Creativity and a Sense of Powerlessness," *Teacher,* Vol. 92, No. 6 (Feb. 1975), pp. 20–26.

chairs and the size of servings for the children. Children in kindergarten often receive more food than they can eat, and hungry adolescents have servings that are too small. Ideas about the decor and the possibility of having music were included. Rearrangement of the furniture, preparation of the food on the site, and decoration of the lunchroom materialized through the planning and work of teachers and students. The lunchroom was used as a learning center for mathematics, reading, and other areas of study. The menu was changed through the establishment of a state-sponsored pilot lunch program. Kohl contends that a creative attitude is as important as creative doing.

Other suggestions by Kohl[28] are for students to create games. "Start-from-scratch projects" such as making cottage cheese, growing bean sprouts, baking bread, sewing a jacket, or preparing homemade cleaning agents are home economics possibilities. How might Chisanbop[29] (counting on your fingers and using them as a calculator) be used in home economics?

Creative activities in the classroom, with the entire school, or with the community may be planned in connection with special days—such as Food Day, Sun Day, and Earth Day,—that pertain not only to the lives of students but to the peoples of the world.[30] Home economics educators may be motivated to consider the creative application of bilingual/bicultural education. Helping students to be comfortable with two cultures can be a challenge. Such a program enforces ideas about diversity in lifestyles and ideas.[31]

Another curriculum focus is on the environment. This may be in the classroom or in the community. In a Baltimore school[32] teachers and students creatively changed the classroom *environment* by removing old desks and replacing them with tables and chairs, rugs, easy chairs, lamps, and the like secured from the warehouse of the department of education. Home economics teachers may seek ways to improve their environment and to help students and parents with more livable, homelike environments in schools.

An *urban development* project[33] involved a group of seventh- and eighth-graders in Philadelphia who interviewed residents and took photographs of what they considered critical environmental prob-

[28] Herbert Kohl, "Creativity in the Curriculum," *Teacher,* Vol. 92, No. 7 (March 1975), pp. 14–22, 24.

[29] Bernadette Lieberthal, "Now It's O.K. to Count on Your Fingers," *Instructor,* Vol. 87, No. 10 (May 1978), p. 72.

[30] "Food, Glorious Food," *Instructor,* Vol. 86, No. 8 (Apr. 1977), pp. 60–61.

[31] Terry Touff Cooper, "Del Pueblo: A School That's Custom-Made for Learning," *Teacher,* Vol. 93, No. 2 (Oct. 1975), pp. 58–61.

[32] Carrie O. Staten, "The School Family That Made a Difference," *Instructor,* Vol. 85, No. 5 (Jan. 1976), pp. 18–21.

[33] Edward L. Stanix, "Cleaning Clementine Street: An Urban Environmental Report," *Instructor,* Vol. 85, No. 5 (Jan. 1976), pp. 48–50.

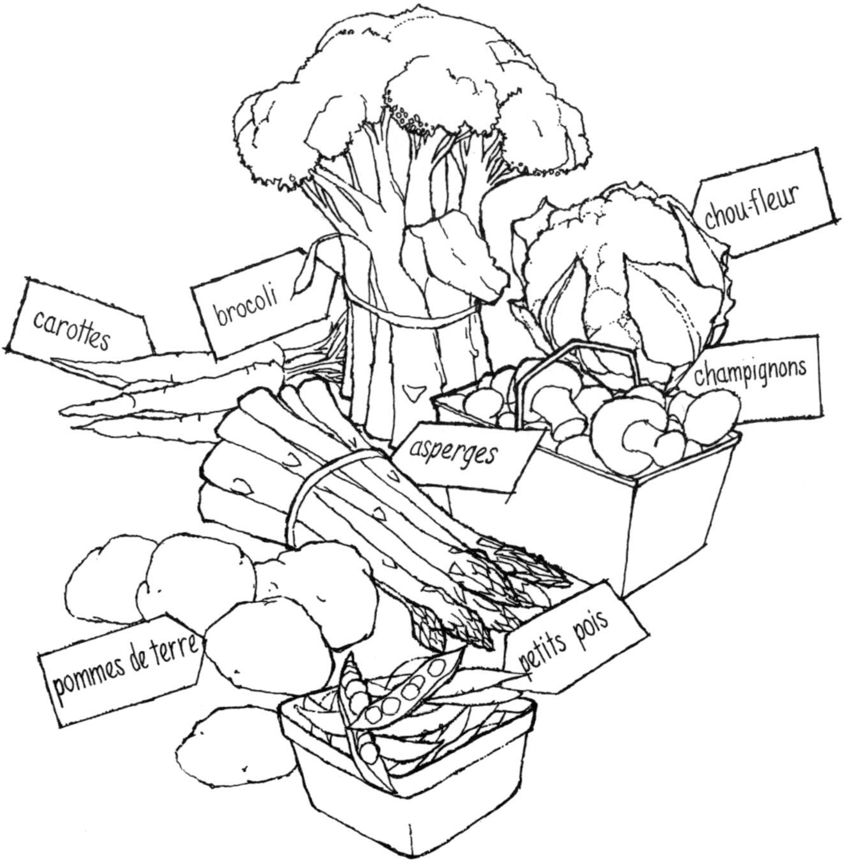

Figure 14–6 Learning the names of vegetables in other languages can be a bilingual and bicultural experience.

lems. Four major problems were identified: abandoned cars, abandoned houses, litter, and graffiti. Efforts were concentrated on one city block, Clementine Street. Litter and trash were removed. Graffiti-covered walls were painted. Many letters accompanied with photographs were sent to the police and city hall. The results were positive, and abandoned cars were removed. Local residents made and painted flower boxes for every home on the street. Students were taught how to repair abandoned houses. A complete record of finances, activities, and equipment went into a financial log book for their report to Project Kare, which had given a small amount of funding. The community and the students evaluated the project and found that it improved their environmental awareness and knowledge of urban problems. This project offers creative suggestions for home economics activities.

The home economics teacher, the home economist in extension, the nutritionist, the home economist in welfare, the home economist in business, and other home economics educators may wish to consider other ways in which creativity may be manifested in their endeavors. Not only will students, clients, patients, and others benefit, but this thrust will reflect favorably upon the profession as a whole.

A teacher can cultivate personal creativity. A self-study to learn under what circumstances original ideas come most readily would be helpful to teacher and students. What brings about creative moods? Authorities indicate that leisure time brings the release of a venturesome spirit and often generates ideas. Too often a teacher stops at the first good idea that comes, which is analogous to working out only one solution to a problem. Trying the new, breaking ground, and deviating from set patterns are all characteristics of the creative teacher.

SUGGESTIONS FOR FURTHER LEARNING

1. Think of the creative teachers you have known. Give some examples of their creative teaching. Were there some common elements? What new dimensions would you add to your concept of creative teaching? Test them in the observation of a number of home economics classes. What further adaptations have you made in your ideas about creative teaching?
2. Keep a log for a day about the evidences of creativity you have noted in life around you. Highlight the feelings associated with your observations.
3. Examine a number of home economics textbooks for ways in which creativity is encouraged. What are your conclusions?
4. Read the following reference for suggestions about creativity: Passow, A. Harry (ed.), "The Gifted and the Talented: Their Education and Development," *The Seventy-eighth Yearbook of the National Society for the Study of Education* (Chicago: U. of Chicago, 1979).

15

Values

Values are an individual's highest priorities. No other influence is so great in our lives and is reflected so much in our personal identification. In an ever-changing world in which children and adults are constantly assailed with conflicting value information from mass media, school, friends, family, employers, and others, the development of meaning and direction in life becomes incredibly complex. Value clarification and development emerge as two of the most important areas in teaching.

Definition

One of the first steps is to define values. Dewey[1] and Raths[2] state that values are the things, ideas, institutions, and processes that we prize. For example, a high value may be placed upon job or professional success, money, family, friends, religion, or personal freedom. The desire not to have something is also an expression of value, such as a lack of desire for material gains. Goals almost invariably reflect values.

Raths, Harmin, and Simon[3] specify seven criteria that must be met to establish the presence of a value. A value must be

[1] John Dewey, "Theory of Valuation," *International Encyclopedia of the Unified Sciences*, Vol. 2, No. 4 (Chicago: U. of Chicago, 1969), pp. 4–6.

[2] Louis E. Raths, "Appraising Changes in the Values of College Students," *Journal of Educational Research*, Vol. 35, No. 7 (March 1942), pp. 559–564.

[3] Louis E. Raths, Merrill Harmin, and Sidney B. Simon, *Values for Teaching* (Columbus, Ohio: Merrill, 1966), pp. 27–30.

Figure 15–1 Childhood experiences have an impact on value formation. (Courtesy of Will Kyselka, University of Hawaii)

Chosen freely.

Chosen from alternatives.

Chosen after thoughtful consideration of the consequences of each alternative.

Prized and cherished.

A source of pride in a choice that may lead to public affirmation.

Acted upon.

Repeated in different situations and at different times.

Identifying these criteria becomes the process of valuing. Often interests, attitudes, feelings, aspirations, goals, convictions, or activities may be confused with values. According to these authors, they are not values but value indicators. However, values may emerge, for example, from an interest or a purpose.

Sources and Dimensions

The actual genesis of a value may be obscure. The impact of home and family, community, ethnic background, school, church, mass media, work, friends, and countless other influences is obvious. The effects of these generators of values vary greatly. Hareven,[4] however, contends that the "family time" is critical and that the family as an institution has great resilience. Kagan[5] indicates that the school, even at an early age, helps the child to appreciate the values of society, but he also credits the family with having an impact on a sense of values or virtue. Of all the mass media, television probably has the strongest impact on values. Through many hours of viewing, children and adults are exposed to many facets of living that have controversial and desirable effects on value formation.

Individuals vary in their backgrounds, so it seems reasonable to assume that they differ in value systems. A student in a Chicago ghetto may have values that differ from those of a young person living as a member of a Hollywood family. Experiences tend to test and modify values. One may outgrow an old value. Values are truly a part of living and involve reflection on complex judgments and actions, according to Raths, Harmin, and Simon.[6] No home economics educator can determine what values are best for other persons, but she/he can help them to clarify and examine the values they possess. This is an ongoing process, for values are not static.

The seven criteria for identifying a value, according to Raths, Harmin, and Simon,[7] tend to sharpen the dimensions of values and may be telescoped into three categories to facilitate value processing. They are choosing, prizing, and acting or behaving.

Valuing and values are included in the affective domain of *Taxonomy of Educational Objectives* as developed by Krathwohl, Bloom, and Masia.[8] These authors define a value as a thing, a phenomenon, or a behavior that has worth. This definition has a personal connotation, in that the individual does his/her own assessing of the worth, and a social interpretation, in that the value may have been derived from social experiences that became acceptable and were internalized by the student. One difficulty for the teacher is to determine when the student's external behavior is compatible with his/her internal commitment.

These educators suggested that values are internalized in the following steps: (1) acceptance of a value; (2) preference for a value; (3) commitment to a value; (4) conceptualization of a value; (5) organization of a value system; (6) generalized set (internal consistency in a

[4] Tamara K. Hareven, "Family Time and Historical Time," *Daedalus*, Vol. 106, No. 2 (Spring 1977), p. 59.

[5] Jerome Kagan, "The Child in the Family," *Daedalus*, Vol. 106, No. 2 (Spring 1977), pp. 33–56.

[6] Op. cit., pp. 36–37.

[7] Op. cit., pp. 38–39.

[8] David R. Krathwohl, Benjamin S. Bloom, and Bertram B. Masia, *Taxonomy of Educational Objectives: The Classification of Educational Goals*, Handbook II: Affective Domain (New York: McKay, 1956), pp. 139–175.

Figure 15–2 One family value may be to encourage children to participate in gardening. (USDA Photo)

system of values); and (7) characterization (values tend to characterize the individual and are the peak of the internalization process). The teacher must determine which stage a student has reached and evaluate his/her performance accordingly.

The challenge to the home economics educator is to encourage students to think clearly about their values, to choose only those that can be accepted with conviction, to use high standards of integrity in selection, and to use their values as guides in their actions. Under these circumstances, personal values will acquire meaning and can be applied to the tasks of everyday living.

VALUES AND HOME ECONOMICS EDUCATION

Home economics, since its inception, has been strongly concerned about values. Caroline Hunt,[9] at the Third Annual Conference on Home Economics at Lake Placid, New York, on June 28, 1901, challenged home economics teachers to be aware of their power in the control of values. She further admonished the teachers to be good examples in their valuations and in prompt revaluations. In a final

[9] Caroline L. Hunt, "Revaluations," in Addreen Nichols (ed.), *Values and Decision-Making* (Washington, D.C.: American Home Economics Association, 1969), pp. 1–7.

warning, she urged home economics teachers to consider freedom the final test to foist their values on their students

Values are mentioned in *"Home Economics—New Directions II,"* [10] a statement intended to redirect the priorities of the profession. Cited are the need for personal and professional value clarification, the role of values in the definition of the family, the reshaping of values in "futuristic thinking and planning," and the acceptance of conflict as an effective mode of clarifying values in "creative adaptation to uncertainty and change."

Home economists in many areas have expressed interest in value clarification techniques and teaching strategies related to values. Home economists in bureaus of home economics in state departments of education, in universities, in extension; home economists in business; nutritionists in clinics; and home economists in other teaching situations have had workshops, have developed kits and literature, and have written articles on the subject. Education in values is an integral part of home economics education.

MORAL DEVELOPMENT

The question might be raised: Are values and morals synonymous? Reagan[11] asks, "What is a moral value, and how does it differ from any other value?"—a question that must be examined in moral education. Reagan concedes that there may be differences of opinion but that such questions will encourage dialogue.

DISTINCTIONS, CATEGORIES, AND PRINCIPLES

Cochrane[12] contends that moral education must rest on moral reasoning, which in turn rests on moral principles. The "first-order principle" is "respect for persons," an important democratic principle. Individuals must examine this and other principles in their many facets and the ways in which they may be implemented in everyday living. This may be the crux of moral education.

Many home economics educators are familiar with the research and the development of distinct levels of moral thinking by Kohl-

[10] Gordon Blivens et al., "Home Economics—New Directions II," *Journal of Home Economics,* Vol. 67, No. 3 (May 1975), pp. 26–27.

[11] Gerald M. Reagan, "Moral Education in Theory and Practice," in "Moral Education," *Theory into Practice,* Vol. 14, No. 4 (Oct. 1975), p. 222.

[12] Don Cochrane, "Moral Education—A Prolegomenon," *Theory into Practice,* Vol. 14, No. 4 (Oct. 1975), pp. 239–243.

berg,[13] which emerged from the thinking of Jean Piaget, John Dewey, William James, and Eric Fromm. According to Kohlberg's theories, at Stage 1, the child sees herself or himself as dominated by other forces, so actions are judged by their physical consequences and by fear of punishment. Stage 2 has the basic motive of satisfying one's own needs, such as, "What can another person do for me?" "How can we agree to act so I will benefit?" Needs of others are not considered unless they are beneficial to oneself. Stage 3 emphasizes a concern about groups of people and conformity to group mores. The image of the "good girl/nice guy" is a strong motivation. Affection is important. Two-way relationships are highlighted. Stage 4 emphasizes a concern for society, with honor and duty valued, along with the preservation of society. During these four stages, a person makes moral choices without making independent decisions. Stage 5 is the level at which there is an internal commitment to principles of "conscience," including respect for the rights, life, and dignity of all persons.

The concepts of these stages of cognitive development[14] refer to the structure of an individual's reasoning and imply the following characteristics: (1) each stage in a structured "whole" or organized system of thought, which means that individuals are consistent in their level of moral judgment; (2) movement is always forward, never backward, which was found to be true in all the cultures studied; (3) thinking at a higher stage includes lower-stage thinking, and (4) stage change depends upon the social experiences of an individual, from which a new stage evolves. Home economics teachers may wish to test the workability of these stages in their educational endeavors.

Conflicts

Moral reasoning is not easy, and persons often become confused in determining a suitable solution to a problem. Deciding between good and evil may not be as troublesome as making a choice about upholding one of two desirable moral principles. For example, Jim and John are good friends. Jim discovers that John is stealing supplies and small equipment at school. Should Jim keep quiet and maintain his friendship with John (loyalty), or should he report John to the authorities (honesty)? Hunt and Metcalf[15] maintain that such a choice is dif-

[13] Lawrence Kohlberg, "The Cognitive-Developmental Approach to Moral Education," *Phi Delta Kappan,* Vol. 56, No. 10 (June 1975), pp. 670–678.

[14] Lawrence Kohlberg and Richard H. Hersh, "Moral Development: A Review of the Theory," in "Moral Development," *Theory into Practice,* Vol. 16, No. 2 (Apr. 1977), p. 54.

[15] Maurice P. Hunt and Lawrence Metcalf, *Teaching High School Social Studies: Problems in Reflective Thinking and Social Understanding* (New York: Harper, 1955), pp. 90–95.

ficult to make and suggest the introduction of a third value, "What is best for the school?" There are other possible solutions, but the point to be made is that moral choices can be frustrating.

Respect for others is given high priority as a moral principle. The meaning of "respect for others" can lead not only to diverse but sometimes to incompatible interpretations. Joh[16] believes that "respect for others" implies a disposition to act properly toward others with all of the relevant moral principles (fairness, truth, consideration of other people's interests, and the like) and that it also implies an objective consideration of the viewpoints and values of others.

Moral value clashes may occur between parents and adolescents, to whom peer approval is important, or between children and parents or grandparents about modes of dress, sexual freedom, church rituals, and the like. There are many other areas of value conflicts that everyone encounters daily. Home economists would do well to brief themselves on current issues in which there are value differences, such as abortion, homosexuality, and test tube babies, and consider ways to approach them in home economics education.

Decision Making and Consequences

Parents and educators must realize that it is impossible to consider all the situations in which students will be faced with making "right" decisions. They can be encouraged to make wise decisions, to select the best alternative, and to become aware of consequences. Consequences may be personal or social, immediate or delayed. A simple example is that of Sam, who removes the only reference book for tomorrow's lesson from the reference shelf and takes it out of the library. The personal consequence may be that Sam is pleased (immediate), or he may have some feelings of guilt (immediate or delayed). One social consequence is that his teacher may commend him for being well prepared (immediate); when she or he learns about his taking the book out of the library, he may be punished (delayed). Another social consequence is that Sam prevented his fellow students from adequate preparation, thus displaying unfairness.

Looking at consequences from personal and social standpoints might be helpful to students in relation to the use of drugs or alcohol, sexual freedom, teenage pregnancy, having someone else punch the time clock for you, cheating on income tax returns, pilferage, shoplifting, cheating on an exam, prejudice, pollution, lying, and similar problems.

Settings where students, young or old, may consider such problems

[16] Jason Joh, "Respect for Persons," *Theory into Practice,* Vol. 14, No. 4 (Oct. 1975), pp. 271–278.

may be in group meetings such as FHA/HERO, in senior citizen clubs, in PTA meetings in which students may participate, in employee groups, in extension sessions, or in concern periods or classes in schools. There are many other possible locations.

TEACHING STRATEGIES

According to Buhler[17] teachers are faced with the dual problem of developing their own values and at the same time helping students to develop an adequate value system. Many individuals find it difficult to clarify for themselves the main directions of their lives. And a teacher should not hand a package of ready-made values to a student. Rather, a student should be inspired to seek and to construct his/her own values.

Teacher's Role

The teacher might ask himself/herself a number of questions, according to Eiss and Harbeck.[18] What kind of model does the teacher present to the students? Are what the teacher says and what the teacher does compatible? Is she/he willing to listen to student viewpoints? Is information about alternatives offered? Have students been prepared to weigh decisions? How are biases handled? Is an opportunity provided for values to be analyzed and clarified?

Coombs and Meux[19] suggest that teachers bear in mind three objectives in the analysis and deliberation related to value issues. They are (1) helping students to make the most rational decisions that they can make; (2) helping students to develop the competencies and attitudes for making rational value decisions; and (3) teaching students how to resolve conflicts between themselves and other members of a group.

The evaluation of values is a special challenge to the home economics teacher. She/he must be concerned not only about the values that a student holds but about his/her ability to identify the values of others. A teacher should encourage students to identify those ideas, things, and ways of living that other individuals appear to cherish or to consider important. Students can then evaluate these values through clarification or identification, discussion, and other means.

[17] Charlotte Buhler, "The Problem of Values and Beliefs in Our Time," *Educational Leadership,* Vol. 21, No. 8 (May 1964), pp. 520–522, 541.

[18] Albert F. Eiss and Mary Blatt Harbeck, *Behavioral Objectives in the Affective Domain* (Washington, D.C.: National Science Supervisors Association, a section of the National Science Teachers Association, NEA, 1969), p. 10.

[19] Jerrold R. Coombs and Milton Meux, "Teaching Strategies for Value Analysis," in Lawrence Metcalf (ed.), *Values Education* (Washington, D.C.: Rational Strategies and Procedures for the Social Studies, 41st Yearbook, 1971), pp. 29–74.

Figure 15–3 What kind of values may a student express in the buying of clothes? (Cereal Institute, Inc.)

Clarification

Many authorities agree that the clarification of values is one of the best methods for helping students to examine the values that emerge in discussions, experiences, relationships, and many other aspects of living.

Raths[20] suggests that students can best examine the content and worth of their values in a climate from which psychological threats have been eliminated. To establish this climate, it is important for the teacher to refrain from passing judgments in general. When a student is permitted to express himself/herself freely without fear of ridicule or contradiction, there is more opportunity for personal values to emerge. Although a teacher must not judge a value as good or bad, she/he must express concern in the ideas suggested by students.

One way to show interest is to listen carefully to what is said. It is also important to remember what a student has said so that it may be incorporated later into the teacher's conversation. Courses and class periods must be organized so that students will have an opportunity to express their beliefs and opinions about the widest possible variety of issues. By helping the students to trace the implications of their

[20] Louis E. Raths, "Clarifying Values," in Robert S. Fleming (ed.), *Curriculum for Today's Boys and Girls* (Columbus, Ohio: Merrill Books, 1963), pp. 323–327.

statements about issues, the teacher is helping them to clarify their values.

Certain techniques are especially provocative. Role playing built around situations of concern to students is good for value clarification. The use of film, filmstrips, and other technological aids to stimulate discussion is appropriate. Literature geared to certain age levels and to contemporary issues and problems can be most provocative.

Teachers must discern and incorporate current issues into class activities. These issues may be related to procedures of government, to barriers for securing a job or an education, to interpretations of religion, to morality or immorality in certain situations, to conflicts between management and labor, to community actions, and so on. Teachers and students must have the courage to face issues and to discuss them, for discussion is the arena wherein values are tested.

Asking certain kinds of questions is helpful in the clarification process. The challenge to the teacher is to ask questions that the student can answer and that challenge his/her values and the tenacity with which he/she clings to them. Such questions may include: "Is this what you mean? Does it make you feel good to think or act this way? Where did you get that idea? Do you believe everyone should think or act this way? Are there alternatives? How would you demonstrate this idea? Why do you think this is important? If the student seems bewildered, the teacher may comment that the question has confounded many persons before and that it requires much thought to answer. Raths[21] suggests asking students to define key words, to give examples, and to trace their change in position or their holding to it. It is important for teachers to be as concerned about student values with which they agree as about those with which they disagree.

If a teacher finds it difficult to draw this clarification process to close, he/she should remember that a debate is not being conducted and that the purpose of the interaction is to search out and build student values. There may be no conclusion, but a teacher can offer reassurance by making comments like "I appreciate your stand," "I see," "I think I know why you feel that way," and "I understand better now." This procedure places the responsibility on the student to look at the idea, behavior, or position and to challenge his/her own thinking. A teacher must not be disappointed if such action does not take place. The atmosphere must be permissive and encouraging but not demanding. When clarifying responses are used often, the effect begins to be cumulative.

Written work can be an effective means of clarifying values. Student logs and written reactions to movies, pictures, fiction, newspaper stories, autobiographies, and poetry often express students'

[21] Op. cit., Ch. 5.

values, beliefs, purposes, interests, or goals. For example, students may tell about the highlights of their summer jobs or other vacation experiences or relate ideas or events in a weekly log or a diary: "My mother was pleased because I gave up playing football to go on a family outing" (found in a girl's log).

Raths[22] suggests using a simple code in the margin of the paper, such as V+ or V−, to raise the questions: "Do you prize this?" or "Are you against this?"

Teachers can collect cartoons that highlight values. Themes may be about money matters, personal or family relations, or managing a home. Each student may be given a cartoon and asked to identify the value illustrated.

Students may be alerted to identify the values depicted by characters in dramatic presentations. The use of puppets, minute dramas, excerpts from plays, pantomimes, and the like often brings values into sharp focus. The implications of holding such values should be discussed freely. Focus in these dramatic situations may be on such value–decision problems as student graffiti on the walls of school and other community buildings, a mother who works as a clerk in a department store and shoplifts presents for family and friends, or parents who object to their daughter's smoking marijuana. Students and teacher will do well to determine situations that

[22] "Clarifying Values," op. cit., p. 513.

Figure 15–4 Students might portray values associated with sports in a minidrama. (Cereal Institute, Inc.)

are pertinent to their locale. Pictures of family situations in advertisements or from magazine illustrations may be analyzed in a similar vein.

Literature provides an excellent resource for value clarification. The readers' values may become clearer as they identify values that are similar to or different from their own. A small book for young children, *Fish for Supper,*[23] might be used as a backdrop for analyzing the place of values in family food habits and in nutrition education, and for values related to certain competencies, such as cleaning fish or household routines. *A Hero Ain't Nothing but a Sandwich*[24] highlights the values of a boy on heroin, of his mother, of his mother's boyfriend, and of his religious grandmother. Students may discuss the values of each character as well as the social influences that may have determined these values. *It's Not What You Expect*[25] describes a summer in the life of a middle-class family. The values of the characters are well defined for students to analyze. Bettelheim[26] believes that folk and fairy tales help children with finding solutions to their inner problems more than any other type of children's literature. Home economists who work with children might explore this idea for possible applications in their own work. Bettelheim suggests, for example, that "The Three Little Pigs" stresses the conflict of the pleasure principle versus the reality principle; "Hansel and Gretel" demonstrates that poverty and deprivation do not improve a person's character; and "Jack and the Beanstalk" encourages the value of greater maturity.

Use of Newspapers

The newspaper is helpful because contemporary values and conflicts are discussed. Students may begin by placing opinions found in newspapers on important topics, such as energy, on a continuum like this:

________________	________________	________________
Find more energy	Conserve energy	Find alternative sources

They should then identify the spot on the continuum where their own values rest. After a discussion among students, see if their values have shifted and why. Another suggestion is to bring in clippings of the amount of money Americans spend on cosmetics, on foods low in nutritional density, on gasoline, on pet food and accessories, and in fast-

[23] M. B. Goffstein, *Fish for Supper* (New York: Dial, 1976).
[24] Alice Childress (New York: Avon, 1974).
[25] Norma Klein (New York: Avon, 1974).
[26] Bruno Bettelheim, *The Uses of Enchantment, The Meaning and Importance of Fairy Tales* (New York: Vintage, 1977), pp. 3–19, 159–166, 183–193.

food shops. What are the implications for values and for the need for reexamination?

The Magic Shop

Students might imagine a magic shop[27] where intangibles may be purchased. Suppose the shopkeeper says that today he/she has love, high grades, and beauty for sale. Which one would you buy? Why? What would you be willing to pay for it? If these items do not appeal to you, which items would you like the magic shop to offer?

Drawings

The drawings of students may reveal their values. Students might be asked to make a drawing of any one of the following:

1. A good mother.
2. The kind of home you would like to have.
3. The best type of vacation you can imagine.
4. The kind of work you would like to do.
5. You and some of your best friends.

The kind of clothes individuals are wearing, the activities depicted, missing elements that might be considered pertinent, and the general mood indicated might show what students consider important.

Dennis[28] and his co-workers examined thousands of children's drawings of a man for certain insights into social values. An analysis was made of the dress, the physical features, the emphasis on masculinity, smiling and nonsmiling faces, the infrequency of work, religious content, the diversity of social roles, and ridicule and humor as depicted in the drawings. These categories may be helpful to home economics teachers in their evaluation of student drawings.

Incomplete Sentences

The way a student completes a sentence will reveal value indicators, hopes, fears, interests, relations to people, and feelings. Here are some examples:

1. My favorite form of recreation is ______________.
2. A good husband (or wife) is ______________.

[27] Ellen Barnes, Bill Eyman, and Maddy Bragar Engolz, *Teach and Reach* (Syracuse, N.Y.: Human Policy Press, 1974). p. 14.
[28] Wayne Dennis, *Group Values Through Children's Drawings* (New York: Wiley, 1966).

3. When I am a father (or mother) I will ________.
4. If I had a $1,000, I would ________.
5. I am proud that ________.
6. I just realized that ________.
7. My favorite magazine is ________.
8. I like to do these things with people: ________.
9. I would like to learn how to ________.
10. I have a strong belief about ________.
11. I wish that ________.
12. If I had more time, I would ________.
13. Something I like to do by myself is ________.
14. The best thing about a friend is ________.

Incomplete sentences clipped from newspaper stories or from advertisements and pasted on a sheet of paper may be used in the same manner.

Many questions may occur to a teacher who is concerned about the values of his/her students. A teacher may ask herself/himself "What is worth clarifying?" Obviously it is not possible for a teacher to respond in a clarifying manner to every question asked or every statement made by a student. No hard-and-fast rules are available. If a student has previously discussed the idea and appears to be trying to clarify a value, it would seem that he/she needs assistance. Because there is no formula for a teacher to follow, she/he can be guided only by insight, past experience, and creativity.

One of the frustrations that may beset a teacher is finding how to deal with students who have a weak structure of values. Raths and his co-authors delineate certain characteristics of these youngsters so that a teacher may identify them more readily. These characteristics include apathy, disinterest, flightiness, uncertainty, inconsistency, overconformity, and overdissension. Granted, these descriptions may typify most students occasionally, but it is the student who manifests such behavior chronically who is in need of help.

Teachers must be aware that thinking appears earlier in the life of a child than valuing. Values are more apt to result in action than thinking because of the conviction with which they are held. Certain processes related to thinking, such as interpretation, comparison and contrast, search for assumptions, planning, summarization, categorization, analysis, and problem solving, are relevant to value clarification.

In regard to needs, thinking, and values, Raths, Harmin, and Simon[29] caution the teacher to look for the cause of the behavior rather than concentrating on the behavior itself. Needs, thinking, and

[29] Op. cit., Ch. 9.

values are similar in that a lack of development of maturity in any or all of them leads to a negative type of behavior.

It is difficult for most teachers to be neutral during class sessions. Each student should be made to feel, however, that values are unique to the individual and may not be desirable for others. If an atmosphere of permissiveness and goodwill pervades the classroom, then teacher and students alike will feel free to challenge and assist one another in identifying and discussing values.

The process of helping students to clarify their values is difficult. The teacher must assiduously apply herself/himself to identifying with students' concerns and to reacting to them in a thoughtful manner. She/he cannot reasonably anticipate rapid changes, for such values as a student may have are often firmly entrenched, and a lack of values is part of a personality pattern that may have been building for a long period of time. Clarification must be repeated over and over to effect a gradual change. This process is especially urgent for those students who have definitely been identified as lacking values. Values of students are revealed in places other than the classroom: at sports events, in personal conversations in the hall, on school committees, and on field trips, as well as in many other situations.

Other Considerations

A home economist in education may wish to think about the role of values education on the job. With regard to content, there are many opportunities to examine values in all areas of the field. For example, in clothing and textiles, students may analyze the values of a particular group according to the clothes that they wear, such as the casual dress of certain youths or the dress of the business person or actor. A home economist in the clothing business may wish to stress value clarification in educational materials related to the use of color, line, function, or other aspects of clothing. A nutritionist may discover value clarification in relation to crash diets to lose weight, the advocates of organic foods, or the diets of athletes. In the area of human development, personal values about aging may be highlighted; this topic is applicable to all age groups. A slide cassette set entitled "Folks Don't Kiss Old People Anymore"[30] may be used as a valuable aid. Other areas of home economics offer many possibilities for value clarification.

Another step, after value clarification, is to help individuals become aware of how they behave or act and how such behavior may change and develop once values are clarified.

[30] Created by Kathy Smith, sound by Tony Smyles, photography by Stephen McBrady, produced by Cullen Schippe, music by Deanna K. Edwards; Slides-Cassette, Franciscan Communications Center, Los Angeles.

SUGGESTIONS FOR FURTHER LEARNING

1. What do you identify as the values of the home economics profession? To what extent, if any, are they in conflict with your personal values? Are there special values that you cherish about your present or future work? Why not reexamine them in the light of change?
2. Find some new resources on values to share with your fellow students or your co-workers.
3. Read widely about moral values such as honesty, fairness, and reverence for life, and consider ways to introduce this important subject into home economics.

16

Nutrition Education

People do not instinctively eat the foods that are most nutritious. They must be taught. Educators, parents, politicians, government officials, and others now realize this fact. Nutrition education cannot be limited to just teaching individuals what to eat. They must also be taught how to select the healthful foods in their markets and how to prepare them at home to retain nutritive values. At the same time, cultural patterns, dietary practices, work, income, and the many other influences that affect eating habits must be taken into consideration.

Since there is considerable evidence that the nutrition of the American people, regardless of social or economic status, is far from adequate, nutrition education becomes an urgent matter. It cannot be a one-time project but must be continuous. Although those persons who have been given instruction in nutrition at an early age generally tend to have better eating habits, the need for education at all age levels is imperative in our changing world.

Nutrition education is successful only to the degree that people are motivated to take the necessary steps to improve their nutrition. Teaching, educational materials, information transmitted by mass media, and other methods of education are of no avail unless they touch an individual in a personal and meaningful manner.

WHO TEACHES NUTRITION?

Many people have a hand in teaching nutrition. One of the most important teachers is the mother. For example, if she believes that eating breakfast is important, then this message will be conveyed to her spouse and her children. Other family members, especially a father, may play important roles. A grandmother, for instance, may say to a child, when she hands him or her a glass of milk, "Drink this; it will make you grow." A neighbor may tell a homemaker to eat onions for a cold. Throughout life, someone is trying to teach other folks about nutrition. It may not be adequate information, but when listeners accept it uncritically, it becomes a part of their nutritional knowledge.

Mass media such as newspapers, radio, television, and magazines bombard the public with diets, enticing ways to prepare food, and other information that has a bearing on nutrition. The knowledge imparted may be illuminating and challenging. Sometimes there is a tendency to go beyond the data that research can uphold. Only the viewer or reader with a sound background in nutrition can judge the accuracy and the truth of the presentations.

Professional educators in nutrition serve in many capacities. A person may profit from nutrition teaching if his or her mother was taught about an adequate diet during pregnancy. Nutritionists in wellbaby clinics and those who work with pediatricians serve mothers or fathers, or both, in a similar manner. Nutritionists and home economists may teach mothers alone or parents about a nutritious diet and meeting particular nutritive needs in infant- and daycare centers and nursery schools.

In schools, an elementary teacher at any grade level is likely to in-

Figure 16–1 A young mother registering in the WIC program. Nutritionists are on the staff for educational purposes. (USDA Photo)

clude some nutrition education in the curriculum. At the level of junior and senior high school, the subject is given more or less emphasis in home economics, science, social studies, and other classes. The coach instructs the members of his athletic teams to eat certain foods so that they will be better players.

Nutrition is taught by many other professionals. Some popular magazines for the home have staff nutritionists and home economists who write monthly columns on the various facets of nutrition, including the selection, buying, and preparation of nutritious foods. Some newspapers offer the same services. Home economists who serve on councils, at institutes, and on boards of experts prepare materials for teachers, reviews of recent research, and special information for particular groups, such as pregnant women, the elderly, and young couples. Some home economists in business or industry give presentations to classes in schools, to women's groups, to clubs, and on television or radio.

Extension home economists communicate various aspects of nutrition to their groups—young to old. A nutrition specialist on the staff helps in planning and with materials. Social welfare agencies usually have a nutritionist on the staff to assist needy families with the problem of providing a nutritious diet for their members. College health departments often have a nutritionist to help students with nutritional problems. Nutritionists are usually found in state, regional, city, county, and other types of government health departments. Whenever it is offered, adult education frequently has a nutrition expert teaching a class. There are many other opportunities to serve, and more nutritionists are needed for this important work.

There are other avenues for other groups to receive instruction. In Los Angeles, a nutritionist was invited to give a two-hour nutrition program for firefighters as a part of their physical fitness program. It was held in their fire stations. The program consisted of the presentation of ninety-four colored slides (cartoon-style) with discussion. The program was called "Eat Heart-ily." Planning nutritious meals, plus shopping and cooking, was highlighted.[1] One hundred twenty-five sessions served 1,500 firefighters. The program was so successful that similar programs were planned for spouses and families.

BACKGROUND INFORMATION FOR PLANNING

The nutrition educator should tailor the teaching and learning of nutrition to the group being taught. Some considerations are life-

[1] Barbara Yee, "Firefighters Learn to 'Eat Heart-ily,' " *Journal of Nutrition Education,* Vol. 8, No. 1 (Jan.–March 1976), p. 31

styles, nutrition knowledge, food buying, nutritional status, food preparation practices, prevalence of food fads and myths about nutrition, and cultural influences. A teenager interested in athletics, for example, may become concerned about nutrition if he/she believes it will improve performance.

Lifestyles

What a person does every day—work, play, and so on—has an effect on nutritional needs and style of eating. For example, the type of recreation a person or family enjoys, whether as active participants or as spectators, will make a difference in planning an adequate diet. The nutrition teacher must be alert to the many changes and ramifications in lifestyles.

Cultural Influences

There are vestiges of their cultural background in most individuals and families in America. Food preferences, the cooking of food, and the style of eating are aspects of cultural differences. A complex system of beliefs influences the use or nonuse of particular foods. Differences in culture may be reflected in rewards; punishments; food for the sick, for children, or for pregnant women. Some families may reveal a number of cultures in their backgrounds, such as a German

Figure 16–2 An adult who prepares his or her own breakfast might enjoy some nutrition education. (Cereal Institute, Inc.)

grandmother, or an Irish aunt, who have left their mark on the kind of food consumed.

Composition of a Family

Adjustments in plans for teaching and learning may have to be made because of the kind of families a nutrition educator is teaching. Are they young couples? What are the ages of the children, and what is the family's familiarity with their various nutritional needs? Does the family include elderly relatives? Is the "family" a single person living alone? Does the family have a single parent? Does the individual or family live in a commune? Are diet modifications necessary for health reasons? What adjustments are made to meet individual needs? The answers to these and other questions are invaluable in working with families.

Often the nutrition teacher is responsible for teaching a group where family compositions may vary considerably and the plan for teaching must be adapted. Sometimes teaching centers on one age level, such as teenagers or the elderly. Even in these circumstances, the teacher cannot assume that the lifestyles are identical. Factors such as size, sex, income, and activities must be noted.

Income

The amount of money available to spend on food varies from that of families on welfare to the affluent. Whatever the financial conditions, nutritive needs must be met. A nutrition educator will profit from being informed about the range in cost of good sources of nutrients in foods. If a family cannot afford orange juice for vitamin C, what are the alternatives?

Work

What family members do for a living has a strong influence on what they do eat and what they should eat. Many family members eat at least one meal at work. This meal may be eaten in facilities at work, food may be brought from home, or the meal may be eaten out, often at a fastfood restaurant. The nutrition educator may give invaluable guidance in selecting such meals. In addition, what is eaten during the remainder of the day must be considered so that the adequacy of the diet is assured. The recommended number of servings from the four basic food groups or other dietary guide may be used as a monitor to determine if nutritional needs are being met. Fruits and vegetables may be deficient. Milk is often overlooked. Assistance in calorie watching may be important if overweight is a problem.

Other work influences are the amount of energy expended on the job and the work conditions in general. Is the work done at night or odd hours so that daily food intake must be adjusted? Working women have to make many adjustments in the planning, selection, buying, preparation, and serving of the food because of time and other factors. If other family members assist in these operations, they may need to be taught, and their competencies should be checked periodically.

Nutrition Knowledge

The information about nutrition held by the person or persons responsible for the family diet is decisive in planning adequate nutrition. In a study[2] of basic knowledge, shoppers varied in their knowledge of nutrition. Younger shoppers (under fifty) scored higher than older shoppers. Women scored higher than men. Shoppers at higher socioeconomic levels (based on education, income, and occupation) scored the highest. The higher the shopper's education, the higher the score on nutrition knowledge.

The shoppers' knowledge of whether or not certain nutrients were readily available in their diets was somewhat uneven. A majority of the shoppers were unaware of the problem of securing adequate calcium, iron, and vitamin D. A majority harbored the misconception that carbohydrate is stored in the body, not realizing that it is stored as fat. Some misconceptions were apparent about other aspects of food and nutrition. Examples are that about one half of the shoppers believed that any food in the supermarket is good for you and that eating anything you like will lead to an adequate diet.

Other results have implications for nutrition education. About half (47 per cent) of the shoppers took vitamins regularly as a precaution —not a need. A majority of the shoppers (57 per cent) said that someone in their family was trying either to gain or to lose weight—mostly the latter.

Food Habits

Clues to nutritional status can be found if the nutritionist knows about an individual's food habits. Why a person eats a certain food is complex. Foods associated with a crisis or an unpleasant event may

[2] *FDA Consumer Nutrition Knowledge Report II, A Nationwide Study of Food Shopper's Knowledge, Beliefs, Attitudes, and Reported Behavior Regarding Food and Nutrition,* Division of Consumer Studies, Office of Nutrition and Consumer Sciences, Bureau of Foods, Food and Drug Administration, Public Health Services, U.S. Department of Health, Education and Welfare, Superintendent of Documents, Washington, D.C., 1976., pp. v–x.

Figure 16–3 Food habits of elementary school children may be assessed by a study of the foods that are rejected or wasted. (USDA Photo)

be avoided in the future. Traditional family foods may be prized. Changes in work, environment, friendships, and the like may alter eating habits. Advertisements in newspapers and on television can encourage the eating of new foods and the discarding of others.

The amount of time allowed for the selection, buying, preparing, and serving of foods varies considerably and affects eating patterns. Many Americans prize speed—as indicated by patronage of fast-food restaurants and carry-out foods that may be eaten while one is riding in a car or bus.

Food Fads and Myths

Many a person holds staunchly to a belief about nutrition. Helping the public to distinguish fact from fallacy is not easy. Sometimes the scientific evidence itself is in controversy. One suggestion is to determine the risk factors and the degree of certainty with which a statement can be made—approximately 35 per cent, 50 per cent, 75 per cent, or 90 per cent. The degree of danger is another element to consider. If the safety of a food additive or a food or its method of preparation is questioned, should any risk ever be taken? With a well-liked food or preparation, people often resist any evidence of risk to their health. This situation presents one of the most difficult problems facing educators. Some type of substitute action may be preferred to regulations. Clever methods of communication coupled with scientific or logical explanations may be a possibility. Considerable thought and research must be concentrated on such problems of nutrition and health.

Food Buying

Food buying is an area that is sometimes neglected in the teaching of nutrition, but it is vital to wholesome diets. This task is not easy, for a shopper is faced with thousands of choices in a supermarket. Teaching consumers to think in terms of the categories of a daily food selection guide will facilitate shopping. Comparing the nutrient density of various foods in the same category may aid in the selection of foods that offer the best buy economically and nutritionally.

Family food preferences have to be considered with every purchase. The use of a wide variety of foods is more likely to contribute to improved nutrition. Reading nutritional labels is another help. Teaching about alternative choices while marketing can alleviate a shortage of food in a certain group because of a freeze, a flood, or some other crisis. In the FDA study,[3] shoppers reported improvements such as reduction of number of trips to the market, making shopping lists, and reading ads before shopping. Looking for dates on products (75 per cent) and for unit pricing (41 per cent) and checking the list of ingredients (46 per cent) were other desirable changes. Other approved shopping behaviors consisted of using less or cheaper cuts of meat, watching for specials, using coupons, and buying fewer sweets or snacks. The wise shopper can save money and have a more nutritious diet if shopping behavior is geared in these directions by nutrition teachers.

Food Preparation Techniques

An appreciable difference in the nutrient quality of the food to be eaten can occur during the preparation of the food. Practices to avoid are soaking food in water for long periods of time and losing water-soluble nutrients. Cubing, mashing, chopping, grinding, or blending will expose larger surfaces to oxidation and will result in vitamin losses. Overcooking and preparing food hours before it is consumed

[3] Ibid., p. x.

Figure 16–4 The kinds of food purchased in a cafeteria reveal nutritional preferences. (Courtesy of Will Kyselka, University of Hawaii)

may lead to less nutritive density. Storing foods in the refrigerator keeps nutritive losses to a minimum.

Baking, broiling, roasting, and other methods of cooking by dry heat are among the best methods for retaining nutrients. Boiling food in large amounts of water, especially vegetables, can be destructive of water-soluble nutrients. Prolonged boiling of vegetables is not recommended. Steaming has advantages. Fat-soluble vitamins may be lost in pan frying. High temperatures over a long period of time can destroy certain nutrients. Checking on food preparation techniques can be illuminating and useful to the nutrition educator.

Personal and Social Influences

The preceding list of influences on the daily diet is not complete. Individual personalities, sudden changes in income or job, and other life happenings may have an important impact. World events, food shortages, inflation, and other effects may have an influence. The teacher of nutrition will be ever aware of the factors that make a difference in a person's or a family's daily diet and its adequacy. The effectiveness of teaching and learning may rest on the completeness of the teacher's knowledge about the background of students and others to be reached.

Figure 16–5 A career couple may share the responsibilities of food preparation. (West Virginia University)

GENERAL OBJECTIVES

Nutrition education can be effective only to the extent that its goals are well defined. The objectives underlying any nutrition program will vary somewhat from educator to educator, from group to group, and from situation to situation. General objectives may be helpful to nutrition teachers and may stimulate their thinking, but in the final analysis, each educator and his/her students will have to determine what they wish to accomplish.

The following list suggests some general objectives.

Related to Goals

1. To reach all ages.
2. To improve both the length and the quality of life of American people through nutrition.
3. To help individuals and families to solve their nutrition problems.
4. To emphasize nutrition in the home, the school, and the community.

Nutrition Education

5. To prepare and disseminate nutritional information to the individuals and groups who need it.
6. To be selective about appropriate approaches to nutrition education.

7. To determine which teaching materials and strategies are suitable for various age levels, groups, specific needs, or situations.
8. To adapt nutrition education to changing times, such as inflation or ready-prepared foods in the market.
9. To utilize all resources effectively.
10. To teach the distinguishing of truth from untruth in nutrition information.
11. To challenge unsound attitudes about nutrition.
12. To recognize family traditions, feelings, and customs whenever possible.
13. To realize the importance of nutritional assessment.

Other Resources

14. To be alert to government programs and action.
15. To work cooperatively with other agencies, mass media, institutions, and others in educating the nation about nutrition.

Some of these objectives may be deleted or altered, or others may be added. Objectives must be fitted to the individual, the group, and the teaching environment.

TEACHING NUTRITION

Reviewing previous chapters in this text will be helpful to nutrition educators, especially Chapters 3–12. Teaching resources and strategies will have to be adapted from situations ranging from one-to-one instruction to large audiences or auditorium-type teaching. The teacher must assess the teaching materials in order to select those most appropriate for the use and interest of the individual or groups to be taught.

Information gained from nutritional assessment, such as actual food consumed, food buying habits, and consistent review of progress or lack of progress in nutritional status over a period of time, is of great consequence. Evidence of maturity in planning the daily diet and coping with related problems is critical.

PLANNING FOR VARIOUS AGE LEVELS

Goals for nutrition education and nutritive needs and problems vary from age to age. For nutrition education to be successful, instruction must be given in relation to each age level to meet the goal of adequate nutrition for all.

Prenatal

The nutritive well-being of a human begins in pregnancy. An important point to teach a pregnant woman is that what she eats during pregnancy will greatly influence her own and her baby's health.[4] Furthermore, by eating a nutritious diet, her husband and other family members, if there are any, will be kept healthy. Desirable eating habits will be reinforced. Other benefits are feeling better and having a greater ability to cope with the stresses of pregnancy, labor, and delivery and less likelihood of developing certain disorders of pregnancy. The possibility of damage from deprivation of certain nutrients for both the mother and fetus is greatly reduced.

Adequate nutrition can reduce the high-risk factor of a small infant of low birth weight.[5] Birth weight reflects intrauterine growth and is considered one determinant of the infant's potential for survival and future health. Special attention must be given to the pregnant teenager.

Teaching materials and strategies may include the use of food models, actual foods, or pictures of food to help the pregnant woman visualize her daily dietary needs in terms of foods. After this information has been taught to her or to the group, then each one may set up a day's foods. The nutrition teacher may demonstrate the evaluation of the diet for nutritional adequacy. In a group, students may evaluate each other's diets as an excellent learning experience. The diet may be checked for possible cost when that is important, for alternatives for certain foods if they cannot be purchased in the market, and for the time and energy required to prepare the day's diet. Other uses of this technique may occur to the nutritionist. For instance, teaching about buying and preparing foods is useful.

In order to supply the additional nutrients within the calories allowed, the nutritionist may wish to examine the foods included for nutrient density. The amount of fat and sugar will bear scrutiny. If these or other nutrients are found in excessive amounts, then teaching to remedy this problem is in order. Prepare the mother to check on such shortcomings herself in future meal-planning. From time to time, a twenty-four-hour or longer recall of the foods eaten will help in the nutritional assessment of the pregnant woman. If one is teaching groups, the students may be encouraged to share experiences about their eating habits and to evaluate them. The nutrition educa-

[4] *Food, Pregnancy and Family Health* (Chicago: American College of Obstetricians and Gynecologists, 1976). A patient information booklet.

[5] Joyce Vermeersch, "Maternal Nutrition and the Outcome of Pregnancy," in Bonnie S. Worthington, Joyce Vermeersch, and Sue Rodwell Williams (eds.), *Nutrition in Pregnancy and Lactation* (St. Louis: Mosby, 1977), Ch. 2.

tor must be alert to misconceptions about foods and the diet that may arise. Explanations about fallacies and the possible shortcomings in the daily diet that may result from adherence to such beliefs are important. Literature at various levels, depending upon the education of the women, is helpful. Slides, posters, and filmstrips about the diet in pregnancy are valuable.

Infancy

Mothers of infants may need assistance in the feeding of their babies for optimum nutrition.[6] A decision that should be made during pregnancy—long before birth—is whether the baby will be breast-fed or placed on a formula for bottle feeding. The mother with the breast-fed child will need to adjust her diet by eating extra servings of certain foods. The process of producing breast milk consumes considerable energy, and the nutrients for the breast milk must be provided in addition to the nutrients needed for the mother's health. Mothers may lose weight if they do not have sufficient calories in their diet. All of these points, and others, must be kept in mind while one is teaching the mothers of breast-fed infants. Some argue that breast feeding is more expensive because of the extra foods required by the mother. Human milk can be cheaper for the baby than proprietary cow's milk formula if economical food choices are made.[7]

The mother who has a formula-fed baby most also maintain a nutritious diet so that she will have good health for the rigors of taking care of her baby and her family.

Both types of mothers will be interested in the foods that are added to the baby's diet to provide the nutrients essential for growth. Sufficient calories and protein of high quality are important for growth.[8] Energy needs depend upon body size and composition, the amount of physical activity, and the rate of growth. Protein recommended for the diet is usually provided by milk plus additional amounts from cereal, strained egg yolk, strained meat, and other foods. Vitamins and minerals are added by these foods as well as by fruits and vegetables.

Mothers may need demonstrations of how to feed a baby, including the desirable equipment. There are many choices in buying baby foods, and mothers may be assisted in making wise buys. In a teaching and learning situation, mothers can compare the same food in different brands and decide on the best buy. Alternatives to some of the most expensive types of baby foods may be studied. In some instances, the cereal, vegetables, fruits, liver, and other foods may be

[6] "Food—from Birth to Birthday" (Rosemont, Ill.: National Dairy Council, 1976).

[7] Bonnie S. Worthington, "Lactation, Human Milk and Nutritional Considerations," in *Nutrition in Pregnancy and Lactation*, op. cit., Ch. 7.

[8] Peggy L. Pipes, *Nutrition in Infancy and Childhood* (St. Louis: Mosby, 1977), Ch. 2.

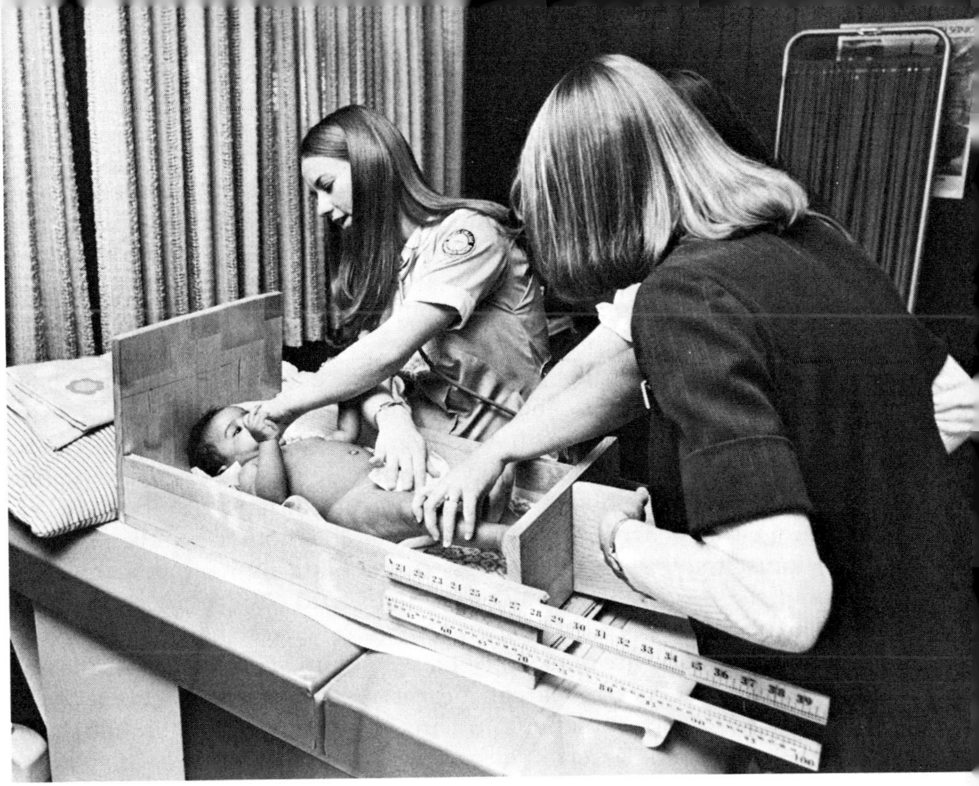

Figure 16–6 Nutritional assessments through specific anthropometric measurements of an infant in the WIC program. (*Lincoln Journal and Star*)

prepared from family foods and strained and chopped according to the age of the baby. These are usually less expensive but do require certain tools and special care in preparation. Demonstrations by a mother or the nutrition educator in the preparation of baby foods can be profitable.

For a broader view, mothers might share with each other what they have learned about feeding their babies. How to take care of a baby during teething might be another helpful topic. The role of the father in feeding the baby may be explored. Teaching a baby-sitter about feeding is another subject for inclusion. Highlighting these situations in role playing can be illuminating. Transparencies, slides and film-strips, plus cassettes, might be used in self-instruction. Finally, mothers can be taught to make nutritional assessments by keeping track of the amount of food and milk the baby consumes from appearance, from signs of growth such as weight and height, and from disposition and other evidence.

Preschool

The development of desirable food habits is an important goal at the preschool age. Learning to eat foods in a daily food selection guide and to become acquainted with many wholesome new foods through tasting and other means is a good teaching strategy. Attitudes toward food are more important at this age than nutritional information. Teaching the parents may raise the level of the daily diet of the child as well as the food habits of the entire family.

Sensory experiences with food will help the children in identification and introduce them to the pleasure of eating many foods. Feeling the outside of an orange, a cabbage, a piece of bread, a nut, a cube of cheese, or other foods can be a genuine educational experience, especially if the children are allowed to discuss the sensations they experience. The feel of foods on the tongue is equally interesting, such as margarine, raw cabbage, and milk. A careful look at a food will encourage the recognition of shapes, colors, and other features. The nutritionist may teach youngsters to speculate by having them think about the inside color of a vegetable or fruit. After they have examined the outside of a cucumber, for example, ask them to tell the inside color. Many are amazed when it is white, not green as on the outside. The smell of foods can be interesting, such as cheese, fresh pineapple, apple, banana, and canned tuna. The sounds that foods make can be fun. Describing the sound of eating celery or crisp bread or peanuts, drinking orange juice, and eating soup are some possibilities.

At meal and snack times children can be encouraged to taste all foods. Peer approval of a food is a strong stimulant to eat. Strategies that incorporate an important food, such as milk, in the diet (unless the child has allergies or an intolerance) are important. Children like to make choices, so provide these opportunities. If fresh fruit is on the menu, children may be given a choice, for example. Children love color in their food. The taste buds are very sensitive at this age, so lumps, burnt food, and disarray on the plate may be objectionable. Also forcing large amounts of food on the children may cause loud protests.

The identification of foods by the use of food models, real foods, or pictures of foods can be a good learning experience, especially if presented as a guessing game. Going to a supermarket and identifying foods are another possibility. The children may enjoy simple cooking, such as making a milkshake or spreading peanut butter on a leaf of lettuce and shaking a few raisins on it before rolling it up (a good finger food). Preparing vegetable sticks or slices and eating them with a cottage cheese dip can be good, and arranging a fruit plate of slices of banana, pineapple chunks, and orange segments can also create an interest in foods.

Parents may be encouraged to have their children help with the cooking at home. Children love to collect the necessary equipment for baking and can help to grease the baking pan or stir something in a small bowl. They may also scrub potatoes for baking. Growing bean or alfalfa sprouts is interesting. Consider the possible safety hazards in food preparation.

Children like to know where foods originate. Taking them to a chicken farm will inform them about eggs and the way chickens grow and eat. Being at a dairy farm during milking can be revealing, although the timing of such a visit may be a problem (milking is done in the early morning and the evening). Peanut butter can be made by putting peanuts in a blender.

Working with Parents to Reinforce Teaching in the Preschool Stage

In teaching parents, determine their current food patterns and habits, and build on them. Which foods of a daily food selection guide seem to be slighted? How may they be incorporated in light of food preferences? Tasting parties may introduce parents to new foods. They may need assistance in the planning, buying, preparation, and storage of foods so that the diet contains as much nutritious food as possible. Another important area is to determine what kind of snacks the children have and, if necessary, to demonstrate nutritious snacks and discuss the purchase of snacks. The selection of foods eaten outside the home may be a good topic for another lesson. Parents are anxious to have healthy children and the nutrition teacher can help

Figure 16–7 Large amounts of sugar should be discouraged in the preschool child's diet. (*Lincoln Journal and Star*)

them to reach that goal. The health of parents can be improved in the process.

Elementary

The development of desirable food habits continues to be an important goal at the elementary-school age. Malnutrition is a greater problem among children of low-income families than in other groups.[9] A lack of one or more nutrients may be found among all children. Foods may not be selected on the basis of nutrient density. For example, certain fruit drinks may or may not be sufficient in vitamin C to make up the daily allowance. Total food intake may be insufficient because meals are skipped or inadequate servings of food are consumed. An omission or shortcoming in one or more of the important food groups, such as milk, will reduce the intake of important nutrients.[10] Ignorance, indifference of family members, eating alone, and other factors may discourage adequate food consumption. Peer approval is important, and friends may influence eating habits. Too much sugar in the diet dilutes the nutrient density of other foods and may affect dental health. Some students consume an overabundance of calories and consequently are overweight, which may lead to health and social problems. The elementary teacher and the home economics teacher who may act as a consultant must be on the alert for evidence of these nutritional problems and plan teaching strategies to alleviate these conditions.

Early Elementary

Some teaching materials and strategies for early elementary students are discussed here. The important food groups can be learned in interesting ways. Thirty or more 3″ × 5″ cards may be used on which pictures of foods related to the food groups are drawn or pasted. Children can help to prepare the cards. A specific food, such as a glass of milk, a slice of bread, or an orange, should be presented. Write the name of the food at the bottom of each card; this supplements the reading program. These cards may be used in several ways. Children may stack the cards in piles, each pile representing a food group. This is a classifying or categorizing activity in which thinking is stressed. Other students may serve as checkers and determine if any mistakes have been made, or students may check each other. An upper student or a teacher's aide may have to help students who are

[9] Peggy L. Pipes and Jane Rees, "Between Infancy and Adolescence," in *Nutrition in Infancy and Childhood,* op. cit., Ch. 7.

[10] Henrietta Fleck, *Introduction to Nutrition* (New York: Macmillan, 1976), pp. 310–311.

having great difficulty with their classifications. The cards may be used to play a nutrition rummy, with three cards from a food group representing a set. The rules are the same as for rummy. Think of other ways to use these cards.[11]

Students may make a daily record of what they eat and evaluate their intake on the basis of a daily food selection guide. Plans by the students may be outlined for improvement. If a child seems embarrassed about his/her intake, assure him/her of confidentiality. This can be a research type of activity if the problem is clearly stated at the beginning.

Sometimes nutrition teaching can stimulate the imagination. Listen for words that children use to designate an illusory creature, such as a "doodlebug."[12] Ask the children to image what a "doodlebug" would eat in order to be strong and healthy, and then compare this "diet" with foods for health required by the children. What is different? The same?

Learning activities that use the Kim series[13] as models have potential. The ideas in "Foods Help Kim Grow" help youngsters to look at the benefits of eating nutritious foods, such as that legs and arms grow longer, and muscles and bones grow stronger in each child's

[11] Harold H. Jaus, "Health: Are Your Lessons Dull?" *Instructor,* Vol. 84, No. 8 (Apr. 1975), pp. 60–61.

[12] Mimi Brodsky Chenfeld, "Doodlebugs and Other Basics," *Phi Delta Kappan,* Vol. 59, No. 7 (March 1978), pp. 479–480.

[13] Mary Schlick, "Kim, the Child Approved Nutrition Teacher," *Journal of Home Economics,* Vol. 68, No. 3 (May 1976), pp. 21–23.

Figure 16–8 In some schools kindergarten children eat lunch in their classrooms. (USDA Photo)

own growing pattern. The possibilities for making nutrition education interesting at this age level are many.

Upper Elementary

The greater maturity of upper-level elementary students can be challenging to nutrition educators. Desirable food habits should continue to receive emphasis. These youngsters often help with the buying and the preparation of food at home and are interested in being good consumers. Scientific approaches appeal to some of these students.

Growth continues to be an important index of adequate nutrition. Sufficient calories and high-quality protein are critical. Girls grow more quickly toward the end of this period than boys. Calories must be adjusted to the activity of the children. Calcium is a very important nutrient because there is considerable storage of calcium in the bones and teeth at this time of growth. Iron is essential for girls, who may experience the onset of the menstrual cycle. Thyroid difficulties may arise, especially in girls, if iodine is inadequate. This period is characterized by a rapid period of growth, so adequate nutrients must be available. Teachers and nutrition educators will wisely incorporate these points into teaching and learning activities.

There are many possibilities for teaching and learning activities for this age level. Role playing, when dealing with real situations, can be practical. Students may wish to construct their own settings. Here are a few suggestions: (1) father and son cooking dinner together for the family; (2) a couple of children from a family shopping for food in the supermarket; and (3) several students ordering lunch in a fast-food restaurant and evaluating the nutritional adequacy—each student has ordered a different meal from the menu.

The preparation of quick, nutritious foods is in keeping with the lifestyle of these students. Fruit, milkshakes, and "munchers" made from a variety of dry cereals to which nuts may be added are suggestions. Delicious pizzas may be made from English muffins or buns cut in two, with toppings selected from soft cheeses, tomato paste, little cooked sausage balls, Vienna sausages, peanut butter, catsup, or deviled ham, and baked in the oven. Take popcorn and find ways to make it more nutritious, such as adding grated cheese to it. These foods and common snacks may all be analyzed for nutritive contribution. Planning nutritious foods for the family at home may be a good learning activity.

Since calcium, iodine, protein, and other nutrients are especially needed during growth spurts, students might plan ways to check on their dietary intake and isolate areas for improvement. Which foods

Figure 16–9 Cereals make a nutritious snack that elementary school children can prepare easily. (Cereal Institute, Inc.)

contain calcium, iron, and protein? What are inexpensive sources? Which foods are preferred? An exhibit might be made of the learnings from this experience so that other students may profit from the knowledge.

Classifying foods according to taste can be a scientific experience. *Hot, cold, sweet, sour, bitter, indescribable, unknown, vague,* or other terms may be applied to the foods tasted. The same foods may be related nutritionally.

Becoming better consumers is another focus for this age level. Bringing empty food cartons to class to study the information on the labels can be revealing. Using cereal boxes, students may evaluate and compare nutritive contributions, cost per ounce, number and kind of additives, and the listing of sugar among the ingredients. How well are the nutritional labels interpreted? Compare the results and see if the nutritionally best buys are among the favorites of the students. A visit might be made to the supermarket to compare costs of various food groups and the results displayed on charts and placed on the school bulletin board. Practical applications in the lives of students may be considered.

These and other activities can be planned by the elementary teacher, the home economics teacher, or other nutrition educators with students or groups at this age level.

Figure 16–10 A study of various grains and their nutritive contributions is fruitful. (*Lincoln Journal and Star*)

Middle and Junior High School

Some of the major goals in nutrition education for youngsters at the middle and junior high level are to teach them to be responsible for their own food selections; to gear learning activities to special interests, such as athletics, complexion, or weight; and to give special attention to the styles of eating, especially snacks.

Stage of Development

The stage of development at this age level has a bearing on the youngster's nutritive needs. The onset of puberty, considerable acceleration in the growth rate, and other complex and important changes are taking place. (See Chapter 4.)

Nutritive intake, particularly the quality of protein, influences growth. Calories should be increased. There is a tendency to acquire adult eating habits. Nutritive needs for boys and girls are indicated separately in the Recommended Daily Dietary Allowances, with higher allowances in some nutrients for boys. If the menstrual cycle has begun in girls, then iron intake demands special attention. Calcium needs are high for important storage in bones and teeth as well as for other physiological functions. The improvement of nutritional status of this age level can be taught through tapping various student interests.

Nutrition for Athletes

Both boys and girls are involved in various types of athletics and are interested in the kind of food that will contribute to their health. The answer is simple: a diet with all the necessary nutrients needed for that particular person. Additional calories and thiamin may be required if the exercise is especially vigorous. Weight is a good guide: if one is losing weight, more calories are required, with an appropriate amount of additional thiamin for the purpose of metabolizing energy. It must be emphasized that no particular food or nutrient has special merit. There are a number of myths about diets for athletes, such as a high meat or high protein diet. The needs for protein are more than adequately met in a varied diet for most athletes.[14] High-quality proteins, such as milk, eggs, meat, and low-fat cheeses, are advised. Vegetarians will need to check their sources of protein for adequacy. Eating large amounts of protein-rich foods requires considerable water for metabolism. This may produce serious dehydration in athletes, which is often coupled with fatigue.

There are a number of learning activities that might be suggested for these boys and girls. A first step is to examine what is being eaten now, and why. Students might keep a record of food eaten for three days or for a week, including supplements, such as vitamins or other concentrates. Intake could be evaluated in terms of a daily food selection guide or the Recommended Daily Dietary Allowances. Is there a lack in any of the food groups or excessive consumption in others? What meaning can be given to these results? How is the diet of a particular student different from or similar to the diets of other students in the class?

What plans might be made to change food habits? How may food dislikes be overcome? Are there ways of preparing the foods in a particular food group, such as milk, so that they will be more acceptable? Some experimental cooking may be the answer. Students with the same food-group problems, such as eating vegetables, may form groups to exchange ideas and to encourage and reinforce each other in their change in food habits. As the diets of students become more nutritious, how do the students feel? Can they see a difference and

[14] Nathan J. Smith, *Food for Sport* (Palo Alto, Calif.: Bull Publishing, 1976), pp. 19–20.

has their performance improved? Are the students well informed about the importance of nutrition in the life of an athlete?[15] Some students may wish to share their learnings with students who are not in their class. They might do this through a bulletin board, a poster, or a sheet of information. In this experience, scientific thinking and behavior modification have been emphasized.

Nutrition and Snacks

Another learning experience for this age level might be a look at snack habits. Sometimes it is easier to look at the shortcomings of others before looking painfully at one's own habits. One way to highlight the role of snacks in the lives of the young is for each student to interview several students who are outside of the class but are of about the same age. The snacks may be categorized under the important food groups. Included in the listing of each food group may be when eaten and where eaten.

[15] Henrietta Fleck and Louise Fernandez, *Exploring Homemaking and Personal Living* (Englewood Cliffs, N.J.: Prentice-Hall, 1977) (see p. 108, "Food for Athletes," in this junior high school text).

Figure 16–11 An analysis of popular snacks is valuable. (Cereal Institute, Inc.)

Analysis of the information may begin with the food groups. Which food group is the most popular? Which food group or groups seem to be neglected? Are snacks high in sugar or fat calories, or low in nutrient density? Do these snack preferences reflect the preferences of the class members? Which food groups would have to be included elsewhere in the day's meals if one is to have a nutritious diet? What about the times for eating? Are there good reasons for eating at those times? What may be the basis for selecting where to eat, such as being with friends, close proximity to food, inexpensiveness, and good food?

Students might examine carefully the information they have gained about what, where, and when snacks are eaten. Are there implications for their own snack habits? Where and how may needed changes begin? Plans or contracts may be made by the students.

Sometimes students carry their interest in other directions, such as studying the snacks of various cultures. Students might study the community for shops where cultural snacks are sold.[16] A small Puerto Rican meat pie made of a ground-beef/pork mixture and flavored with garlic is an example.

Other Experiences

Other learning experiences for these boys and girls might be how to make wise selections of foods in the school cafeteria, in fast-food restaurants, or on a date; how to be a better food shopper for the family; and how to prepare nutritious meals for the family so that food habits might be improved.

Senior High School and Older Youth

Need for Nutrition Education

Teenage boys and girls need nutrition education because their health, for the rest of their lives, may reflect the eating habits of this age. Teenage boys need more calcium, phosphorus, iodine, magnesium, and iron than at any other time in life. Energy needs are higher. Girls complete their growth earlier than boys. Teenage girls have the poorest eating habits of any age group, according to dietary studies. Being figure-conscious causes them to skip or to skimp on meals. Frequently nutritious foods are omitted. The goal of a trim figure lures them to "crash" and faddish diets that may be quite inadequate nutritionally. These situations are serious, because girls need the essen-

[16] Dolores Malo-Juvera and Lorraine Boykin, "La Marqueta: A Food Habits Learning Experience," *Journal of Nutrition Education,* Vol. 7, No. 2 (Apr./June 1975), pp. 58–59.

Figure 16–12 The nutritive needs of a student with learning problems requires special attention (U.S. Office of Education, Bureau of Education for the Handicapped)

tial nutrients for optimum development at this age. The increasing number of teenage pregnancies is alarming. Pregnancy places an additional stress on the girl when she may already be malnourished. (See Chapter 5.)

Out-of-School Youth

Out-of-school youth may be in college or at work. Some are married and have family responsibilities. Getting a job and staying employed may be a problem. Low income may cause anxiety. Living independently requires skills for living that youth may or may not have.

Weight-Loss Diets

One type of learning experience may deal with weight-loss diets. Many individuals place themselves on a diet without consulting a physician. This tactic should be discouraged. One way to determine the adequacy of a diet for weight loss is to take a daily menu from a number of diets and have the students evaluate these menus against a daily food selection guide. The results can be quite revealing. The number of calories should be checked, because many diets are below the 1,200 calories usually recommended by physicians. These dietary characteristics can result in an intake of nutrients at a dangerously low level. Water-soluble vitamins, protein, and carbohydrate are not stored in the body, so body functioning may be hampered if these are not supplied in the daily diet.

Sometimes students are not aware of the caloric content of foods. Making lists of nutritious foods that are low in calories according to a daily food selection guide is helpful. From these lists, interesting daily menus and snacks may be planned.

Other aspects of a weight-reduction regimen are weighing oneself regularly, establishing goals, being informed about nutrition, and having a positive attitude. Belonging to a group or having a partner for the sharing of ideas and for mutual reinforcement is helpful. Behavior modification ideas may be explored.

Nutrition Problems

Eating food of low nutrient density is a habit of many youths. These foods may be classified according to a daily food selection guide to highlight the little contribution most of them make to the diet. A consideration of alternatives may bring to light a number of desirable possibilities, such as plain salted popcorn, plain puffed cereals, raw vegetables, tea, and unsweetened beverages for snacks.

Individuals at this age level may be on a vegetarian diet. A lacto-vegetarian or a lacto-ovo-vegetarian can manage an adequate diet. It is difficult to plan a vegetarian diet that is nutritionally adequate without animal sources of protein. Some B vitamins may have to be taken as supplements because of the low nutrient density of B_{12}, B_6, and riboflavin in a strict vegetarian diet. The inclusion of protein pairs, such as legumes and cereals, makes a more nutritious diet. Vegetarians may analyze the nutritional adequacy of their diets and make plans for improvement. Where to find the best buys in fruits and vegetables and the other foods allowed is a good problem to discuss. The cost of foods in health stores can be enlightening.

Students in this age spectrum may need assistance in planning their daily diet, in economical food buying, in food preparation techniques to salvage nutrients, or with the selection of food when eating away from home. Sources of information for help with nutritional problems may be important. Sources of government bulletins and other literature should be made available.

Adults

The adult years bring many family, work, and community responsibilities—a strenuous time of life. Adequate nutrition for optimum health is a plus in coping with these problems. The age spectrum for this group is wide, from the early twenties to the fifties. Working women who have home and family responsibilities in addition to a job may need special assistance in nutrition education. According to the government's Ten-State Nutrition Study, the prevalence of deficient values in iron appeared to be most significant in both female and male adults. Low-income adults had the highest prevalence of deficient values. Protein intake was closely correlated with caloric intake. Nutrient intake for calcium and vitamins A and C approached or met the standards. Overweight was a common problem among adults. The use of oral contraceptives may disturb the metabolism of certain nutrients, and dietary adjustments may have to be made.

Food Fads and Fallacies

The bombardment of halftruths and fallacies from television, radio, newspapers, magazines, and books has left us with many misconceptions about nutrition. The wide use of vitamin and other concentrated nutrient preparations is alarming. The Food and Drug Administration conducted a national survey on health practices and opinions.[17] The belief that vitamin preparations will give one pep is so widespread as to be characteristic of the society as a whole. This idea is contrary to qualified medical opinion, which believes that fatigue is seldom due to deficiencies of nutrients—especially in the absence of other symptoms. Women are more likely to use vitamin preparations than men. Megavitamin therapy has a strong hold on the population for curing colds, impotency, circulatory problems, acne, arthritis, cancer, and a host of other ills. Often these vitamins are taken without the benefit of a physician's advice, but upon the suggestions of friends and relatives, an advertisement, or other nonprofessional sources. An overload of vitamin intake may have serious consequences, especially with fat-soluble vitamins. People have a stronger concern about vitamins than any other nutrient.

Teaching Strategies

Surveying the needs and interests of adults will enlighten the home economics educator about desirable teaching and learning experi-

[17] *Final Report, A Study of Health Practices and Opinions,* Food and Drug Administration, Department of Health, Education, and Welfare, Washington, D.C., 1972, Ch. 1, pp. 68–69, and Ch. 2.

ences. Because of the high interest in vitamins, it might be helpful to demonstrate the vitamin content of nutritious foods. Using the bulletin *Nutritive Value of Foods,*[18] which is a valuable contribution to any family library, adults might plan foods to provide an adequate supply of vitamin C, vitamin A, or one or more of the B vitamins. Food models or actual foods might be used to dramatize the amount of food required. Students might compare the price of the food with the price of the vitamins they take. The bulletin might be scrutinized for a number of foods supplying the vitamin so that a variety of foods may be used. The least expensive sources might be surveyed. Other nutrients, such as calcium and iron, may be studied in a similar manner. Many adults are unfamiliar with the sources of nutrients in foods.

In working with low-income families or with families in the middle class who are concerned about inflation, home economics educators may discuss ways to reduce food costs. Adults may bring copies of their favorite recipes to class. Are there less inexpensive ingredients that might be substituted, such as nonfat dry milk instead of fresh milk, a less expensive fat, a bouillion cube instead of canned broth, or

[18] *Nutritive Value of Foods,* U.S. Department of Agriculture, Home and Garden Bulletin Number 72, Superintendent of Documents, Washington, D.C., 1977.

Figure 16–13 Comparing the costs of three preparations of beef liver can be enlightening in an adult class. Liver and bacon is the most expensive; liver and onions, the least expensive. (Swift & Company)

homemade cracker crumbs? Students can help each other with suggestions. The revised recipe might be prepared and a sample brought to class for the other students to judge. The class may explore other ways to save food money during shopping for food. Class members may share ideas or shopping tips, such as using coupons, looking for specials, or buying the least expensive and the best green vegetable rather than determining ahead of time what the vegetable will be.

Working women may need advice on quick processes for making decisions about family food management. One way is to use a daily food selection guide as a criterion. When planning shopping lists, the shopper may consider daily food for all family needs, such as family members who may be eating alone at home or who may need brown-bag lunches, so that adequate servings of essential food groups are included. Additional suggestions may come from the U.S. Dietary Goals as a reminder to watch the amount of salt, sugar, total fat, animal fats, and the number of calories. The entire family may discuss ways to help with the shopping, preparation, serving, cleanup, and individual nutritional assessment.

If adults persist in diets in which important nutrients are lacking, then a discussion of the consequences of such actions might be appropriate. The same might be done about the effects of too much sugar, too much fat, or too many calories. Changes may have to be made slowly. In the case of sugar, this ingredient might very gradually be decreased. Becoming accustomed to eating fruits in juice rather than canned with sugar is one step. Some of the adults may have tried other successful plans that may be shared.

Senior Citizens

The elderly segment of the population is rapidly increasing in numbers. These elderly adults are probably the single most economically deprived group in the nation. Restricted income limits the buying of nutritious food, food preparation facilities, and other amenities of life. This age group has more health problems than any other group, and many can be traced to inadequate nutrition. Another problem is lack of transportation, which restricts mobility, food shopping, and social interaction.

In regard to nutritional status, the adequacy of diet in early life is related to health and well-being in later life. Some diets of the elderly are low in calories, and protein may consequently be inadequate. Calcium and asorbic acid may be in short supply.

The federal government, in cooperation with the states, funds various programs for the aging.[19] One program provides at least one hot-

[19] Rules and Regulations, Title 45—Public Welfare; Chapter IX—Administration in Aging, Social and Rehabilitation Service, Department of Health, Education and Welfare; Part 909—Nutrition Program for the Elderly, *Federal Register,* Vol. 37, No. 162 (Aug. 19, 1972).

lunch meal to be served five or more days a week. Each meal must provide at least one third of the Recommended Daily Dietary Allowances. When feasible and appropriate, special menus should be available to meet particular dietary needs arising from the health needs, the religious requirements, or the ethnic backgrounds of participants. Supportive services supply transportation, health and welfare counseling, nutrition education, shopping assistance, and recreational activities. Individuals must be at least sixty years of age and pay for the meal what they think they can afford. No one is denied participation because of inability to pay. Settings include public schools, churches, town halls, public housing, senior centers, and homes for the aged. The program has proved successful from the nutritional standpoint and from the standpoint of the social advantage of eating with others. Another program, "Meals on Wheels," is a service of bringing one hot meal to a housebound person or couple.

Nutritionists have assisted with the nutrition education portion of the federal- and state-funded projects. Many individuals seek help on how to prepare meals in the limited facilities of one room. Men especially often request this assistance. An appliance, such as an electric skillet, can be used for the preparation of many foods. It may be too heavy for some to use. A hot plate is used by others. A double boiler is efficient because two foods can be cooked at the same time. A potato baker can be used for other foods than baking potatoes, such as broiling meats, and preparing escalloped potatoes, macaroni and cheese, and other casserole dishes, as well as heating breads in a small pan that fits into the baker.

Some elderly people need to be urged to eat sufficient food that is nutritious. Help in planning easily prepared but tasty food may be

Figure 16–14 Senior citizens enjoying a nutritious noon meal in a school facility. (USDA Photo)

necessary. How to shop for one or two persons may present a problem, so tips on this subject are welcome. With friends in the senior center, the older adults may prepare one of their ethnic dishes, and the results may be used in a buffet. How to make their daily food more nutritious may be a good topic for discussion. Some of the elderly may need assistance in planning their modified diets. Instruction may be given to several persons who are on the same diet.

OTHER TYPES OF NUTRITION EDUCATION

Instruction in nutrition reaches individuals and families in many other ways than previously described. Within the academic structure, medical and dental students, nurses, dental hygienists, health educators, and other health-care professionals receive instruction. Nurses and medical students would profit from studies and instruction in normal and therapeutic nutrition, for example, nurses frequently give dietary advice to patients.[20]

In medical colleges or schools where such instruction is given, medical students, under the supervision of a nutrition professor, have an opportunity to appreciate the role of nutrition in the total health-care program by having experiences with a variety of patients. One outcome is to see the relation between diagnosis and the diet prescription. In some medical colleges, medical students work with a nutritionist in community health programs to broaden their experience.[21] The Medical College of Virginia, Virginia Commonwealth University School of Dentistry, and the Dietetic Internship of the Medical College of Virginia Hospital work cooperatively in a program in which a dental student and a dietetic intern counsel a patient about dietary needs.[22] The shift in dentistry from a disease-oriented to a health-oriented discipline emphasizing prevention sharpens the role of clinical practice in nutrition for dental students. Similar programs are to be recommended for dental hygienists, who are often responsible for nutrition information while discussing dental health with patients. This change is already evident in the offices of some dentists, who encourage sugarless candy and gum and the use of fresh fruit and vegetables for snacks. Above the dental chair may be a mobile of a daily food selection guide, and around the office are posters

[20] Julie M. McDaniel, "Diet Therapy in the Nursing School Curriculum," *Journal of American Dietetic Association,* Vol. 70, No. 3, (March 1977), pp. 285–286.

[21] At the New Jersey College of Medicine and Dentistry under the supervision of Dr. Elizabeth Munves, Ph.D., R.D., Professor of Dietetic Medicine.

[22] John G. Odom, Dominick P. DePaola, and Ann E. Robbins, "Nutrition Education for Dental Students: A Conjoint Approach," *Journal of American Dietetic Association,* Vol. 72, No. 1 (Jan. 1978), pp. 56–58.

and other wall decorations that highlight nutritious food for healthy teeth.[23] Health educators and other health-related professionals need to receive nutrition education in order to incorporate it into total health education.

Dietitians and nutritionists teach nutrition in other situations. As the incidence of malnutrition among hospital patients has become more evident, so have the services of a clinical dietitian specializing in nutrition assessment and therapy. This clinical dietitian participates with other services in total health care, as well as planning, implementing, and evaluating nutritional prescriptions. Educating and involving the patient in his or her nutritional health-care plan and instructing other staff members are other responsibilities.[24] There is a strong trend toward the participation of nutritionists in comprehensive health-delivery systems that involve both therapeutic and preventive care.[25] These nutritionists must have competencies in identifying nutrition-related health problems, in exploring educational and interviewing techniques, in communicating in a teaching situation involving individuals or a group, in understanding values and lifestyles in their relation to health and nutritional status, and in communicating with other professionals. Experience in counseling and working in community nutrition programs is essential. The rationale for these community programs is that nutrition and dietary factors are keys to the prevention of many crippling, killing, and costly diseases. Some of the programs that require nutritional counseling are prenatal care, services for well infants, and early periodic screening diagnosis and treatment programs for children (which may reveal such nutritional problems as iron deficiencies, growth retardation, obesity, and dental defects). Nutritionists also work with WIC, a special supplemental food program of the U.S. Department of Agriculture for pregnant women, infants, and children, who are high nutritional risks. Cardiovascular clinics and city, county, and state health departments employ nutritionists in a variety of programs.[26]

Hospital dietitians teach patients about their prescribed diets and about home applications. Nutritionists teach in many types of clinics, including those for adolescent obesity, for youths with nontraditional food patterns, and for drug addicts.[27]

[23] Harry R. Tolly, D.D.S., Lincoln, Neb.

[24] Joanne E. Wade, "Role of the Clinical Dietitian Specialist in a Nutrition Support Service," *Journal of American Dietetic Association,* Vol. 70, No. 2 (Feb. 1977), pp. 185–188.

[25] Maureen Thieles and Jean H. Hankin, "Training Nutritionists for Comprehensive Health Delivery Systems," *Journal of American Dietetic Association,* Vol. 70, No. 2 (Feb. 1977), pp. 189–191.

[26] Mildred Kaufman and Frances Hoffman, "Dietetic Interns Learn About Their Community," *Journal of American Dietetic Association,* Vol. 71, No. 5 (Nov. 1977), pp. 527–530.

[27] "Nutrition Services in a Free Medical Clinic (Michigan State University)," *Journal of American Dietetic Association,* Vol. 72, No. 1 (July 1977), pp. 52–53.

Educators in nutrition may participate in television or radio programs on current nutrition topics, write newspaper releases on the shortcomings of the American diet, interpret the U.S. Dietary Goals, or may give talks to various groups. Dial-a-Dietitian is generally organized by a local dietetic association so that the public may call and ask questions about nutrition that are later answered by an expert in the field. Nutrition is being taught to the cadets of the Police Academy in New York City. The opportunities for service are many.

A FINAL WORD

Nutrition educators must be ever alert to the changes that will have an impact on their teaching. How do changes in dietary guides make a difference? Certain components of the diet, such as specific nutrients, and consequently certain foods, may be increased or decreased. The effect of the energy crisis on food production and on food preparation in the home is another consideration.[28] These are only a few of the political and social changes that must be considered.

All nutrition educators will wish to assess their teaching. What evidence is available that students, patients, or other audiences are improving their food habits and eating more nutritious food? Has their list of food preferences increased, with more foods of greater nutritive density? Has weight been lost or gained? What signs of improved nutrition are evident?

In whatever manner nutrition education takes place, educators will face greater accountability. What was done and what was accomplished will have to be documented for later scrutiny by administrators or evaluation teams. Has the nutritional well-being of the students or the patients been improved, and to what extent?[29]

A summary of a paper on nutrition education prepared by a panel of the National Nutrition Consortium raises the following questions: "What Information Do Consumers Need About Their Food Supplies? What Type of Nutrition Information Does the Consumer Need? How Should Nutrition Information Be Provided? and What Should Be Done to Improve the Knowledge Base on Which Nutrition Education Is Based?"[30] Nutrition educators may wish to analyze these questions and to make changes or additions or to consider ways to implement them.

[28] Marjorie Devine, "Ecology of Human Nutrition: Systems and Synergisms" in *Living in America, Home Economics Education for the Third Century,* Department of Community Service Education, The New York State College of Human Ecology, A Statutory College of the State University, Cornell University, Ithaca, N.Y., 1977, pp. 44–68.

[29] Johanna T. Dwyer, "Point of View: Challenges in Nutrition Education of the Public," *Journal of American Dietetic Association,* Vol. 72, No. 1 (Jan. 1978), pp. 53–55.

[30] M. C. Nesheim and Helen A. Guthrie, "Statement on Nutrition Education—A Summary," *Journal of American Dietetic Association,* Vol. 72, No. 1 (Jan. 1978), p. 66.

SUGGESTIONS FOR FURTHER LEARNING

1. Compile the most important legislation related to nutrition and nutrition education. What are the gaps? How may present legislation be improved and at which levels?
2. Here are some references for teaching nutrition.

Bisbee, Joyce. "Consumers and Food Making Choices." *Forum* (J. C. Penney) (Fall–Winter 1977), entire issue.

"Everybody Needs Food." *Learning,* **6** (Dec. 1977), 39–46.

Illinois Teacher

"Better Health Through Better Nutrition." **17** (Jan.–Feb. 1974), entire issue.

BeVier, Karen, and Ellen Z. Hooker. "Patient Education." **19** (Sept.–Oct. 1975), 32–38.

"Cereal or Sugar." **18** (Jan.–Feb. 1975), 161–163.

Feitshans, Sandra. "Children and Food—A Natural Combination." **17** (Sept.–Oct. 1973), 46–51.

"Junk, Junk Foods Before They Junk You." *Instructor,* **87** (Jan. 1978), 30.

"Nutrition Lifestyles and the Quality of Life." **19** (March–Apr. 1976), entire issue.

McNutt, Kristen W. *Nutrition Education Materials.* Washington, D.C.: Nutrition Foundation, Office of Education and Public Affairs, 1974.

Nutrition—What's In It for You? A 1974 kit with filmstrip and cassette plus other teaching materials. May be borrowed from your local J. C. Penney dealer or order from J. C. Penney Company, Inc., Education Relations Department, 1301 Avenue of the Americas, New York, N.Y. 10019.

Ritchie, Jean A. S. *Learning Better Nutrition.* Rome: Food and Agriculture Organization of the United Nations, 1967.

Short, Sarah H. *Innovative Teaching of Nutrition.* Chicago: American Dietetic Association, 1973. A kit.

Sonneberg, Lois. "Food Specials on Three Levels." *Learning,* **6** (Feb. 1978), 117.

17

Education for Work

Work is the central and most binding continuity in the life of most individuals from sixteen to seventy years of age.[1] Work is central to living because, in general, it provides the major social and psychological framework for forty to fifty years of the life cycle. Work structures and limits experience, reduces or opens options, influences time schedules, and in many ways has a powerful impact on life.

Through a job or jobs most men and women maintain their connection with the human community, which keeps changing with social and economic conditions. It is through daily work that an individual examines his/her self-concept, his/her feelings and attitudes about work, the tasks that confront him/her and his/her expectations for future relationships and rewards. Work is strongly related to the family and has a major influence on the lives of family members, for their circumstances may depend on choices made in regard to work. The role of work in the lives of individuals and families is of particular interest to home economics educators.

CONCEPTS OF WORK

The concepts of work and the esteem in which work is held differ from culture to culture, from age to age, and from one social class to another; one's view of work seems generally to emerge from ideas held by family, friends, and the people in the community. The Greek

[1] W. E. Henry, "The Role of Work in Structuring the Life Cycle," *Mental Health Digest,* Vol. 4, No 3 (March 1972), pp. 1–2.

Figure 17–1 Through many types of work men and women maintain connections with the community and the nation.

philosopher Socrates believed that work was an expedient; the Roman poet Vergil stated in the *Georgics,* poems on the life and labor of peasants, that work was a necessity and a curse. Work today is defined as something more than mere strenuous exertion, but it is still true that the nature of these work concepts has a powerful influence on an individual's attitude toward a job. Neff[2] states that "the adult ability to work is the product of a long series of individual experi-

[2] Walter S. Neff, *Work and Human Behavior* (New York: Atherton, 1968), Ch. 2.

ences, events, and circumstances, which occur in a very complex matrix of social demands, expectations, and mores." Although there is considerable literature on the factors that produce or deter work efficiency, there is an underlying assumption that most individuals possess the ability to work. Neff questions this concept and believes that there is great variation in people's ability to work.

Work cannot be reduced easily to indices of mental and muscular energy as work technologists are inclined to do. The human qualities of the individual must also be considered. In addition, Neff contends that because work is not an instinctive human activity, an individual must learn to be a worker. This learning process varies greatly from person to person.

The role of the worker is regulated by social norms in the culture of which he/she is a part, and certain kinds of behavior are expected in a frame of prescribed functions. Neff delineates "necessary" conditions for work that include the required physical and mental capacities, plus a willingness to learn about the job. There are also the "sufficient" conditions tied to social behavior, including dress, speech, and ways of relating to peers, subordinates, and superiors.

Although work has been the major means of making a living, it is generally viewed as drudgery, and a persistent dream of humans has been to relieve themselves of work. For that reason, work and leisure are often associated. Although working hours have been reduced, a person may use the additional free time, according to De Grazia,[3] by spending more time in travel to and from work, by "moonlighting" or undertaking several jobs, or by working overtime more frequently.

For most persons, existence depends upon work. If people did not work, there would be chaos in the universe. Work may be associated with pain, greed, courage, ingenuity, humor, harshness, dreams, and a host of other concepts. Work has great variety; it extends from someone working with thousands of other employees to the craftsman who works alone.[4]

Terkel[5] contends that working brings daily meaning to life, the essentials of living (food, clothing, and shelter), plus cash, recognition, and hopefully some surprise and excitement. Sometimes work is less than satisfying, and according to Terkel, one hears statements such as "I'm a robot," "I'm caged," or "I am an object."

The youth of today differ from their parents in their concepts about work.[6] More emphasis is placed on the salary and the security of a job

[3] Sebastian De Grazia, *Of Time, Work and Leisure* (New York: 20th Century Fund, 1962), p. 64.

[4] "America at Work," a photo essay, *Senior Scholastic*, Vol. 108, No. 7 (Apr. 6, 1976), pp. 30–32.

[5] Studs Terkel, *Working* (New York: Avon Books, 1975), pp. xiii–xiv.

[6] Robert J. Havighurst and David Gottlieb, "Youth and the Meaning of Work," in Robert J. Havighurst (ed.), *Youth*, The Seventy-fourth Yearbook of the National Society for the Study of Education (Chicago: U. of Chicago, 1975), p. 147.

Figure 17–2 Youth are interested in work that gives service to society.

by the older generation. Young people are less concerned about these priorities. Stress is on the benefits of a job to others in society, on working with people and not things, and on challenge, achievement, and responsibility.

VOCATIONAL EDUCATION

Some type of vocational education has been considered important by people from the days of Hammurabi. In America, with the signing of the Smith-Hughes Act in 1917, vocational education was justified, according to Barlow,[7] on the grounds that it ought to be an integral part of an individual's total education. It seems sensible that the concept of vocational education be applied to all types of work and to all people. Some interpretations of vocational education divorce it from liberal education. In reality, both are essential and complementary because each helps the individual to make a maximum contribution to society.

[7] Melvin L. Barlow, "The Challenge to Vocational Education," in Melvin L. Barlow and Herman G. Richey (eds.), *Vocational Education,* Sixty-fourth Yearbook of the Society for the Study of Education, Part I (Chicago: U. of Chicago, 1965), Ch. 1.

Federal Aid to Vocational Education

Financial support from the federal government has been responsible for advancing numerous programs in vocational areas. There is considerable controversy over the favorable and unfavorable influences of federal aid to public education, the critics claiming that vocational education has narrowed its offerings in consequence of such aid or that programs have been developed only to meet immediate needs. There is no proof to support these criticisms. A major contribution of the federal acts has been the development of standards in vocational education, including standards for administration and supervision.

The Smith-Hughes Act, passed in 1917, appropriated funds for the promotion and development of agricultural, trade, and home economics education. The George Barden Act, passed in 1946, broadened the Smith-Hughes Act provisions for vocational education to include preparation for distributive education and vocational guidance. Funds appropriated through these laws had to be used under the public supervision and control of state or local boards of vocational education, which in turn worked closely with the federal agencies.

The Vocational Education Act of 1963 (Public Law 88—210) was considered a legislative milestone. A panel of consultants on vocational education, whose recommendations influenced the content of this act, concluded that vocational education reaches too few people. The central purpose of the act is to assist the states to maintain, extend, and improve existing vocational education programs and to develop new ones. A corollary objective is to provide part-time employment for youths who need jobs in order to continue their vocational education and to provide instruction so that individuals of all ages and in all communities shall have access to vocational training, or retraining, of high quality. Those eligible for this training may still be in high school or may have completed high school or may be adults who need upgrading or new skills. All students must use this preparation to enter the labor market. Persons with educational handicaps, such as the need for remedial reading or training in other basic skills, also benefit. The act also establishes, through funding, auxiliary services, such as teacher education, special demonstration and experimental programs, the development of instructional materials, the review of the manpower available and job opportunities, state administration and leadership, and research.

Funds provided under the George Barden Act were continued until 1968 for the support of home economics programs that offered preparation for homemaking and family living.[8] The Vocational Education

[8] Mary Lee Hurt, "Vocational Home Economics, Present and Future," *Journal of Home Economics,* Vol. 64, No. 5 (May 1972), pp. 26–32.

Amendments (Public Law 90—576) continued the support of occupational education and homemaking but with some variations. Part B of Title 1 of the amendments[9] provided grants to states on a matching basis and according to a state plan "to assist them in conducting vocational education programs for persons of all ages in all communities of the States, which are designed to insure that education and training programs for career programs are available to all individuals who desire and need such education and training." Special allocations of funds are made for occupational training programs for disadvantaged and handicapped youth and adults. Funds are also provided for the support of research, exemplary programs, cooperative work–study programs, and curriculum development in vocational education. Home economics programs have benefited and expanded from sharing these funds.

In addition, Part F of Title 1 of the Vocational Education Amendments of 1968[10] provides funds to states on a matching basis for "Consumer and Homemaking Education." At least one third of the funds made available under this section are to be used for programs in depressed areas or areas of high unemployment. Funds allocated to the states for the purposes of Part F of the amendments may be used to help support consumer and homemaking education programs in local schools and for ancillary services and activities to ensure quality in these programs. The requirements to be met in order for local programs for youth and adults to receive approval are[11]

a. The program will encourage greater consideration of the social and cultural conditions and needs, especially in economically depressed areas;
b. The program will encourage preparation for professional leadership in home economics and consumer education;
c. The program will be designed for youth and adults who have entered or are preparing to enter the work of the home;
d. The program will be designed to prepare such youth and adults for the role of homemaker or contribute to their employability in the dual role of homemaker and wage earner; and
e. The program will include consumer education as an integral part thereof (including promise of nutritional knowledge and food use and the understanding of the economic aspects of food uses and purchase).[12]

[9] Public Law 90—576, Oct. 16, 1968. *Vocational Education Amendments of 1968,* Title 1, Part B, p. 9.

[10] Ibid., Title 1, Part F, p. 22.

[11] Bureau of Adult, Vocational, and Library Programs, U.S. Department of Health, Education, and Welfare. *Regulations for State Plan Programs,* Vocational Education Amendments of 1968. Washington, D.C., Apr. 1969, p. 10. (Material for administrative use only.)

[12] Part in parenthesis added in Public Law 91—230; H.R. 514, Apr. 13, 1970, p. 69.

The Vocational Education Amendments of 1976 identify areas of concentration for teachers of consumer and homemaking education:

a. Participation of both males and females to prepare for combining the roles of homemaker and wage earner.
b. Elimination of sex stereotyping through curriculum materials that deal with women working outside the home and men assuming household responsibilities, and with the changing of career patterns of both men and women.

Figure 17–3 Sex stereotyping is discouraged by law and spirit in education.

c. Greater consideration of conditions and educational needs in educationally depressed areas.
d. Outreach programs for the aged, young children, school-age parents, single parents, handicapped persons, and educationally disadvantaged persons.
e. Emphasis is to be placed upon parenthood education, nutrition education, consumer education, and the management of resources.
f. Homemaking is considered a vocation. This is justified because homemakers, as a rule, have the major responsibilities for the home, equivalent to a full time job.[13]

Home economics teachers will wish to study the implications of the Vocational Acts and their amendments for their program so that their planning will be more effective. A wide range of home economics vocational programs are available throughout schools in the United States. Programs vary to meet the needs of individuals and families. Other influences on such programs are the availability of resources, the support of the school administration and the members of the community, and the innovative interpretation of the teachers in the development of the program. Before planning a program, the teacher in home economics occupational education may wish to review the major influences on vocational behavior.

VOCATIONAL BEHAVIOR

There are many facets of work behavior to consider, along with their relation to each other. Unfortunately, research and study in this area are somewhat limited.

Why People Work

Basic to the planning of a program of job preparation for students is an understanding and appreciation of the reasons that people work. The motivations are varied and complex. "Paid" work appears to be important to many citizens. Social factors, such as opportunities for work, the environment of the job, co-workers, government regulations, and unions, may influence job choices. Personal abilities, the amount of preparation for work, family and peer influences, and health are among other considerations in work selection. Personal attitudes, desires, potential satisfactions, or freedom may determine whether a person works for money, to serve others, to be with people of similar bent, to improve society, or for other purposes.

[13] Lowell A. Burkett, "Latest Word from Washington," *American Vocational Journal*, Vol. 51, No. 9 (Dec. 1976), p. 9.

Attitudes Toward Work

It is necessary for teachers to determine whether student attitudes toward work are positive or negative. Is work something that can be satisfying, or is it sheer drudgery? Is it a means to some end, such as wages, or does it make a contribution to the life of the individual? What kinds of work do the young people being taught consider appropriate for themselves?

A number of techniques might be used to solicit this information. Students might be asked to prepare a two-column sheet of paper. On one side would be listed "What I Would Like About a Job" and on the other side, "What I Would Dislike About a Job." Students might share and discuss their ideas. Another possibility is to categorize the items on their lists and then apply them to possible jobs. Students might rate items on their list from the most desirable to least desirable and from most objectionable to least objectionable. If rapport is good among the students, they might challenge the job characteristics listed as being incompatible with what they know about the student.

Social Values Related to Work

Shindler-Rainman[14] advances these recommendations, which have social connotations: (1) a wide range of exciting choices in the work world should be offered to all students—male and female, handicapped, and majority or minority; (2) help all students to look at their multiple roles as related to home, sex, work, and other areas of living so that these roles may be blended for greater fulfillment; (3) provide many community opportunities for securing firsthand career-exploration experience; and (4) open the world of work as widely as possible to all individuals through cooperation with industry, government, education, and other agencies or avenues.

Psychological Benefits of Work

Work can command a concentration that excludes worry, loneliness, or restlessness; it may even provide an opportunity to get rid of aggressions. A girl or boy who works as a nursery-school aide may lose some hostile feelings or unpleasant thoughts in the course of caring for energetic three-year-olds.

At work, people learn to control themselves to a greater degree than they may in the midst of the family. In addition, they must learn

[14] Eva Shindler-Rainman in a talk to home economics educators at the annual meeting of the American Vocational Association in Atlantic City, Dec. 1977, summarized in *Forecast for Home Economics,* Vol. 23, No. 6 (Feb. 1978), pp. 62, 80.

to coordinate their work with that of others, to communicate, and to be sensitive to the ideas and needs of fellow workers. Individuals who work together are inclined to relate to one another much as they do to family members. Reactions on the job reflect the amount of give-and-take in families and the type of power structure to which persons have been accustomed. To a working teenager, the employer may seem to play the role of a father or mother.

Work gives one a feeling of being a part of the world, of knowing what is going on. Persons who are unemployed often do not come to grips with reality. That someone needs one's help gives a feeling of worth; for that reason, too, unemployment can have devastating effects. Work is important in fulfilling a person's basic needs for achievement and recognition, for one's self-concept is partially influenced by what one does. If one is proud of one's work, and especially if the employer takes time to praise that good work, self-esteem is sustained at a high, wholesome level. Furthermore the manner in which one is regarded by others is determined, to a certain extent, by the way he/she earns a livelihood. When an individual feels that he/she must apologize for work, the effect on the personality can be detrimental.

THE WORKING WORLD

Youth Unemployment

Millions of youth roam the street every day looking for work. This situation is found not only in America but worldwide. This unemployment is present in both good and bad times and gives rise to serious social tensions.[15] In the United States more young blacks suffer from unemployment than any other youth group. They are followed in number by other minority-group young people, then by white girls, and finally by white boys, who suffer the least of all. The plight of youth in urban centers is more critical than in other areas of the country.

A number of reasons are advanced for youth unemployment. Many youths have few marketable skills. Some are dropouts who lack the necessary credentials, such as a high school diploma. When they do find jobs, the pay is low, the work is boring, and there is little or no opportunity for advancement. Career and job counseling in school may have been inadequate. Many become discouraged and discontinue looking for jobs.

Many women have entered the labor market so there are fewer jobs available. Wage unemployment occurs when wages rise above the

[15] Editorial, *Business Week* (Dec. 20, 1976), p. 80.

Figure 17–4 Many youth are out of work and may be bored, confused, and angry.

point where employers can pay workers, especially inexperienced workers.[16] Lack of union membership denies work in some part-time and seasonal jobs. The postwar baby boom has increased the number of teenagers, so competition is greater. Licensing boards sometimes increase requirements and thus exclude teenagers. Teenage unemployment leads to more crime, and drug addiction and less income for families.

Griffin[17] cites a number of variables that bear consideration for vo-

[16] *News, Subject: Jobs* (Washington, D.C.: Chamber of Commerce of the United States, Jan. 1977), p. 1.

cationally prepared students. They are (1) the availability and location of jobs for youth; (2) certain attitudes of job-seeking youth; (3) the preferred sex and age groups that employers are seeking; (4) the number of youth identified as looking for temporary or part-time jobs; (5) patterns of unemployment for nonwhite youth; and (6) shifts in ages in the population, plus movements from one section of the country to others (such as from North to South). Manpower planners in large cities and rural developers are giving consideration to more jobs for teenagers and young adults. Federal, state, and local governments are paying attention to this problem. Vocational educators must stay alert to legislation that is being projected to meet some of these problems.

Sex Stereotyping

Vocational education is charged in the 1976 amendments with erasing sex stereotyping by opening vocational education courses to everyone. Girls and women may be encouraged to go into higher-paid jobs, such as plumbing, electrical work, and mechanics. In the Eli Whitney Vocational High School in Brooklyn, New York, students take ten of fourteen workshops in different vocational areas during the freshman year. A decision about specialization is made in the sophomore year. Girls are now taking cabinetmaking, machine shop, radio repair, and upholstery.

In the Illinois State Department of Education, a special curriculum for grade 7 through first year of community college was planned and field-tested to counteract sex stereotyping. The results were encouraging, according to John Washburn, a member of the Research and Development Department of the Vocational and Technical Agency in Illinois. In North Carolina, a statewide project called the New Pioneer Program uses brochures, tapes, and filmstrips to overcome sex bias among both teachers and students. Director Amanda Smith reports that more than a thousand girls are now in agriculture and seven hundred are in trade and industrial programs. Male enrollment in nutrition and home furnishings has doubled. Director Smith and staff meet every month with local directors to encourage boys and girls to examine and change their options.

Women

Although both men and women are served in vocational home economics programs, women have encountered unique situations and problems. More women continue to enter the labor market steadily

[17] Dean Griffin, "Youth Unemployment: Can Voc Ed Do Anything About It?" *American Vocational Journal,* Vol. 52, No. 7 (Oct. 1977), pp. 24–25.

year by year. The projection is that 47.1 million women will be working in 1987. The reasons for this development are changing social values and lifestyles, the fact that more young married women are looking for jobs, rising educational levels, the decline in the nation's birthrate, inflation, the lowering of real incomes, and federal laws that have increased hiring opportunities for women.[18]

Women continue to work in a somewhat limited range of occupations, mostly clerical and service jobs. The gap between the wages of men and women widens in favor of men in spite of the creation of the Equal Employment Opportunity Commission. Some women are moving into administrative and managerial positions at all levels.

WAGE-EARNING INSTRUCTION

Wage-earning preparation for high school students, out-of-school youth, and adults is a responsibility proper to the home economics program. This responsibility extends to more than teaching a student the skills for a single job: it means assisting him/her to adapt to the present and future worlds of work. In light of the rapid changes occurring in our world, it is difficult to envision the kinds of work that students will be doing even ten years from now. Education must be accepted as continuing for an entire lifetime.

Wage-earning preparation should be dignified as *education,* not mere *training.* According to Dale,[19] *training* connotes short-range, limited goals. *Education,* by contrast, connotes long-range goals with unlimited horizons and ends and means that change with time. Home economics teachers must not fall into the trap of giving a narrow interpretation to instruction for wage earning. Programs should be designed with vision, creativity, flexibility, and a deep regard for human values. Work is an integral part of life, a fact that must be reflected in teaching.

Preliminary Planning

There are several ways in which home economics may contribute to an orientation to the world of work and to the preparation of youth and adults for gainful employment. Students from the elementary level through high school may be enlightened about work through a course or a minicourse or throughout the consumer and homemaking program. The topics to be covered are the kinds of work and the abilities they require, the meaning of work, feelings about work, the im-

[18] "Women, Their Impact Grows in the Job Market," *U.S. News and World Report* (June 6, 1977), pp. 58–59.

[19] Edgar Dale, "Education or Training?" *The Newsletter,* Vol. 21, No. 1 (Oct. 1965), p. 1.

pact of work on family members, and the contribution of work to individuals and society. Education for gainful employment focuses on the preparation of youth and adults with the knowledge, attitudes, and skills to become employed in an occupation related to the field of home economics. With the assistance of the school administration, an advisory council, parents, and students, the teacher will work to plan the most effective ways to prepare students for the world of work.

In planning the curriculum for wage earning, the teacher will do well to consider the total educational needs of the students. Competence in the basic skills of reading, writing, oral communication, and arithmetic are important, for they will be needed on the job as well as in other life activities. Students must have other subjects, too, such as social studies and the arts and sciences, to prepare them for effective living and satisfying work. The better educated the individual, the greater his/her motivation and ability to solve life's problems.

Home economics has a special charge to prepare students for a stable and happy home and family life. Family members require special attention to prepare them for the roles of wage earner and homemaker. To be successful in both areas is a challenge, but many learnings can serve both purposes. The selection of clothes; human relations; creativity; the management of time, money, and energy; the assumption of responsibility; and the development of a positive self-image are some of the areas that are important to the woman on the job as well as the woman/man in the home. But the girl, the boy, or the adult who plans to work must also be provided with information about selecting and finding a job, the skills required, and the ethics and attitudes that will let them develop an appreciation of the meaning of work. Instruction should also give attention to a student's special personal and social needs.

The Wage-Earning Curriculum

The first step in planning a curriculum is the selection of an advisory committee or council, as mandated by the 1976 vocational educational legislation as a condition for federal funding. A number of suggestions are offered here for the selection and role of these committees or councils.

Attitude

Ely[20] contends that "the professional vocational community" must manifest a strong and positive belief in the need for these committees to ensure the effectiveness of the program.

[20] Ron H. Ely, "How to Organize and Maintain a Productive Advisory Committee," *American Vocational Journal,* Vol. 52, No. 3 (March 1977), pp. 37–39.

Types of Committees

Nerden[21] suggests at least two main types of advisory committees for most vocational schools. One is the school committee that works directly with the overall administrator of the school's vocational programs, such as home economics and industrial arts. The other committee is the curriculum advisory committee that works with one area, such as home economics or occupational education, but coordinates with the school advisory council. The school committee advises on the school's vocational program in such activities as recruiting and enrolling students, placing and following up on graduates, making feasibility studies, influencing legislation at federal, state, and local levels, improving public relations, and studying comparative costs of instruction. Members of the school advisory committee are often representatives of employers, management, labor, and education.

Possible members of the home economics occupational curriculum advisory committee may be representatives from the chamber of commerce, a labor union, or an employment agency; managers of businesses or agencies that typify the kind of occupations for which students are being prepared, such as the administrator of a food-service establishment, a day-care center, or a hospital; a guidance counselor; an interested parent; former students; or a personnel official. The people selected should:

1. Manifest an interest in occupational education.
2. Represent varied interests within the community.
3. Have the time and energy to be helpful.
4. Have something to offer to the program.
5. Be competent in an occupational area pertinent to the program.
6. Be able to visualize the impact of the program on the student, the school, and the community.

Occasionally consultants who are experts in a specific area may be added. The advisory committee studies, interprets, suggests, and recommends but does not establish policy. That is the province of the school administration and the faculty.

Appointees to a new or ongoing council are more helpful if they are informed about the responsibilities of a member of the advisory committee and about the vocational program. It is assumed that each appointee has been discussed and cleared by the overall administrator of vocational programs, the top administration in the school, and the

[21] Joseph T. Nerden, "Advisory Committees in Vocational Education, A Powerful Incentive to Program Improvement," *American Vocational Journal,* Vol. 52, No. 1 (Jan. 1977), pp. 27–29, 35.

school board. Invitations to the advisory committee are generally extended by the school.

Organization of the Advisory Committee

Regular and well-planned meetings (at least three or four a year) will enable the committee to work more effectively. An agenda should be sent to each member before the committee meeting. A constitution and bylaws may be developed to guide the committee's endeavors.

Faculty might sensitize themselves to the unique contributions that each committee member may make to the program or how she/he may be of assistance in other ways, so that the services of the committee members may be utilized to the fullest extent. The results are a better program and interested and satisfied committee members.

Functions of the Advisory Committee

The advisory committee may suggest instructional procedures and materials; identify critical objectives; provide work experiences, student placement, and follow-up; improve community service and public relations; and plan space and equipment; utilize community resources; and periodically review the development of the curriculum. Suggestions may be offered for staffing, evaluating the program, forecasting future trends, increasing the relevance of the program to community needs, and promoting greater community status.

Identification of Areas and Plans for Centers for On-the-Job Experience

The courses to be taught in occupational education will depend upon the availability of jobs, the recommendations of the advisory board, the vocational interests of the students, the facilities in the school and in the community, and a competent staff. When the home-economics–related occupation or occupations have been chosen, a thorough study of each is undertaken, including content, student experiences, ways to evaluate student needs, and the like. Some suggestions for the major areas are offered here.

Food Service

The restaurant business is one of the fastest growing industries in America. Home economics can prepare students for jobs in this area, such as short-order cook, preparer of cold foods such as salads and

Figure 17–5 Fast-food restaurants offer job opportunities.

sandwiches, vegetable cook, general cook, and chef's helper. *Fast-food restaurants*[22] have a special appeal for the public and offer many opportunities for jobs. Special fast-food preparation techniques plus rapid production would be important skills. *Institutional feeding* in places such as schools, hospitals, employee cafeterias in industry or offices, and mass feeding for airplane service has interesting job possibilities for which vocational students may be prepared.[23] Certain large companies *prepare meals for large groups on a contract* basis for use by companies, agencies, or institutions. Regional and ethnic foods have become nationalized in large-quantity food production, such as pizza, tacos, and fried clams. The preparation of food for *vending machines* in airports, bus depots, visitors' lounges in hospitals, and other places is another possibility. Other types of food service might be explored.

One type of job possibility related to food is the test kitchen aide, who assists in the preparation of experimental and new recipes for new or old products in the food industry. Other possibilities are catering for parties or special occasions such as weddings; specializing in the preparation of a certain food, such as birthday cakes, jams, jellies and preserves, and salad dressings (some students begin in a

[22] "Fast-Growing Careers in Fast-Food Service," *Forecast for Home Economics,* Vol. 23, No. 1 (Sept. 1977), p. 132.

[23] "Training for the Food Trades," *CO-ED,* Vol. 23, No. 1 (Sept. 1977), p. 32.

small way and then develop their own business or shop); and becoming a dietary aide in a hospital, who helps in food service to patients or in other ways. The possibilities in the food service area are unlimited and depend on the ingenuity of the students and instructors.

Clothing Services

Students in the area of clothing may be prepared to work in dry-cleaning shops or alterations departments or may work at repairing clothes or dressmaking. A graduate with artistic ability may be an aide to a clothing *designer.* With some previous experience, a former student may plan a small *boutique* that features clothing accessories, needlework, patchwork, or other services.[24] A *small clothing factory* in a community or in an urban area may offer job opportunities for which the ability to sew on an industrial sewing machine would be a necessary skill.[25]

The world of retailing offers many opportunities for students who are also business-minded. Clerking in a department store is a good way to get experience and to learn about this field. Stock personnel, assistants to buyers, fashion coordinators, window display designers, are other areas of employment.

[24] "Stepping into the Fashion World While Still in High School," *American Vocational Journal,* Vol. 51, No. 1 (Jan. 1976), pp. 40–41.
[25] Virginia F. Thomas and Sandra Plumb, "Exploration of Home Economics Related Occupations in Clothing," *Illinois Teacher,* Vol. 20, No. 2 (Nov.–Dec. 1976), pp. 85–89.

Figure 17–6 The world of retailing offers many types of positions.

Pattern companies, sewing machine companies, and industries that provide accessories for home sewing, such as thread companies, often employ people skilled in clothing construction to test their products. With experience, demonstrations may be given to the public. Other positions are available, such as work in consumer relations in industry, but additional experience and education are required.

Child Care and Development Services

Students who have demonstrated an interest in working with infants and small children will find job opportunities, especially in urban areas. Infant and day-care centers, nursery schools, and family day-care homes are sources for positions such as child-care aide. These child-care facilities must be licensed in most states or by local government for the purpose of protecting the users of these services.[26] Staff may have to meet certain minimal requirements.

Child development aides may work also in institutions dealing with handicapped children, in hospitals in which children are long-time patients, in orphanages, and in other types of institutions.

The family day-care centers are located in homes. Sometimes the mother of a small child may care for other children as well. This type of care (usually limited to four children) is subject to regulation in many states. Older students and adults interested in this area may consider this situation as a work possibility.

In all of these positions, a strong background in the development of children and skills in feeding, dressing, toileting, and providing activities that foster total development are necessary.

Home Furnishing Services

Students may work in department or furniture stores or specialty shops in home furnishing services. Work might involve making home accessories, such as pillows, curtains, draperies, and chair cushions. Jobs in refinishing and reupholstering furniture, rewebbing cane chairs, and the like have potential.

Being a secretary or a receptionist in the home decorating department in a store or shop is a start in providing some of the experience necessary to become a decorator's aide. This aide may search for fabrics, furniture, and accessories that are appropriate for a customer's layout. A sense of color and design, a knowledge of furniture types, and a familiarity with fabrics for the home are important in this type of position.[27]

[26] Ivalee McCord et al., *Child Care Handbook* (Washington, D.C.: American Home Economics Association, 1975), p. 7.

[27] Lee Tarp, "An Interior Design Class Accepts a 'Client,'" *Illinois Teacher*, Vol. 21, No. 1 (Sept.–Oct. 1977), p. 53.

Cooperative programs may be planned with other vocational education areas. For example, a student may learn to upholster in the industrial arts department and combine this skill with other aspects of home furnishings as preparation for working in a shop that renovates furniture. A knowledge of architecture will help in ideas about coordinating the inside and outside looks of homes. Team teaching of home economics with architecture and the building trades, for instance, is a possibility in the preparation of a decorator's aide.[28] Decorating for offices and public buildings, such as banks, can be exciting.

Home Management and Consumer Services

Students who enjoy organization, efficiency, and management of resources would like the home management and consumer services areas. Many positions are opening in these services. In urban areas, for example, there are businesses that provide daily, weekly, or seasonal house cleaning. Students are hired and paid by this business, not by the homemaker. In addition to the cleaning personnel, some businesses provide the cleaning equipment and supplies. Workers within a cleaning crew are experts in cleaning one area, such as bathrooms, living rooms, or kitchens. The homemaker is billed for the services by the company. These workers render a specialized service that has status and negates some of the problems of being supervised by the homemaker.

In an institutional setting, housekeeper aides may meet a potential need. Hotels, motels, hospitality centers, and similar institutions usually have an executive housekeeper who supervises the aides.[29] Such positions involve cleaning rooms, changing linen and other supplies, checking on conditions in preparation for the next tenant, and being an aide to the executive housekeeper. Hospitals, nursing homes, convalescent homes, large office buildings, school dormitories, and the like have housekeepers or maintenance personnel and hire aides.

For adult students, men or women, preparation for becoming a homemaker–home health aide[30] presents an opportunity for service. Health and welfare agencies recruit the aides to care for children, the aged, the chronically ill, and other incapacitated family members in their homes. The responsibilities may include managing the home, planning nutritious meals within the budget, doing marketing, and carrying out other instructions from a professional supervisor. This service may be arranged by the social service department of a hospi-

[28] Milton L. Baca and Laine Bransford Fisher, "Two for One in Vocational Education," *Illinois Teacher*, Vol. 18, No. 1 (Sept.–Oct. 1974), pp. 41–44.

[29] Job Focus: Executive Housekeeper, An Expanding Career Field," *Forecast for Home Economics*, Vol. 23, No. 4 (Dec. 1977), p. 46.

[30] Sponsored by the National Council for Homemaker–Home Health Aide Services, Inc., 67 Irving Place, New York, N.Y. 10003.

tal, a nursing home, or other facility, while a family member is hospitalized or later, during a convalescent period.

Home Call Inc.[31] arranges for the discharging of home responsibilities for the elderly. A home economist in the community supervises the service. High school students and other available persons may take care of the home periodically, do shopping, prepare some meals, take the person to a doctor, see to other health-care needs, mow the lawn, be a companion, or render whatever service an elderly person needs.

In the consumer service area, assistance is needed by food companies in neighborhood surveys, taste tests in a bus terminal or other busy thoroughfare, or home tests of new products. Helping to man an exhibit booth at a convention that is highlighting new foods or new angles on familiar products is a good learning experience. Sometimes this work takes place in supermarkets, where samples and information are dispensed about new foods, detergents, cleaning agents, small equipment, and a host of other products.

Homemaking as a Vocation

Home economics has to demonstrate again and again that homemaking is a vocation. One question to be answered is what the financial worth is of the services provided by family members.[32] Computing the possible wages based on prevailing hourly wage rates for the various types of work done in the home is one way of calculating the value of such services, which amounts to thousands of dollars. Although not included in the gross national product at this time, it is estimated that the GNP could be increased by one fourth if unpaid household work was included.[33] Nelson raises the question whether the value of homemaking should be calculated solely on household chores. Other contributions of the homemaker and other family members are the management of all resources and the physical, intellectual, and emotional development of all family members at all ages through companionship, supervision, and concern. The ideas advanced here can be fruitful for further discussion and action.

Developing a clear-cut definition of a homemaker would be helpful. FHA/HERO chapters have made a challenging contribution through their project "Who Is the Homemaker?"[34] The idea projected is that it is everyone who lives in a home and has responsibilities for that

[31] Home Call Inc., 20 N. Court St., Frederick, Md. 21701.

[32] Kathryn Walker and Margaret E. Woods, *Time Use: A Measure of Household Production of Family Goods and Services* (Washington, D.C.: Center for the Family, American Home Economics Association, 1976), Ch. 1.

[33] Helen Y. Nelson, "The Unpriced Services of the Unpaid Homemaker," *American Vocational Journal,* Vol. 52, No. 7 (Oct. 1977), pp. 36–38.

[34] "Who Is the Homemaker?" *Teen Times,* Vol. 33, No. 1 (Sept.–Oct. 1977), entire issue.

home—a refreshing facelift of the former homemaker image. Students and teachers might ask themselves about next steps in this image-changing problem.

Field Experiences

Throughout the vocational program in home economics, provision should be made for many actual experiences, such as observation, partial participation, and full participation. Not only is personal and professional development enhanced, but the transition into the working world is smoother. Some in-school laboratory experience may be provided in facilities such as the school cafeteria and the nursery school. These experiences must be supplemented with other experiences in a well-rounded program. Some students are sent to an area vocational school that cooperates with the local school for actual occupational training. The area school generally serves several schools in the area. Joint agreements may be made between two or more schools to share the resources so that students in occupational education will have an effective program.

In some work–study programs, students have an opportunity to study and to have work experience in the community. Scharf and Wilson[35] make a plea that work experience not be confined to economically deprived students and that the occupational skills be coupled with the human development of each student. Boston High School, for example, whose student body is composed largely of dropouts, troublemakers, grade repeaters, and parolees, planned an exciting work–study program[36] that had three main goals: to improve academic abilities, to strengthen student motivation, and to help students develop salable job skills and desirable attitudes toward work. With dedicated teachers and cooperative businesses, the project results in each student's gaining what is comparable to three years of working experience. Upon graduation, a job is assured, attendance in school has improved measurably, and the spirit of the students and their active role in the program have been inspiring. Most important is that the students return to society's mainstream and make a contribution.

Job Analysis

A detailed description of each home-economics–related occupation is necessary for planning. Such a description includes a typical work

[35] Peter Scharf and Thomas Wilson, "Work Experience: A Redefinition," in Galen Saylor et al., "The High School/Promises to Keep," *Theory into Practice,* Vol. 15, No. 3 (June 1976), pp. 205–213.

[36] Jane Hauser Hoyt, "The Story of Hard-Nosed Boston High," *American Education,* Vol. 12, No. 5 (May 1976), pp. 11–14.

plan by hours, days, weeks, months, and year; duties fully delineated; types of equipment that will be used; the amount of standing, sitting, stooping, and other physical exertion; parts of the job that are repetitious and parts that vary; and amount and kind of supervision given. The kind of decision making that is necessary is important. The environment—indoors, outdoors, hot, noisy, air-conditioned, or odorous—might be included as well as the kind of work location, such as behind a counter. Age, physical requirements, kind of preparation needed, such required materials as uniforms or tools, and union membership requirements are other points to be added.

Ladders and lattices related to an occupational field are helpful to student and teacher. Identifications, such as entry-level, semiskilled, skilled, semiprofessional, managerial, or professional, represent the ladders.

Evaluation of Student Progress

A teacher will wish to determine the degree to which the behavioral objectives have been reached for the group and for each student. Students should be encouraged to evaluate themselves. Checklists of competencies, short written reports about their work experience, talking into a tape recorder about their progress, getting reports from supervisors in the field, laboratory performance, evidence of personality development from comments of other students and from teacher observation, and the employability of students are some of the sources of evidence for evaluation. The adequacy of the facilities and the community work centers for preparing students should also be evaluated.

Plans for the future should be based on the information gained. Are new programs needed? Are there students in the school who are not being reached? Are there adult groups in need of a course to improve their potential for being employed? Have all avenues for recruiting dropouts been surveyed? Are there ways to cooperate with teachers of other areas of vocational education, such as distributive education for the preparation of students for jobs in business? Are there gaps in the public relations programs? Have comprehensive records been maintained for purposes of accountability and of selling the program? What is the plan for the follow-up graduates?

Transition to the World of Work

The traditional prediction is that a young person—boy or girl—achieves adult identity through his or her first job.[37] The severe youth

[37] Robert J. Havighurst, "More Youth Than Jobs," in Ralph W. Tyler (ed.), *From Youth to Constructive Adult Life: The Role of the Public School* (Berkeley, Calif.: McCutchan, 1978), Ch. 8.

unemployment has challenged this fulfillment of a cultural dictum. Some youth find part-time jobs. In the regular market, however, according to a review of the literature by Barton,[38] two thirds to three fourths of the employers do not employ anyone in a regular job until the ages of twenty or twenty-one years. What will sociey and education do with youth during the period from high school graduation until reaching this age?

Other problems, according to Barton, are that the *local labor information* is inadequate, although the national information from the Bureau of Labor Statistics is highly accurate and efficient. *Placement services* for this age level are practically nonexistent. A shortage of *counseling services* is evident, especially for the non-college-bound. The transition from school to work is not easy.

The Special or Handicapped Student

The preparation of the special or handicapped student for work is another challenge and is mandated in vocational education. Godia[39] gives a number of good suggestions. A personal commitment by the teacher to help these students will influence the entire program. Looking at each area in home-economics–related occupation education to determine where these special students may develop skills for a job is one of the first steps. What can students do sitting down, for example? What kind of simple equipment may be improvised? These students should be prepared for entry-level jobs, but the teacher should also look for students who may progress beyond this stage. They should be prepared for concrete working situations as fully as possible. These students may take more of the teacher's time, but with the use of volunteers and other students, plus patience, the task can be done.

The teacher may work with the special education specialist for assistance in teaching these students. Supervisors in the field may require some in-service education. If the situation is discussed with the advisory board, perhaps they can help to prepare the way for these students to get jobs.

Special vocational youth clubs[40] have been formed to encourage these students. The Coordinated Vocational Academic Education program (CVAE) in Georgia is designed to meet the special needs of potential dropouts through the interaction of academics and the vocational laboratories. An extension of these clubs is the Vocational

[38] Paul E. Barton, "Problems of Youth in the Labor Market," in Ralph W. Tyler (ed.), *From Youth to Constructive Adult Life: The Role of the Public School* (Berkeley, Calif.: McCutchan, 1978), Ch. 9.

[39] Louis Godia, "Program Changes to Accommodate Handicapped Students," *American Vocational Journal,* Vol. 53, No. 3 (March 1978), pp. 29–32.

[40] Ruth Gibson, "New Kid on the Block: Youth Clubs for Special Needs Students," *American Vocational Journal,* Vol. 52, No. 6 (Sept. 1977), pp. 34–36.

Figure 17–7 The special or handicapped student can be prepared for work.

Education Awareness Program (VOCA), which provides leadership and citizenship enrichment through school and community activities in school newspapers, school beautification projects, lunchroom cleanups, and the like, to give only a few examples of the many endeavors. Over 6,500 students in Georgia belong to VOCA.

The Teacher

What kind of teacher is best suited for the programs described? Home economics has been confronted with the problem of identifying similarities and differences in consumer and homemaking education and occupational programs.[41] Sumner contends that teaching processes and techniques and curriculum are the same for each program but that the basic goals differ. The consumer–homemaking teacher prepares for the vocation of homemaking and the occupational teacher for wage earning.

In the preparation of the teacher of home-economics–related occupations, an opportunity for actual experiences in the working world is important. Here the teacher will acquire competencies that will be taught to students, as well as a knowledge of the working world. Additional awareness of organization, financing, layouts, personnel, employer–employee relations, customers, profits, and other facets of the business and institutional world seems imperative.

Suggestions for Consumer and Homemaking Programs

The innovative teacher will discover ways to incorporate education for the world of work in every area of the consumer and homemaking program. An examination of the meaning of work to a student, to the family, to the community, and to the nation can be quite fruitful. Using the discussion method, students can share meanings, attitudes, problems, feelings, and other reactions to work. An analysis of what makes work pleasant or unpleasant can be valuable. Examining work choices and the reasons for the choices is a good experience. Looking realistically at the world of work—the kinds of work available, the preparation needed, the personal charcteristics required, the compensation, and so on—is another suggestion. Above all, sharpening student perceptions about the place of work in their total living pattern and the contribution of each person's work to the betterment of society is urgent.

Inside or outside of the school, work experiences can be simulated. In the foods laboratory, foods might be tested as they are in test kitchens. The same can be done for fabrics or ready-to-wear garments. Helping in the nursery school or kindergarten will give information about the work of a child-care aide. The teacher should survey the community for other experiences. Again this experience might parallel the study of a subject, such as child care, foods, or clothing construction. A series of posters depicting professional and nonprofessional careers in home economics might be used for class

[41] Sue Sumner, "The Transition from Teaching Consumer Homemaking to Occupational Home Economics," *Illinois Teacher*, Vol. 27, No. 2 (Nov.–Dec. 1977), pp. 19–91.

discussions, as a resource for students exploring careers, or for bulletin boards. A description of each career might accompany the illustration.

Studying want ads, visiting an employment agency, talking to a personnel officer, making out an application, having an interview for a summer job, and similar experiences help to prepare a student for the world of work.

SUGGESTIONS FOR FURTHER LEARNING

1. A number of important issues related to jobs and work are raised in Chapters 8, 9, and 10 of:

   Tyler, Ralph W. (ed.). *From Youth to Constructive Adult Life: The Role of the Public School.* Berkeley, Calif.: McCutchan, 1978.

   Read these chapters and select what are, in your opinion, the most important issues. Discuss them with your classmates and revise them, adapt them, delete them, or add them to your former ideas.
2. From time to time, vocational education comes under attack. Read the following references and find some on your own. Clarify your own stand.

   Eggington, Everett. "Is Vocational Education Meeting Its Objectives?" *Phi Delta Kappan,* **59** (Apr. 1978), 533–534.

   Harriman, Lynda C. "Changing Roles: Implications for Home Economics." *Journal of Home Economics,* **59** (March 1977), 12.

   Rogers, David. "Vocational and Career Education: A Critique and Some New Directions." *Teachers College Record,* **74** (May 1973), 471–511.

   Wirth, Arthur G. "Issues Affecting Education and Work in the Eighties: Efficiency Versus Industrial Democracy, A Historical Perspective." *Teachers College Record,* **79** (Sept. 1977), 55–67.

18

Professional Preparation and Development

Home economics educators have been exposed to and influenced by teachers and teaching at an early age and for at least a total of sixteen years.[1] Some of these experiences have been rewarding, others may have been negative, but all have left an impression. The educational behavior of a home economist in a teaching situation will reflect motives, goals, and concepts that have emerged from her/his personal experience of teachers. Home economists should analyze the meanings of teaching in a very personal manner and think about what teaching is and why they hold these beliefs. Is teaching a job, interaction with students for optimum development, a highly structured process, or a social commitment, or does it allow of other interpretations?

TEACHING AS A CAREER

In the decades ahead, teaching as a career will reflect the massive changes predicted for education, including increased instruction by computer and other technological aids, new emphases in curriculum, and shifting patterns in the operation of schools, according to Ryan and Cooper.[2] Many alternative approaches are being considered. After years of acute shortages of teachers, the 1970s ushered in an era

[1] Benjamin D. Wright, "Our Reasons for Teaching," *Theory into Practice,* Vol. 16, No. 4 (Oct. 1977), pp. 225–230.

[2] Keith Ryan and James M. Cooper, *Those Who Can, Teach* (Boston: Houghton, 1972), p. 144.

of surpluses. Students who consider teaching must realize that it is a competitive career. Home economics has excellent potential for broadening its base for teaching possibilities. There are opportunities to teach in day-care centers, to work with retarded children and their parents in the area of personal and family living, to teach the ten million or more handicapped homemakers to reach greater independence in their family responsibilities, to enlarge the ways in which adults are reached in continuing education, to help the twenty million or more senior citizens with their problems as homemakers and consumers, to teach abroad, or to work with the producers of technological aids in the preparation of software, such as home economics programs for the computer. These are only a few of the positions that students may wish to consider in addition to teaching at the elementary, middle, and high school levels.

The structure of the profession demands scrutiny. At present no career line exists for a teacher. Excellence is usually rewarded by promotion out of the classroom into administration or supervision. Job requirements present a problem. A beginning teacher is expected to be highly skilled in all aspects of teaching and human relations and to continue in these responsibilities during the ensuing years. The demands on the beginning teacher are awesome, and the prospects for promotion of an experienced teacher may be deadening. A few schools are experimenting with different categories of teachers with different job requirements and salary scales. All are participants in classroom teaching, but some use their leadership competencies in an area such as long-range planning, whereas others may be in charge of in-service programs. Students and beginning teachers may wish to look into the implications of these possibilities for the future of education in relation to their career plans.

Characteristics

Teaching, according to Fischer,[3] can be frustrating, fatiguing, and demanding. Teachers are the butt of many unkind jokes and are criticized endlessly. Yet, when the problems of the world in general and of youth in particular become especially critical, people in every walk of life turn to that important person, the teacher, for answers. A high value is placed on the educated person in our society, and the need for superior teaching is urgent.

When a student teacher or a new teacher begins to be concerned about the choice of a career, he or she might ask a number of ques-

[3] John H. Fischer, "Why Teach?" Guest Editorial, *NEA Journal,* Vol. 51, No. 4 (Apr. 1962), p. 31.

tions. What would a perfect job be like? Write down its attributes, and match them against teaching. What are the results? Is teaching the best choice?

Other considerations might be, Is teaching a stepping stone to something else or is it a lifetime career? Will this kind of work be as appealing five or ten years from now? What unique personal contributions can be brought to teaching? Does being a teacher fit in with other personal plans?

A teacher or a student teacher also might ask, Am I competent for the job? What are my strengths and weaknesses in the three components of home-economics teacher preparation: general education, professional education, and specialized education in home economics content?[4] Do I have a clear concept of the job's requirements? What would be my relations to the community? To whom is the home economics teacher responsible on the job? What interrelationships are important? Am I enthusiastic about the job?

A clear-cut notion of what success (or failure) on the job means is helpful. Consider the special feelings, senses, equipment, abilities, and experiences associated with teaching home economics. What kind of pressures can be expected? Will these pressures be a challenge or a frustration?

The Future

What can student and beginning teachers expect of the new roles to be assumed by teachers in the education of the future? In the past, the teacher served as an entire instructional system—teaching all aspects of a subject; assuming extra responsibilities, such as lunchroom, hall, and playground duties; and operating his/her own technological equipment, in addition to many other functions. In contrast, this new teacher will become the director of an instructional system, according to Ryan.[5] Having at her/his disposal many instructional aids, such as simulators, videotapes, and computer-based learning systems, the teacher must be prepared to be a skillful diagnostician who is aware of the abilities and potentials of the students and of the system of instruction to be applied, with the greatest sensitivity and intelligence. Supporting the teacher in this activity will be specialists and paraprofessionals.

[4] Home Economics Teacher Educators, *Competencies for Home Economics Teachers* (Ames: Iowa State U.P., 1978), p. v.

[5] Kevin A. Ryan, "Where Are We Going and How Do We Get There?" in Roy A. Edelfelt (ed.), *The Teacher and His Staff: Differentiating Teaching Roles* (Washington, D.C.: National Commission on Teacher Education and Professional Standards, 1969), pp. 76–77.

STUDENT TEACHING, FIELDWORK, OR APPRENTICESHIP

Student teaching or similar preparation is an essential and integral part of the preparation of a teacher. In addition, the teacher–educator and the students must give consideration to the kind of experiences a student has had in and out of school prior to student teaching and the impact of these experiences on educational maturity.

Pre-Student-Teaching Experiences

The trend is to plan teaching experiences prior to student teaching for a number of reasons. Students have a chance to gain insights into their liking of and feeling about teaching. An opportunity is provided a student to discover strengths and weaknesses, both personally and professionally, in order to attempt necessary changes.

It is helpful if each student analyzes experiences that have contributed to effective teaching and those that might be valuable in the future. Do experiences include assisting with Girl or Boy Scouts or

Figure 18–1 Prospective teachers will find that experience with small children is broadening. (U.S. Department of Labor)

Camp Fire Girls, teaching Sunday or church school, supervising playground activities, camp counseling, or working with other children or youth groups? Was there any experience in teaching adults? In high school, did the students have opportunities to be a teacher, media, or other type of aide? Has there been any experience with handicapped individuals?

What kind of part-time jobs were learning experiences, such as clerical work, checkout work, baby-sitting, delivering papers, or yard work? Some students have their own business, in which they make and sell something such as food, accessories, or crafts. Learning to work with others, judging people, and assuming responsibility are among other benefits to be derived from these opportunities.

Knowledge of the community is helpful, such as knowing community services, particularly for the poor; the way a community governs itself; community programs; beautification projects; and cultural emphasis. Being alert to such problems as poverty, divorce, crime, child abuse, and teenage pregnancy and how the community is handling them can be valuable information in a teaching position later, no matter what its geographical location.

How many home economics programs have been observed? This might include classroom observation at different grade levels, the education of adults through extension, community agencies, or evening classes in high schools or through other auspices, and senior-citizen education programs. How is teaching done through television or radio?

Students who do not plan to do educational work in classroom situations may have experiences in educational work in hospitals, clinics, department stores, advertising agencies, public relations firms, food services, family or home economics magazines, social service agencies, public utilities, home economics departments, business, or other areas. Some of these experiences are desirable for all home economics educators.

In many colleges, professional experiences begin in the freshman year in connection with regular courses.[6] Students may observe or work with children, youth, or adults in community agencies or institutions. Other activities may be a familiarity with the markets that a consumer uses or interviewing families about pertinent areas such as grocery shopping, home management, or interior decoration. Home experiences during vacation or the summer that correlate with college laboratory experiences can strengthen areas of specialization, such as in food, clothing, consumer education, child development, or family and personal relations. Flexibility in planning is usually encouraged so that a student may concentrate on particular needs.

[6] Ryan and Cooper, op. cit., pp. 242–246.

Evaluation is built into the planning so that progress in learning may be determined and new needs surveyed.

Transition

Bridges between courses and student teaching have been suggested by Ryan.[7] Beginning with paraprofessional tasks, the college student is given the advantages of assuming some adult responsibilities and of being placed in contact with pupils. Next, the college student may serve as a resource person for pupils, helping them with references, written papers, or playing educational games. Progressing to teacher's aide is the next step. Assignment to one teacher or a team of teachers will give the student a working relationship with experienced teachers and firsthand experiences in observing and studying teachers' roles. Concurrently with these experiences, a college course may simulate a hypothetical home economics class that concentrates on common teaching problems, such as pupils' errors in preparing a recipe or sewing, the problems of a slow learner, student disinterest, or a parent who complains about a grade received by his daughter.

The curriculum may include certain clinical exercises in a school, such as following a student through all his/her classes for a day, studying a problem student in depth, and discussing perceptions with the teacher or guidance counselor. Looking for evidences of thinking in one student during a class period and discussing the experience with the teacher is another possibility. The results of these clinical exercises might be further analyzed on campus with other prospective teachers. Tutoring one or several students is helpful in identifying learning problems. Establishing and executing a plan for solving the problems and evaluating the entire experience follow. Becoming acquainted with a student and his or her problems will bring many insights to the future teacher.

Microteaching has proved to be exceptionally valuable in preparing students for the full responsibility of a classroom. Videotaping, so the student may view herself/himself alone or with other students, brings strong reactions and much discussion. Depending upon the previous experiences and the maturity of the students, it is suggested that each student teach a small group of other students in the college classroom to gain confidence and valuable feedback. This type of teaching may be done also with adults or teenagers in community work undertaken by the student. Frequently focus is on a specific skill, such as questioning, leading a discussion, or giving a demonstration.

[7] Ryan, op. cit., pp. 80–82.

Students may consider the potential of other college experiences, such as working with a club or the student council, working on the college newspaper or magazine, assisting with freshman orientation, and presiding at meetings or giving reports. Outside of the classroom, participation in political activities, consumer groups, or other community improvement movements promotes the personal development of the student. Having aesthetic experiences will make one a more interesting person to students. Working in the ghetto, helping the aged and the handicapped, and serving as aides in hospitals, orphanages, or other institutions are valuable experiences. Experiences that require some responsibility, that lead to the development of skills that provide encounters with real people and real situations, and that require problem solving will contribute to the personal and professional development of the student.

Purposes of Student Teaching or Apprenticeship

The primary purpose of student teaching is to provide student teachers with the opportunity to assume the teacher role in an actual teaching situation under the guidance of a skilled, practicing or master teacher. During this experience, the student teacher has a chance to add evidence in determining if this is the kind of work she/he would like to do, and if it is, to gain some insights into probable success in future teaching. Through such firsthand experience, it is hoped that her/his philosophy of education will be refined and made functional and that her/his value system will be clarified to a greater degree. It is hoped, too, that a better understanding will be developed of students, of the processes of learning, of the effectiveness of various teaching methods and materials, of the use of techniques of evaluation, and of the interrelatedness of the various kinds of knowledge. Student teaching is a period of exploration and of continuous self-evaluation, during which the student teacher will be able to determine needs for further study and development. In many respects, the first-year teacher is merely continuing student teaching, except that she/he has more autonomy and more responsibility.

Opportunities to work and think with many different individuals and groups, including students, teachers, administrators, parent groups, and civic groups, and to test the effectiveness of her/his ability to communicate and her/his awareness of the need for and the ways to create good public relations are important.

The student teacher or apprentice should have the experience of a teacher's full working day and should be able to see the relationship of each day's work to the plans for the week, the semester, and the school year. She/he should become familiar with the many routine responsibilities that are part of teaching, including the preparation of

Figure 18–2 Observing and assisting a nutritionist in a clinic is a valuable experience. (National Center for Health Statistics, Rockville, Md.)

reports, business matters, faculty meetings, class preparation, the ordering of supplies, and other managerial responsibilities.

Other home economics educators may be provided with experiences that simulate the situation in which they plan to work. This experience may be in dietetics, business, social welfare, extension, public utilities, or other areas. Broad experiences in the field will enhance later preparation.

STEPS IN STUDENT TEACHING, FIELD EXPERIENCES, OR APPRENTICESHIP

Each institution has its own method of placing students in schools, hospitals, extension centers, businesses, utility companies, and the like, requirements for entering this phase of education, and plans, organization, and supervision of the actual experience. Certain steps, however, are common to most student teaching or apprentice experiences.

The first step is for the student teacher to become acquainted with the supervising teacher and with the school. In the home economics rooms, she or he might observe what equipment is available and where it is located, what the routines are, how the teaching is conducted, what the students are like, and what general atmosphere prevails. Note, too, how the teachers seem to relate to one another and what the means of control are. Other observations include what is put into the display cases and what kinds of materials are on the bulletin boards. Through observations and through talking to students in a general way much is learned about what the school seems to value.

During the first days and weeks, a student will help the supervising teacher in any possible way, perhaps by getting out supplies and teaching aids. In some schools, the next step may be leading part of a class, such as giving a demonstration, showing a filmstrip, or helping to supervise during a laboratory period. The student progresses from teaching one full class to additional classes, ultimately to a full day's teaching, at a rate adjusted to increasing competency.

In addition to these experiences in the home economics department, the student teacher might assist with out-of-class events, such as clubs, FHA/HERO, hall or cafeteria duty, assembly programs, and field trips. Attending parties, sports events, faculty meetings, or advisory council sessions may prove valuable. Every student teacher should try to discover other opportunities for adding to personal development.

Many persons are interested in helping the student teacher to have a superior teaching experience. Regarding his/her progress, the student teacher will have periodic conferences with the supervising teacher, and from time to time, her/his college supervisor will also visit and discuss development. The principal and other school administrators may observe and offer valuable suggestions, and the city, county, or state supervisor may also make visits.

Figure 18–3 Working with FHA/HERO is important.

The First Day

The first day is critical in the minds of students and beginning teachers. It is quite common for a person to have anxiety prior to a new experience, particularly if the experience is an important career step. Most of these worries are groundless, for everyone is ready to offer a friendly and sympathetic helping hand to student and beginning teachers.

Good advice to the new teacher is to be professional from the first day. Begin a daily diary, which will be very helpful in the analysis of professional growth, weaknesses, strengths, and the steps that can be taken for improvement. If the young teacher recognizes quickly that students usually know much less than she/he does, anxiety will be greatly eased. The first day is only the gateway to the total experience of student teaching; it is what follows that is really critical.

Before beginning the first teaching day, the novice teacher will presumably have become familiar with all aspects of the classroom or classrooms, the school's routines, and, of course, class organization plans. Be in the room before class arrives, greet the students cheerfully, be especially well groomed and attractively dressed, and generally create the impression of being, and intending to remain, in charge. Many a teacher has lost the interest and the control of students by being inefficient, indifferent, and haphazard on the first day.

Handling Problems

Of concern to student and beginning teachers is discipline. Here are a few practical suggestions. The new teacher should learn the student's names quickly, organize the seating and working arrangements to facilitate control, give more do's than don't's, stand or sit where an eye can be kept on every student, turn her/his back on the class as little as possible (have the students do the writing on the blackboard), anticipate difficulties before they arise (stop petty misbehaviors in an informal yet businesslike way), control emotions, try to remain calm even when annoyed, bring into participation any student whose attention seems to be wavering, and remember that good planning and stimulating class sessions encourage classroom control. Student–teacher relationships are reflected in each other's behavior.[8] When a teacher "loses control" of a class, it is the students, or some students, who have gained control. Sometimes it is assumed that teachers act and students respond. That is an oversimplification. Students are usually not passive. A teacher must be expert in group dynamics.

[8] Phillip C. Schlecty and Helen E. Atwood, "The Student–Teacher Relationship," *Theory into Practice,* Vol. 16, No. 4 (Oct. 1977), p. 285.

THE BEGINNING TEACHER

Each fall there are thousands of beginning teachers. Most are filled with hope and expectations but also with qualms about the new role. The classroom, once so familiar in many ways, takes on new and different dimensions. By doing careful planning, by being well informed, and by having a workable philosophy, the new teacher can keep the first year from being the ordeal so often depicted.

Sizing Up the Teaching Situation

Many factors have direct and indirect effects on a teaching situation, and a careful analysis of them will give the young teacher greater insight into the community, the school, and himself or herself. One of the most potent influences is the value system prevailing in the community. What are the dominant positions in regard to politics, community improvement, religion, art, morals, education, civil rights, involvement in world affairs, and the like? Who holds these positions? Are values democratically oriented? Are the positions inclined to be liberal, conservative, or neither?

What is the educational climate of the school? Is there an eagerness to learn and to experiment and a spirit of cooperation? Are the facilities designed to encourage learning? Do parent–teacher groups flourish? Are dropouts a problem? Is the school a good place for students and teachers to grow?

In every situation, some individuals or groups have more power than others. This phenomenon is evident in the administration, on the school board, on the faculty, in the student body, and in the community at large. Who are the most influential members of the faculty? What is a new teacher's position with them? Power groups shift from time to time, and it is important to identify them and to consider how they may affect one's teaching role.

A careful exploration of the way changes are made is valuable. Who is involved—students, teachers, administrators, individuals in the community, others? What is the impact of the state legislature? Are teachers informed about contemplated changes? To what extent is the home economics teacher free to plan for and use her/his facilities, program, and general organization? An examination of the areas in which changes take place is equally important. Is the emphasis on curriculum, student behavior, rules and regulations, and policy making, or on other aspects of school functioning? The frequency and nature of the changes are pertinent.

A consideration of the responsibilities of various persons is also helpful. Are the functional distinctions of teacher and administrator clear-cut? What are the functions of the school board, the guidance personnel, and the student government? What can be expected of the custodial staff? Are there any guidelines about professional and community commitments?

How is the school organized and operated? Is the administration democratic, autocratic, or laissez-faire? Are the policies established by teachers put into practice? How is the administration's efficiency rated? Is considerable effort spent by administrators and faculty in manipulating, propagandizing, informing, or cooperating with the community? What is the attitude of the school toward problems of the home economics department?

What is the work of the guidance department in the school? Does it assist students who demand attention beyond the amount that the classroom teacher can give? Does it control the enrollment in the home economics department? Do its counselors appear to be well informed about home economics so that they can advise students accordingly? Does it give information about students entering home economics classes so that the teacher may help them better? What is the attitude of the teachers toward the guidance department?

Day-by-Day Teaching

No two days of teaching will be exactly alike; each day will have its joys and its problems. But it behooves each teacher to take the long look—to find evidence of progress and to analyze the "whys and the wherefores."

Every teacher can expect classes to have a bad day now and then. She/he may find that Mondays, rainy days, or the day before or after a holiday, a sports event, a party, or other such deviations from regular routine have an effect on student behavior. The observant teacher can learn when to expect such days and to plan in advance for them. Those days may be best for quiet work; reading a story; browsing in books; looking at pictures, filmstrips, or slides for special enrichment; playing quiz games; or perhaps something more lively. Once such a day has passed, it is sensible to return to regular activities and not to refer to the slump, according to Gans.[9] Of course, the teacher, too, will have off days, with special plans for doing the best under the circumstances.

Finding time to give individual help, which is very important in student development, may be difficult for the busy young teacher, hence she/he should encourage students to make their problems known and should allow time for helping them. Special times may have to be set aside, such as a question-and-answer session at the beginning of a class period. If many needs are expressed, it may be

[9] Roma Gans, "How to Get 'Off Days' Back on the Track," *Grade Teacher*, Vol. 83, No. 8 (Apr. 1966), pp. 50–51.

necessary to incorporate them into the class work in order to find the solutions to these problems. Another possibility is to plan certain periods when students work individually on what Gans[10] calls what-I-need-most projects. The teacher must display a consistently reassuring attitude toward those asking for help. She/he must assume that students reaching for assistance truly need and want it. Volunteers or student aids may be useful at such times.

Learning how to handle criticism from persons who are uninformed about or unfamiliar with home economics or who have had unfortunate experiences in a home economics classroom is pertinent. These critics may indicate disapproval in many ways. They may avow that boys and girls are best taught about homemaking at home. Some—notably school board members—may believe that home economics is too expensive to be taught in school. Answering this charge may require a comparison study of pupil costs in home economics with similar costs in science, music, industrial arts, or other more-or-less comparable subjects.

Teachers must realize that it is necessary to live with critics—to be ignored, after all, would be worse, for that would mean that the public is unaware of home economics. Criticism should be thought of as a source of strength instead of demoralization. It can be a challenge to revise, to reconsider, and to improve many aspects of our profession. Teachers should try to meet unfair criticism calmly, with facts and tactful arguments. Sometimes a touch of humor can encourage enlightenment.

Some Instructional Approaches

A new teacher has much to learn about the students for whom he/she has responsibility. From many sources—standardized test scores, cumulative folders, personal observations, teachers' lounge discussions, the school nurse, comments of students about themselves and other students, and the viewpoints of guidance counselors—certain expectations may be formed, according to Beattie and Deichmann.[11] Teachers should keep an open mind about the potential of any student, because research[12] indicates that teacher expectations can affect pupil performance. When teachers were led to expect greater intellectual growth in certain children, these children, although chosen at random, demonstrated IQ gains beyond those of

[10] Roma Gans, "How to Give Them That Priceless Gift—Individual Help," *Grade Teacher,* Vol. 82, No. 3 (Nov. 1965), pp. 23, 44.

[11] Ian Beattie and John Deichmann, "Teacher Expectations," *Instructor,* Vol. 81, No. 2 (Oct. 1971), p. 19.

[12] W. V. Beez, "Influence of Biased Psychological Reports on Teacher Behavior and Pupil Performance," in M. W. Miles and W. W. Charters, Jr. (eds.), *Learning in Social Settings* (Boston: Allyn, 1970).

the children not selected. When teachers were led to believe that children were bright, their grades improved. It is interesting and somewhat frightening to contemplate what the results might have been if the teachers had been lead to expect poor performances from selected students. In other words, misplaced expectations about the ability of a student can be destructive. Sometimes expectations are communicated in negative ways, such as "That is better than I expected," or "That is good—for you." Evidence points to the desirable results of believing that a student has greater potential than she or he may show.

A new teacher may be asked to use instructional techniques that are new to her/him. In an ungraded or open school, for example, students may come not from one class but from several levels. Often students may be assigned to classes because of common interests or for other educational reasons. Students usually enjoy working with persons of different ages. In some schools, this is called *vertical teaching.*[13]

Team teaching is common in many schools. The primary goals of team teaching are to do a better job of individualizing instruction, to develop independence in learning among students, to deal more effectively with the differences among students and their styles of learning, and to plan a broader, richer, and more challenging program of instruction. To accomplish these ends, many teaching techniques are employed. These include large-group instruction, small-group teaching for five to ten students, remedial work, independent study, the use of community resources, and the use of instructional materials and technology. There is a challenge to develop and to experiment with different approaches, techniques, and innovations. The stimulation of working with others on the same problems can lead to professional development and to meaningful curriculum development. Team teaching has considerable potential for home economics.

Many beginning teachers will be assigned to schools in the ghetto. For the past decade, teachers in these schools have been increasingly under fire because of their inability to educate the children of the slums and to provide them with the essentials for success in school and eventually in society. Home economics teachers generally have been successful because their teaching can be adapted to the specific needs of these students. The problems to be combated include a high rate of absences—approximately 40 per cent of the students do not come to school on any given day. There are racial and political conflicts. Vandalism and theft may be daily occurrences; students often

[13] Roy R. Wilson, "We Formed a Vertical Team," *Instructor,* Vol. 79, No. 8 (Apr. 1970), p. 129.

wear coats and outer apparel throughout the day to prevent losing them. Many students are drug addicts and some are pushers. Students often live in rat- and roach-infested tenements. Many students lack the skills to perform well in school.

The situation may be highly discouraging, and obviously much patience, perseverance, and ingenuity are required. Working with these students can be very satisfying because basically they are eager to learn, have potential, and can be reached. In Thomas Jefferson High School in Brooklyn, Lorrance[14] describes how one school formed an organization called "Seekers," dedicated to the principle that beautiful relationships can exist between people if they consciously work to build them. The Seekers planned a "Love Project" as an exercise in giving and sharing. In spite of reservations voiced by the faculty, the students planned four activities: a "Cookie Fest," a "Book Fest," a "Toy Fest," and a "Music Fest." The Cookie Fest was under the auspices of the home economics department. Over eight thousand cookies (two per student) were baked by faculty and students. A student passing by the home economics room commented, "You know they smell better than pot." Students distributed the cookies during homeroom periods. Although the gifts were not received cheerfully by all students, many responded positively. The students who had baked the cookies were pleased to see other students enjoying their efforts at giving. At a later date, home economics students baked bread and took it to a neighboring high school and shared it with their students as another part of the Love Project.

For the Book Fest, faculty members and local residents donated books to give to students. Toys were collected and made for the Toy Fest and delivered to patients in a nearby hospital at holiday time. For the Music Fest, singers toured the school building, imparting the spirit of the Love Project. In one short month, the atmosphere of the school changed markedly. Other projects have been planned. These ideas may trigger other innovations for the teacher in the slums.

Experienced teachers over the years have given the new teacher hints for survival. One of them is to hang on to a sense of proportion, according to Richstone.[15] The teacher should watch for student overreactions. Some of them may reflect insecurity. An attempt to understand the student can be helpful. What is causing the undesirable behavior? Looking at a student's records, talking to her/his parents or a previous teacher, and having a conference with the student and listening to his/her story may be revealing. If there is need to reprimand a student, the teacher is wise to criticize the act and not

[14] Arleen Lorrance, "The Love Project," *Today's Education, NEA Journal,* Vol. 60, No. 6 (Sept. 1971), pp. 74–77.

[15] May Richstone, "For a Brand-New Teacher," *Instructor,* Vol. 81, No. 1 (Aug.–Sept. 1971), p. 80.

the student. The activities should be varied so that students will not become restless and inattentive.

Keeping a sense of balance is essential. Purposes may not be realized as quickly as anticipated. There may be limited resources, pressure for results, and many claims on time, but it is sensible to submit with good grace to what cannot be helped. Having a contemplative mind as well as an active mind is useful. Not everything, especially in important matters, has to be decided in a split second. Judgment may be deferred for several hours, or overnight when feasible. This delay permits a rehearsal of the variables and the possible solutions.

Home economics educators in nonschool situations may face similar teaching climates in their first jobs. Being well prepared during fieldwork or apprenticeship and having personal motivation and interest will enhance confidence. Effective instruction will be reflected in raising the achievement goals of students, encouraging greater cooperation among individuals and groups, developing creativity, and increasing the enjoyment of teacher and students in learning.[16]

EVALUATION

Student and beginning teachers in all areas of home economics education must adjust to the fact that they are being evaluated, that is, watched and judged. It is easier for a teacher to accept evaluation if she/he is aware of the ways in which the evaluating is being done. Obviously being evaluated are attitude toward teaching, psychological maturity, ability to adjust, cooperativeness, and readiness to accept constructive criticism and suggestions. Originality in applying knowledge of the subject matter; ability to maintain classroom control, as well as students' reactions to the teacher and to the climate of the classroom; and knowledge of and ability to understand students and to adapt to their special needs are included. Other criteria are personal appearance and demeanor, personality, enthusiasm, and eagerness to learn and to maintain good relations with others.

But the teacher should also expect that observers will want to know if she/he is encouraging students to ask questions; stimulating them to find answers; using many materials; and encouraging students to be creative and original. Helping students to feel that they are a vital part of class activities and organization, assisting them to achieve their level of ability, and recognizing their uniqueness are also marks of good teaching. The good teacher also varies and adjusts experiences and assignments to individual differences and puts to work the principles of learning; both are equally important.

No student teacher or beginning teacher ought to feel that she/he

[16] William W. Wattenberg, "The Ecology of Classroom Behavior," *Theory into Practice,* Vol. 16, No. 4 (Oct. 1977), p. 256.

has to be a paragon. It is extremely important, however, for teachers to look closely at their ideas. They must know what they believe in, the stage of their professional development, and what direction they are taking. In the classroom, a teacher cannot avoid communicating personal attitudes and goals.

Competencies for Home Economics Teachers[17] may be used as a basis for certification and for evaluation by local schools, school administrators, state supervisors, and others. This document was designed primarily for a home economics teacher entering the profession. Increased depth in professional education and competencies that develop with service may be necessary for the evaluation of experienced teachers.

A very young teacher will also evaluate the extent to which he/she has helped each student to achieve utmost potential. The complexity and interrelatedness of the world appears to hinder this goal. Yet linked with the very forces that tend to mold persons into conformity are clamors for greater creativity, uniqueness, and vitality. The more involved the world around us becomes, the more pressing is the need for diversity and for individuality.

Closely related to their individuality is the teacher's concern about students' excellence. The demand for talent is especially urgent in our technological, affluent, and internationally oriented society. It is hoped that everyone will soon uphold the idea that each individual should be encouraged to achieve excellence, with no limitations on the area of endeavor. Because research findings frequently indicate that the home is a powerful influence on the development of excellence, home economics, with its concern for the improvement of home and family living, may find it worthwhile to give special scrutiny to this matter.

Teachers cannot confine their actions to the classroom. They must be sensitive to their responsibilities as citizens and to the traditions of the nation, must understand and feel democratic tenets deeply, and must consider themselves public servants who are dedicated to helping others build a good society. Only to the extent that a new teacher can identify with these roles and display competency in their fulfillment can she/he be certain that the choice of teaching as a life profession is right for her/him.

SUGGESTIONS FOR FURTHER LEARNING

1. Keep a daily diary or reaction journal during your student teaching or first months of teaching. Record from day to day the following:
   a. Aspects of your teaching in which you excelled, and why.
   b. Aspects of teaching in which you did less well, and why.

[17] Op. cit., pp. vi–vii.

   c. Incidents highlighting your relations with students and an analysis of your strengths and weaknesses in dealing with students.
   d. What you consider your most important problem and how you propose to solve it.
2. Write a short story or a poem or draw a series of sketches or cartoons that depict your dreams and hopes as a teacher. Read for suggestions: Dorothy Needham, "What Is It Like to Be a Teacher?," *Teacher,* Vol. 90, No. 6 (Feb. 1973), pp. 62–64.
3. Analyze experiences that are pertinent to your teaching. Consider the possibilities of using of these experiences in your résumé.

19

Public Relations

What home economics does and represents must be publicized, for the strength and effectiveness of a home economics program depends to a large degree on the understanding and support it receives from the school, institutions, businesses, agencies, and the community. Abraham Lincoln observed that "Public opinion is everything—with it, nothing can fail; without it, nothing can succeed." In this age of mass communications and fast selling, the best program in the world cannot wait to be discovered. The public must be led to it.

DEFINITION

Public relations—as the name indicates—is relations with the public. In other words, public relations consists of everyday dealings with students, clients, patients, customers, teachers, administrators, individuals, and groups in the community or elsewhere. These interactions should foster an approving attitude in the public so that it will support home economics—its staff and its programs—in schools, agencies, institutions, and the mass media.

Home economics educators must distinguish between public relations and publicity. Publicity is intended to get the attention of the public. A news release about an upcoming FHA meeting is publicity, but if the story of the FHA meeting is a part of a plan to show how home economics reaches beyond the classroom for the personal and social development of students, the publicity news item becomes public relations.

MAKING PUBLIC RELATIONS WORK

The first requisite for a successful public relations program is for every home economist to have a strong and positive belief about the importance of the profession and to demonstrate this belief. Members who are indifferent to or openly negative about the profession can bring real deterioration in public relations in general and in opinions held by the members of various publics.

Public relations can succeed only with the high degree of commitment of every member of a program that is sustained, not sporadic. Communications and messages must be well conceived and presented[1] and must be evaluated continously. The assumption of a sincere, personal responsibility by each professional is needed if goals are to be reached. A realization by each member that he or she is representing home economics through words, actions, and attitude is essential. An effective program requires planning, organization, leadership, the use of many talents, and great dedication.

IDENTIFICATION OF THE PUBLIC OR PUBLICS OF HOME ECONOMICS

Home economics has many publics to consider, rather than "the public." A public consists of individuals who have common concerns or interests in such areas as economics, geography, culture, education, age, and family. A home economics educator may ask, "What does home economics have to offer the rich, the poor, single parents, working women, single men, adolescents, pregnant teenagers, laborers, business men and women, or a host of other groups." Bear in mind that individuals may belong to several publics, such as being both a parent and a working mother. The challenge is to point out the benefits that the profession offers and to influence these groups so that they will be predisposed favorably toward the profession and its offerings.

For the purposes of discussion, publics may be loosely grouped into certain categories.

Publics on the Job

Other employees

School, company, agency, club members

Office and clerical workers

Boards of education

Food service personnel

Boards of directors

Students, clients, patients, customers, and others served by home economists

[1] *Public Relations Guide,* Educational Services, Proctor and Gamble, Cincinnati, Ohio, 1975, p. 2.

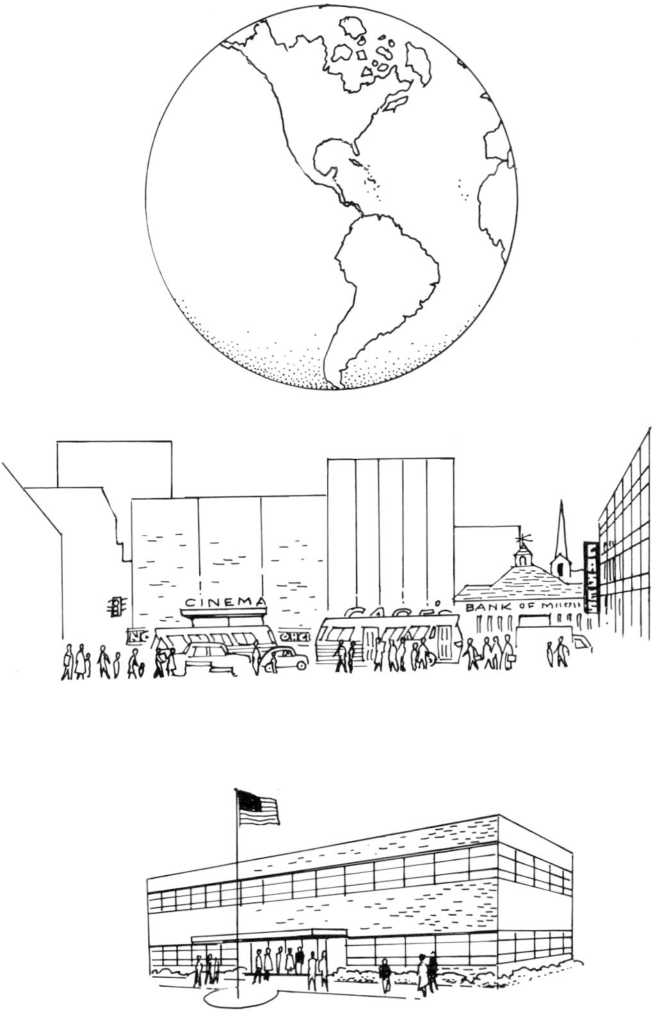

Figure 19–1 Publics to be reached are one's school, neighborhood, and the wider community.

Administrators
Custodians
Personnel directors
Guidance counselors
Parents of students
Alumni of the school

Community Publics
Parents
Service clubs—men's and women's
Youth groups
Grange
Labor groups

- Civic groups—men's and women's
- Personnel connected with newspapers and magazines
- Personnel connected with radio, television, and other media
- 4-H clubs
- Extension clubs
- Church groups
- Librarians
- Personnel in clinics
- Business
- Industry
- Professional groups
- Governing body

Wider Community

Individuals encountered casually on bus, plane, train; socially; while shopping; and county, regional, state, national, or international groups.

The home economics educator might begin to contemplate public relations by considering the publics in her/his own situation. Employees outside the department are a very important public because of their many dealings with individuals in the school and the community. The guidance counselors are in a strategic position to point out the advantages of home economics not only in the high school program but also as a profession. The alumni should be kept informed so that their information on home economics is up-to-date.

The key personnel of the mass media—newspapers, magazines, radio, and television—must be cultivated, for they are the access to the widest audience. Other professional groups, legislators, governors, senators, persons in Congress, White House personnel, and government agency personnel are other important publics.

In contacts with all these publics, the home economics educator is the embodiment of the home economics program. She or he should examine all contacts as potential interpreters of home economics, for word-of-mouth public relations is very effective. When a professional explains home economics to one person, that person is the first link in a lengthening chain of communication.

PLANNING FOR PUBLIC RELATIONS

Some types of public relations go on without conscious effort. Parents may discuss the home economics program with each other; students, patients, clients, and others served may describe experiences to other students. Conscious campaigns, however, demand planning.

Preplanning

Before planning a campaign, assess the present situation. Finding the answers to questions such as the following[2] may be helpful:

What are the present goals?
Have these goals been achieved? If not, why not?
Are the goals realistic?
How do the various publics see home economics?
What kind of image do home economists wish to project?
What strengths are mentioned?
What weaknesses are highlighted?
To what extent are the publics uninformed?
Which publics are being reached and which are being neglected?
Who are our most important publics? Do groups change from time to time?
Are the most important points and benefits being emphasized?

Which strategies have been successful? Unsuccessful? These and other points must be faced objectively, with sound judgment and discrimination, so that planning for the future will be effective. Further questions might be, Should goals be sharpened or redefined? What needs to be done differently? What important changes in strategies appear desirable? What would the profession like to have happen? How may this be achieved? How will future trends in the profession influence planning?

Planning

The basic steps in outlining a strong program include:

1. Establishing clear, well-defined, and achievable objectives.
2. Identifying the publics.
3. Identifying appropriate targets within the publics.
4. Planning a specific program.
5. Planning the budget.
6. Setting up a calendar.
7. Planning workable strategies.
8. Making decisions about media and tools.
9. Planning evaluation.

In establishing the objectives for a public relations program, the home economics educator might consider the goals of the place of

[2] Ibid., p. 3.

employment, the school, the home economics profession, and the personal goals for the program as they relate to the needs, problems, interests, and desires of publics within and outside the school. People are most attentive to public relations messages that identify with their problems and desires.

In weighing the long list of publics to be reached, a teacher will realize that equal attention cannot be given to all of them at the same time. In beginning a campaign, consider a number of points. Decide which groups are sympathetic and which need to be sold, what the sympathies of the strongest community groups are, and what groups have the greatest need for education about home economics. Select a few groups that can be handled competently; then make a concerted effort to reach them. Sometimes it is good to start with easier groups or those that are already in sympathy in order to make strong allies of them. It can be very discouraging to tackle the most difficult group first, especially for a teacher with little experience in public relations, who must gradually develop know how.

Next the home economist plans the program, analyzing each desired objective for the best way to achieve it. Consider fresh ideas that will lend themselves to showmanship,[3] which is essential if one is to compete for the time and attention of the publics.

A decision must be made as to who will participate. The more people involved, the greater will be the benefits. If this effort is a part of a total school program, the students can probably assist. For instance, if the teacher believes that a public—say, the parents of students—are uninformed, even misinformed, about the home economics program, a public relations program might be built around some or all of the following activities:

1. A monthly or quarterly newsletter to parents or in-house outlining activities in the home economics department or giving professional advice.
2. An open house for parents or other publics featuring exhibits, activities, and demonstrations.
3. The appointment of a parent, community, advisory, or professional group.
4. A column in a local newspaper giving advice about nutrition, use of energy, or being a good consumer.
5. Television or radio programs about home economics department activities.
6. Soliciting questions about the home economics programs from

[3] Genevieve Callahan and Lou Richardson, *Show-How and Showmanship* (Ames: Iowa State U.P., 1966), Ch. 1.

Figure 19–2 Letters to parents can be effective.

parents and other publics and using their reactions in public relations planning.
7. A plan developed by each student for his/her parents.

If other publics are to be reached, the home economics educator can make a similar analysis of their particular needs and the best ways to reach them.

A calendar of plans is a great help in this type of program. The success of the program will be more certain if it is carried out step by step and according to schedule.

Some kind of budget is necessary for most public relations work. The teacher must know what funds, if any, will be available for such items as postage, photographs for news stories, and materials for exhibits and posters. The amount of available money need not be the sole determinant of the extent of the program, for with ingenuity, a great many activities in the regular home economics program can be worked into the public relations program.

In planning the public relations program, survey the tools and the media available. For example, will students who are clever help in the preparation of posters, bulletin boards, or exhibits? Are the local radio and television stations receptive to programs? How may the school paper or a local newspaper be used? A home economics educator will make a very careful analysis of personal skills, too. There may be a general awareness of the meaning of home economics and the objectives of the profession, but each home economist must also know how to dramatize a message to get it across to the public. Sensitivity to the interests and vulnerabilities of the individuals involved is important. For example, what would be the best way to convince a mother who fancies that she can teach her daughter or son everything about homemaking at home that the student will nonetheless benefit from the school's home economics program? Certainly the mother should not be made to feel self-conscious or out-of-date. If the mother thinks of home economics primarily in terms of cooking and sewing, the teacher might start from that point to invite the mother's attention to the scope of contemporary home economics education.

Any public relations program is best introduced through methods that will give it the widest possible appeal. People generally want to know what difference home economics will make in their own lives, so it is desirable to highlight the benefits by personalizing the program. The public is generally more interested in what home economics is doing for Jim and Mary Student than it is for a host of faceless statistics. School board members and administrators are often more willing to appropriate funds for a program when they can see boys and girls managing money more expertly, selecting their own sensible wardrobes, improving their health through knowledge of nutrition, caring for small children, and generally assuming an active and satisfying role in family living, all directly as a result of home economics education.

Last, very definite plans must be made for continuous evaluation. A simple diary or some kind of chart for recording progress toward the program's goals may be maintained; a scrapbook of photographs, programs, news releases, and the like is helpful. The teacher can look for tangible evidence of a change in the public's attitudes toward home economics. Increase in course enrollment is such a piece of evidence.

Feedback—evidence discerned from comments by or discussions among administrators, students, and the people of the community—

must be analyzed in terms of objectives. If a mother comments that her daughter's improved eating habits seem to be a result of a nutrition unit, if students regard the home economics teacher as approachable, if fellow faculty look upon her/him with respect and confidence, her/his public relations are progressing.

STRATEGIES FOR PUBLIC RELATIONS

There are limitless ways in which relations with the public can be improved. The person-to-person approach is among the most powerful. Simple and direct, it can do much to develop goodwill and to achieve purposes. A teacher must realize that her/his own attitude about home economics can be very contagious. Enthusiasm, competence, and a friendly interest in others will pay dividends. Talking to parents, teachers, or business people as they are encountered in the community or at school activities offers opportunities for the direct approach.

Talks

Students can do a great deal to assist with talks and speeches in the promotion of better public relations. One department had a speaker's bureau of students who gave talks and demonstrations on the best buys in food for adequate nutrition, homemade fashion accessories, tasty and nutritious foods of other cultures, careers in home economics, step and time savers for the working woman, food fads and fallacies, and similar topics. These talks were given to classes in the elementary grades and in high school and to community groups. The English department cooperated, and, needless to say, their students profited as well as those in home economics. Program chairmen of various organizations are often interested in program suggestions, such as student talks or a panel discussion by teacher and students.

Teachers can contribute to public relations by the talks they give. Reporting about the home economics department to the faculty, groups of administrators, or boards of directors, or to the board of education; discussing a topic of interest to a parents' group or to a school club; speaking before a community organization; or being the luncheon speaker at a civic service club meeting are some examples. The local home economics groups might profit from a speaker's bureau.

For effective speaking, a teacher may wish to bear in mind some of the following suggestions. A well-prepared speech is confined to the topic, geared to the interests of the audience, and timed accurately. Many a potentially successful speech has been made less effective by the attire of the speaker, such as distracting jewelry or inappropriateness of dress. Mannerisms such as wildly waving the hands, constantly clearing the throat, or twirling a pencil, can be distracting.

An effective speaker gains the attention of his/her audience immediately. Citing some important facts related to the content of the talk, raising a thought-provoking question, using an unusual quotation, or alluding to a pertinent experience are some good openings. If visuals or props are used, they must be large enough to be seen well and must have a definite bearing on the talk. Good aids enhance understanding. Being positive in tone rather than negative is an asset. Any attempts to impress an audience with polysyllabic words is discouraged. Speaking directly, simply, distinctly, and slowly keeps the attention of the audience. An ending that suggests action or some inspiring thought is effective.

Pitfalls, fears, and other hindrances to a good speech are minimized when a teacher has enthusiasm and interest. Talks can make an important contribution to an improved image of the profession, so it behooves a home economist to use this form of communication to the best advantage.

Displays and Demonstrations

Some schools have found clinics of various types helpful. One school had a laundry clinic; demonstrations and exhibits were set up in the gymnasium. Adults could go from station to station to see the latest ideas in the laundering of synthetic fabrics, points on selecting a detergent, ways to take care of easy-care garments, and ways to secure the best service from a washing machine and dryer. This clinic idea can be adapted to other areas of home economics. Having demonstrations or clinics specifically for working mothers is another suggestion. An open house has many possibilities.

If you are having an open house or a mother's tea, exhibits will help tell the home economics story. Student participation can ensure greater interest. Students can demonstrate how to sew knitted or vinyl clothes; how to glamorize convenience foods; how to reduce pollution at home; or how to make the most efficient use of portable electric equipment, such as a skillet, as an energy saver.

A theme should be chosen for each exhibit, such as how science is applied in the home; scientific implications for every area of home life can be explored. Principles of physics might be demonstrated with small household equipment. Acids and alkalies in food preparation may be shown in experiments. Suggestions can be offered for the best methods of removing the different kinds of dirt found in a home.

Similarly the applications of art in the home can be demonstrated. Basic principles of art relating to line, color, and design might be

Figure 19–3 Participation in a health fair may impress the guests. (USDA Photo)

demonstrated in clothes, tableware, kitchen equipment, or home furnishings.

One interest-catching device is to take one article at a time from a large hatbox, an oversized purse, or a small chest, each article related to a point in the talk. In a talk about influences in daily living, the collection might include a dollar bill, a clock, keys, a shopping list, a baby doll, a toy chair, and a first-aid kit. A few comments about each item and how it relates to the home and personal living might be made. The interest of the audience is sustained through anticipation of the next article.

Silly hats are another device for emphasizing points. For example, the title of a skit may be a takeoff on a Broadway play, like "How to Have a Happy Family by Trying." One student may be the commentator, and as each specific point is made, a girl or boy might appear wearing an outlandish hat. The advice to think about relationships broadly would be illustrated by a very large hat. The point "avoid concentration on trivia" would bring on stage a tall boy wearing a very small hat. To remove outmoded concepts of family living, a girl with a scarf around her head would appear carrying a broom, as though she is about to clean house. Again humor will accentuate the points.

Displays and exhibits may be placed in key spots thoughtout the community; in stores, libraries, clinics, professional offices, or museums. Community auditoriums, theaters, and other places where people gather are good sites for displays. Local, county, and state fairs provide an excellent opportunity for telling the home economics story.

A picture story about a home economics department might be displayed in a library, in a store window, at a clinic, or on school bulletin boards where all may see it. Photographs of school activities may be made into a scrapbook for parents to look at during their visits to school or at an open house. Photographs may also be used to illustrate an annual report to the school administration.

Flyers or handout materials might be given to the librarian to hand out with books; students may distribute them to customers at the end of the checkout counters in a supermarket, providing approval has been secured; the local utility company may be willing to include a leaflet with utility bills. Handout material on suggestions for child feeding might be placed in the waiting room of a doctor's office or in a clinic. A library might be grateful for career packets from the American Home Economics Association.

Advantage should be taken of special "weeks," such as Book Week, Fire Prevention Week, or American Education Week as the focus for displays. During Book Week, for example, a librarian, either in the community or in the school, might be encouraged to arrange an exhibit of books about the home or the family.

Newspapers

Newspapers are an excellent medium through which to keep home economics before the public. Establishing and maintaining friendly contacts with local newspapers is essential. Even in large cities, there are newspapers in different sections of the city or in the suburbs that may be pleased to publish properly prepared news about home economics. It is a good idea to visit the newspaper office personally, to explore editorial reactions to the idea of such news and to identify the editors who would handle it. The teacher should find out when releases are due and how editors like to have news stories prepared.

If she/he expects to make friends with editors, the teacher should bear the following points in mind when writing news releases:

1. The topic of a news release must be timely. If possible, the release should be turned in well in advance of an event. Something that happened last week is stale news and will not interest an editor.
2. Releases should be typed double- or triple-spaced on 8½″ × 11″ plain white paper. In the upper left-hand corner of the first page of the releases, the following information should be given: the name, address, and telephone number of a person whom the

newspaper can call to verify points in the article reliably and quickly; the name of the school or organization from which the story is originating.

3. In the upper right-hand corner of the first page the date of the release should be given, particularly if it is exclusive, that is, if it has not been given to any other newspapers.
4. Only one side of the paper should be typed on.
5. About one third of the way down from the top and centered in the width of the page should be typed the heading or title of the release. The body of the story should begin three or four lines below the heading.
6. Ample margins should be left at the left and at the right. The purpose of the space at the top and the margins is to permit the editor to make notations for the typesetters.
7. The first paragraph in a news story is called the *lead.* It comes as a surprise even to people who have read a newspaper daily for years to realize that newspaper paragraphs rarely contain more than one sentence, yet in a properly written news story *all* of the story's basic information—the *who, what, when, where, why,* and *how*—should be in the first paragraph or two. When all of the essential information is in the first paragraph, the editor can cut remaining paragraphs without real loss to the story.
8. Succeeding paragraphs develop the lead paragraph. If possible, news releases should be complete on one page.
9. The entire release should have sparkle, interest, and attention-getting news. The material should be fact, not opinion.
10. Good, sharp action photographs enhance a news story. Pictures for public relations must tell a story in a swift, direct manner. A combination of words and photographs conveys a much stronger message than either alone. Good pictures are not happenstance. They must be carefully planned. The kind of picture desired must be conceived by the person who is going to take it. Emotional appeal and action strenghten the value of a photograph.

The home economics teacher will have to decide what is news. Here are a few possibilities:

The announcement of a scholarship winner who will study home economics in college.

Student volunteer work in the community (a good human-interest story).

A story about a play school set up for preschool children in connection with a child development unit.

The visit of a homemaker from a foreign land who tells a class about family customs in that land.

The preparation of traditional family recipes and a discussion of the origin of each recipe.

Boys and girls working together in classes in home economics.

The cooperation of local business firms in certain class activities.

The exchange with students of other countries of tapes of student conversations on family festivals, community projects, and class activities.

Editors may be interested in an occasional student-written column about pointers on child care, nutrition, energy saving, and other areas of home economics.

In one school, students in home economics classes wrote fillers for the local newspaper. These were one- or two-line comments that were used to fill up a newspaper column. These fillers included timely items about food buying, the care of children, microwave cooking, credit, sources of information for shoppers, and other aspects of home economics. Suitable topics might be pointers on sewing items made of felt, simple dishes for increasing children's milk consumption, evidence of how saving a few cents on a grocery item can mount to dollars in a period of time, making popsicles, how to study the roots of family foods, or ways to watch calories.

The task of writing news releases might be shared by teachers and students and perhaps with other departments as well. The English teacher, the art teacher, and other teachers with whom cooperative projects are done may be interested in working with the home economics teacher in putting out news releases. It is always important to check with the school on plans for releases so that duplicates are not sent. In writing news releases, it is important to bear in mind that the readers are not professionals but are people from many walks of life and various educational backgrounds. The teacher must consider the best way of making her/his story understood so that it will have a universal appeal.

A distinction should be drawn here between a news release and a news story of an event. News releases are notices of forthcoming events provided by the school. News stories are accounts of the event after if has happened and are written by the newspaper's correspondents or reporters. Sometimes the releases written by student reporters or the teacher are rewritten by the newspaper staff. Frequently the newspaper, if notified well in advance, is willing to provide a photographer to take appropriate photographs to accompany the story. If the school has a "stringer reporter," a student paid by the newspaper to submit stories or to cover certain events, the home economics teacher might cooperate with him/her.

Bear in mind that editors are eager for news. When a teacher can give it to them briskly and succinctly written, while it is fresh and new, the possibility for securing space in a newspaper should be good.

Radio

Radio has never been a more powerful medium of communication than it is now. In practically every home in the United States there are one or more radio sets, in addition to car radios and many portable radios. The total potential radio audience is enormous. Unless a broadcast is confined to a very limited area locally, the possibility of reaching large groups of people is great—often an audience of millions. The local radio offers a splendid opportunity for improving public relations in the community.

Radio stations are as eager to have news releases as newspapers, and they can be prepared in much the same way. For example, a home economics teacher wrote a news release on an aspect of home management entitled, "Have a Philosophical Approach to Homemaking," that was distributed by the Associated Press. It was broadcast over two thousand stations having a collective potential audience of millions. Following are some suggestions on how the radio might be used successfully.

Figure 19–4 A radio program reaches a wide audience.

1. Topics adaptable for radio programming include interesting class activities; ways to cut the food budget; family camping; home sewing; government resources for the family; ways to recycle clothes; or the use of food stamps. Other possibilities are the various aspects of home care of the sick, cooking out-of-doors, inexpensive ways to have fun, or understanding one's parents. It might be a good plan to make a careful study of the particular interests and problems of homemakers or, if the station is local, of people in the community.
2. A home economics teacher may be asked to give a talk on a radio program. The topic of the talk may be specified by the radio station, or it may be mutually agreed upon by the teacher and the station. All the points of good public speaking are important in radio broadcasting. Because it is difficult to hold a radio audience for any length of time, radio talks should be short. Three five-minute talks, for instance, are often better than one fifteen-minute talk—if nothing else, they give triple exposure, as well as an opportunity to reemphasize points. Such talks might be segments of a regular program with an established audience.
3. A teacher may have the opportunity to be interviewed on radio. The types of questions and the areas that will be discussed are agreed upon beforehand. There is still considerable allowance, however, for spontaneity, so the teacher must be very careful about what she/he says and the extent to which she/he is expressing opinion rather than fact.
4. The round-table discussion is adaptable for radio. This might consist of a panel of home economists, a teacher and students, or a teacher, a parent, and a student. Three people is probably the most desirable number so that the audience can identify them easily.
5. Some home economics teachers have been fortunate enough to have their own programs on local stations. This is generally a ten-to-fifteen-minute session and does require considerable work, but it is well worth it. On some programs, the teacher might, after a little experience, be able merely to outline beforehand the important points, giving her or his talk in an informal manner. The wide range of possible topics from home economics can well serve as subjects for weekly discussions. From time to time the teacher may wish to have students participate.
6. Dramatic programs can be given on radio with considerable effectiveness, but they do take a great deal of preparation and should be given very well or not at all. Cooperation from the speech or dramatics teacher may ensure an impressive program.
7. Fillers are generally one-, two-, or three-minute human-interest

stories about activities in classes, in home economics clubs, or in community activities. Some statistics about the profession, such as number of teachers, dietitians, home economists in business, and other careers, can be presented in an interesting manner for this type of filler.

8. Spot announcements generally come at the time of a station break and vary in length. They provide an opportunity for announcements about adult classes and the like. The United Nations has been very successful in using spots consisting of little songs, catchy tunes with simple lyrics conveying a powerful message. Original songs might be tape-recorded and used to highlight important points, such as new food uses (zucchini or yogurt bread) or how children might be taught at home to strengthen school learning. Great care must be exercised, however, not to borrow without permission from copyrighted music and lyrics, for serious repercussions could result. Students in the music department might compose the music, those in home economics writing the lyrics.

Television

Television is one of the most effective forms of communication. It is a medium that promotes intimacy, and it thrives on informality. People feel as though they are sitting in the front row and that the speaker is talking directly and personally to them. This feeling is a real advantage in the communication of ideas, but attention must be gained promptly or the audience will be lost. Someone has suggested that a television program should be prepared and presented as though it will be the only opportunity to reach people with a certain message. This thought implies the necessity of extremely careful planning. The effect of color on television must be considered. Here are some ideas for possible television programs.

1. Helping teenagers to select a nutritious lunch in a fast-food restaurant.
2. Highlights of a home economist on the job.
3. Becoming a better buyer, illustrated with actual articles. For example, in a program on the buying of sweaters, not only should points be made about shopping for a sweater in the store, but it might be desirable to show a good buy in a sweater and a poor buy after each has been worn for about a year.
4. Safe and efficient ways of storing food.
5. Suggestions for combating high utility bills.

SUGGESTIONS FOR FURTHER LEARNING

1. Read newspapers, listen to the radio, and watch television with the intent of developing ideas for use in home economics public relations. Share your reactions with class members. Are there common points to consider in all of these media?
2. Evaluate the public relations materials of professional organizations, such as the American Home Economics Association, the American Dietetics Association, and the American Vocational Association. Do the same for FHA/HERO materials. What impressed you? Have you any suggestions to offer for improvement?
3. Consider possible subjects for the content of a three-minute film that might be used on television for the purposes of public relations.
4. Read the following references for additional suggestions:

   Conarre, Richard R. *Public Relations for Professional Organizations.* (Westport, Conn.: Walden Public Relations, Inc., 1977).

   So, You Have Been Elected Publicity Chairman. (Los Angeles: Occidental Center, 1150 South Olive, Los Angeles, Calif. 90051, 1976).
5. Read:

   Yankelovich, Daniel. *Home Economist Image Study, A Qualitive Investigation,* Washington, D.C.: American Home Economics Association, 1974.

   React to the results of this study. What implications do you see for public relations?

20

Legislation and Grantsmanship

Home economics educators are urged to develop a political awareness and to participate in political action as a professional responsibility. Home economists have had a concern for human and public affairs for many years.[1] For example, the June 1919 issue of the *Journal of Home Economics* had an article that urged members of the American Home Economics Association to support a bill that broadened the definition of vocational home economics.[2]

LEGISLATION

The need for home economists to be more concerned about legislation is critical, especially in these days of strong lobbies and other influences that may have an effect on legislation bearing on home economics. The legislative process is a major means for facilitating educational and social change. Grantsmanship is included here because legislation has a vital role in the funding of many home economics programs.

Many benefits can accrue through group and individual action by professionals. More and more decisions are in the hands of the people most concerned.[3] This power, if wisely used, can bring needed and

[1] Rosetta Robinson, "Public Policy at the Grass Roots," *Journal of Home Economics* Vol. 65, No. 4 (Sept. 1976), pp. 21–23.

[2] E. N. White, "A New Program for the Promotion of Home Economics in the Schools," Vol. 11, No. 6, pp. 261–269.

[3] Sharon McKee (ed.), *A Handbook, How to Work with Government: Federal, State and Local,* Association for Educational Communications and Technology, 1201 Sixteenth Street NW, Washington, D.C. 20036.

important changes to families and home economics. The active involvement of more members of the profession will bring greater productivity in legislative planning. In the process, members of the legislative and executive branches of federal and state government will become better informed about home economics and its contributions.

There are many opportunities for home economists to give leadership in the legislative process through dispensing the information that is basic to a bill. When some members of the profession are involved, other members become interested in participation and consequently also become better informed.

Public Policy

Critical to legislative action is the development of public policy. "Public policy is the culmination of activities initiated by individuals or groups that affect the lives of other individuals or groups in society."[4] These public policies are adopted and implemented by means of public laws, programs, or institutions. Examples of public policies that have had legal implementation, or are being considered, are nutrition programs for the elderly, child- and spouse-abuse programs and policies, and equal educational and work opportunities for women and youth.

Making public policy into law is preceded by the political process of making a law. Here home economists can have input, starting from the very first draft of any bill, that will have an effect on the social and educational interests of the profession. From a practical standpoint, professionals must be aware of the parameters of the proposed action, such as financial limitations, the biases and priorities of key legislators, the clamor of constituent views, and the reality of political compromise. In spite of these hazards, organized home economists can make an impression through communicating concerns in strong and effective terms directly to the legislators involved.

Framework for Action

The Public Affairs Division of the American Home Economics Association (AHEA) gives direction to the legislative issues, but implementation rests with the public affairs committees in each state.[5] This is the "grass roots" approach. There are a number of functions performed by these state chairpersons and their committees. Information is supplied to state association members on legislative issues

[4] Robinson, op. cit., p. 21.
[5] Ibid., pp. 21–23.

Figure 20–1 Home economists may communicate concerns about a bill directly to legislators.

of concern and on the ways that members may become involved in them. The state chairpersons communicate with legislators about special concerns of the profession regarding particular pieces of legislation. Home economists have expertise about families, and they can convey their availability as consultants in this area to the legislators. Working with other groups, such as the League of Women Voters and educational groups, strengthens the overall efforts. Other functions of the state chairpersons are to stimulate membership participation and to plan strategies for action.

Legislative Decision-Making Process

In order for home economists to participate in political action, it is important for them to become familiar with the steps in legislative decision-making. Knowing when constituent influence is more potent and effective is essential.[6] One suggestion that may be overlooked is to initiate an idea for important legislation by making a suggestion to any legislator—the right of every citizen. This idea must be given to a representative of the committee that is involved in this type of legislation. A Congressman or Congresswoman of the constituent, although not a member of the appropriate committee, might appreciate knowing about this action and may encourage the committee member to whom the suggestion was made.

[6] McKee, op. cit., p. 13.

Other critical periods for making suggestions are when the bill is being drafted, while it is in committee, during the testifying at hearings about the bill, and while it is being marked up and changed after the hearings. During the debate in the legislature or Congress, letters, telephone calls, or telegrams may be sent expressing approval or disapproval of the bill or parts of it. If there is a bill favored by home economics and there is a question of a possible veto by a governor or the President, then strong opinions and feelings should be communicated at this point. Becoming acquainted with the staff of legislators, giving them suggestions, and voicing approval or disapproval at any of these stages can be very effective.

Strategies for Action

Examples of strategies of public affairs committees in various states are described by Robinson.[7] A list of legislative resource persons—home economists who could provide expertise if needed—was compiled by the state of Louisiana. An exhibit of legislative concerns was developed in Arizona. A program for training home economics legislative interns was designed by the state of California. A legislative brunch in Montana for home economists and legislators gave them an opportunity to interview each other and to become acquainted with common interests. In Minnesota, legislators were invited to attend the Center for the Family/J. C. Penney forum on "Stress in the Family," prior to the AHEA's annual meeting. Mutual policy interests were fostered in a workshop sponsored by the Iowa Dietetic Association, the Iowa School Service Association, and the Iowa Home Economics Association, with an Iowa Senator as the speaker. The Ohio state home economics association has a part-time paid position for a public affairs coordinator to help identify legislative priorities, write a legislative newsletter, and plan legislative workshops. Illinois sponsored receptions for government officials, legislators, and declared candidates at which home economists had an opportunity to express their views and to develop good working relations. In addition to several other activities in Pennsylvania, the public affairs chairperson is a representative on the Citizens Advisory Council and the Women's Legislative Exchange. The Wisconsin home economics association worked on changes in policy that would benefit families, such as nutrition programs and good buying habits.

Other strategies are for individual members of the profession to work for the election of government officials who appear to favor home economics interests. Of course, the candidate may not win but

[7] Op. cit., pp. 21–23.

Figure 20–2 Home economists may work for the election of government officials who support legislation favorable to home economics concerns.

might win the next time around, and the experience of influencing voters is invaluable. Another strategy is to pinpoint the person or persons with power and to establish good working relations with them. Those individuals who influence the power people must not be overlooked. It is important to understand the motivations, interrelationships, and goals of the people in power.

Legislators and power persons are busy individuals, so be clear, succinct, and dedicated in discussions with them. Compromise is a part of politics, so analyze carefully ahead of time possible adaptations and changes that might be made without demolishing the goal. Working in the legislative arena requires alertness, patience, perseverance, and "keeping ahead." The involvement of home economists in legislative decision-making can be exciting, challenging, and satisfying.

Sometimes home economists ask or are asked to testify at hearings at the federal or state levels. The most important point is to be well prepared because the comments and the questions can be difficult and devastating. Testimony may be given in the form of a written statement. Another procedure is to give oral testimony and leave a written statement for future reference. This testimony is placed in the hearing record with the comments and the credentials of the person

Figure 20–3 Testifying at hearings is another contribution a home economist can make.

testifying. A free copy of any particular hearing may be secured from your Senator, Congressman, or Congresswoman.[8]

A home economist who testifies must explain any technical or scientific language for clarity and ease of understanding. If possible, details can be humanized for greater interest. A short testimony is appreciated. Charts and other aids may illuminate major emphases. Important points should be highlighted, and a summary at the end is helpful. If there are friends of the home economist on the committee holding the hearing, sending them advance copies of the testimony is courteous. This sort of occasion can be used to publicize home economics. Newspaper stories may be accompanied by photographs of those testifying. Writing personal thank-you notes to members of the committee helps to build bridges for future relations. Another good practice is to write letters to those committee members who were especially interested and gave encouragement during the testimony, according to McKee.[9]

Working cooperatively with other groups is a good strategy.[10]Planning legislative action with such groups as those who work for adequate homemaker and other services for the elderly is an example.

[8] *Nutrition and the Elderly—1977, Hearings Before the Select Committee on Nutrition and Human Needs of the U.S. Senate,* Ninty-fifth Congress, First Session, Chicago, Ill., Nov. 14, 1977; Rockford, Ill., Nov. 16, 1977; and Moline, Ill., Dec. 12, 1977. (An example of a hearing report.)

[9] Op. cit., pp. 37, 41, 47.

[10] Margrethe Plum Ahlschwede, "Involvement: Present and Future," *Journal of Home Economics,* Vol. 68, No. 4 (Sept. 1976), pp. 18–20.

The same might be done in city and community planning. Other possibilities are working with architects or architectural organizations to promote better homes for families and for special population groups, such as the elderly, the handicapped, and the poor. Clergymen and religious congregations can be helpful in securing legislation for social action. The media—personnel associated with newspapers, magazines, radio, and television—can also be valuable. Home economists are urged to identify other groups. Being a lobbyist is a good strategy because it provides an opportunity to persuade committee members and other legislators about bills important to home economics.[11]

Communications Networks

Staying in communication with all members and with legislators is a challenge. The New Jersey Home Economics Association established a "telephone tree." Designated members telephone other members from a list, and they, in turn, telephone five other members. This branching continues until all members have been reached.[12] Such an arrangement requires careful preplanning so that the network will be ready when needed. Having enough flexibility to meet different situations is another consideration. Members may need to be reached quickly or, in the event of a sustained campaign, less frequently.[13] Large states may have to be organized into regions. The chairperson and members of the state public affairs committee act as the major contact in a network. Adequate records of this method of communication should be maintained and listings kept up-to-date for the purpose of future reference. For less urgent matters, the newsletter will suffice.

The information communicated to each member must be of consequence, with clear directions for suggested action. The sources of the information may be at the national level, such as the American Home Economics Association, the American Vocational Association, the Home Economics Education Association, or from newsletters of other professional organizations that have input pertinent to home economics. Other sources may include a supportive legislator, the staff of a legislator, or a committee member. Feedback, in which members reverse the system and call the contact person about action that was taken, is important. A network may be developed with other associations so that each may share information that would be helpful to the

[11] *Home Economists in Public Affairs, Priorities, Realities, and Risks,* Third General Session, Annual Convention, American Home Economics Association, On-the-Spot Duplicators, Inc., Washington, D.C., 1978. Cassette.

[12] Robinson, op. cit., p. 23.

[13] McKee, op. cit., p. 7.

others. The important part of any communications network is to facilitate action.

Political Role of Professionals

Professionals are being pushed into the political arena. A greater awareness of politics is emerging. Politics is interpreted by Black[14] as a concern for "general decision making at all levels by those entrusted with legislative and executive power." No longer should decisions be made by legislators without input from the professionals concerned. Action is necessary to protect professional interests.

Preprofessional education for home economists in political involvement is urgent. Education in the past often leaned to an uncritical acceptance of legislative decision-making. Now educators and home economists are more politically active.[15] This step may mean a change in behavior for some professionals. Objective discussion of controversial issues among students and members of the profession is to be encouraged. Real experiences in the political system provide the necessary practical experience. How may this important education be facilitated for students and for professionals in inservice education? Legislative workshops are one answer.

[14] Theodore M. Black, "The Political Role of Educators," *Educational Leadership,* Vol. 34, No. 2 (Nov. 1976), pp. 122–125.

[15] Gerald Ponder, "The Teacher as Activist," *Theory into Practice,* Vol. 10, No. 5 (College of Education, Ohio State University, Columbus, Dec. 1971), pp. 363–369.

Figure 20–4 A legislative workshop is effective in informing professionals about possible roles and responsibilities.

Professionals and politicians often have distorted views about each other that may hamper desirable working relationships.[16] Some professionals contend that politicians have short-term views of the world and often compromise on issues of great importance. Often decisions are made without analysis or reflection. Politicians are often considered somewhat unethical, and many are poorly informed about education and home economics. Politicians often express the belief that professionals act as though they were the only group to maintain standards, that they do not always communicate clearly, and that they lack continuity in their efforts. Equally irksome is educators' lack of appreciation of the difficult job of negotiation, refining, compromising, and pleasing as many constituent interests as possible. Halperin suggests that these viewpoints be submerged and that an effort made by politicians and professionals alike to work on common problems.

Professionals must be alert to the legal aspects of the work that they do.[17] Lawsuits for malpractice are not unknown, and some dietitians, for example, carry malpractice insurance. There have been cases of teachers being sued for failure to teach adequately. Legal liability is a serious subject, and professionals may wish to give thoughtful attention to the matter. The legislative aspects of the problem might be explored.

In looking to the future, home economics educators may wish to survey possible areas for needed legislation that may be brought to the attention of the American Home Economics Association for exploration and discussion. An analysis of current and pending legislation and the probable consequences for families and education is urgent.[18] Before legislation is initiated, it should be rigorously examined for its impact on the profession and on families, so that changes can be proposed before the legislation is enacted.

GRANTSMANSHIP

A home economics educator who is a successful writer of proposals for grants can be the recipient of many benefits. This is true for professionals in all areas of service. This is a resource that too few home economists have used.

The most important advantage is that visibility, credibility, and

[16] Samuel Halperin, "Politicians and Educators: Two World Views," *Phi Delta Kappan*, Vol. 16, No. 3 (Nov. 1974). pp. 189–190.

[17] William A. Hassan, Jr., "Legal Issues Facing Dietary Practice," *Journal of the American Dietetic Association*, Vol. 70, No. 4 (Apr. 1977), pp. 355–360.

[18] Blaine R. Porter, Editorial, "Reflection on Government Impact on Family Life," *Family Perspective*, Vol. 10, No. 2 (Spring 1976), pp. 1–3.

prestige are brought to the profession, to the school or agency with which the home economics educator is associated, and to the individual or individuals who are the recipients of the grant. In addition, there is an opportunity to test an idea to which considerable thought may have been previously given but for which the time, the urge, or the funds did not exist. It is a great satisfaction to know that a grant may improve curriculum or an understanding of students or may help in many other ways. A grant not only affects the immediate situation but may assist hundreds or thousands of other home economics educators in their work. In this manner, the level of the entire profession is raised.

Making the Decision

Getting a grant takes know-how, credibility, patience, diplomacy, homework, hustling, and even luck.[19] Unfortunately many will offer only discouragement to the potential grantee with statements such as "You have to have 'pull,'" "There isn't any money anymore," "You have to develop a special language to write a proposal," or "Only old-timers get grants, not newcomers." All of these statements can be debunked. There is money if one is familiar with the sources. Funding agencies are interested in encouraging the neophyte who has submitted an innovative proposal. A clear, well-written document without flourishes is preferred.[20]

There are several ways to gain input before making a decision. Talking to friends, fellow workers, or other professionals in the community about their experiences in grantsmanship may be helpful. Many schools, colleges, and institutions have an office of research and development that can give one an overview of what is involved and perhaps some broad ideas to consider for proposal writing. Reading professional journals about the kind of research that is being done may be inspirational. Research reports given at national or state conventions can be helpful, especially if one converses with the researcher. A review of past personal experiences in research is good; they may include papers written in college, assistance of a minor nature with a research project on a part-time job, discussion of projects with someone in the family or neighborhood who does research, or participation in courses in which research in that field was critiqued.

[19] Harry Jackson, "Grantsmanship, A Science in Itself," *The Lincoln Star,* Feb. 14, 1978, p. 7. Story about two chemists at the University of Nebraska—Lincoln and how they secured funding for a brilliant idea.

[20] Constance H. Kravas and Donald C. Ordick, "Winning the Grantsmanship Game," *Phi Delta Kappan,* Vol. 59, No. 8 (Apr. 1978), pp. 536–539.

Figure 20–5 Cooperating with one's school or college research and development office is helpful when seeking a grant.

Steps to Proposal Writing

The preliminary steps to proposal writing include answers to certain questions dealing with getting started. Types of proposals, sources of grants, sources of ideas, and information about proposal writing are points to consider for success in this undertaking.

Getting Started

The suggestions about evaluating previous experiences that touched on research are good beginnings. The analysis of personal feelings and attitudes toward developing a project for funding is important because enthusiasm and perseverance are critical to this type of endeavor. An appraisal of interests and capabilities will help one to focus on an idea or ideas to be used in this process. Making a list of possible projects will start other ideas flowing. Each individual would probably have quite a different list. A small project might be appropriate for a minigrant. These vary in amount but usually are for small sums—a few hundred dollars.

Here is an example that has many implications for home economics. The magazine *Instructor,* for elementary school teachers, has given minigrants of $250 to a teacher with an innovative idea for a project. One year, a special education teacher won a grant.[21] The request was for "funds to equip a classroom for intermediate educable mentally retarded students, for experiences in nutrition, cookery, and comparison shopping, and a 10-week shopping budget for ingredients (stove, sink, and refrigerator already available)." The students studied nutrition, planned meals, and prepared a shopping list with approximate prices. The class visited the supermarket, priced the food to be purchased, and made their best choices. Back in the classroom, the students prepared, served, and ate the meal. Cleanup and evaluation of each experience followed.

The teacher, Karen Kazmark, stated that in addition to the above learnings, language stimulation, sensory-perceptual awareness, motor skills, social living skills, and personal gratification were included. The possible transfer to the daily lives of the children was another exciting plus. This project idea could be adapted to many other areas of home economics and could be used with other types of students requiring special education. With the emphasis on mainstreaming, a search for other sources is possible.

Another way to begin is to invite a fellow staff member in the school or agency where the home economics educator is employed to share in an interdisciplinary project. A consumer education project is a possibility and may include the departments of business education, social studies, and home economics. Such a project might be planned as an elective course, open to all students and taught by teachers in all three areas with some creative angles that would increase the potential for funding, such as wide use of community resources or student evaluation of the services and goods available. Another angle is the organization of students with some expertise in consumer education who might handle a hot line to help other students with consumer problems.

A teacher may be interested in preparing individualized study packages on different areas of home economics for students with reading problems; such a project might be funded by the state departments of home economics and education or by other sources. This same idea might be used with bilingual students and tested for effectiveness.

Reading in professional journals, including the *Home Economics Research Journal* and the *Journal of Nutrition Education,* to gain ideas

[21] "Instructor $250 Mini Grant Winners," *Instructor,* Vol. 83, No. 2 (Oct. 1973), p. 28.

about projects that have been funded would be helpful. Newspapers and magazines also describe funded projects.

At this stage, the home economics educator in search of a grant may begin to crystallize the main idea. Answers to the following list of questions will give structure to the idea:[22]

1. What is innovative, unique, or different about this idea in comparison with others in the area?
2. Would authorities in this area endorse the idea?
3. Do project director and other workers have adequate credentials?
4. Who would be served or benefit from the project—locally, regionally, or nationally?
5. How may the idea be evaluated?
6. Is the idea appropriate to the locale of the project—school, agency, community, or other situation?
7. How many workers would be involved in the project, and are they available?
8. What would be the length of time for the project?
9. What type of financial support would be required under categories such as staff, facilities, materials, etc.?
10. What proportion of your time would be needed—full or part time?

Other questions may also have to be answered. The idea for the project should be so clear that it could be written in one sentence or a small paragraph.

Sources of Information About Funding

Locating a potential donor means sifting through many sources to find the one or the ones that might be interested in the proposal. One way is to pinpoint the federal agency, the foundation, the professional organization, or the other sources that have previously indicated interest in this area. Sometimes there are geographical limitations; particular needs, such as economic or operational, to be pinpointed, and other criteria may have to be met. Try to arrange a budget that is within the range of possible funding.

Federal Funding

A number of valuable directories and other materials can be helpful. For federal grants, the *Catalog of Federal Domestic Assistance,* se-

[22] *Grantsmanship: Money and How to Get It,* Marquis Academic Media, Marquis Who's Who, Inc., 200 East Ohio Street, Chicago, Ill. 60611, 1978.

cured from Superintendent of Documents, describes more than one thousand programs administered by many federal agencies.[23] In the U.S. Office of Education, U.S. Department of Health, Education, and Welfare, funding possibilities may be found in agencies dealing with international education or community colleges. State departments of education or state colleges may have federal funds channeled to them. Social and Rehabilitation Services, also a part of HEW, gives funds to state agencies for the handicapped and for vocational rehabilitation and thus may be a potential source of funds for programs dealing with the handicapped. The U.S. Department of Labor is concerned about vocational schools and institutions, manpower administration, and state departments of vocational education.

The magazine *American Education,* published by the Superintendent of Documents, is invaluable for information about funding. Each issue has an article on "Federal Funds," which describes a federal funding program and examples of funded projects. Once early in each year, there is a review of that year's Office of Education funded programs.[24] Information includes the type and purpose of assistance, the authorizing legislation, the total dollars available for appropriation, who may apply, and where to apply. Those who are interested should consult the magazine of the latest year for information.

The fund raiser must be alert to changes in government grants; some are always being discontinued and others originated. The *Federal Register* is a good source of information for these changes. Reading *Washington Dateline,* an AHEA publication, is informative.

The Congressmen and Congresswomen and Senators from each state are interested in the funding of projects, and their offices may be contacted for information and assistance. Knowing the legislation that has been enacted in the area of interest is helpful. Securing and reading the original bill will often uncover possibilities.

Funding by Foundations

The approach to foundation funding is quite a contrast to the approach to governmental funding. Many foundations are family-oriented and may concentrate on an area in which the family has concerns (such as the Kennedy family's interest in retarded children). The objectives of the foundation must be well defined by law, and this definition establishes the focus of the foundation. Foundations with an interest in various aspects of the family, women, children, and the homes are possibilities.

[23] Philip Des Marais, *How to Get Government Grants* (New York: Public Service Materials Center, 1977).

[24] Gwendolyn D. Smith, "Guide to OE-Administered Programs, Fiscal Year 1978," *American Education,* Vol. 14, No. 2 (March 1978), pp. 27–35.

Wise potential grantees will inform themselves about foundations in general and later those in particular that may be helpful. *Foundation News,* published by the Council on Foundations, Inc. (888 Seventh Avenue, New York, N.Y. 10019), has a bimonthly "Foundation Grants Index." Recently reported foundation grants of $5,000 or more are organized by foundations in each state. In addition, there is an alphabetical list of recipients, which permits interested individuals to locate schools and organizations with similar interests; also listed is the amount of funding given their projects. The subject index is another aid. The Foundation Center also publishes the *Foundation Directory.*[25] Another service rendered by the Foundation Center is to provide printouts of foundation-funded projects in key subject-matter areas. Annual reports of foundations are available at the center. Descriptions of the projects funded and the amount of the grants supplied are included. From this information, a grant seeker may select potential donors for her or his project.

One should study these reports in detail to discover certain patterns in the granting, such as geographical or project preferences, duration of support, number of times a grantee may be supported, or restrictions on the use of the funds. Knowing someone on the board of directors, or an officer, may be an avenue for additional information. In examining the annual reports, the potential grantee may recognize a former recipient; if so a discussion about her or his experience may further information. An analysis of all potential donors must include the degree of compatibility between the projects under consideration by the home economics educator and the interests of the foundation. Such an analysis will foster desirable working relations.

Other Sources of Funding

Federal funds may be channeled to other sources, such as states, universities, or colleges. The state home economics supervisor may have suggestions about funding. Corporations, in addition to foundations, may be sources of small grants in areas that reflect their interests. Professional organizations, such as the American Home Economics' Center for the Family, fund research projects or other proposals that are compatible with their objectives. The Association for the Supervision and Curriculum Development Small Grants is related to critical issues in education. The American Association for University Women and Women's Business may be an appropriate source. Magazines often offer minigrants for projects in which they are interested.

Caution must be exercised so that a grant is not sought from a

[25] Marianna O. Lewis (ed.), *The Foundation Directory* (New York: Columbia U.P., 1977).

source that may have goals in conflict with those of the profession. The opportunities for funding are many, but the potential grantee must search for them and be discriminating in choice.

Writing the Proposal

The information acquired to date may be sufficient for the applicant for a grant to begin writing a rough draft of the proposal. This task will quickly highlight gaps of knowledge and expertise. Sometimes a proposal is written by one person, and sometimes with others. Battaglia[26] recommends teamwork.

Components of a Proposal

Detailed guidelines for writing a proposal are generally given for government grants. These rules must be followed in great detail unless otherwise indicated. In writing for foundations or other sources, the directions may not be so strict. A general outline is discussed here that may be adapted if necessary.[27]

Introduction. The introduction should be a carefully worded statement that gives an overview of the area of concern. Hopefully, the introduction will arouse interest and communicate the idea of the proposal so well that the reader will comprehend the entire proposal. This opening should be short and not full of tedious and technical details.

Background of the Problem. This section or background reviews the origin of the idea and the professional experiences of the potential grantee that may have encouraged the idea for the proposal. Sometimes a small pilot study has been done that has excited the writer. Pertinent statistics and other information about conditions on the social scene, for example, if skillfully used, can further establish the need for the project.

A review of similar projects and how this project differs from others is discussed. If it is a research proposal, a section on related studies is usually a separate component. The unique contribution of this project must be related, as well as the specific benefits of this work, in other words, "Who will benefit from this undertaking?" Sometimes the proposal writer will compare this project with other

[26] Carmen L. Battaglia, "How to Ask for Federal Funding," *American Education,* Vol. 13, No. 6 (July 1977), pp. 6–9.

[27] Lawrence F. Locke and Waneen Wyrick Spirduso, *Proposals That Work, A Guide for Planning Research,* (New York: Teachers College Press, Columbia University, 1976), pp. 5–9.

work that has been done and indicate how it differs or is similar in methodology, in the sample used, in the assumptions made, in the philosophical approach, or in the interpretation of results. At all times, there should be clarity of concepts and theories.

Statement of the Problem. A clear and concise statement of the problem with which the investigation is concerned is critical. The writer will use this statement as a guide for the entire undertaking. Questions of inclusion, deletion, and pertinence can be answered quickly by a look at the statement of the problem. Methodology, interpretation of data, selection of the sample, and other parts of the study are interpreted in light of the statement. In research projects, a hypothesis or hypotheses are given. A general statement of what is to be accomplished strengthens the problem statement.

To have a clear, well-defined problem is a source of great satisfaction because other aspects of the study are thereby given direction. The problem must be stated separately, so that it will be highly visible to prospective donors.

Site of the Study. A description of the location of the project is usually included in the body of the proposal, but sometimes it is considered a part of supplemental materials, depending on the directions of a possible donor. This description includes where the work will be done—in or out of the school or agency with which the investigator is associated. The support systems—such as administration of the school, institution, or agency; other departments; and community and other resources as related to the project—are described. Special facilities, equipment, or other needs that have to be met may be mentioned.

Procedures or Methodology. If the statement of the problem is clear and reasonable, then it will be easy to indicate the logical steps to be taken or the questions to be answered to solve the problem. These are sometimes called *subproblems.* Special care must be taken that each step, question, or subproblem is clearly stated and measurable, so that the action necessary to secure pertinent information or results will emerge easily. A detailed explanation about the selection of the sample, such as availability, suitability, representativeness, and adequacy, is essential. The application of sound principles to sample selection is imperative.[28] Each subproblem and the appropriate method or procedure for supplying the information desired is discussed. In addition, the collection of data that result from the action taken must be discussed in detail. A demonstration of how each step

[28] Norma H. Compton and Olive A. Hall, *Foundations of Home Economics Research, A Human Ecology Approach* (Minneapolis: Burgess Publishing, 1972), Ch. 9.

is related to the main problem is important so that gaps, inconsistencies, and other weaknesses may be spotted.

Other aspects of this portion of the proposal include advancing arguments that are adequate to support statements about the validity, reliability, and objectivity of the study. See Chapter 13 for additional information. The pinpointing of dependent and independent variables is important, especially if the proposal is research-oriented.

This section must be scrutinized and reworked again and again if one is to avoid conflicting statements and procedures, unsound standards, inadequacy, unrealistic methodology, and confusion. Like a jigsaw puzzle, each part must be in place and supporting all other pieces to present a total picture of a workable proposal.

Analysis of Results or Data

Plans are designed for the way that the data will be analyzed for meaning and implications. This analysis is generally done subproblem by subproblem to determine to what degree each step has met the demands of the project. These data are summarized as a basis for determining final results. How well the problem was or was not solved, according to expectations, will identify the degree of success of the project. Reasons for the results will be sought.

Conclusions, Evaluation, and Implications

It is best to state the results succinctly and clearly. In addition, comparisons should be made with the results of similar studies and with the theories on which the project was based.

The investigator will evaluate the entire study for strengths and weaknesses as well as for changes to be recommended for similar studies in the future. This information is invaluable to the investigator in planning other work in the field and to other proposal writers.

Implications may be given about the possibility of further studies in this area, *about implications of the study for the profession,* and about the methodology for this type of project.

Inquiry About Funding

All of the steps involved in writing the proposal were delineated first because a grant seeker must be well versed in all aspects of the project in order to answer convincingly any questions that might be raised. Inquires may be made directly to government agencies that have funds for such projects under consideration, but the home economist's school, college, university, institution, or agency may already have this information because of its prior involvement. The same may be true of other sources of funding, such as foundations.

If the place of employment permits, a person-to-person discussion with the funding agency is desirable. During the conversation, there will be evidences of interest or disinterest in the project. Preferences of the funding agency may emerge. Suggestions may be given for the presentation of the project in a more favorable light.

If the travel distance is too great, then a letter may be the first contact. The letter should be clear and brief, yet generate strong interest in the project. The following points may be covered: referral to the funding agency's interest in this area, a description of the ways that the proposal under consideration by the investigator matches these interests, and the amount of funding required for the project.[29]

Supplemental Materials

If the search for funding for the project is successful, certain supplemental materials are usually required. The *period of time* of the project may be on the cover of the proposal or included with the supplemental materials. The *credentials* of the staff, judges, consultants, experts, assistants, and other resource persons are included. The experience of special strengths of the applicant that are pertinent to this project may be emphasized. A detailed *budget* must be planned to allow for direct and indirect costs, such as inflation and fringe benefits for staff. Travel, if necessary, and publication costs, as well as other budgetary demands, should be carefully checked. The need for accountability is obvious. If *special equipment* is required, it should be described, and if it is not available, the possible costs should be noted. If *human subjects* are used, instructions for them and consent forms are added. *Interview schedules, evaluation instruments, tests,* and *similar items* are included. Sometimes *supplemental bibliographies* are requested. An outline, usually of major headings, may be requested for the *final report.* The list of requirements should be carefully checked for the inclusion of all items and for their accuracy.

Reports

In addition to a final report, most funding agencies require some form of periodic report about problems and progress. A favorable impression will result if reports are well done and on time. The reports should be candid, with honest admission of delays, failures, or temporary setbacks. Accomplishments deserve attention, too. Visits to

[29] *Grantsmanship: Money and How to Get It,* op. cit., p. 7.

the site of the project are often made by representatives of the funding agency. These visits require careful preparation. Helpful suggestions may be offered to the investigator.

The final report depends upon the requirements of the government, the foundation, or the other source of funds. The following are usually included: an overview of the project, the results, and an honest evaluation of the outcome. Suggestions for similar projects may be included.

Requests for a report of the project may come from interested persons. What is sent may be the final report made to the agency, or it may be a one-page abstract. Consideration should be given to publishing an account of the project in a professional magazine. In this way, members of the profession are alerted to the contribution and may be inspired to plan projects on their own.

Next Steps

Hopefully doing a project was a positive experience and plans will begin for additional investigations. If the first project was small, it may serve as a pilot study for a much larger project. Through research and other studies, every home economics educator can add to the prestige and knowledge of the profession.

SUGGESTIONS FOR FURTHER LEARNING

1. Do further reading on your own about pending legislation at the federal or state levels. Select a bill that interests you and examine it for possible consequences to families, education, or both, if enacted. If the consequences would be adverse, consider steps in voicing your concern. Enlist others in a campaign to discourage the bill.
2. Project yourself into the future, when you will be teaching. What kind of projects or research would appeal to you? Why not start a file folder with ideas for projects, clippings, and sources of funds. Make changes when new ideas come to you. Someday you will be ready to write a proposal.

21

Professionalism

What is a professional? What are the criteria for being a professional? What is the process of becoming professionalized?

ELEMENTS OF PROFESSIONALISM

Characteristics

Weigley[1] suggests that too little attention has been given to the process and to the meaning of professionalism. Moore[2] believes that professionalism is a dynamic, ongoing process and is not static. Thus professionalism reflects the past, the present, and the future. Brown[3] states that the most accepted characteristics of a professional is being altruistically motivated or service oriented. Other values, stated by Nosow,[4] are that members of the profession are bound by a sense of identity: that professional status is a continuing one; that generally values are shared by members; that definitions are projected to sort members and nonmembers; that professional community has power

[1] Emma Seifrit Weigley, "The Professionalization of Home Economics," *Home Economics Research Journal,* Vol. 4, No. 4 (June 1976), pp. 253–259.

[2] Wilbert E. Moore, *The Professions: Role and Rules* (New York: The Russell Sage Foundation, 1970).

[3] Marjorie Brown, "Home Economics and Professional Values," in *The Field of Home Economics—What It Is* (Washington, D.C.: American Home Economics Association, 1964), p. 20.

[4] Sigmund Nosow, "The Nature of a Profession: Home Economics, a Particular Case," in *The Field of Home Economics—What It Is* (Washington, D.C.: American Home Economics Association, 1964), pp. 33–49.

over its members; that the parameters of the profession are reasonably clear; and that membership is controlled through the selection of trainees and the preparation process.

Brown[5] further identifies a profession by certain characteristics, such as (1) a profession has a body of knowledge that members must master to enter the profession; (2) this knowledge is not identified as technical skills but as a "systematic body of abstract principles derived from empirical research and logical and honest analysis"; (3) professionals place a high value on rational and rigorous thinking, discrimination, and an openness in the examination of ideas and actions; (4) preparation at a college or university is prolonged because of the complexity of the knowledge; (5) the profession has a monopoly on this knowledge, which is readily identified by professionals; (6) the body of knowledge that the profession considers its own contributes to and is necessary for the good of society; and (7) only members in the profession can be considered qualified to pass on the competencies needed to practice in the profession. Lastly, a professional has an esteemed position in society that grants the right to have a voice in legislation and other public affairs as related to competence.

Steps to Professionalism

Caplow[6] suggests four steps: (1) the creation of a professional organization; (2) the provision of a title and an academic area that can be monopolized; (3) the development of a code of ethics; and (4) adequate political action to strenghten barriers to entry into the profession through such means as licensing, registration, and certification. Implied in these steps are that the admission and the final qualification of a professional are established by the professional organization.

Another phenomenon is the accreditation of departments, schools, and colleges of home economics in academic settings. Accreditation is first granted by a general accrediting agency representing the academic sector to determine if home economics is an eligible profession. When it is accepted for professional accreditation, the professional organization, the American Home Economics Association (AHEA), is responsible for accrediting the home economics departments, schools, and colleges. One of the important purposes of accreditation is to upgrade the profession. The institution seeking accreditation does a self-evaluation and establishes objectives. A site visit by an accreditation team of professionals checks all credentials, may make suggestions for improvement, and rates the institution.

[5] Op. cit., p. 21.
[6] T. Caplow, *The Sociology of Work* (Minneapolis: U. of Minnesota, 1954).

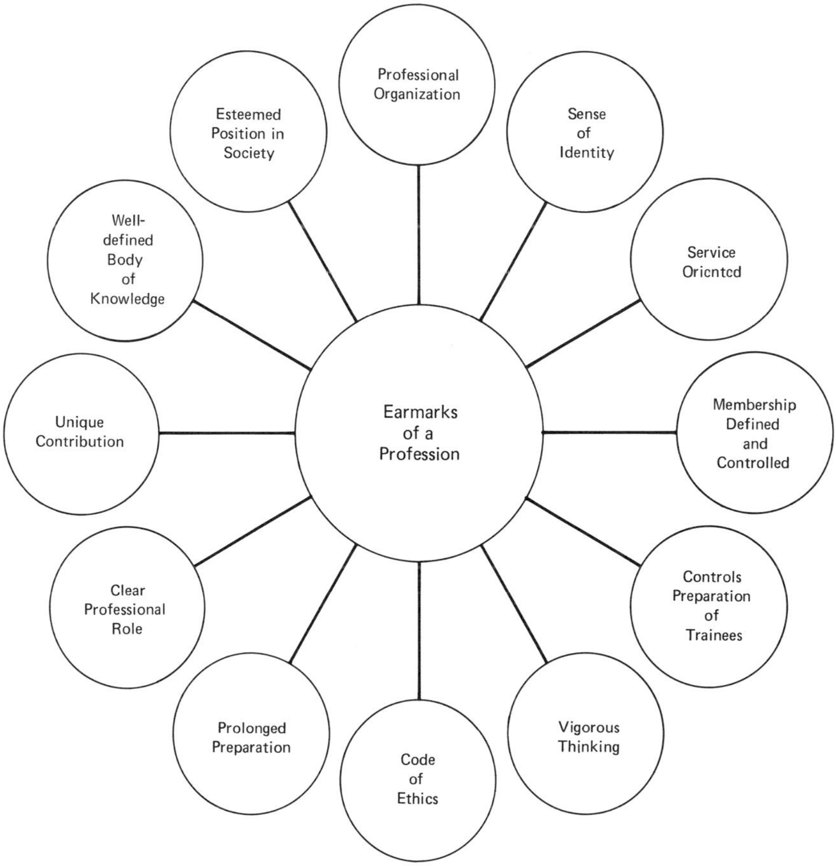

Figure 21–1 Components of a profession.

The faculty and the team discuss the situation and mutually agree on the next steps.

Name

The name of the profession was determined at the 1899 Lake Placid Conference. Prior to that date, names such as *home science, domestic science, domestic economy,* and *household arts* were used. The purpose of selecting *home economics* was a bid for acceptance and prestige.[7] The association with economics in that title was meant to encourage inclusion in the college curriculum.

Other names had been suggested, such as *ecology,* but Ellen Richards indicated that botany had already appropriated that word. Mrs.

[7] Weigley, op. cit., pp. 256–257.

Richards did suggest *euthenics,* or the science of living, but it never gained widespread use. The AHEA has formed committees to consider name changes in recent years, but it has failed to find a name change that was approved by the members. About 82 per cent of the home economics units in higher education have retained the traditional name. In other cases, the names vary. *Ecology, family, human development,* and *consumer* are some of the words found in these titles.

Professional Organizations

Among the largest professional organizations in the nation is the American Home Economics Association. Home economics educators may find other organizations of interest. Educators in nutrition may belong to the American Dietetic Association. Some home economists may find it helpful to belong to both organizations. Special interest groups may belong to other organizations. Home economists who are engaged in vocational home economics are encouraged to belong to the Home Economics Division of the American Vocational Association. The Home Economics Education Association, affiliated with the National Education Association, is a voluntary organization of home economics educators and others interested in home economics instruction in schools and colleges. Everyone should belong to the AHEA.

All of these professional organizations hold meetings and have publications, including newsletters. Many committees work on basic issues and problems as well as on plans for organization and in similar areas. This work is reviewed and approved or disapproved in committees. If approved, the committee report is presented to the assembly of delegates (or similar group) for review, discussion, and vote. If thus approved, appropriate actions or guidelines have to be established. Some of these organizations have workshops, seminars, and other special meetings for professional development. Members who belong to a professional organization have an opportunity to become acquainted with other members and to share ideas as well as to work together on common causes.

The AHEA has a foundation established in 1962 as a nonprofit education and scientific corporation with restricted or unrestricted funds for the advancement of home economics in the broadest and most liberal manner.[8] Among its many projects have been inner-city fellowships for home economics educators, establishing the Center for the Family, project grants for research and development efforts, helping launch the *Home Economics Research Journal,* and awarding national and international fellowships. The American Dietetics Asso-

[8] *The American Home Economics Association Foundation* (Washington, D.C.: American Home Economics Association, Pamphlet, n.d.).

ciation has a foundation that disburses funds for scholarships and special projects—over $30,000 per year.

Home economics has an International Federation of Home Economics (IFHE), the only world home economics organization. Dues are paid through the American Home Economics Association. The 1976 IFHE Congress had more than 1,000 participants from fifty-eight countries. Members throughout the world participate and have consultative status with such international organizations and the United Nations Educational, Scientific, and Cultural Organization (UNESCO), the Food and Agricultural Organization, the United Children's Fund (UNICEF), and the Council of Europe. The publications are the *IFHE Quarterly* and the *Annual Report,* printed in English, French, and German.

There is also an international section in the AHEA for home economists interested in international home economics. Forty-three states are linked with eighteen Latin American countries in a two-way exchange of cooperative programs, arranged by Partners of the Americas. Sister Cities is another channel for cooperative effort and professional linkages, such as Denver–Nairobi, Kenya, and Phoenix–Shiraz, Iran.

Coalitions

A coalition of the Home Economics Education Association, the American Home Economics Association, and the Home Economics Division of the American Vocational Association has been formed and deals with the area of vocational home economics education. Some of the major purposes of this coalition are to increase and to enhance communications and to mount a unified front on issues related to vocational education. Each organizational representative reports and interprets action of the coalition to the members of her or his professional organization.

Home economists would do well to become acquainted with the possibility for the use of coalitions in many areas of home economics. A coalition is a group of people with differences in background skills and expertise who work together to realize common goals[9] that they cannot reach alone. The ability to identify diverse abilities and contributions in groups other then home economics is important. It is a good idea to match coalition members with the audience to be reached. Being a member of a coalition is a valuable experience in being a team member and submerging personal grievances and pur-

[9] Jo Lynn Cunningham and Elizabeth Christy Hughes, "Energy Coalition Opportunities (ECO): A Force for Families," *Miniworkshop, Energy: Awareness Education and Use by the Child and Family,* Annual Meeting, American Home Economics Association, On-the-Spot Duplicators, Inc., Washington, D.C., 1978. Cassette.

poses so that the group goal may be reached. Each particular coalition will have a defined constituency, but here are some broad areas to consider for membership: research-and-development persons, manufacturers (such as for windmills and solar energy, in the case of energy awareness), experts in marketing, behavior modification experts, advertising and public relations personnel, family and child development specialists, representatives of government agencies and the courts, educators, school administrators, legislators, other professionals, and members of volunteer groups.

A professional coalition to which the American Home Economics Association belongs, along with the American Association of Family Services Association of America, the American Association of Marriage and Family Counselors, and the Family Service Association, was formed to have greater input into the planning of a future White House Conference on the Family, called by President Carter. Their publication, *Cofo Memo,* (Coalition of Family Organizations) reviews legislation and other governmental action pertinent to the group. The coalition is working at the state level toward the passage of certain legislative bills of interest. It is quite possible that this coalition will become a permanent organization and will work on other items than the White House conference. Home economists may consider other areas in which it would be profitable to form coalitions, temporary or permanent, for professional and public policy purposes.

Professional Standards and Governance

A professional organization, and usually a state regulatory agency, determines who shall be admitted to the practice of a profession. Certification and licensing are under the jurisdiction of a state agency, with the advice, in most cases, of members of the profession. Registration is generally governed by the professional organization. One of the purposes of licensing and certification is to prevent persons who do not have the qualifications from teaching or practicing.

Regulation of a profession is important to its status and recognition. Home economics educators are urged to be alert, so that proposed regulations reflect consistency, flexibility, creativity, and high standards. These prescriptions should not be static or lock-step in nature, but geared to change and professional needs.

EMPLOYMENT

Preparing to be a home economics teacher is the prologue. Beginning the work that may take years of the potential teacher's life is at hand.

Resources

The first step is to determine how much the college or university will assist in securing a position. Will certain faculty, with whom the student is well acquainted, be helpful, and in what ways? Is there a bulletin board that has notices about available jobs that are worth considering? Is there a college placement office? Friends and other students may give suggestions for jobs or advice about filling out application forms or having interviews. An alertness to possible leads for positions can be helpful.

Writing a Résumé

Bostwick[10] contends that the purpose of a résumé is to secure an interview. This is an accepted form of initial communication with a prospective employer. The way a résumé is written and its appearance can have an important effect on a prospective employer. The law forbids discrimination, so it is not necessary to indicate race, religion, or political affiliation unless related to the position. The salary desired is best not mentioned, because that is negotiable.

The résumé is geared to the job objective and includes a compilation of the relevant important information about oneself. The same résumé cannot be used for all purposes. The information should reflect fitness for each particular position. When possible, give concrete

[10] Burdette E. Bostwick, "Step One: Planning and Preparing the Resumé, the Covering Letter, and the Broadcast Letter," in *Finding the Job You've Always Wanted* (New York: Wiley, 1977), Ch. 4.

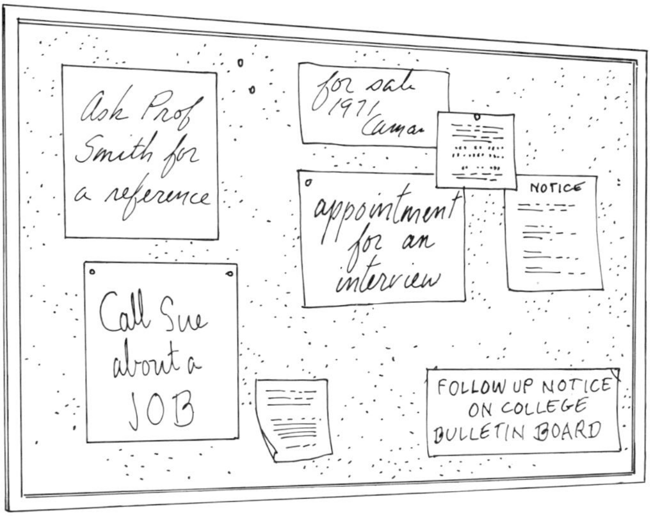

Figure 21–2 Job-getting resources on a personal bulletin board.

examples, even personal qualities, such as motivation or intelligence. A résumé should be written in an interesting, crisp, and personal style, but it should not be too technical.

A covering letter accompanies a résumé. This letter is a means of introducing the writer, giving the purpose of the letter, and asking for an answer. Résumés should be kept up-to-date with the addition of the new job experience or more education.

Keeping adequate records on file in a college placement bureau is often a prerequisite to one's finding a position. An inventory of the persons who are most qualified to give one recommendations should be reviewed periodically. It is courteous to gain permission for recommendations and to ask each time if a person's name may be listed as a reference.

Planning

One of the most critical factors in finding a job is the extent to which the job represents what the job seeker wants. Often an individual will grab any job, and for the moment, that may be the only solution. The most helpful course is for a person to spend the time to plan his or her life, including work for a lifetime. This planning can begin early in life—the sooner the better. Alternatives, options, and even second, third, and fourth career choices might be included. Bolles[11] strongly advocates this kind of planning. Once a person writes down a few short-term goals and them adds a few long-term goals, she or he has made a beginning. Ideally plans should be made for the total life span. Life mission, goals, role, and/or contributions must be defined and reflected in these plans.

Certain roadblocks to this planning must be faced. The outlook of some persons is limited, so they need to be inspired to broaden their parameters through new experiences, reading, and talking with others. Others may have vague notions about the kind of work they plan to do, and so they may visit persons in home economics work, talk to them, obtain some experience in it, and secure other information.

A lack of incentive or "push" can be a deterrent that may not be easy to solve. Possible causes may be explored through counseling and pinpointing areas of interest. One of the most common excuses is lack of time, which may allow one to postpone this important step indefinitely. Bolles notes that a year's work is about 2,000 hours, so the hours involved in thirty to fifty years of work can be awesome. Would it not be profitable to take a few of these many hours to plan for a future that could bring more pleasant and effective living? Even

[11] Richard Nelson Bolles, *What Color Is Your Parachute? A Practical Manual for Job Hunters and Career Changes* (Berkeley, Calif.: Ten Speed Press, 1977).

if a number of years of employment have passed, it is still not too late to plan. A husband or wife, a relative, a close friend, or an associate may be willing to help one check on plans and to make suggestions. Life plans should be reveiwed from time to time, in light of new interests or life changes.

One might make an inventory of the personal skills that can be used to facilitate plans. This inventory should include suggestions for seeing to any skills that are lacking or need honing. Dividing plans into time spans is illuminating. The identification of risks at any stage of these plans is part of the planning process. Risks are not negative; they are a part of forward movement. A recognition of the factors that control one's plans, such as family responsibilities, philosophy of life, or goals, adds thoroughness to the planning. The thread of basic purposes should be apparent in all planning.

Getting a Job

Securing a position can be a positive learning experience. Learning about oneself as well as about the availability and types of positions can contribute to development.

Irish[12] claims that many jobs are secured through a grapevine or network of friends, relatives, former employees, faculty, and acquaintances in the community. The secret of finding a job has never been pinpointed in exact detail. Many factors influence the outcome, such as the availability of jobs, the qualifications of the applicant, and personal characteristics of the applicant, such as wages desired, perseverance, alertness to all possible leads, and a well-organized plan of attack.

Interview

The interview is one of the most important parts of getting a job.[13] Often many interviewees are present. Here are some possible questions: Why did you select teaching? Tell us about your student teaching. What were your activities and interests in college? What would you like to know about us? What are your greatest strengths? Weaknesses? How would you maintain discipline? What method of evaluation would you use for your own teaching? How did you select your major? How would you respond to slow learners, handicapped students, or students with low motivation? What is your opinion of unions? Are you informed about "Bloom's mastery of learning"? (See

[12] Richard K. Irish, *Go Hire Yourself an Employer* (Garden City, N.Y.: Anchor Press/Doubleday, 1973).

[13] William D. Ernest, "35 Questions You May Be Asked in an Interview," *Instructor*, Vol. 85, No. 7 (March 1976), pp. 42, 48, 50.

Figure 21–3 The interview is a critical part of finding a desirable job. Both individual and group interviews are important.

Chapter 3.) What have you read lately? These or similar questions will have to be answered.

Job Benefits

Often teachers fail to examine the benefits associated with a position. Are there provisions for a pension upon retirement, Social Security benefits, and health insurance? Is there a plan for regular increments or promotions? Is the environment stimulating, that is, do faculty discuss new ideas, their latest reading, or suggestions for changes that might be made? Are faculty encouraged to be creative and experimental in their teaching? Are teaching materials and supplies adequate? In what ways do faculty work together? Is this school a place for teachers to grow? What might be other considerations about benefits on the job?

Multiple Roles

Many teachers have family and community responsibilities in addition to teaching. Finding the best way to juggle all of these commitments so that none are slighted requires management, a philosophical outlook, and the wise utilization of available resources, including contributions of family members, students, and others. Sufficient time for planning and establishing priorities can facilitate extra income, in the light of inflation and perhaps a static income, might be welcome. Retirement is not an end but a part of life that deserves positive attention.

IN-SERVICE EDUCATION

Lifelong learning pertains to teachers as well as to other adults. State certification agencies and schools sometimes require some evidence of outreach or periodic additional education. Most professional organizations demand some type of in-service education of their members.

Status of In-Service Education

Edelfelt and Lawrence[16] suggest that some programs of in-service education do not contribute to the renewal and further development of teachers. But there are some exciting programs that are improving instruction.

Planning

The effectiveness of in-service education depends upon a plan for action that involves, for the most part, federal and state departments

[16] Roy A. Edelfelt and Gordon Lawrence, "Inservice Education and the State of the Art," in *Rethinking Inservice Education* (Washington, D.C.: NEA, 1975), p. 9.

Figure 21–4 In-service education is demanded of most teachers.

of education, colleges and universities, professional organization, schools and school boards (which have become increasingly influential), and teachers and educational personnel. There is a special need for each teacher to initiate and direct self-improvement as a part of the plan.

Some of the reasons for staff development, according to Dillon,[17] are declining enrollments, public dissatisfaction with student achievement, and the general pressures of society on the schools. With fewer students, there will be fewer new teachers coming into the system with fresh ideas and other points of view. Teachers may not be so specialized. The home economics teachers may have to teach a course in health or some other area. Staff will have to cope with public criticism. One way has been to emphasize "back to basics" programs, which may have to be stressed in all areas of instruction, including home economics. The public pressures the school to prepare students so that there will be fewer social ills. It is not realistic to saddle the school with the total responsibility in this area; the family and the community must also be social agents. But the school might reexamine ways to do its share, which may include the implementation of new coping mechanisms and management. There may be influences that are unique to a particular school. Readers may wish to consider other influences on continuing education.

The first step is to assess staff needs for development. Answers must be found for such questions as "What are we doing well? Fairly well? What should be terminated? What needs immediate attention?[18] For home economics teachers, the needs for development might include teaching in the affective domain, reaching more parents, mainstreaming, bilingual education, and working with other departments and staff to plan interdisciplinary programs. In specific schools, teachers may identify a particular need. If a teacher has students with multicultural backgrounds, information about the similarities and differences of these groups might be important for better human relations and education.

From these general goals, one or more teachers may select the goal that is most urgent to them. Resources will be surveyed and studied. The research and theories related to the area will be examined. Plans for action will emerge, including implementation in the classroom. How to measure success will be planned, and suggestions for change will be formulated. Then the same teachers, or others, will progress to another goal to meet their needs.

There may be some deterrents to planning, such as lack of time,

[17] Elizabeth A. Dillon, "Staff Development: Bright Hope or Empty Promise?" *Educational Leadership,* Vol. 34, No. 3 (Dec. 1976), pp. 165–170.

[18] James L. Olivero, "Helping Teachers to Grow Professionally," *Educational Leadership,* Vol. 34, No. 3 (Dec. 1976), pp. 194–200.

money, and commitment.[19] Time is important for developing competencies, as well as for practicing and refining knowledge and skills, testing applications in the classroom, and evaluating progress. Funds may be allocated by the school or secured from state or federal agencies or from other sources. Most important is the willingness, perseverance, and drive to accomplish improvement that reflects educational purposes.

Professional Organizations

There are many ways in which professional organizations contribute to professional development. The American Dietetic Association has used satellite technology, known as *Stardate*,[20] as a tool in continuing education for registered dietitians. The dietetics program was included as a part of the biomedical communications satellite program sponsored by the Department of Health, Education, and Welfare. The satellite communication is basically a relay procedure. The broadcast signal is initiated from one earth station (six earth stations have been funded and are located in Bethesda, Maryland; Lexington, Kentucky; Bozeman, Montana; Denver, Colorado; Seattle, Washington; and Fairbanks, Alaska) and goes to a satellite, which relays the signal back over an area identified as the *footprint* to a receiving terminal.

In the first experiment, the signal originated in Bethesda, and the remote earth stations were Denver and Seattle, which received the signal simultaneously. There were two modules, "Financial Management Planning for Nutritional Care," presented by Rachel Hubbard, Ph.D., R.D., of Ohio State University for three sessions, and "Patient Nutritional Assessment," offered in four segments by Margaret Simko, Ph.D., R.D., of New York University. As the instructor taught, students in Denver and Seattle could see and hear and could be seen and heard in other locations. Participation of all stations is thus facilitated.

The effectiveness of this type of continuing education with modules will be assessed in other types of situations, such as use by affiliated dietetic associations and with different formats. This technique has exciting potential and hopefully will be commonly used.

The American Home Economics Association has held preconven-

[19] Lyle M. Ehrenberg and Donald S. Brandt, "Improved Student Learning: A Necessary Goal of Staff Development," *Educational Leadership*, Vol. 34, No. 3 (Dec. 1976), pp. 205–209.

[20] William K. O'Connell, Stardate 1. "Continuing Education via Communications Satellite"; Rachel M. Hubbard and Anita R. McCormick, Stardate 11. "Workshop on Financial Management for Nutritional Care"; 111. Margaret D. Simko, Catherine Cowell, and Judith Gilbride, "Workshop on Patient Nutritional Assessment," *Journal of The American Dietetic Association*, Vol. 73, No. 3 (Sept. 1978), pp. 270–280.

Figure 21–5 Participation in a national organization benefits members and the profession. (Courtesy of the American Home Economics Association)

tion workshops in various areas, such as "Nutrition Update—Accent on Youth," sponsored by the Food and Nutrition Section. During the 1978 convention, a large number of successful miniworkshops were held in professional and subject-matter sections. The choice was wide so that members might select a miniworkshop that was pertinent.

From time to time, professional organizations have workshops at the local, state, or national levels to meet special needs, such as the FHA/HERO workshop in 1978 for home economics teacher educators and teachers. Professional organizations have publications, kits, cassettes, and other materials that contribute to professional development. Cassettes of sessions of annual meetings are helpful to members who cannot attend. Teachers might benefit from attending a national meeting, workshop, or seminar of an educational association, such as the Association for Supervision and Curriculum Development. Reading the magazines of other professional organizations can also contribute to teacher development.

Challenges and the Future

Examination of national and world changes will give home economics educators a perspective on the changes and adaptations needed in home economics education for the future. If we plan now, the future will be more easily controlled.

Changes

Here are some trends for contemplation:[21] the high mobility of families (an average of fourteen moved in a lifetime), the shift in work patterns to adapt to employment needs, and the increasing number of women in the labor force (predictions that in the future 90 per cent will be working). What meaning do these social happenings have for home economics education, so that students and families might be helped in their adjustment?

Some other changes to consider are those in lifestyles, including eating patterns; unemployment, especially of the young; the greater numbers of the elderly; less space for homes; poverty; inflation; and the role of government as related to the family. This list is not complete, but it is a start.

Resources

To teach effectively in a changing society requires that teachers have good sources of information. Reading widely to broaden knowledge is one possibility. What, for example, are the social indicators[22] saying about the status of the family, income and consumption, trends in health and health care, social mobility, work–life patterns, and other influences on home economics education? What are leading authorities saying about children and families?[23] How may a teacher discover what it is like to be old?[24] How may government and government publications be of service?[25] Reading the daily newspaper can be informative.

Being active in the community, attending professional meetings, being a concerned member, and exchanging ideas with other teachers can be invaluable. Talking to individuals, wherever one is, can inform one about people's concerns and interests. Other resources may be explored.

Contributing, Understanding, and Sharing

A home economics teacher may find it enlightening to ask the question, Whom am I reaching with my professional expertise? It may be

[21] Joyce J. Osternig, "Home Economics and the Dynamics of Change," *Journal of Home Economics*, Vol. 69, No. 5 (Nov. 1977), pp. 36–38.

[22] Conrad Taeuber, "America in the Seventies: Some Social Indicators," *Annals of the American Academy of Political and Social Science*, Vol. 435 (Jan. 1978).

[23] Kenneth Keniston and the Carnegie Council on Children, *All Our Children, The American Family Under Pressure* (New York: Harcourt, 1977).

[24] Robert N. Butler, *Why Survive? Being Old in America* (New York: Harper, 1975). (Look for other references.)

[25] Robert Ferber et al., *Selected Aspects of Consumer Behavior*, prepared for the National Science Foundation, Superintendent of Documents, Washington, D.C. 1977, #NFS/RA 77-0013. One example of thousands of government publications.

disconcerting to realize that students are largely the recipients. To reach more people may require the establishment of networks. What networks for communications are open now?[26] Fellow home economics teachers and other teachers in the school; home economics teachers and other home economists in the community, county, state, and nation; personnel in certain agencies; and people in business and industry are only a few of the networks that a teacher might establish for broadening his or her background, sharing ideas, and stimulating activities. Writing a note of appreciation or sending questions to a television or convention speaker or to the author of an article can develop a different type of network.

In what ways may a teacher share ideas and make a contribution to the profession? One way is to describe a highly successful teaching strategy to a group of home economics teachers at a local meeting. Not only may this be helpful to the teachers in attendance, but these teachers will tell others. If the reception of the talk was enthusiastic, the speaker might consider the possibility of writing a short article for a professional magazine. As a result, an audience of close to 100,000 readers may profit from the idea. Another possibility is to present this same idea at an in-service group meeting at school and, if the other teachers approve, to adapt the idea for an educational magazine. Home economics teachers often underestimate the value of speaking and writing as a service to the profession and as a source of great personal satisfaction. A lack of time or a fear of writing or speaking is a lame excuse.

Perhaps students in the classroom have worked on an exciting project on energy conservation or recycling or on a study of cultural traditions associated with home and family. Would the local radio or television station be interested in having the students make a presentation? This is an example of sharing expertise with the community. The audience may be in the thousands of listeners. Although a teacher's first responsibility is to the students, that does not preclude the sharing of ideas with a wider audience.

Next Steps

One challenge is to reconsider what constitutes "good" home economics education. Most areas of education have been criticized almost since the beginning of schools. Even Socrates complained that children were disrespectful to their teachers and were tyrants in their homes. Mannino[27] challenges home economists to orient themselves

[26] Saul B. Cohen, "Networking, Educational Program Policy for the Late Seventies," *EDC News,* Issue No. 10 (Fall 1977), pp. 1–4.

[27] Fortune V. Mannino, "An Ecological Approach to Understanding Family and Community Relationships," *Journal of Home Economics,* Vol. 66, No. 3 (March 1974), pp. 9–13.

to the entire family and not to confine all their efforts to an individual family member. Teachers can gain a greater understanding of the individual from the context of his or her family life. In addition, the family should be educated in terms of its environment, the local and wider community. "Good" home economics education may wish to consider one focus as being on the entire family and its setting.

Teachers might ask themselves if certain home economics content is now less pertinent to daily living. Sharp distinctions in masculine and female roles are not emphasized today, for example. What new emphases should be included? The ecology, families as educators, interdisciplinary projects, death and dying, multisensory perceptions, and consumerism are some possible considerations.

Reaching beyond the classroom through satellite, television, telephone, computer assistance, and other types of instruction offers a great challenge. The establishment of family centers in communities, where assistance may be given in any area of home and family living, has great potential. Home learning centers and home-based study, through the use of books, other literature, kits, technological aids, and other devices, provide possible involvement of the entire family and have been under discussion for some time but need to be given greater impetus. In the future, teachers may have to be prepared to work in these innovative programs.

Along with the "good" home economics program, teachers may ask themselves, What are the unique contributions of home economics to the total education of the student? Answers to that question would also justify the existence of home economics in the schools. Would a review of excellent practices in the past, such as the family life centers of 1939 (see Chapter 6), have merit for programs of the future? Belated recognition of problems such as drug abuse, teenage pregnancy, ethnic and intercultural misunderstandings and tension can make solutions more difficult both now and in the future.[28] All of these ideas, plus many more, may serve as input in the design of teaching and learning for the days ahead so that home economics may nurture and support families and family members. Thus the greatest possible potential for the good life is reached.

SUGGESTIONS FOR FURTHER LEARNING

1. Draw a sketch that would identify networks that a home economics teacher might use for gaining information and ideas for self-development. Draw another sketch of a network of persons or groups that would gain from your professional expertise.

[28] Harold G. Shane, "Making Tomorrow Work in Education," *Educational Horizons*, Vol. 54, No. 3 (Spring 1976), pp. 111–118.

2. Look at the characteristics of a professional and identify the ways in which the development of each characteristic might be assured.
3. What kind of career planning have you done for the future? How do you feel about planning ahead and, specifically, about the plans that you yourself have made? What represents the peak of your professional ambition? Read the following reference.

   Focus on Careers. Washington, D.C.: American Home Economics Association, 1977.

   Have you been influenced to make any changes in your planning?

Index

B

C

G

H

I

J

K

L

M

O

P

S

U

V

W

	DATE DUE		
Mar 4 '81			
Mar 24 82			
OCT 1 '86			
FE 23 '99			